African Rifles & Cartridges

AFRICAN
Rifles & Cartridges

The experiences and opinions of a professional ivory hunter
with some thirty years of continuous living in the African
Bush—who has used all of the various calibers
and most of the suitable cartridges, and with
them killed the many species of big game
found on the continent of Africa.

by

JOHN TAYLOR
(Pondoro)

DRAWINGS BY
E. STANLEY SMITH

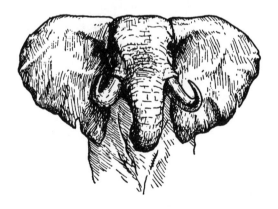

SAFARI PRESS, Inc.

P.O. Box 3095, Long Beach, CA 90803, USA

African Rifles and Cartridges by John Taylor. Special contents of this edition copyright © 1994 by Safari Press. All rights reserved. No part of this publication may be used or reproduced in any form or by any means, electronic or mechanical reproduction, including photocopying, recording, or any information storage and retrieval system, without permission from the publisher.

The trademark Safari Press ® is registered with the U.S. Patent and Trademark Office and in other countries.

Taylor, John

Safari Press Inc.

1994, Long Beach, California

ISBN 1-57157-222-8

Library of Congress Catalog Card Number: 94-067700

10 9 8 7 6 5 4 3 2

Readers wishing to receive the Safari Press catalog, featuring many fine books on big-game hunting, wingshooting, and sporting firearms, should write to Safari Press Inc., P.O. Box 3095, Long Beach, CA 90803, USA.
Tel: (714) 894-9080 or visit our Web site at www.safaripress.com.

CONTENTS

TO

ALI NDEMANGA
*who stood nobly by me when
times were mighty lean*

Foreword

My object in writing this book was threefold:

Firstly, to amuse myself during a period of enforced inaction owing to the fact that my rifles, cameras, kit and equipment, and pretty well everything else I possessed in the world, were stolen whilst I was away at the war;

Secondly, because my good friend Tom Samworth, who publishes it, asked me to; and

Thirdly, in the hope that it may be of assistance to American sportsmen who will be thinking of taking a run out here to Africa for a smack at the big fellows, as they did in days gone by, by describing the most suitable weapons for different types of hunting. It is really lamentable to think of the costly, useless weapons that unscrupulous gunsmiths—or let us give them the benefit of the doubt and say "ignorant"—used to foist onto inexperienced sportsmen coming out to Africa for the first time, in those palmy days between the two World Wars.

Further, there is such an enormous collection of different calibers from which to choose that the beginner may well be excused for feeling somewhat lost when trying to make up his mind as to which he should get. He will find no lack of men to advise him; but the trouble is that their advice is so contradictory that he finishes up no better off and no wiser than when he started! Most writers of big game hunting books devote a short chapter towards the end of their book to rifles; but in the vast majority of cases these men, having found weapons which give them reasonable satisfaction *in the type of country in which they are hunting*, cease experimenting, and just use and recommend those particular weapons. They seem to forget that there are widely different types of country all of which require different types of weapon if the best results are to be obtained; that their readers may have had vastly less experience than they have had; and that the particular rifles which proved so satisfactory for them might be quite useless, if not positively dangerous, in some other part of the continent. A great many of these books must be read if all the ground is to be covered; some of them, being out of print, are extremely difficult to obtain; and it is almost impossible for the beginner to sum up amongst so many widely divergent opinions when he himself knows nothing whatever about it. "Damn it!" he'll say, "here's one fella swearing by the double .577 Nitro-Express for elephant; and here's another who vows that the .416 Magazine is the *only* elephant rifle; whilst here's still another hero who uses nothing but a .275 (7mm) carbine! They're all three experienced professional hunters—which am I to follow?"

That is no exaggeration. There have been men who used just those calibers and wrote books about it. Accordingly, since I know from my own experience how difficult it is for the complete tyro to choose the best and most suitable guns, it occurred to me that if the whys and wherefores of the various weapons, and the requirements of the different species of game under widely varying types of country, were collected and published in one volume and discussed by a practical hunter, who could explain just exactly why this or that type of weapon was better than some other, it might help to clarify matters.

This has been done for India by Major Sir Gerald Burrard Bt. D.S.O. in his excellent little volume "*Notes on Sporting Rifles*" and for America by Elmer Keith in his most informative "*Big Game Rifles and Cartridges*" but so far nobody has attempted it for Africa. It is my earnest hope that this book may fill that gap—which so badly needs filling—and possibly save some beginner from the costly and heartbreaking disappointments that once were mine thru using utterly unsuitable rifles.

My authority for venturing to offer advice on such an important subject is based on nearly thirty years of professional elephant hunting. And when I say "thirty years" I mean just that; because I hunt from 11½ to 12 months a year and not merely three or four months at a stretch as is so often the case when a man speaks or writes of "My Twenty-five Years Big Game Hunting" or something of the sort. During the years I have been hunting I have experimented with practically everything that has appeared on the market from .256 to .600, both inclusive. Some of the calibers I have had two or three times so as to check up on the notes I had made in the past concerning their behavior. Admittedly, my hunting consists almost exclusively of elephant, rhino, buffalo and man-eating lion; nevertheless, I have shot practically every species of game in Africa, since when trekking from one district to another one must shoot for the pot, and there are generally many mouths to fill. (There are no automobile "champagne" safaris about elephant-hunting; you walk with porters.)

Apart from my own personal experience, I have discussed rifles with a great many other hunters and sportsmen and read everything I can lay hands on dealing with my chosen profession. I have endeavored to deal with my subject and discuss the various rifles from the point of view of practical hunting, and so far as possible to avoid technicalities. I have done so because in the first place my knowledge of theoretical matters is insufficient, and in any case I have a notion that the practical aspect will interest a greater number of sportsmen—especially beginners.

However, there are one or two small points connected with ballistics which cannot be entirely ignored, so I have just touched on them as briefly as possible. It cannot be too often repeated that a weapon that may prove perfectly safe and satisfactory when used in sub-Tropical or sub-Arctic regions, may prove dangerous if taken to the lower altitudes in the Tropics. The pressures generated by Magnum medium and small bores are steadily mounting up and are in some cases approaching the practical limit for satisfactory results, and even for safety. If that is the case in temperate climes, such weapons could not be considered safe for use in the Tropics where the heat can be such that it cannot be appreciated or even understood by those who have never experienced it. All nitro powders are affected by temperature: the higher the temperature the more violent the combustion, and therefore the higher the pressure generated. This is a point that must not be forgotten or overlooked, especially by Americans who are so keen on handloading their own shells and boosting the standard velocities of the factory-loaded ammunition. Any increase in velocity must spell a corresponding increase in chamber pressure. As I shall be showing later on, there is no real call for these super-high velocities for general African hunting. Accordingly, if the delightful little squibs and squirts that produce these terrific speeds show very high pressures in the States, it would be better to leave them back home when coming out here to Africa.

It would certainly seem that the American rifle manufacturers have a magnificent opportunity right now to grab the African market. Except for large bores, which were almost exclusively

British, Germany had the market during the years between the two wars. Her cheap Mausers were obtainable from one end of Africa to the other, and shells for them could be bought in almost any store. It was only the professional hunter who was tackling dangerous game almost daily, and whose life, and the lives of whose trackers and gun-bearers, depended upon the utter and absolute reliability of his rifles, who insisted always upon the best grade British rifles—double or magazine. Such weapons would be very much more expensive than corresponding German rifles; but there was no question of their reliability. We know that fine custom-built doubles and magazines were obtainable in Germany, yet there is no getting away from the fact that the vast majority of experienced hunters, of all nationalities including German, used British-built doubles when tackling dangerous game at close quarters in thick cover. But quite apart from regular hunters, every farmer and planter would have his rifle, and usually two. These would almost invariably be cheap German Mausers. American rifles would certainly be very much more reliable than those cheap German things, and could yet be produced very much more reasonably priced than they could in Britain—judging by the pre-war prices of some Winchester .375 Magnums I saw in British East Africa. And what's more, they were of better quality and finish than any of the lower-priced British rifles.

In the tables of ballistics I have headed one column "Knock-Out Value." I am fully aware that many ballistic experts would look very much askance at these figures, but I do not care because I do not pretend that they represent "killing power;" but they *do* give an excellent basis from which any two rifles may be compared from the point of view of the actual knock-down blow, or punch, inflicted by the bullet on massive, heavy-boned animals such as elephant, rhino and buffalo. Theoretical, mathematical muzzle energy lays too much stress upon velocity at the expense of bullet weight; whereas my figures permit the heavy bullet to come into its own in spite of its more moderate velocity. Practical experience bears out these figures in an altogether remarkable manner as I shall show in due course. Accordingly, I have included them in the ballistic tables as it seemed the obvious place for them.

It may be thought, at any rate at first glance, that I have overly stressed the possible dangers that lie in wait for the unwary and the careless, to say nothing of the inexperienced. I should not like to think that I am giving the impression that African big game hunting consists of eternally leaping out of possible death-traps into even more precarious situations. It is nothing of the sort. Big game hunting can be just as dangerous as you wish to make it. Sometimes, generally owing to your own inexperience, it can be a good deal more dangerous than you would wish; but that is all. It is merely that from time to time I have seen inexperienced amateurs doing such fantastically stupid things, and arming themselves with such utterly unsuitable weapons, and without in the least realizing what horrible risks they were running, that I have risked being called an alarmist. But let me add right now that you can hunt literally for years without ever finding yourself in a tight corner— but, by the same token, you may find yourself in that tight corner the very first day you go out! The glorious uncertainty as to what is going to turn up next is one of the great attractions of African hunting.

I must express my very real thanks to Major Sir Gerald Burrard Bt. D.S.O. for his kindness and courtesy in permitting me to use the trajectory tables out of his *"Notes on Sporting Rifles."*

I have also to acknowledge the kindness of the Editors of the *AMERICAN RIFLEMAN* and the British journals *GAME & GUN* and the *FIELD* for permission to work into the following pages various articles or parts of articles of mine which, either in a somewhat similar or entirely different form, have from time to time appeared in those excellent magazines.

I should also like to take this opportunity for expressing the real debt of gratitude I owe to my friend the late C. Fletcher Jamieson, the Rhodesian professional, for the promptness with which he answered my S.O.S. for photos with which to illustrate this book.

I should like to make it quite clear, here and now in the commencement, that I have no financial interest of any description whatsoever with any firm of gunsmiths or ammunition manufacturers. What praise I have to bestow upon, or criticism to make of, any particular weapons is based solely and entirely upon the merits or otherwise of those weapons. I have tried to deal with my subject and discuss the various rifles in the most impartial manner possible, but I am only human and if I have let myself go a mite now and then it is simply because of the intense pleasure and satisfaction I have always derived from using certain weapons built by certain firms. And I trust that you who read will bear this fact in mind, and make allowances.

It is an astonishing thing how little the average man in Africa knows about the rifles he uses—it is but a very small exaggeration to say that all he really does know is that the bullet comes out of that end which has a hole in it! America is the home of rifle shooting, and there is no doubt that Americans are very much more "rifle-minded" than the British. Nevertheless, conditions are so very different in Africa from what they have been accustomed to in America, that I trust and hope that this book may be of value to any who intend to try their hand on African game.

JOHN TAYLOR

Portuguese East Africa
March, 1948

(AUTHOR'S NOTE:—I regret to have to say that my friend Fletcher Jamieson of Rhodesia joined the Silent Majority just as this book was about to go to press. His untimely death is a real loss to the big game hunting world, as his magnificent photos, which go to illustrate this book, clearly show. There are so few *genuine* hunters left, that we can ill spare him. One can but hope that he has found his Happy Hunting Grounds wherein the breeze is ever favorable and the tuskers all big'uns.)

ABBREVIATIONS

B.P.	Black powder
D.B.	Double barreled
F.S.	Feet per second
Ft.lbs.	Foot pounds weight
H.V.	High velocity
M.E.	Muzzle energy
M.V.	Muzzle velocity
S.B.	Single barreled

African Rifles and Cartridges

CHAPTER I

Definitions and Details of Rifles

Sporting rifles were originally divided into but three categories: Large Bores, Expresses, and Miniatures. However, with the introduction of smokeless powders, those definitions were no longer sufficiently comprehensive. Various attempts were made to coin new definitions which would include the old black powder weapons as well as their more modern nitro-firing counterparts, since thousands of them were still in use. However, the definitions finally chosen were none too happy, tho doubtless the best they could get. The trouble was that there was too big a difference in the power developed by the new nitro-firing weapons with their metal-jacketed bullets, and their black powder predecessors, to permit of their being classed together. Considerable confusion arose thru the careless manner in which men referred to their rifles, both verbally and on paper, and, of course, thru ignorance on the part of those who heard or read.

During the transition period from black powder to smokeless, around the turn of the century, it was absolutely imperative to indicate whether the rifle in question fired black powder or cordite. But in the writing of their books those who had been accustomed to black powder weapons rarely bothered to do so; tho others who had recently taken to cordite were usually more particular. Then, when cordite finally and completely superseded black powder in Africa, men ceased to differentiate and assumed it would be taken for granted that they were referring to nitro rifles. That was okay as far as it went; but unfortunately there were still diehards in India who persisted in using black powder weapons of similar calibers, and could not see that it was only fair to their readers to definitely describe them as such.

I

During this period Large Bores were defined as rifles the caliber of which was not smaller than .600; Medium Bores as rifles the caliber of which was not greater than .600 nor less than .400; and anything under .400 as a Small Bore. But as black powder weapons became obsolete, it obviously became necessary to revise the definitions of sporting rifles. For instance, if you were to refer to a .600 in Africa as a medium bore, your listeners would gape at you and ask you what on earth was your idea of a large bore if you considered a .600 as medium. In view of the fact that the .600 is the most powerful sporting rifle that has ever been placed on the market, and that men not unnaturally associate caliber and power, it's palpably absurd to retain definitions at the present day which seem to indicate that such weapons as the .577 and .600 bores are of but medium power—particularly when it's remembered that the old black powder weapons that made this classification necessary are no longer used in Africa and are rarely seen other than in some museum. In the same way, there is far too great dissimilarity in power and utility between, say, the .240 and the .375 Magnum to permit of them both being arbitrarily classed in the same group as small bores.

Consequently, since I am dealing principally with Africa and African hunting, and since there is more big game hunting in Africa than in any other part of the world, I shall use thruout the following pages the definitions I always use and which are those most generally used and understood thruout Africa, and which, I think, are those that are gradually coming to be used everywhere. Here they are:

LARGE BORE. A rifle the caliber of which is not less than .450".

LARGE MEDIUM BORE. A rifle the caliber of which is not less than .400" nor greater than .440"(11.2mm).

MEDIUM BORE. A rifle the caliber of which is not less than .318" nor greater than .375".

SMALL BORE. A rifle the caliber of which is less than .318".

MINIATURE. A rifle the M.E. of which is less than 1,500 ft. lbs.

MAGNUM. A rifle the M.V. of which is not less than 2,500 f.s.

No mention is made of black powder rifles because, as I have said, such weapons are no longer used. It will, therefore, be understood that when I speak of a rifle by its caliber I am referring to the modern nitro-firing weapon and not to its old black powder predecessor unless I definitely use the words "black powder" or the letters "B.P." in connection with it—i.e. black powder .577 or .450 B.P. Express, or something of the sort. In this way there can be no confusion or misunderstanding.

Auctor: What exactly is implied by the word "Express"? It seems to be used pretty indiscriminately by writers and gunsmiths in their catalogs. And you might say a bit more about the use of the word "Magnum." It appears to be more widely used than your definition would seem to imply.

Lector: The original "Express Train" rifle was introduced by Purdey somewhere around the middle of the last century, 1856 I think it was, and ever since then the word "Express" has been used to denote a high velocity weapon. The British ammunition manufacturers use it in connection with all sporting rifle ammunition as distinct from military calibers. Actually, as used today it really has no meaning and is rarely employed except when referring to a black powder weapon of that group.

Originally the word "Magnum" implied a cartridge having a larger powder capacity than the accepted standard for that caliber. In the case of rifles this almost always meant a bottle-shaped shell—a case of larger caliber having been necked down to take the smaller bullet. Where large bores and shot guns were concerned it meant a longer shell than the normal length for that gauge, and to the present day British wildfowlers and duck hunters use it in connection with their 2¾" and 3" chambered guns; it is used in the same way for the 2¾" 12-bore "Paradox"-pattern ball-and-shot gun. There are still one or two gunsmiths who like to use it when describing some of their pet calibers which are not magnums according to modern reckoning, presumably in the hope of implying that they are more powerful than others, tho it is obviously absurd to so distinguish them when there is no corresponding caliber from which to do so. Many cartridges which come within the magnum group are not so called simply because there never was a lower velocity shell of that caliber from which to distinguish them.

As I have already mentioned in the Foreword, I have no intention of entering into a theoretical discussion of ballistics, internal or external; but there are one or two small points that must be touched on in passing, because they are of very real importance to the practical hunter. For instance:

PRESSURE. Black powder generated low pressures and was not affected by changes in temperature. It was, therefore, an almost ideal propellant for Tropical use. Unfortunately, however, the disadvantage of smoke outweighed all else. When the nitro-glycerine powders came in cordite was found to be the best of them, in spite of its very real disadvantages. Its own temperature of combustion is very high, whilst it is very sensitive to changes in atmospheric temperatures—the higher the temperature the more violent the combustion, which spells an immediate increase in chamber pressure and velocity. The still more modern nitro-cellulose powders are very much better because their temperature of combustion is lower, whilst they are not affected to anything like the same extent by variations in climatic conditions.

Nevertheless, I think it can be safely stated that *all* nitro powders are affected to a greater or lesser extent by increases in atmospheric temperatures. With the modern craze for higher velocities chamber pressures are steadily mounting up; and altho such cartridges might prove quite satisfactory when used in cold countries, you have no warrant for supposing that they would prove equally satisfactory in the great heat of the Tropics.

I am not exaggerating when I say that it is impossible for the ordinary man to grasp his barrels tightly with the naked hand after walking around in the midday sun for an hour or so in some districts out here, and that without a shot having been fired thru them. True, all Africa is not so bad as that; but a very great deal of it is, including some of the best big game districts, and there is no telling when you may be persuaded to try a hunt in one of them. Stiffness in extraction of a fired shell, owing to its having been expanded to too great an extent by excessive pressure, could have very serious consequences. Consequently, if you are trying to make a choice between two rifles of approximately similar power, other things being equal, always choose the one that shows the lower chamber pressure.

Nearly all the best and most powerful British cartridges were designed for and loaded with cordite since it was found to be the best and most reliable of the then new nitro-glycerine powders, and for a long time was the only one used. When the early nitro-cellulose powders came in it was found that none of them would give the same ballistics in many of the larger bores. Consequently, if the cartridges used in these larger rifles were now to be loaded with nitro-cellulose, the rifles would have to be re-regulated and re-sighted. If any gunsmith would undertake the work of re-regulating doubles, the cost would be very high. Accordingly, it was realized that to change the ballistics of these cartridges would be manifestly unfair to the hundreds, if not thousands, of users of these rifles. Besides, even altho cordite has many disadvantages when compared with the nitro-cellulose powders, there is no getting away from the fact that it has stood well the test of just over half a century.

All British cartridges that could be loaded with nitro-cellulose without interfering unduly with their ballistics are now so loaded; but the others continue to be loaded with cordite. Nitro-cellulose powders are, in comparison, but slightly affected by temperature changes and generate very much lower temperatures themselves on combustion. I take it that all modern American powders are of the nitro-cellulose type, or Neonite. At least it would be in the last degree improbable that they would be introducing new weapons designed for cordite at this late date.

I am not really in a position to discuss powders, because hand-loading of large bore ammunition is something unknown in British territory. The British, as I have said before, are nowhere near so rifle-minded as the Americans—except in their colonies they get little opportunity to shoot a rifle, other than miniatures. I doubt if there is a chronograph station in the length and breadth of the African continent. It would be extremely unwise, to say the least of it, to hand-load nitro-express shells without having each batch tested for pressures and velocities—particularly when they are for use in double rifles. In my case it would be out of the question, because I am a tent-dweller and have no facilities for setting up a powerful reloading machine.

In the days of muzzle-loaders, of course, everybody was a hand-loader from necessity; and when the early breech-loaders came in some men continued to "roll their own." And I shouldn't be at all surprised to learn that this was in large measure the cause of the numerous misfires from which they seemed to suffer. The early anvils may not have been too good a fit; some of the men may not even have known that anvils were essential! (I've seen an otherwise reasonably intelligent man reloading fired paper shot gun shells—poor economy at the best of times—without fitting anvils in the caps, or primers. I asked him what on earth he thought he was doing, and when I explained my question his reaction was: "Oh, so that's what those little things are for!" He then told me that he *was* becoming somewhat discouraged with this hand-loading on account of the number of misfires he experienced!)

I was quite fascinated when I first heard of American hunters nearly all hand-loading their own ammunition, and reckoned that this was a game that would surely suit me—and started studying the advertisements. However, on reading Keith's book what horse sense I possess rose up and scattered my day-dreams to the four winds with a number nine moccasin! I don't suppose that any man living knows more about rolling his own than Elmer Keith does, or has had more experience, yet Keith relates numerous occasions when he had misfires and hangfires with his own shells. Well, a misfire may occasion no more than a disappointment and some profanity when it takes place with non-dangerous game at long range; but it's a very different matter when you are tackling the big fellows that can hit back and they're only maybe a few feet away. Under these conditions a misfire is something you just cannot risk; whilst as for a hangfire . . . Well, picture it for yourself: You've just fired one barrel and now find yourself being charged by an elephant or a buffalo; your rifle misfires; you dare not wait that five seconds, in case it's a hangfire, to open the breech; you break the breech, take hold of the shell—and then have that 75–100 grains of cordite let go! . . .

I experienced a number of misfires in my early days before I took to using Kynoch ammunition; and for many years past have ordered my shells direct from the factory, soldered up in airtight 50s or 100s, and as I have mentioned elsewhere in this book, have personally only experienced one misfire ever since—I have never experienced a hangfire. Well, just look at the confidence that gives me. It matters not what experience you may have had, nor how certain you may feel that your nerve will not fail you in a tight corner, if you have not absolute, positive confidence in both your rifles *and their ammunition*, you cannot hunt dangerous game with assurance. Confidence is half, or more than half, the battle; but that confidence must be extended to your rifles and ammunition— shared equally between all three of you.

Following on the adventure wherein I was so nearly killed by a wounded elephant, and which you will find described elsewhere in this book, I lost my nerve entirely and was positively scared sick for some considerable time afterwards whenever it was necessary for me to approach a herd in thick cover. But I gradually came to realize that with a thoroly reliable rifle in my hands, loaded with equally reliable ammunition, there was no earthly need for me to be scared. Had I not had that supreme confidence in both rifle and shells, in all probability I should have quit elephant-hunting then and there.

I reckon that any man who attempted to roll his own nitro express shells for use in powerful double rifles which he intended to take against dangerous game in the Tropics, and didn't know exactly what he was doing and didn't have a pressure barrel at hand and an up-to-date chronograph station within reasonably easy reach, would be qualifying for the bug-house—if not for the Styx.

I've seen such incredibly foolish things done in Africa, some of them by men who had been hunting all their lives, that I'm half scared to mention them sometimes for fear of being accused of over-exaggeration. However, I'll risk it here. What would you think of a man who had an old double hammer .577 Black Powder Express chambered for the 3″ shell and regulated for 167 grs. of powder and a 610-gr. bullet who used 2″ Snider cartridges loaded with 70 grs. of powder and a 480-gr. bullet for lion "because they were cheaper"? And who then couldn't understand why he failed to kill the lion (the barrels would not be grouping within maybe six or eight inches of one another)! And the same man who then used 3″ .577 Nitro-Express ammunition in the same rifle for elephant: 100 grs. of cordite back of a 750-gr. metal-jacketed bullet showing a velocity of 2,050 f.s. for a chamber pressure of 14 tons, whilst his rifle was regulated for a velocity of 1,650 f.s. and proved for only 10 tons pressure? And that isn't all! The original strikers had long been broken and this hero calmly used nails from a packing case instead! He told me they sometimes stood up to three or four shots. . . . True, he never hunted alone; but always had three or four rifle-armed native hunters along with him; nevertheless, it shows you that African big game hunting is not quite as dangerous as some would like to have us believe. It must not be imagined, however, that I am recommending this sort of procedure.

Then there was another fella, a man who had spent his whole life in the Bush and done an immense amount of hunting. Somebody told him there was a wounded buffalo not far away, so out he went; his only weapon being an old 10.75m. (.423) Mauser from the muzzle of which he had lopped off an inch or so because it had become bell-shaped, his foresight was only tied on because he hadn't yet had time to solder it, the bore was so badly worn and rusted that he had hammered his bullets square so as to make them touch the bore at least somewhere; his right eye had failed and he had only recently started to learn to shoot off his left shoulder, never previously having bothered to practice; he knew nothing about the buffalo: who had wounded it? where or how hard it was hit? Nothing. With one cartridge only for his worn-out old gun, off he went to deal with that buffalo. But the Gods must have taken pity on the old fool—he was getting on for 70—because the buff was dead when he found him.

Auctor: You seem to have wandered quite a piece from the pressure you started discussing.

Lector: What if I have? It's all part and parcel of the same thing: the necessity for not using a cartridge which generates too high a pressure, or which in any other way might prove unreliable.

I am surprised that this most important ballistic element is so completely ignored by gunsmiths in their catalogs; yet it is of the very utmost importance in the case of rifles intended for use in the Tropics.

VELOCITY. But the same gunsmiths are by no means so reticent concerning the velocity developed by their rifles. There is no question of the advantage of a high velocity when it's a matter of shooting at long range, since the high velocity flattens the trajectory and so to a great extent eliminates the bug-bear of judging distance. That was the primary object of boosting velocities. There are other advantages connected with penetration and expansion of bullets; but practically all these are in connection with long range shooting. In fact, unless your bullet weight is carefully chosen, too high a velocity at close range can be a decided disadvantage thru causing your bullet to disintegrate on impact if it happens to strike even a comparatively light bone.

I have long been inclined to think that there has been too much of a rush to velocity whilst ignoring bullet weight, at least where

African shooting is concerned. There are certain gunsmiths who had splendid medium bore cartridges that were eminently satisfactory for general use, but who, to comply with the demand for higher velocities and flatter trajectories, sacrificed their bullet weight in order to boost its speed without unduly increasing the pressure. But in my considered opinion those rifles are by no means so generally useful as they were in their original guise—the flattening of the trajectory only becoming noticeable beyond the range at which animals are usually shot with such a rifle out here.

There is a lot of misunderstanding about this question of velocity. Inexperienced men have heard someone saying something about the extraordinary killing effect of high-velocity bullets, or perhaps read something somewhere about it, and instantly jump to the conclusion that they have the secret at last; velocity! velocity! there's your answer! But they entirely overlook the all-important point: if a given bullet with a very high striking-velocity is so much deadlier than an identical bullet with a lower striking-velocity, then what is the "critical" striking-velocity at which this increase in killing power first becomes apparent, and below which it is not seen? That this enhanced killing power is there is indisputable; there is a wealth of evidence in support of it; tho the *reason* for it is still wrapped in mystery.

It has been observed time and again that when the striking-velocity is really high a new factor becomes apparent. These high-velocity bullets seem to possess a peculiar property of "shock" which appears to paralyze the animal's entire nervous system; but to obtain this effect the striking-velocity has to be not less than about 2,350 f.s. at the moment of impact. In other words, you require a rifle with a muzzle velocity of not less than 2,500 f.s.; what is now referred to as a "Magnum."

It was the .280 Ross, somewhere about 1910 if I remember rightly, which revolutionised our ideas as to the requirements of a sporting rifle, and with which this peculiar killing property was first noticed. There was a rush to buy a Ross rifle; but men overlooked the fact that the little light 140-gr. expanding bullet would disintegrate all too readily if it happened to hit a bone on all but the smallest of animals, and thereby dissipate its killing power before reaching the vital point. After one or two men were killed by lions which their .280s failed to stop, it was discarded other than for the pot. But it served its purpose in showing us the enormous advantages of a high striking-velocity, provided the bullet was heavy enough to hold together.

But I do not think that the reasons for this "pole-axing" effect have ever been explained. Some years ago an intensely interesting discussion, in which I took a small part, ran thru the pages of the British journal, *GAME & GUN*, and evoked such wide-spread interest that it ran on for a couple of years. It dealt with this question of "Velocity and Killing Power." We even persuaded surgeons and medicos to give us their views, but finished up not much wiser than when we started. Nevertheless, a great deal of interesting matter was brought to light from a considerable variety of keen hunters, sportsmen and riflemen generally from all over the world, and their varied experiences.

It was shown that if an animal was hit by a bullet of sufficient weight and of suitable pattern, so as not to smash up on impact, he was either killed instantly where he stood or, if the bullet struck remote from an immediately vital spot, he was totally paralyzed and incapable of moving until either finished off with another shot or left to keel over himself, stiff-legged, like a child's toy. One instance was given of a Scotch stag being shot with a Winchester .220 Swift rifle at somewhere in the vicinity of 300 yards range. The sportsman stated that the stag never flinched (he was using a Zeiss telescope sight) and he thought he had missed clean. He was about to fire again, when the stag collapsed. It never moved from the spot upon which it had been standing, yet the little 48-gr. slug, which had mushroomed perfectly, had only penetrated about two inches into the brisket. Numerous other instances were given of this extraordinary paralyzing effect. But what causes it? What is there in the speed of penetration to cause complete paralysis of the nervous system? Because it is to be noted that if the bullet enters and then disintegrates it does not produce instant death; it seems to rely upon its lacerating properties.

One theory that has been put forward is "that there is a phe-nomenon of 'shock' differing in its features from any with which we are acquainted. That the passage of a projectile of a given di-ameter, at a high velocity, thru tissues of high liquid-content, sets up a violent 'wave' (of pressure or oscillation) at right angles to its course and against the inertia of the surrounding tissues. This 'wave' of mechanical shock, transmitted thru and indefinitely far around the tissues about the axis of the bullet's course, directly (and far more extensively than the bullet itself could) affects the functions of all vital structures and elements it reaches—in short, a blow against all the minute cells comprising living tissues—but, without causing as much visible laceration as certain expanding, or disrupting, bullets of smaller bore and higher velocity are known to." That's the theory offered for examination.

It might be asked, "But what the devil does it matter? We know that the modern Magnums are deadlier than their lower velocity counterparts; very well, why worry? Just use one and be satisfied." That's all very fine; but if we knew the reason for these things, it might be possible to produce a light rifle that would be suitable for use against dangerous game. I defy any man to show that he can use a heavy rifle equally as quickly and equally as effectively at the end of a long hard day, when he is dog-tired, as he could have when he started out in the morning, or as he could an appreciably lighter weapon.

But it must be remembered that all this deals with a m.v. of not less than about 2500 f.s. if the bullet is to have sufficient speed left by the time it gets out to where the animal is standing. So it will be seen that it is quite absurd to imagine that any small increases in velocity below that "critical" speed will have the slightest effect on the killing power of the rifle. Where all normal weapons are concerned, and suitable bullets chosen, the killing power of the weapon is dependent upon the correct placing of the bullet. High velocities can only be obtained at the expense of bullet weight, or a big increase in the weight of the rifle if recoil is not to become excessive; and light bullets are not suitable for heavy animals, since in expanding form they tend to break up all too quickly and when used as solids they cannot inflict a sufficiently heavy punch. A very high velocity is totally unnecessary at close ranges and, since it can only be obtained at the expense of bullet weight, is to be looked at very much askance when it's a question of tackling dangerous game—for them, bullet weight is essential.

ENERGY. Surely the most misleading thing in the world—where rifles are concerned. Gunsmiths invariably quote it because, particularly since the advent of the Magnum, it is decidedly flattering to their weapons. Personally, however, I take little notice of these figures. They're quite useless if you are trying to compare any two rifles from the point of view of the actual punch inflicted by the bullet. Muzzle energy is far too dependent upon velocity and tends to ignore bullet weight; but it's the weight of bullet that matters when it's a case of knocking down some beast at close quarters.

In the right hand column of the opposite tables I have given figures which I have labeled "Knock-Out" blow. I do not think there is any necessity to go into the methods I employed to arrive at the formula I used, suffice it to say that the final figures agree in an altogether remarkable way with the actual performance of the rifles under practical hunting conditions. They permit of an immediate comparison being made between any two rifles from the point of view of the actual punch delivered by the bullet on heavy massive-boned animals which are almost invariably shot at close quarters, and enable a sportsman to see at a glance whether or not any particular rifle is likely to prove a safe weapon for the job. In the case of soft-skinned non-dangerous game, such as is generally shot at medium and long ranges, theoretical mathematical energy may possibly prove a more reliable guide, provided a suitable weight of bullet is chosen for the weight of animal against which it is to be used. But here it does not really matter so much, because it is unlikely to be a question of life or death.

To explain what I mean when I say that my figures give a surer and more accurate indication than do the figures for mathematical energy, let us take the case of the .416 and .470-bore rifles:

If you take a frontal head shot at an elephant with a .416 and miss the brain by a small amount, you will probably not knock him out. His hindquarters will give way and he will squat there like a huge hog for a few moments then, if you don't finish him off at once, he will heave to his feet again, slew around and clear off. But if you had taken the shot with the .470, and missed the brain by the same amount, that elephant would have been knocked out entirely, unconscious, and would have remained down for anything up to about five minutes—yet the theoretical energies of the rifles are the same. The point is that my figures allow the heavier bullet thrown by the .470 to come into its own—as it does in actual practice—whereas theoretical energy would seem to make the .416 just as powerful. It would seem to make it even more powerful

Practical Striking-Energy

Rifle	Pressure tons	Bullet grs.	M.V. ft.secs.	M.E. ft.lbs.	Knock-out value
.600	14.0	900	1950	7610	150.4
.577	14.0	750	2050	7020	126.7
.505	15.0	525	2300	6180	86.25
.500 rimless	?	535	2400	6800	90.3
.500 3-inch	16.0	570	2150	5840	87.8
.476	16.0	520	2100	5100	74.2
.475 N≝2	15.5	480	2200	5170	71.7
.475	15.0	480	2175	5030	70.8
.470	14.0	500	2125	5030	71.3
.465	14.0	480	2125	4820	67.7
.425	18.5	410	2350	5010	58.5
.423 (10.75mm.)	14.5	347	2200	3750	46.1
.416	17.0	410	2350	5010	57.25
.405	17.0	300	2200	3240	38.2
.404	16.0	400	2125	4020	49.0
.404	16.0	300	2600	4500	45.0
.400 3-inch	16.0	400	2125	4010	48.6
.375 Magnum (H & H)	18.0	300	2500	4160	40.1
.375 Magnum (H & H)	18.0	270	2650	4220	——
.375 Magnum (H & H)	17.0	235	2800	4100	——
.369 Purdey	17.0	270	2620	4120	——
.366 (9.3mm.)	16.5	285	2175	3000	32.8
.360 N≝2	14.7	320	2200	3450	36.2
.350	16.0	310	2150	3190	33.3
.350 Magnum (Rigby)	17.5	225	2600	3380	29.25
.333	18.5	300	2200	3240	31.4
.333	18.0	250	2500	3470	——
.330	18.0	165	3000	3300	——
.318	19.5	250	2400	3200	27.25
.318	19.0	180	2700	2920	——
.300 Magnum (H & H)	18.5	150	3000	3000	——
.300 Magnum (H & H)	18.5	180	2700	2920	——
.300 Magnum (H & H)	18.5	220	2350	2700	——
.280 Halger	22.5	100	3800	3210	——
.280	18.0	140	2900	2610	——
.275 Magnum	18.0	160	2700	2590	——
.275 (7mm.)	18.0	173	2300	2040	15.6
.270 (Winchester)	21.0	130	3100	2770	——
.260 (B.S.A.)	18.0	110	3100	2350	——
.256	19.0	160	2400	1980	13.5
.250 (Savage)	19.0	87	3000	1720	——
.246 (Purdey)	18.0	100	2950	1940	——
.242 (Vickers)	19.5	100	3000	2000	——
.240 (Holland & Holland)	17.0	100	2950	1940	——

than the .465, yet you would find the latter hitting the heavier punch if you were to use both weapons. That the punch delivered by the .416 is sufficiently heavy for all normal requirements is immaterial and irrelevant; the point is that it does *not* hit so heavy a punch as does either of the other rifles mentioned, and my figures clearly show this.

These ballistic tables are by no means complete, but they show all those rifles in general use in Africa at the present time. I have omitted all those which have been rendered obsolete by their more modern counterparts, altho they may still be used occasionally by those who own them. Of the older weapons I have retained just a few that are perfectly capable of holding their own against more modern rifles, and in a few cases even surpassing them, but that have gone out of fashion simply because of this craze for higher velocities. Experienced men would have no hesitation in using some of those older weapons, and some still do.

I have only worked out the Knock-Out value of certain small bores to show that they cannot be considered safe weapons to take against dangerous game at close quarters in thick cover, altho a few men used them in the past with considerable success. They are seldom used nowadays by experienced hunters; but the books that those men wrote are still extant and beginners might be inclined to believe that there is no very good reason why they should not also use them successfully today. I have heard that argument used on more than one occasion, both in connection with rifles for African elephant as well as for tiger in India. It must be remembered that when those men were doing most if not all of their hunting, the elephant were still unsophisticated and spent most of their time in the open. It was for all practical purposes virgin country and the elephant had not yet learnt what the song of a rifle meant. If you are lucky enough to find your elephant in the open, you can still kill him just as easily with a .275 as you could with a .577; but the point is that you mighty seldom find your elephant so obliging. Nowadays they spend the daylight hours in thick bush and heavy forest. Under such conditions those men would be absolutely lost with their little small bore squibs. But I shall have more to say in this connection later.

I do not know if the same method is used to determine pressure in the States as in Britain. The British use tons instead of pounds, and I dare say they reckon them with their long ton instead of with the American short ton; but the pressures of the few American cartridges in the list have been reduced to agree with the British readings; so that even if they are not identical with those obtained in the States, they can be taken to be relatively correct for the purpose of comparison.

For use in very hot countries pressures running over 20 tons to the square inch are not recommended. Some of the very best British gunsmiths have wisely reduced the velocities of some of the Magnum medium and small bores from 3,100 to 3,000 f.s. so as to be absolutely on the safe side should the rifles ever find their way out to the Tropics. For all practical purposes of sport there is nothing to choose between velocities of 3,000 and 3,100; but the reduced pressure that results from the lowering of the velocity can be a very real advantage.

ACTIONS. There are really only two main types of rifle in general use in Africa at the present time: doubles and Mauser-actioned magazines. The old Farquharson falling-block single-loader, that was so popular in days gone by before it was superseded by the Mauser, is rarely seen now. It was a splendid action, one of the very best that has ever been designed; strong, simple, silent and reliable. Its one weak point was the extractor; the design did not lend itself to permit of much leverage being available for primary extraction, and the result was that if the chamber was at all pitted, or if a very high pressure cartridge was used, the fired shell would sometimes stick in the chamber. It was usually the fault of the owner for allowing his chamber to become pitted; but there it was, and I am afraid that there are a good many more pitted chambers in Africa than clean ones. At the same time, there can be no doubt that if magazine rifles were barred from sport as, in my humble opinion, they ought to be, the combined brains of the gun trade thruout the world would be brought to bear on this question of primary extraction and some improvement or modification of the existing action would appear which would once and for all render it as sure and as certain as it is on doubles. I shall have more to say concerning single-loaders later.

I have frequently been asked why doubles should be so infernally expensive. Well, you have only to examine a *fine* double to realize the immense amount of work that must go into it to produce the finished article. The material used thruout must be of the very finest quality if the weight is to be kept down without sacrificing strength, because the action is not naturally so strong as that of a falling-block or Mauser bolt-action. Then the locks are vastly more complicated and must be most carefully made if they are to do their duty satisfactorily and reliably. The assembly of the barrels and action requires more care than in the manufacture of a high grade watch—I have heard it referred to as accurate as a transit theodolite. Then the attainment of the irreproachable balance of a fine grade double, which is one of its greatest advantages, is a matter calling for the expert craftsman.

But the greatest trouble in the manufacture of double rifles is to get the two barrels to group together; if they don't the weapon is not merely useless, but positively dangerous. To the uninitiated it might seem that all that is necessary is to clamp the barrels absolutely parallel with one another. If that was done the right barrel would shoot to the right of the mark, because its axis is situated to the right of the centre of gravity of the weapon; and in the same way, the left barrel would shoot some inches to the left of the same mark for the same reason; its axis being to the left of the centre of gravity. Accordingly, the two barrels have to be set so that they are converging towards the muzzles. The amount of convergence will vary with every caliber and velocity, and also with similar rifles firing the same shell; because, as everybody must surely know by now, rifles have individualities just as ships have. And these hand-made doubles far more so than machine-made magazines. No rifle shoots the same from a fixed rest as it does from the shoulder, so that an absolutely first-class rifleman is needed to see to the regulating. The only known method of regulating double rifles is by trial and error in the hands of an expert.

It is an education in itself to visit the workshops where best grade doubles are being made; they are made almost entirely by hand, and there you will see grandfathers working at the same bench with their grandsons. They work, quite literally, to the thickness of a layer of smoke. A piece of the mechanism is passed over a flame, placed against the part where it will have to work, examined, touched gently with a piece of the finest emery or a scraper, again passed over the flame, and once more put in position. And so it goes on until the master craftsman is satisfied that the

fit is perfect—neither tight nor loose.   Such weapons take from
five to six months to build.   No cost is considered, no detail
thought too small; the one idea being to produce a perfect example
of the gunsmith's art.   They cannot, and will not, be hurried.   Is
it any wonder that such weapons cannot be sold cheaply?   And
don't forget; when you buy a best grade double you *know*, you
know beyond possibility of doubt, that it will not jam, misfire,
or otherwise let you down.   I have never even heard of one of these
weapons breaking down, much less experienced it.

Once upon a time cheap double rifles were obtainable, but they
no longer are for the simple reason that they proved so disappointing in use that men ceased buying them.   The firms that once built
them are either out of business or else turning out magazine rifles
and cheap shot guns only.

Altho many British firms build under-and-over shot guns, I
only know of one who makes a habit of advertising rifles of this
type, and that is Westley Richards.   He has asked me not to say a
great deal about these weapons because he does not expect to be
able to make any more for some considerable time.

The principal advantage claimed for this pattern of weapon is
that its narrower line helps you to get on your target quicker than
the more conventional side-by-side weapon.   In other words, you
get all the advantages of a single with the quick second shot and irreproachable balance of a double.   It is also claimed that they are
more generally accurate, that is, the two barrels group more closely
than they do on the side-by-side rifle.   That is all that concerns
the shooter; but the gunsmith has his side of it too.   Since, apart
from the locks, which are common to all types of double rifle, the
regulating of the barrels is by far the most tedious and tricky part
in the manufacture of a double rifle, he likes the under-and-over
because the work of regulating the two barrels is by no means so
difficult.   He also claims that the breech-locking devices are much
stronger on the under-and-over.   At the same time there is an immense amount of extra work entailed in the action mechanism,
especially in regard to the under bolting.   The result is that these
weapons are considerably more expensive than their side-by-side
counterparts.   They are also about a quarter of a pound heavier
than a side-by-side rifle handling the same shell.   But to offset
that there is the better balance, due to the greater concentration of

the available weight between the hands, which in turn is due to the fact that considerably more metal is required in the action because of its much greater depth.

Personally, I consider that the general idea of the under-and-over is sound. There is no question of its strength; at the same time it's but fair to mention that I have never even heard of a best grade side-by-side breaking down. Then with regard to "getting on your target quicker;" this is probably so in the case of a scatter gun, at least when the precision called for in competitive trap shooting is considered—witness the fact that all the crack trap-shooters in the States use the single alignment; but with a rifle the matter is rather different: you don't see your barrels when aiming a rifle as you do your barrels when using a shot gun; it's your sights you're concerned with. In the case of a rifle I should be inclined to think that it's more a personal matter than one on which one should generalise.

With regard to accuracy; a fine under-and-over should certainly be more accurate than an equally good side-by-side. Because the two barrels of the former do not swing in opposite directions when each is fired, as they inevitably must with the latter type, since the axis of the two barrels are situated one on either side of the centre of gravity of the weapon. In the under-and-over the two barrels are in the same plane, the movement of the muzzles under the shock of discharge will be in the same direction—the difference will only be one of degree; the muzzle of the upper barrel will be thrown slightly higher than that of the lower, because its axis is higher above the centre of gravity. The barrels being super-imposed upon one another, there will be no "flip." There is no reason why the under barrel could not be made to shoot as accurately as any rifle under the sun, at any range, owing to its rigidity. The upper barrel will probably shoot a trifle higher, but the difference will be negligible in sport.

Altho the action is so strong it really does not matter, neverthe-less I would suggest that the front trigger be arranged to fire the lower barrel, because it being so deeply sunk in the action body there can be little or no strain on the action when it's fired—and one barrel almost always gets more use than the other.

I've heard it suggested that the wider gape, that is, the greater distance thru which the barrels have to fall so as to permit of the lower one being reloaded, would be a serious disadvantage when tackling dangerous game, as it might tend to slowness. On paper that might be so, but in actual practice I doubt if there would be any noticeable or appreciable hiatus. I've never used one of these rifles myself—tho I've long promised myself to get hold of one whenever I could—but I've discussed them with two men who had used them. They both had liked them: one was a .425; I forget what the other was, but it was something pretty small. Both men spoke of the accuracy and ease of handling; tho the fellow with the small bore—I rather think it handled the .250/3000 Hi-power shell—complained about the weight. But he didn't realize that these very fast shells need a heavier and stronger weapon than might be imagined on account of the pressure generated to produce these very high speeds. I must admit that I cannot remember the fella with the .425 saying anything about slowness in reloading.

But if a scope sight is to be mounted as a more or less permanent fitting it can be mounted much more neatly on a side-by-side and less likely to be damaged or become entangled in things.

Auctor: Have you ever used a double rifle firing rimless cartridges as used in magazine rifles? Are they equally as reliable as those handling flanged shells?

Lector: No, I have never actually used one myself; but I know of several men, amateurs, who use them and they appear to be perfectly satisfied. It is generally considered that on account of the difficulties in designing suitable extractors for rimless shells, they do not function as well as with rimmed cartridges. That is what gunsmiths and others will tell you; but Westley Richards has been building doubles for rimless shells for many years, and it is inconceivable that a firm with Westley Richards' enviable reputation would build and continue to build costly best grade double rifles of a type that were not one-hundred per cent reliable and satisfactory. He has, of course, his own patent extractor which he claims acts as perfectly with rimless shells as it does with flanged. Altho, as I say, I have never yet had an opportunity of testing such a weapon, I know that if somebody was to present me with one now I should use it with every confidence.

Incidentally, it may not be out of place to mention here something that refers to rimless magazine rifle cartridges being used in double rifles. Not long before the outbreak of the recent war, a

certain sportsman who was so fond of the 10.75mm that he had a
a costly double rifle built to handle it, sent the rifle and two different lots of ammunition around to be chronographed because at
that time the Germans were stepping up some of their velocities,
and it was doubtful if those cartridges would group accurately in
the double rifle which had been regulated for the standard ballistics. One lot of shells gave normal velocities and there was no
difficulty in extraction nor evidence of any abnormal pressure; but
the second lot showed considerably higher velocity and extraction
was very difficult. There was every indication of excessive pressure, and in one case a complete separation—the head of the shell
coming away and leaving the body of the case stuck in the chamber. Yet in spite of the stiffness in extraction, the extractors did
their duty.

Auctor: But what precisely is the object of having a double firing rimless shells when there are plenty of equally good flanged cartridges to choose from?

Lector: Just that it enables you to have both double and magazine handling the same shell, which is a great boon in that it saves
you having to bother about a multiplicity of different kinds of ammunition for all of which you will probably be wanting at least
two different kinds of bullet. I have often thought that a battery
consisting of an open-sighted 26″-barreled double .425 and a 25″-
barreled aperture-sighted magazine .425 would take an immense
amount of beating for general all-around work amongst dangerous
game.

Double rifles can be fitted with either side locks or box locks.

Auctor: What advantage, if any, has the side lock over the box
lock? I notice that practically all gunsmiths fit their best grade
guns and rifles with side locks, and they certainly have a more im-
posing appearance and give greater scope to the engraver than box
locks; but are they really any better? And if so, in what way?

Lector: Owing to its design, which necessitates less of the bar of
the action having to be cut away to accommodate the limbs, the
side lock action is stronger than the box lock. Altho Westley
Richards, who introduced the Anson & Deeley, the first hammerless action, has brought out improvements which make his special
action, with its hand-detachable locks, almost as strong as a side
lock. A further advantage of the side lock over the box lock is

that the design permits of a more perfect trigger release, and this is very important to the marksman.

The box lock has less than half the number of moving parts required in a side lock, and since machine work can be used satisfactorily to a greater extent in its manufacture it is possible to build a box lock weapon and sell it at a lower price than an equally good side lock weapon. Do not have anything to do with a cheap side lock—it can never be reliable.

Side lock weapons are sub-divided into two types: Bar-actions and Back-actions. The back-action is the strongest of all actions; but owing to its design it's rarely possible to get quite such a perfect trigger release as you get with the bar-action. Some of the very best makers, such as Purdey and Holland & Holland, do away with the forward extension of their lock plates on their bar-actions and reinforce their actions at the angle—the weakest part—with additional metal. An excellent plan.

The principal disadvantage of the ordinary box lock, from the point of view of the practical hunter, is that you cannot examine it as you can the side lock to see if any moisture that may have gotten in is properly dried out and the lock cleaned and oiled; but to offset this, there is the fact that the box lock is more naturally waterproof than the side lock. Westley Richards' hand-detachable locks can, as the name implies, be removed without any trouble and are quite unique. I must say that I like to be able to absolutely satisfy myself concerning the inner comfort of the locks on all my rifles, particularly those that are taken against dangerous game—rust is insidious stuff; however, it is only fair to admit that I have never even heard of the locks of a good rifle breaking down.

Some men declare that they can see no advantage in hand-detachable locks; but to me the advantage is very real. Human nature being what it is, locks which require turnscrews to remove them will not be removed and examined as often as will locks that can be removed by hand without any tools whatever being needed. In wet weather your locks should be examined frequently; it is astonishing how quickly and how easily rust *can*, and sometimes will, form. Besides, it is very easy to burr the heads of the screws in the lock plates if you are tired, and if you succeed in making a bad mess of one of them you may cease bothering about it and just let the locks take pot luck in future. Holland & Holland's side locks and Westley Richards' box locks are by far the simplest and most convenient to remove for periodical examination.

The Mauser-pattern bolt-action is the only type of magazine rifle seen nowadays in Africa. The Mannlicher-Schoenauer, with its revolving magazine, was very popular in days gone by because many men claimed that reloading was easier and smoother than with the box magazine of the Mauser and Lee actions; and it is still occasionally seen with the 6.5mm (.256). However, it would seem that its revolving magazine could not be adapted to the larger and very much longer shells of the Magnums and other more powerful introductions. The Mauser is very strong and comparatively cheap, whilst given a high grade weapon it is very reliable. All really powerful magazine rifles are fitted with this action.

CHAPTER II

Double vs Magazine

THERE ARE, AND DOUBTLESS ALWAYS WILL BE, TWO CLASSES OF HUNT-
ers; those who prefer doubles, and those who prefer magazines.
Since I am so often asked the question: "Which is the better of
the two?" "Which would you advise me to get?" and, "Why
should one be so much preferable to the other when there are experienced and successful exponents of both types?" that I have decided to devote a chapter to a thoro discussion of the matter here
in the beginning of the book and before coming to the individual
rifles and their calibers for different purposes.

Let me voice an aphorism to start with: The type of weapon
you prefer and in which *you* have most faith, is the best *for you*. It
matters not whether it is a shot gun, hand gun or rifle you are
considering for any particular purpose, within reasonable limits
you will always perform best with the type of weapon that most
appeals to you. That is sound rifleman psychology. But don't
forget that just because a certain type of weapon is the best for you,
it doesn't necessarily follow that it will therefore as a matter of
course be the best for the next fella. And it will be noticed that I
have qualified that statement with the words "within reasonable
limits." Naturally, you don't need me to point out that just because you are a whale of a 'chuck-hunter with some super hotted-up
.22 fitted with a 12-power target scope that you would do equally
as well with your pet bull-pup when using it against Africa's lions.

But before we can discuss the best type of rifle for any particular kind of shooting, it is most necessary to know something
about the conditions under which the shooting will take place.
If you go to any gunsmith and tell him you want a battery of rifles
for big game shooting, the very first question he will ask you is:

In what part of the world do you intend to hunt, and what animals do you expect to be shooting? We can dispense with the first part of the question; but it is necessary to consider the second. African hunting takes place over a wide variety of different types of country, from the bare open plains to the densest and most impenetrable bush and heavy forest; whilst the game varies from the elephant, the biggest and heaviest of all, to the little dik-dik, a tiny antelope little bigger than a well-grown hare. Non-dangerous game is so plentiful and so comparatively easy to hunt, that a man is not considered a "Big Game Hunter" altho he may have spent his life hunting such animals, some of which, the eland, for instance, run up to more than 1,500 lbs in weight. In Africa, "Big Game" should read "Dangerous Game." A man is not considered a big game hunter unless he is known to have spent considerable time hunting dangerous game: elephant, rhino, buffalo and lion. And a big game rifle is a weapon suitable for such work.

Speaking broadly, most African hunting takes place in what may be described as semi-open scrub, and consists of shooting the heavier varieties of soft-skinned non-dangerous game and occasional lion. Where you find game in any quantity there will you almost certainly find lion also. Now in this sort of country anybody with any pretensions to calling himself a hunter should be able to get well within 200 yards of his quarry. Even on the great open plains of British East Africa, these plains are not usually dead level but gently undulating, and except in districts where the game have been much shot-up, anything over 200 yards is long range shooting. Occasionally it may be necessary to take a shot at around 250 yards; but normally such are very rare. In the closer bush, shots will usually be taken well under 150 yards; whilst in thick cover you need hardly consider anything beyond 100 yards. All in all it can be stated that the average range at which most African shooting takes place will average out between 75 and 175 yards, with just an occasional shot at 200. Dangerous game are shot at very much closer ranges. Having fewer enemies than the non-dangerous animals they are not usually on the alert to the same extent, and therefore are much easier to approach. In addition, they prefer closer cover which also helps the hunter when stalking them. Generally speaking, anything over 40 yards is a long shot at elephant; and much the same applies to rhino in bush country. I calculate that the average range at which my elephant have been shot would probably work out at somewhere between 12 and 20 paces—frequently very much closer. Buffalo are usually shot at ranges varying between 20 and possibly 120 paces. No greater mistake can be made than to indulge in long range target practice at dangerous game—assuming that you can see them at long range. Get as close as ever you possibly can, and then make dead certain of your shot.

There is one rule that is, or should be, as immutable as the Laws of the Medes and Persians: *Never attempt to press trigger against dangerous game until you can clearly see your way to either kill or cripple.* On no account must you fire into a potentially dangerous animal until you can see what part of him you are firing at. Do not run away with the idea that you will find your game standing out in the open offering beautifully clear broadside shots the way you sometimes see them in photographs. Those animals are practically all photographed in reserves wherein they never hear a rifle speak and have long learnt that man is not dangerous. Further, most of the photos are taken from hides or blinds around water-holes and have been there for a long, long time to enable the game to become accustomed to them, before the photographer takes up his position in them. Conditions are very different when you are hunting with a rifle.

Unwounded, an animal is unlikely to attack; but if you just clout him anywhere at all with a dum-dum bullet you are asking for trouble, real trouble. An animal rarely charges instantly on feeling the lead; it is during the following-up business that you have got to be on the look-out.

One of the primary requirements of any rifle is accuracy, and theoretically a single, with or without magazine, will always be more accurate than a double at the longer ranges. But theory does not always coincide with practice, and in actual practice the human element plays a big part. The conditions under which game are shot are very different from those you find on the range. Where best grade weapons are concerned—and I do not consider any other kind—experience has shown that a fine double will shoot more accurately than the average man is capable of holding at ranges running up to at least 200 yards under practical hunting conditions. At ranges under 150 yards a double will shoot as closely as could ever be needed in practical sport; whilst for close range work there is nothing whatever to choose between double or single from the point of view of accuracy.

Balance is another extremely important requirement of a sporting rifle. No single can ever be so well balanced as an equally good double, for the simple reason that there is not the same concentration of weight between the hands with the former as there is with the latter. You cannot take snap-shots with an ill-balanced weapon with anything like the degree of certainty and accuracy you can with a well-balanced weapon. Personally, when tackling the big fellows at close quarters in very thick cover, or at night when they are raiding the food crops, I consider balance of far greater importance than accuracy. Any good rifle will have all the accuracy you could possibly require when you are reckoning your range in feet, not yards. Under such conditions I would very much prefer a moderately accurate weapon which was irreproachably balanced to the most accurate rifle that has ever been built, if the latter was not well balanced.

I had this most forcibly brought home to me, many years ago, when I was carrying an old double-hammer .450 N $\stackrel{o}{=}$ 2, 28" barrels and a very short stock. It was a brute of a thing, no attempt at balancing it ever having been made; yet, incredible tho it may seem, it was supremely accurate—it must have been a fluke, but there it was—I have seldom used a more accurate double rifle. I was badly off for meat for my men, so, on encountering a troop of zebra at about 25 yards, I swung up the rifle for a quick snap-shot at the stallion and, forgetting what weapon I was using, pressed the trigger as the butt settled into my shoulder. Normally with this rifle I had to quite literally heave up the muzzles with my left hand to get the sights in line. At the shot the zebra lurched and bounded away; only to pull up again 10 or 15 paces away just as I finished cocking the left barrel. I again swung up the rifle for another quick shot at him; only to have the same thing happen once more. It was only now, when I came to reload, that I realized that it was this brute of an old rifle that I was using. The third shot was centrally placed. On examining the zebra I found that one of the shots, probably the first, had blown off his near fore hoof, and that the second had smashed his leg, the same one, just below the knee.

When shooting with a perfectly balanced, perfectly fitting double rifle at close ranges it is not necessary to think about the sights at all; just look at the spot on the animal in which you wish to place your bullet, swing up the rifle, and press the trigger as the butt settles into your shoulder. It's an incalculable asset when taking quick shots at close quarters. I do not doubt but that one's eyes do actually take note of the sights, but you are not conscious of doing so.

Weight is usually put forward as a grave disadvantage of doubles, and there is no question that cheap doubles are very much heavier than better quality weapons; but nowadays you can have a best grade double built to weigh but 4 ozs. more than a magazine firing the corresponding rimless shell. In my experience it is a mistake to use *too* light a rifle. If you are tired or a mite out of breath a featherweight rifle absolutely refuses to keep still if you want to take a shot; but if the weapon has a bit more weight in it it settles down much more steadily in the hand, its weight helping enormously to overcome those involuntary little tremors of your arms that are the result of your fatigue—and you are often fatigued in the African Bush. It must be remembered that a double, thanks to its balance, shortness and compactness, "handles and carries" much more easily than its actual weight might suggest.

Then with regard to reliability: I do not see how any magazine can be regarded as being as reliable as a good double. Things, leaves and twigs and grass-seeds and bits of sand and grit, can get into the action of a magazine far more easily than they can into a double. The bolt lever of a magazine can get hung up on a trailing vine or creeper or something of the sort; there is no similar excrescence on a double, its smooth outline offers nothing that could become entangled with either foliage or clothing, or festooned with long grass. Then an inexperienced sportsman can give himself a serious jam at a critical moment if he fails to draw back his bolt sufficiently when reloading with a magazine, after his first shot fails to stop the charge and he in his excitement tries to rush things. With a double the second shot is always there and is absolutely certain. And I think it is this knowledge, this absolute certainty, that is the reason of the double's great popularity amongst big game hunters. It's true, if there's no jam, three or possibly four shots could be fired more rapidly from a magazine than from a double, but if you are within a matter of feet of your quarry it's the second shot that counts. The greatest exponent of the magazine couldn't hope to get off his second shot as quickly as could a man with a double. I grant that twigs and things can fall into the breech of a double when it's broken for reloading and so prevent it closing until they've been removed; but nothing of that sort can interfere with the firing of the second shot; it is there and waiting on you.

Then there's the question of silence: one seldom hears this spoken of or mentioned in writing except, of course, by other staunch upholders of the double; but personally I consider it of the very utmost importance. No matter how careful you may be, you cannot avoid the metallic clatter of the bolt when reloading with a magazine rifle. It frequently happens that game stands motionless after the first shot, quite unable to place the danger zone; if you want a second shot you can get it with a double; but the inevitable clatter of a magazine will stampede them before you are ready to fire with that type of weapon. And if that's important in the case of non-dangerous game, it's a thousand times more so where dangerous animals are concerned.

Also in this connection, you can carry two different types of bullet all ready for instant action with a double rifle, whereas you can never have more than one type ready to fire with any pattern of magazine weapon, hence there is the very real advantage that if necessary you can draw one of those cartridges and substitute another with a different pattern of bullet when close to game without scaring them. If you are only reasonably careful there need not be a sound of any sort. But with *any* pattern of repeating rifle there must inevitably be a loud metallic clatter when you try to change cartridges.

I have already mentioned that one of the great attractions about hunting in the African bushveld is that you are liable to meet-up with almost anything at any moment, and usually at pretty close quarters. *You must be quiet in all you do.* Any metallic noise of any sort and your quarry will go like rockets. Silence, silence, silence, should be your watchword when in the Bush. You get to like silence, you know, when you come to learn what real silence is. In fact, you soon come to rate silence as equally valuable as that other priceless hunting asset—*patience.*

Let us see how it pans out with elephant: Elephant-hunting usually implies picking up the spoor shortly after daybreak and following it until you come to where they have halted for their midday siesta. You will generally find, if it's a herd you've been following, that they've spread out and are in a rough horse-shoe formation resting and dozing in whatever shade they can find. If you drop the leader with a clean brain shot, you will usually find that the remainder of the herd just stand around, ears up and trunks up, unable to place the danger zone and waiting for the Master bull to give them the line of retreat—they not knowing that he's dead. Because in dense bush or heavy forest it's often extremely difficult to say just where a shot has been fired if you haven't been expecting it. The unavoidable clatter as the bolt of a magazine is drawn back and then pushed forward again will inevitably disclose your position to the herd and lose you a second shot.

Even the sharp "click" of the ejectors in an ejector double rifle is enough to start the stampede if the elephant are close. Because in very thick cover you must never fire your left barrel until after you have reloaded your right: it must be kept in reserve in case of a sudden and unexpected attack from right beside you on the heels of the shot that you may have fired at some other member of the herd. But with a non-ejector there need not be a sound of any sort whilst you reload the barrel you've just fired: there is no sound as you open the breech and remove the fired shell, slip it into a pocket or down the front of your shirt or anywhere at all where it won't make a noise, or scorch hell out of your bare hide; slip another cartridge into the chamber; and then, holding the top lever over with your thumb, quietly close the breech and let the lever come back into position. Then with both barrels once more fully loaded, you can move quietly around until you spot another good tusker. You drop him, and still have your left barrel in immediate reserve in case some brute of a tuskless bull or a peevish cow takes a notion to drive you out of it or kill you.

With every ejector double rifle I have ever owned in the past, I have had to remove the ejector springs when tackling elephant in very thick cover, because of this "click" as the breech is broken. Further, if the springs are very powerful, and they always are, the empty shell will frequently "ring" as it is thrown clear of the breech; besides there is always the possibility of it striking your chest or shoulder and falling down with a clatter against the breech or butt of the rifle; and even if that don't happen, then it's almost certain to fall on the only stone within a radius of a hundred square miles. But easily worst of all is the loud "clang" as the breech is closed; and you can't avoid it, because the closing of the breech has to compress the ejector springs so as to "re-cock" the ejectors. Any metallic sound of any sort is, quite naturally, entirely foreign to the Bush and therefore spells danger to the herd. I very much prefer non-ejectors for this sort of work; tho admittedly there are occasions when ejectors might be an asset. Still, in my experience, such occasions are mighty few and far between and are far more than offset by the number of occasions when they are an infernal nuisance. Accordingly, being a very poor man, I have my doubles built as non-ejectors, as I cannot see the fun in paying forty or fifty dollars for ejectors which I should not be using.

Now if an ejector double rifle is too noisy when tackling game at close quarters, how much more so must a magazine be? Because the noises referred to are nowhere so loud as the clatter of the bolt of a magazine rifle. I have had magazine enthusiasts tell me that I make too much song and dance about this question of silence that I have just been discussing, and that they have never found it so important. But the point is that they have no means of knowing how many times they would have gotten a second shot had they been using a non-ejector double instead of their beloved magazine. It's true that game will usually stampede on the heels of the first shot, and then sometimes will stand around in the most extraordinary way no matter how many shots you fire; but there can be no question that, generally speaking, any metallic noise will scare them if you are close. Then they put forward the contention that if you are lucky enough to find a party of elephant in a clearing you can sometimes bag three or four with a magazine where you could hardly expect to get more than two with a double. Well, that has not been my experience. If the game are going to stand, they'll stand, no matter how much noise you make; and the more you shoot the more demoralized the remainder seem to become. My biggest bags have invariably been made with double rifles. In any case, if the animals are in the open there is nothing to prevent the double-barreled man from using his general-purpose medium bore as well as his heavy weapon.

Another very real advantage of the double rifle is that it's really two weapons in one. The locks are entirely separate from one another. If one "side" of your double happened to break down, you could still continue hunting with the other, using it as a single-loader. I know a man who has been doing so for years. I sold him a little double hammerless .450 B.P. Express by Holland. Not satisfied with leaving well-enough alone, he had to strip the locks—his only tools being what he had in his motor-truck! He smashed something in one of the locks, could not get it repaired out here, and has used the rifle ever since as a single-loader. He is quite satisfied.

It will be apparent from the foregoing that I prefer doubles to magazines. I do, and always have done so. But as we set out to compare the advantages and disadvantages of both types, it's only fair to give the magazine its due. A well-made Mauser-actioned magazine is very strong and comparatively cheap. Price is the great snag about the double. A man who is accustomed to the magazine action can do fine work with one of those weapons. But I cannot help feeling that the greater number of the magazine school are men who either have never used a really fine grade double or those who had previously done so much shooting with magazines that they didn't feel confident without those three or four shells in reserve.

I am by no means alone in my preference for non-ejectors; a very keen German hunter with whom I was friendly used best grade British-built doubles and invariably removed his ejector springs when hunting in thick cover; he had had considerable experience. And I am most certainly not alone in my preference for doubles generally, at least where dangerous game are concerned. You will find that most experienced hunters, both of the past and present day, used and use this type of rifle when tackling animals that can hit back.

In America shooting with the single barrel is almost universal, yet it is noteworthy that American sportsmen when coming out to Africa or Asia usually arm themselves with powerful doubles in addition to their magazines; Rainsford used a double .450 Rigby for heavy game; the Roosevelt party had double 500/.450s;

House used a double .450; Clark a double .470 and a double .465; Sutton a double .600 which he later changed for a double .577, and a double .465 in Africa, and when he went on to Indo-China he took the .465 and a double .400 instead of the .577; Martin Johnson, the game photographer, had a pair of double .470s; Carl Akeley used at least one if not two powerful doubles, but I forget their calibers; Packard had at least one double; Vanderbilt a double .600 and a double .470; one could go on indefinitely as the list is almost inexhaustible. Altho these men had probably never used a double rifle before coming out to Africa, they realized that there must be something in it, that the double must have something the magazine hadn't, or why did all these Britishers use them, both professionals and amateurs.

The British had evolved the double rifle before the magazine was even dreamt of, so as to secure greater fire power; yet when the powerful magazine was introduced, giving its still greater fire power, how come it failed to supersede the double? How come experienced hunters of all nationalities continued to use and stoutly recommend the double rifle in preference to it? And the answer is as I have tried to explain in the foregoing paragraphs: the absolute reliability of the good double; the certainty of the second shot, and the silence and lack of movement with which it can be operated; irreproachable balance so essential for quick *and accurate* shooting.

The double possesses another advantage which I have not previously seen in print, altho I consider it of great importance, and that is the rapidity with which it can be gotten ready for action in an unexpected emergency. Its safety slide, of the shot gun pattern, is in exactly the right position on top of the grip for your thumb to come naturally in contact with it. Provided you insist on a decent sized slide, shaped to the thumb and deeply file-cut or checkered so that a wet thumb won't skid on it—and not one of those wretched little flat slides that some gunsmiths love to fit "because it looks neat"—you can snick it forward into the firing position whilst the butt of the rifle is actually on its way up to your shoulder: there is not an instant's delay.

Let me give you a concrete example or two from my own experience to press home the point:

On one occasion I was trekking thru a patch of thick thorn-bush in which I was unaware that there were any rhino. It was in the days before I had learnt that the hunter must always carry at least a light rifle himself. I had given my rifle, a Manton double .470, to my gun-bearer to carry muzzle-foremost on his shoulder immediately in front of me so that I had only to reach forward my hand, if necessary, to grab it off his shoulder, and so that I would know immediately if he dropped out of the march to tie up his sandal or answer a call of nature or anything of the sort. I was not hunting; just passing thru. Suddenly there was a crash and a snort in the bush on my left. It was a rhino, and he was much too close to be pleasant. I grabbed the rifle off the boy's shoulder and snicked forward the safety catch with my right thumb as the barrels dropped into my left hand and the rhino's head broke thru the bush beside me. There was no time to even bring the butt to my shoulder much less in which to aim. From a range of about a foot I fired with the butt on a level with my waist. As I fired I twisted my body slightly, and it was doubtless that slight twist that saved me from being impaled; his horn only missed me by inches. He tossed me over his head; but I guess it was merely the up-throw of his head as he fell, because my first shot had killed him. Naturally, I gave him another when I came down just to make doubly sure; but I don't think it was necessary. Still, his head, which was all I could see of him, was upright and I was taking no more chances. Now I am positively certain I could never have gotten the safety of a Mauser action across from the right to the left side of the bolt in time; further, unless the rifle had been fitted with an abnormally short barrel, it might have been impossible to get the bullet into the rhino at all even supposing I had been able to get a shot off before he got me.

Then there was another occasion when I was charged without the slightest warning by a buffalo bull that some coon had wounded the previous day with an old gas-pipe muzzle-loader. I hadn't the remotest idea that there was a wounded buff anywhere in the district and was making my way thru long grass over my head to get to a place where I knew I'd find buffalo. By this time I had learned my lesson and was carrying a rifle myself, a double .450 N $\stackrel{\underline{o}}{=}$ 2, my gun-bearer carrying my second rifle. I was carrying it on my right shoulder, butt foremost. Hearing a rush thru the grass, I heaved down on the butt and as the barrels dropped into my left hand, my right thumb again snicked forward the safety just as the buffalo's head appeared on my immediate left. I fired with the butt of the rifle clasped between my right forearm and side, and had to jump aside or the buff's nose would have whipped the legs from under me as he fell and his momentum carried him forward. I am quite convinced that I could not have gotten a Mauser into action in time on that occasion either.

One could continue recounting such incidents for a long time; but I guess the two given are enough to show that the double's advantages are not merely theoretical, but are genuine practical advantages. They show themselves again and very clearly when you are following up a wounded lion. Remember, the advantage is all with him; he is motionless, whilst you are moving; he will choose his spot and will merge into his background so perfectly that you will almost never spot him until he launches himself forward in his charge; his rush will come from close quarters and at an altogether unbelievable speed. But, and this is the point, he will generally loose a savage snarl the instant before he hurls himself forward. It's true there will be but a split second between the snarl and the rush, but at least it gives you the direction in which to look. And because of the speed with which the first shot can be fired from a double on account of its perfect balance, you may be able to get a bullet into him while he is still a more or less stationary target. If it knocks him down, even tho it fails to kill, you should be able to finish him then and there with your second barrel. On the other hand, if he is already under way before you fire, you have a much better hope if you are using a double rather than a magazine. Because the whole secret of stopping a charging lion with certainty is to wait until he is close, really close, before firing your first shot; and it stands to reason that you can safely let him come much closer when armed with a double-barreled weapon than you dare with a magazine, because if the shot is not too well-placed you can give him the second barrel without the slightest difficulty, movement, fumbling, delay, or risk of a jam.

Commander Blunt relates a story concerning that well-known amateur hunter, the late Sir Alfred Sharpe. He writes:

". . . He had had some miraculous escapes, two of which he reckons were due to using a double barrel instead of a magazine rifle. On one occasion he was tackling two elephant in open country without any kind of cover and grass knee-high, when one of the elephant charged him. Having fired his two rounds and accounted for his beast, he was attacked by the other. As the boy carrying his ammunition had bolted, and as there were no trees to climb, he went to ground, lying down and watching the elephant as he came towards him."

Now how could any man, finding himself in a predicament of that description, honestly blame it on his rifle? When all is said and done, the finest double rifle that has ever been built cannot reasonably be expected to fire more than two shots without being reloaded! On a case of that sort I say that if there is any blame floating around it should come home to roost on the sportsman's own shoulders for bucking more than one elephant with a double rifle and not having a single solitary spare round of ammunition on him. Granted that wealthy sportsmen are not accustomed to, and do not care about, carrying any unnecessary weights; but surely two spare shells, or even only one, in the pockets of your shirt cannot be termed an excessively heavy load.

But altho the double is undoubtedly preferable for dangerous game at close quarters, it must not be imagined that you cannot hunt without even a reasonable degree of safety and satisfaction with a magazine. You certainly can. Some of the most experienced hunters use and prefer magazines, tho admittedly they are in the minority. The usual battery consists of a medium bore magazine for general use, and a large bore double for dangerous game. Except, of course, for those who prefer either a large bore or large medium bore magazine for the dangerous animals. There are some men who use large medium bores, such as the .400 and .404 for everything. I have noticed that many magazine enthusiasts have the notion that the double-barreled man invariably blazes off both barrels into every animal at which he shoots, and that is the idea of having two barrels. Nothing could be farther from the truth. It's a fact that nervous men have been known to make a practice of firing both barrels together; but as I have shown, one of the greatest advantages of the double is having that sure second shot *in reserve*—you cannot have it in reserve if you fire it needlessly.

Auctor: When you were speaking of the silence in which the non-ejector double could be reloaded, it occurred to me that there was a point there in connection with magazines that you might have mentioned. You might have pointed out that most men using these weapons, and wishing to see the result of their first shot, lower the butt from their shoulder and then reload. The result is that there is an appreciable hiatus between the firing of the first shot and the clatter of the bolt. Whereas, had they instantly whipped back the bolt and slammed it forward again on the heels of the first shot, and without waiting to lower the butt from their shoulder, in very large measure the clatter of the bolt would have merged, as it were, into the disturbance of the first shot and whilst the animals' ears were still ringing with the report. Well, what do you think of it?

Lector: You've got something there, son. That's sure sound reasoning; but how many men do it? I don't know whether animals' ears ring like ours do when a powerful rifle is discharged in our direction and unexpectedly; but I see no very good reason to suppose they don't. Seems to me if men reloaded as rapidly as you suggest with their magazines they would not be so liable to scare the remainder of the herd; but they would need to do a good deal of dry-practicing in camp or there would be a grave risk of giving themselves a jam thru not drawing the bolt back far enough. And I can see many a fella cutting his chin or cheek with the bolt thru not raising his head sufficiently—and I guess that would be the end of his experimenting. Still, there's no doubt you're right; and I dare say there are many magazine enthusiasts who do as you suggest, but I can't say I have ever seen it advised anywhere. Tho I've used many magazines from time to time, most of my shooting has been done with doubles and single-loaders; yet I can recollect shooting four buffalo in rapid succession with a scope-sighted .375 Magnum magazine without shifting the butt from my shoulder. I don't seem to remember that I had any particular difficulty in doing so either. All the same, I don't like recommending anything that might tend to make an excitable man rush his shot. I can picture such a man jerking his trigger in his anxiety to get his hand to the bolt lever with the minimum delay.

Auctor: You've been speaking thruout of the ordinary Mauser-type of safety which has to be twisted across from the right to the left side of the action before the rifle can be fired. But I gather that the Americans have several modifications of the Mauser action now with safeties that move horizontally across from one side to the other to permit of scope sights being mounted low down. It would seem that those types would permit magazines to be gotten ready for action much more easily than the conventional Mauser safety. Do you know anything about them?

Lector: I'm afraid not. The only powerful magazine rifles I have ever seen or used have been fitted with the ordinary Mauser safety. Whether or not the American firms will be persuaded to build large bore rifles now that Germany is out of the running is a question I cannot answer. But it would sure be a pity if they don't. I've seen those safeties advertised, and they certainly look as tho they should be very much better than the normal type provided they are equally as reliable. That has always been one of the very strongest arguments in favor of the Mauser—its strength and re-liability—provided of high quality. Still, I cannot imagine the American firms with such fine reputations as the Winchester have, for example, turning out anything that was not reliable. But I can't speak of them from personal experience yet; tho I hope to be trying one of them in the not too distant future.

It's understood, of course, that when you are following-up a wounded beast you will carry your rifle at "the ready" with the safety in the firing position, irrespective of what sort of weapon it is; but it would be inadvisable to go wandering around like that when just hunting. Personally, when carrying a magazine rifle and hoping for a shot I used to carry the safety in the vertical position instead of over to the right. In this position there is no fear of blowing your tracker's head off, as the rifle cannot be fired; but the safety can be pressed down into the firing position on the left of the action by your thumb with the least possible delay if a quick shot is called for. I found it very satisfactory.

Incidentally, talking of carrying rifles reminds me of a rather peculiar incident that occurred many years ago. I was carrying a double-hammerless rifle myself and my gun-bearer was carrying a double-hammer rifle in front of me. We were hunting in fairly thick bush, but nothing to write home about—I have hunted in very much worse stuff than that. I suddenly noticed that the hammer of the right lock of the rifle on the boy's shoulder was at full cock. I stopped him, lowered the hammer, and cautioned him to be more careful, pointing out that he must have been day-dream-ing not to have felt the hammer being cocked. It struck me as strange, because I hadn't noticed many trailing vines or creepers that could have been responsible; besides the hammer takes quite a deal of drawing back.

It passed out of my mind as we continued the hunt; but twenty minutes or so later when I again happened to glance at the old rifle, to my astonishment—and considerable indignation—there was the right hammer again at full cock! I again stopped the boy and this time bawled him out some as I once more lowered the offending hammer—the rifle, of course, was loaded. The lad protested that he had felt nothing, and just couldn't explain it. Naturally I blamed him; and to show him that the fault must have been his, I exchanged rifles with him and told him I would carry the double-hammer weapon muzzles foremost on my shoulder as he had been doing, and that it was utterly impossible for one of the hammers to be cocked without my feeling the drag and preventing it.

So we continued the hunt, my gun-bearer stalking ahead of me in high dudgeon, his sense of justice outraged and showing in every line of his back; I more mystified than angry. After about twenty minutes or half an hour I decided I had carried the old rifle long enough to prove my point, and once more stopped the boy with the intention of again exchanging rifles, as the old hammer weapon was a good deal heavier than the brand new hammerless one. "See now," I began in his own vernacular, "you will have noticed that the bush thru which we have been coming has been just as thick, if not even thicker, than that thru which we came when you were carrying this rifle; but when I carry it," I went on loftily, not even bothering to look at it, so certain was I that all was well, "the hammers do not get cocked. See!" And I handed him the gun, taking the hammerless weapon from him. But when I saw a smile twitching the corners of his mouth, I looked down and there to my horror and unspeakable amazement was the *right hammer again at full cock!*

I expect you are awaiting the answer. So am I; I have been waiting for more than a quarter of a century! To my boy, of course, the answer was quite plain; obviously it was a case of witchcraft. Somebody must have put a spell on the old gun, which anyway was much too heavy to give any self-respecting gun-bearer to carry, and it was quite time I discarded it. I discarded it certainly, but it was not because of that cocked hammer! A curious incident. I had never seen it happen before, either with that rifle or with any of the other double-hammer rifles I have had; nor have I ever had anything of the sort happen since. Yet there it was, three times in the one morning within the space of maybe an hour and a half.

To sum up: there can be no question that the double rifle is better and preferable in every way—except cost!—with which to tackle dangerous game at close quarters, and sure to prove more suitable and satisfactory to carry when hunting any game in thick and fairly thick cover wherein a quick shot may be called for. At the same time there is no need to become disheartened and postpone your proposed African expedition indefinitely just because you don't feel that you can afford a battery of costly best grade doubles: you can get along splendidly with good magazine rifles if you like that type of weapon—many good hunters do.

CHAPTER III

The Large Bores

Altho these rifles are defined as calibers ranging from .450 upwards, I always reckon that there should be a sub-division for the .577 and .600 bores, they are so much more powerful than anything else in the group and far too powerful for anything but elephant and possibly rhino. Further, they are really too heavy for the average man to carry around himself, as he would need to do when hunting rhino in thick bush. Consequently, I like to class them by themselves as "Ultra Large Bores" and deal with them separately as second rifles, for that is really what they are, and it is as second rifles that they show their worth. By "second rifle" I mean a weapon that the hunter does not carry himself, but normally only takes over immediately before the shot to get the benefit of the full power when a particularly difficult or tricky shot is called for.

For example: suppose a hunter armed with a double .400, .450 or .470, a rifle that is which he can carry easily and yet which has adequate power in case a sudden and unexpected shot is called for, has followed two or three good tuskers into a dense, matted tangle of bush. It's a physical impossibility to maneuver around owing to the density of the bush and the fact that it's practically all of the "hawk's-bill" thorn variety. He can only see bits of one of the elephant, but can hear all three of them. No vital spot is showing into which he can slip a bullet. If the gentle breeze is fitful it may carry the scent of man to the elephant any moment; one step and they've gone and he probably won't see them again that day, if ever. If he waits too long for a better opportunity the light may fail. What's he going to do?

If the rifle in his hands is the only weapon he possesses, he can't do anything except hope. It's of no earthly use blazing off at elephant and trusting to luck if you can't put your bullets in a vital spot. Whoever coined that fatuous expression "fill him full of lead" merely shows his ignorance and utter lack of knowledge and experience of elephant-hunting. You can fill an elephant as full of holes as any colander, and still you may lose him; in dense bush you will seldom get more than one shot at the animal, because the instant he moves you lose sight of him. But if our hunter has a .577 or .600 along with him, he can take it over now and, because of the tremendous blow it delivers, can slam a heavy bullet from it into that tusker's head with the certainty that it will stun him for an adequate length of time to enable him to tear his way thru the tangle of bush intervening and still be in plenty of time to give the elephant another shot to finish him before he has recovered consciousness.

A .577 will keep an elephant down for anything up to about twenty minutes; a .600 for close on half an hour. There is no question about this. In days gone by, when these calibers were more widely used than they are today, it not infrequently happened that a careless hunter, having dropped his elephant with a head shot, cut off the tail and sat himself down for a smoke and a rest. After a while he got up and returned to camp; but when his men went out to cut out the tusks, they found that the elephant had come-to and cleared off minus his tail. I have shot two or three tailless elephants, and have heard of quite a few others. At least one of mine had a .600 caliber bullet in his head: the men brought it to me after they had chopped out the ivory; and I have little doubt but that they would have found similar slugs in the others had they taken the trouble to look for them.

Somewhere in this book you will find a photo of an elephant's skull that my friend Jamieson dissected. It will give you an excellent idea of what it's like and why such a tremendous dunt is required to stun an elephant. Those little air-cells that make it look like a honey-comb act as shock-absorbers. In the case of other animals, the bones of whose skull are more or less solid, the shock of the bullet is transmitted directly to the brain and they are quite easily stunned; but not so with elephant. Fifty of my Knock-Out values are necessary to bring an elephant down with certainty, but they won't keep him down other than momentarily;

more than 60 values are needed to stun him. With values ranging between 60 and 80 you will probably keep him down for 5 or 6 minutes provided the bullet hits pretty close to the brain. So that in view of the density of the thorn it will be seen that our hunter friend could not have hoped to bag his tusker with any real degree of certainty with his regular rifle, as it would probably have taken him too long to get into a suitable position from which to take the second shot.

Now that is the way either of these great rifles should be used, unless you are a man of quite exceptional physique. To carry one around all day and expect to be able to use it quickly and effectively in an emergency is but a pious hope, you just won't be able to do it. And that's why so many men were disappointed when they were trying to use one of these ultra large bores. Had they done as that fella we were just discussing did, and had a regular rifle packing a decent punch to carry around, all would have been well; but they only had some featherweight medium or small bore squirt in addition to the big gun. That combination is all wrong. Their light rifle was too light, that is, lacked power, to permit them to rely upon it in thick cover or when following-up a wounded beast that might have gone some considerable distance, and so they had to take over the heavy weapon and carry it for long hours at a stretch. I don't care what your physique may be, you just cannot carry a rifle weighing 13 to 16 pounds where the going is hard and you are picking your feet up till your knees touch your chin as you bend down to go under something else, and all in a sweltering atmosphere for hours on end, and then expect to be able to use that big gun efficiently at the end of it all when you suddenly come on the wounded and savage beast that you have been following all day.

There is the other side to it also; if you had taken the first shot with the big gun, then you probably wouldn't have had to follow far. Because my experience was that if you hit an elephant or rhino with a .577 or .600 anywhere within reasonable distance of a vital spot, he was yours. But don't get me wrong there. I'm not suggesting that these big guns are infallible. They're not; no gun is. You can't merely blaze off into the "brown" of a beast and expect to pick him up just because you are armed with a .600-bore. You've got to aim and squeeze your trigger with the .600

just the same as you have with your .22. Which is a little point
that has brought more than one man to grief—if nothing worse.
They got the notion that with the .600 in their hands they were
safe no matter what happened. There was one who rushed so
hurriedly after an elephant he had wounded that he ran straight
into him and was killed by the elephant, which had ambushed
him, before he could fire another shot at all. It's true the result
would have been the same no matter what rifle the fella was carrying; but the cause of it all was the ridiculous over-confidence the
fella had in the .600. The elephant died a short distance away.

I had a Jeffery double .600 once upon a time, and a double
.577 by Westley Richards later. I was mighty fond of my .600
and did good work with it; but I had a double .400, also by Jeffery,
to carry around, only taking over the .600 when closing my beast.
I shot some 60 or 70 elephant with it, and did not lose a single
beast hit. I considered it a magnificent weapon. But then I was
a whole lot younger and stronger in those days: I very much doubt
if I could use it today. I didn't keep the .577 long because it was
fitted with single-trigger mechanism and was the only weapon I
possessed so fitted. (It's obviously a mistake to have one weapon,
gun or rifle, fitted with single-trigger and the others all double-
trigger, and vice versa.) My .600 weighed 16 pounds and was regulated for 100 grs. of cordite and a 900-gr. bullet. With that load
and weight I found it pleasanter to shoot than the 13¼ pounds .577
which was regulated for 100 grs. of cordite and a 750-gr. slug;
but it must not be imagined from that that the .577 was anything
of a man-killer—it certainly wasn't.

Men who haven't used these big guns get queer notions about
them. Admittedly, either of them is quite capable of knocking
you for a home run if you were to try standing on one leg when
shooting them; but then nearly any gun bigger than a .22 rim-fire
would do the same under similar circumstances. I never experienced any unpleasantness or discomfort either at the time of firing
or later. The greatest number of shots I can remember firing from
either of them "at a sitting" was five from the .600, and these
killed five grand tuskers.

Both these weapons are a legacy from the days of black powder
when large bores were essential for elephant, altho the .600 never
saw the light of day in black powder form. But the .577 had made

a great name for itself as an Express ever since Holland had built the first to special order for the late Sir Samuel Baker. For a considerable time after cordite superseded black powder, big bores and great power were still considered the prime requisites of an elephant gun, and it took a long while for men to realize that all the power necessary for normal requirements could be obtained from appreciably smaller calibers and much lighter and handier weapons. Nevertheless, I do not think that the ivory-hunter, the professional elephant-hunter, is really properly armed without one of these big guns in his battery, even altho he only uses it occasionally. There will arise occasions when he will be enabled to bag two, three, or even several elephant if he is using one of them, where he could not reasonably hope to bag more than one, or at the very most two, if he is armed with any less powerful weapon. Not a single one of those elephant need be killed outright; it will be sufficient if they are knocked out. He can then stroll around and finish them off with a lighter rifle to save the costly ammunition.

But I do not think that I would recommend the casual hunter or visiting sportsman to invest in one. They would use it so seldom that there would be grave risk of it causing them to flinch thru thinking too much of muzzle blast and recoil on the rare occasions when they would use it. Further, long years of experience have shown that there is really no need for such tremendous power— other than in the cases just given. But the visiting hunter is not shooting for his livelihood, he is here simply for sport and pleasure, there is no call for him to battle his way thru those matted tangles of thorn. At the same time, if you feel you would like one of these great weapons, there is plenty of precedent for you to follow and you will find yourself in good company. Some of the most successful professional elephant-hunters used them.

Sutherland used a pair of double .577s, and is said to be the first man to shoot a thousand elephant;

Pearson, who could also claim his thousand, used a similar pair;

Banks, also a four-figure merchant, was another to use a pair of .577s amongst other things;

Anderson used a double .577;

Hunter used a double .577;

Larsen used a double .600; and there are many more.

Now let's take these two grand cartridges up separately—and in detail.

.600 NITRO-EXPRESS: Case 3″; Powder 110 grs. Smokeless; Bullet 900-gr. Metal-covered; Pressure 14 tons; M.V. 1,950; M.E. 7,610.

Case 3″; Powder 100 grs. Smokeless; Bullet 900-gr. Metal-covered; Pressure 11 tons; M.V. 1,850; M.E. 6,840.

The most powerful sporting rifle and cartridge that has ever been produced. But there really was never the slightest need for it. Back in the days when it was introduced men were still imbued with the notion that an elephant gun must be of large caliber and great power and weight. With the .577 already available the .600 was redundant. Nevertheless, there were men who used it—I was one of them—with great satisfaction and success. But you definitely need physique above the average to handle this weapon effectively in an emergency.

I have an American friend who used one in days gone by, and he told me that on one occasion his hands and arms were so cramped and tired from carrying it, that when he was at last offered a shot he simply could not take it! He said that he had to rest for an appreciable time, during which period he several times tried to aim but just couldn't make it. He was foolish, of course, because, since he hadn't been following a wounded beast, there had been no need for him to have been carrying the .600 all day; he ought to have been carrying his lighter weapon, and only taken over the .600 when at last closing his quarry. That is the method the rest of us employ.

If for any reason you think you would like a .600, I would strongly recommend you to have your rifle built and regulated for the reduced load of 100 grs. of cordite. It makes it much pleasanter to shoot, and you will find that it has all the power you could possibly want. I am not alone in saying so; Major Powell-Cotton used a Jeffery double .600 considerably and spoke very highly of it; a Dane I knew, Carl Larsen, used a similar weapon in both Portuguese East and West Africa, and was equally pleased with it. I was very fond of my little Jeffery which was regulated for the 100 grs. load, as are all Jefferys. I forget the maker of my first .600; but it was built for the full 110 grs. charge, yet I cannot

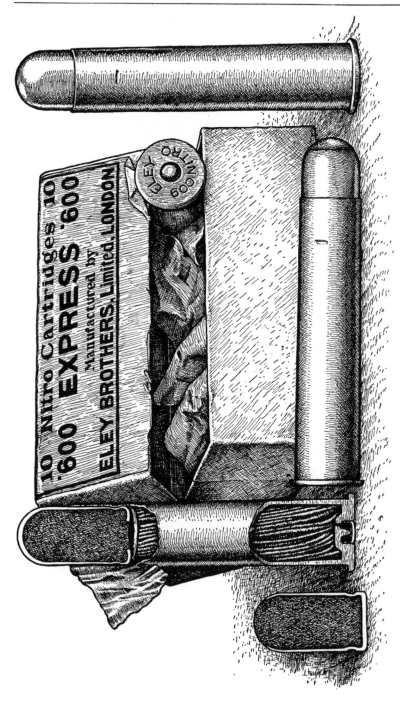

THE .600 NITRO-EXPRESS

say that I found the Jeffery any less powerful when it came to actually killing something; the reason, of course, being that there is so much power to spare that you don't notice if a bit of it is missing.

Most men who use the .600 seem to use the soft-nose bullet because of the damage it does on lung shots when it sets up. There is no doubt about that; but personally I didn't bother with soft nose because they would have been useless for frontal head shots, altho I gather they will kill on a side brain shot. However, I always load all my rifles with full-patch bullets when after ele-

---

.600 NITRO-EXPRESS.

The .600 was primarily designed and intended as an elephant *STOPPER*. It was fully realized that no man would arm himself with a .600 and a .600 only—he would be bound to have some lighter weapons in his battery. The idea of the .600 was always that it should be used as a second rifle, particularly when it was a case of tackling elephant in very dense cover, and when following-up a wounded animal when there was a very good chance of being charged. The cartridges illustrated here are typical of the older and original .600 shells made by Eley Bros. You will notice the peculiarly blunt nose of these bullets. Well, the idea behind that shape was *stopping* power. It was felt that the blunt nose would cause greater resistance to be encountered than would a sharper nose— on exactly the same principle as in the case of the blunt bows of a barge or lighter meet with much greater resistance than do the clean, sharp bows of a racing yacht.

There are certain firms that have always made a great feature of the .577 as an elephant rifle, in fact as *the* elephant rifle, and amongst other things point to the much deeper penetration of the .577. Sure, the .577 has deeper penetration than the .600, but what of it? The .600 has ample penetration to kill any elephant— so what more do you want? I grant you that the .577 is capable of driving its 750-gr. solid right thru an elephant's head on a broadside shot and then thru a tree 5 or 6 inches in diameter—I've seen it done—but it won't kill that elephant any deader than would a .600 after driving its 900-gr. slug into his brain. Provided you have sufficient depth of penetration to kill from all reasonable angles, there is nothing to be gained by additional depth.

The more modern Kynoch ammunition has a slightly less bluntly shaped bullet. I do not think there was any real need to alter the shape, beyond the fact that some men who didn't bother to do much thinking for themselves listened too closely to these statements that the .577 had much deeper penetration than the .600, and never thought to ask if that was the same thing as saying that the .600 failed in penetration—they took it for granted and squealed until the makers changed the shape of the .600-caliber slug. Actually, the amount of alteration is very slight and in no way interferes with the .600's well-known stopping power, which is very definitely greater than that of the .577.

The .577 was always more widely used than the .600, but that was because it was already very popular from its Black Powder days (the .600 was never a B.P. weapon), and could be built considerably lighter than the .600.

phant, and consider it by far the most satisfactory, since they can be used with certainty for any shot where the soft-nose cannot.

I have heard it said that the bullet for the .600 is too heavy for the powder charge. Now that can only mean that the trajectory is not sufficiently flat, or that the bullet lacks penetration. It's quite clear from this that the men who make such remarks have never used a .600. In the view of the close ranges at which elephant are shot, *any* nitro rifle has as flat a trajectory as you could possibly require. Remember, 40 yards is a long shot at elephant. About the only times you may be called upon to fire beyond that distance are on those rare occasions when you may find your elephant in a small clearing or at the water and there are a bunch of cows, calves and immature animals between you and the big bull. When this happens it might just sometimes happen that you will have to fire at the exceptionally long range of 70, 80, or possibly even 90 yards. Well, your .600 has a flat trajectory for 100 yards, so what are you worrying about? In any case, since you will probably shoot more accurately at long range with a lighter rifle, why not use it? Every man who possesses a .600 is bound to have a smaller-calibered weapon for general use—what's to prevent you using it if such a long shot is called for?

Whilst as for penetration, it's only necessary to remember that you can only kill an animal dead. You can't kill him any deader by driving your bullet clean thru him than you can by driving it into a vital spot. He can only be killed the once. I've had considerable arguments over this question of penetration and the .600, and on one occasion, having killed a good bull with a frontal brain shot from my .600, I shoved a piece of young bamboo into the wound as far as it would go, and then withdrew it and measured it against the 24″ barrels of the rifle—it was fully 3 inches longer. Well, in the name of all reason, what more do you want than that?

I remember shooting a buffalo bull between the eyes one day at a range of about nine feet when he lifted his head to look at me thru the grass. I was using the soft-nose bullet and it split his head open much as you can split open a watermelon by bouncing it on a rock.

To give himself the greatest possible benefit under all conditions, I certainly reckon that the professional ivory-hunter should have either a .577 or .600 in his battery, altho he may only want it once or twice in a twelvemonth; but I would not recommend the casual sportsman to do so. He would use it so seldom that there would be an inevitable tendency to flinch when doing so, thru thinking too much of muzzle blast and recoil; in addition, he would find the weight a handicap unless of exceptional physique.

.577 BLACK POWDER EXPRESS: Case 2¾"; Powder 160 grs. Black; Bullet 520-gr. Lead Copper-tubed; Pressure 10 tons; M.V. 1,725 f.s.; M.E. 3,440 ft.lbs.
Case 2¾"; Powder 160 grs. Black; Bullet 560-gr. Lead Solid; Pressure ?; M.V. 1,650; M.E. 3,380.
Case 3"; Powder 167 grs. Black; Bullet 570-gr. Lead Copper-tubed; Pressure 10 tons; M.V. 1,725; M.E. 3,770.
Case 3"; Powder 167 grs. Black; Bullet 610-gr. Lead Solid; Pressure ?; M.V. 1,650; M.E. 3,690.

It was the late Sir Samuel Baker who had Holland & Holland build him up the first of these .577 Expresses after the British had adopted the .577 Snider as their Service caliber. It became his favorite rifle, and he used it all over the world for all kinds of big game, including even some of the smaller American antelope. It proved immensely popular thruout the big game hunting fraternity. Neumann, that great elephant hunter, preferred it to all other calibers until the introduction of Rigby's .450 Nitro. After the 3" shell appeared, the 2¾" gradually disappeared, both as a black powder weapon as well as in its more modern guise as a nitro-express.

Not only was the black powder rifle the most popular of all calibers for tiger shooting in India, but some of the greatest lion-hunters of the past used it in preference to anything else. Yank Allen, for instance, did practically all his lion-shooting with a double .577 and there has been no more successful lion-hunter

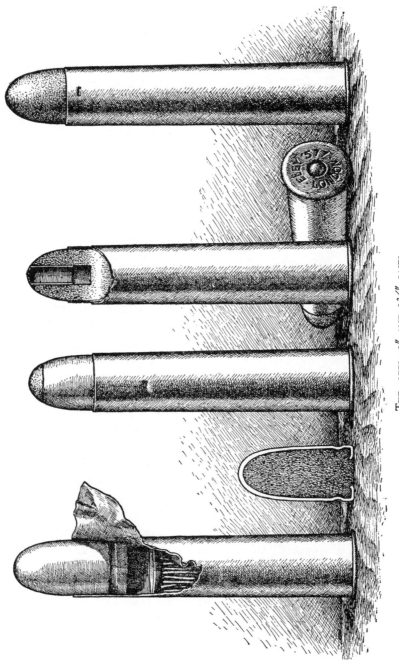

THE .577s—3" AND 2¾" CASES

than he was. Today, to avoid the smoke nuisance, this shell is loaded with 75 grains of cordite and a 650-gr. solid, soft lead, metal-based bullet. In this guise it still remains the favorite of many tiger-hunters in India. They contend that its big soft lead bullet is better in every way to anything in the .450–.470 group with their metal-jacketed slugs. I fully agree with them in that, where lion and tiger are concerned; but personally reckon that the 410-gr. bullets thrown by the .416 and .425-bore rifles are even better.

If I was concentrating on tiger or man-eating lion to the exclusion of everything else, I shouldn't hesitate: I would almost certainly have a double .577 built to handle the modern .577/75/650 load. Such a weapon need not weigh more than around 10½-pounds. Now, altho I kill quite a few man-eaters, I cannot afford to have such a weapon nowadays because it would be quite useless for thick-skinned game such as we get out here. There is no question that the big solid soft lead bullets thrown by these weapons are the best all-around expanding bullets that have ever been designed—I have never known one break up. They invariably mushroom perfectly, and lose no weight. The copper-tubed slug should only be used on non-dangerous soft-skinned animals. Using the solid hard lead bullet I have killed elephant and buffalo, but, of course, only with heart and lung shots.

.577 NITRO-EXPRESS.

In the cartridges shown here, the two outer are the 3″ and the two inner the 2¾″, one of the latter being the old black powder load—as witness the copper-tubed lead bullet. It will be noticed that the nose of these bullets is considerably less blunt than that of the .600-bore bullets illustrated elsewhere. It was undoubtedly because of this that the .577 got its name for much deeper penetration than the .600, plus, of course, its higher velocity. There is no question that it has deeper penetration than the .600, but since the .600 has as deep penetration as you are ever likely to require, I cannot see that this deeper driving of the .577 is such a tremendous asset as its supporters would have us believe.

The solid bullet shown in section is a typical nickel-jacketed bullet without any outstanding points about it. The envelope is well-reinforced, not merely at the nose, but well down its whole length. The plain soft-nose is much too massive to set up on anything lighter than a rhino or possibly on a frontal shot at a buffalo.

(This is a good place to call the reader's attention to the fact that all of the illustrations of cartridges shown in this book are reproduced to exact size of the cartridge; bullet reproductions likewise. These exact dimensions have been reproduced just as closely as modern printing methods will allow.)

.577 Nitro-Express: Case 3″; Powder 100 grs. Smokeless;
Bullet 750-gr. Metal-covered; Pressure
14 tons; M.V. 2,050; M.E. 7,020.
Case 2¾″; Powder 90 grs. Smokeless;
Bullet 650-gr. Metal-covered; Pressure
11 (?) tons; M.V. 1,950; M.E. 5,500.

The full-powered .577 Nitro was widely used by professional
elephant hunters during the first quarter of the present century.
It had made a great name for itself originally as a B.P. Express
and, of course, became a vastly more powerful weapon in its new
Nitro Express guise. It took the old timers a long while to realize
how enormously enhanced was the killing power of the various
Expresses with the new loading, not only on account of the higher
velocity, but even more so because of the much deeper penetration
of the metal-jacketed bullet. Accordingly, since in the days of
black powder it had been essential to think in terms of large bores
and heavy weapons where elephant hunting was concerned, it
seemed but natural to still do so, and provide yourself with the
heaviest and most powerful rifles made. And so you will find that,
with but a few exceptions, nearly all those hunters, both professional and otherwise, who shot most of their elephant during the
first two and a half decades of the present century, had at least
one if not two .577s in their battery. The exceptions were principally those who did most if not all of their shooting in fairly
open country wherein the elephant had not been shot-up to any
very great extent; but in thick bush and heavy forest, the .577 was
almost a *sine qua non.*

It is, of course, a magnificent killer—it literally crumples up
elephant—and can be built considerably lighter than the .600;
nevertheless, there are comparatively few men who can handle it
really easily and effectively in an emergency if they happen to be
tired. The vast majority of experienced hunters today will tell
you that you are simply "over-gunning" yourself with one of
these great rifles, and that you will do much better work with
something in the .450-.500 group. Such few of the old-timers as
still exist have been compelled to lay aside their beloved .577s and
take to lighter weapons as the years told their inevitable story,
and at last they realize that they could have done so long ago;
that the enormous power of the .577 is really unnecessary. I

possessed one myself years ago, a 13¼″ lb. Westley Richards, and it sure did great work for me amongst the elephant, rhino and buffalo; it's much too powerful for anything lighter.

I have amusing recollections of one elephant I shot with it. He was standing on the far bank of a small stream from which he had just had a drink. The bank was about eight or nine feet high and a sheer drop. A tree covered his head and shoulders but he was a big fellow and I had seen his tusks. I fired from about 50 paces, a long shot at elephant, and placed my 750-gr. slug well up on his hip. He must have been standing on the very brink of the bank, because when his hindquarters gave way he tumbled straight down into the stream, backwards, in the attitude of a dog sitting up and begging. There were only about two or three inches of water in the stream, and I could feel the thud of his landing come up thru the soles of my feet. He rolled completely over, so that when he raised his head he was facing me. Another bullet between the eyes finished matters. But to this day I can see the astonished expression on his face just before I squeezed my trigger!

I was a very powerful man, physically, before I went into World War II, and could handle such a rifle with ease; but it's a very different story today. Remember, the rifle that may seem light and easy to handle in your gunsmith's showrooms, can become heavy and leaden when you are dog-tired at the end of a long hard day. Long years of experience have shown that the various weapons in the .450–.500 group have all the power necessary to enable you to safely tackle any animal anywhere.

I have once or twice heard inexperienced men talking about the .577 and .600 bores, and it would seem from what they said that they had the notion that with a .577 in their hands they would be perfectly safe no matter what happened: that they would only have to pull trigger, and no matter where they hit the beast he would instantly crumple in his tracks. This is a dangerous illusion.

There was a man who was badly mauled by a lion altho he was using an 8-bore throwing a slug of 1257 grains. It had the fault, common with those old cannons, of double-discharging unless the left lock was kept at half-cock. When the lion charged the man fired, the gun double-discharged, which knocked the fella backwards, and before he could do anything the lion was on him. He was only saved by a plucky gun-bearer coming to his assistance with another rifle. It was found that the huge bullet slung by the 8-bore had blown out the lion's canines on one side of his mouth, taking half his jaw with them—which was probably why less damage was done when the lion got hold of the hunter. What happened to the second bullet from the 8-bore I don't know. But it just serves to show that no matter what the weapon is, you've got to hit the animal reasonably near to a vital spot if you want to stop him.

The 2¾" .577/90/650 is one of the few shells with which I have not had personal experience. I have only once seen a rifle chambered and regulated for it; but did not get a chance to speak to its owner. Theoretically, it should be a very effective weapon for close range work; and on account of its low chamber pressure, with modern steels could be built very light for a weapon of that power. I don't think it can ever have had much of a vogue; men wanting a .577 would almost all have gone the whole hog and gotten themselves the full-powered weapon. This 2¾" shell was, of course, also developed from its black powder predecessor. Its Knock-Out Value runs 104.

However, the general consensus of opinion nowadays is that the enormous power of these big rifles is more than offset by the inevitable concomitant of great weight, and that a theoretical mathematical muzzle energy of around 5,000 ft.lbs. is amply for all normal requirements. And I entirely agree—that is, when recommending rifles for the occasional hunter. If you are thinking seriously of a .577 or .600, then think of it as I suggest—as a second rifle.

And now for the main group of large bores.

John Rigby pioneered these back in '98 by introducing the .450 Nitro, which immediately became a stock caliber thruout the British gun trade. To those accustomed to black powder weapons with their lead bullets, it was a revelation. The enormously enhanced penetrative power of the metal-jacketed bullet made it an astounding killer. I have not included these .450s in the ballistic tables because, some years ago, the British prohibited all weapons of .450 caliber both in India and the Sudan. Consequently, these rifles are only built to special order nowadays. However, they can be and still are widely used thruout other parts of Africa, tho naturally they are becoming somewhat elderly now since if a man wants a new gun of that power he buys one of the corresponding bores. But there are many .450s still floating around and you can occasionally pick up a good used one at an appreciably lower price than one of its contemporaries in the .470 group on account of its more restricted market. Accordingly, since I shall frequently be referring to them and since you can hardly pick up a book on African big game hunting without seeing them mentioned, I shall give full details of them here.

As I said just now, Rigby brought out the first of them by taking the old 3¼" Black Powder Express shell of that caliber, loading 70 grs. of cordite into it back of a 480-gr. bullet. It gave a M.V. of 2,150 f.s. for a chamber pressure of 17 tons to the square inch and a corresponding M.E. of 4,930 ft.lbs. K-O value 66.3. Holland & Holland then reckoned that it would be a good thing to reduce the pressure a bit, so they took the 3¼" 500/.450 B.P. shell and loaded it with 75 grs. of cordite and a similar 480-gr. slug. This brought the pressure down to 15½ tons for a M.V. of 2,175 and M.E. 5,050, K-O value 67.1 Then Jeffery, I think it was, decided to go one better and designed a massive 3½" shell specially for cordite, loaded it with 80 grs. of cordite and the same bullet. It showed a pressure of a mere 13 tons, the lowest pressure developed by any nitro-express rifle, for ballistics that were otherwise identical with those of Holland's 500/.450, whilst the K-O value was, of course, also the same. He called it the .450 N$\stackrel{\text{o}}{=}$2.

In those days there was nothing between .450 and .500, nor was there the slightest need or demand for anything. The .500 was never very widely used, and has tended to be somewhat overlooked, because in days gone by it was almost invariably built far heavier than it need have been—somewhere around 12-lbs.; the result was that if a man reckoned he wanted something more powerful than one of the .450s, he usually went the whole hog and got himself a .577 or .600.

Today, however, you can have a double .500 built to weigh but 10½-lbs. It's a magnificent weapon for elephant, rhino and buffalo; but the bullet is really too massive for lion. Even in soft-nose-split form it will rarely meet with sufficient resistance to remain in his body on a broadside shot. Which means that a great deal of its power will be wasted; but what is of even greater importance, there will be grave risk of it wounding one of his companions without you knowing it. There is no such thing as too much power where elephant are concerned; the limit of power that should be used being dictated solely by the weight of rifle that the hunter can use with ease and certainty. But where lesser animals are concerned, it can be a serious mistake to use too much power. Admittedly, it's better to use too much power than too little; but when suitable weapons are available, why not choose one of them?

Now, while there's no such thing as too heavy a bullet for elephant, the position is rather different when we come to lesser game. Except for rhino, the solitary animal is the exception in Africa. And if you are using either too heavy a bullet, or a bullet of the wrong pattern, it will almost certainly go clean thru the animal at which you are firing and will often wound maybe several of his companions. It can hardly be described as good sportsmanship to indiscriminately wound; whilst if the animals are of the dangerous types you may be building up a load of trouble for yourself that you may regret for the remainder of your days. Even if you are not the victim yourself, you should remember that there are other, and quite inoffensive, folks who may be the ones to suffer.

I once met up with a fella who was shooting buffalo in a pretty densely populated district. There were small native kraals, or villages, scattered about all over the place and the buffalo used to come in herds and devastate their food crops. Like most good buffalo districts, there was a lot of long grass and more or less thick scrub and bush. There was also a lot of wild fruit of a type much in demand by the coons, from which they distilled their hooch. This fella belonged to that school which lets rip at anything he can see with hair on it, or anything that moves, without waiting for a clear shot at a vital spot or even being sure what kind of beast he is shooting. He also believed in emptying his magazine into the stampeding herd in the hope that at least one or two of his shots would get home. Needless to say, they rarely did. But the result of all this was that there were wounded buffalo all over the district—and there are few more dangerous things than a wounded buffalo in long grass and scrub, particularly when you don't know they are there. Women and kiddies going out to collect firewood and fruit would stumble across these wounded animals unexpectedly, and naturally had not the agility to avoid the charge when it came. Five women, three kiddies and two elderly men were either killed or seriously injured during the seven months that elapsed from the time this hero started operations until I appeared on the scene. I had been sent for by the authorities to see if I couldn't rid the district of these wounded buffalo. The first thing I did was to ask them to chase that fella out of it!

Now I'm no police-cop; I'm not even a game ranger or warden. I'm just a poor divil of an ivory-hunter—(and poacher!; but let's whisper it)—but if there's one thing I can't stand, it's indiscriminate wounding. I only brought that fella in here to show what can happen when there are wounded animals left around. He hadn't the guts to follow them up and finish them off himself. What he used to do was, hand his rifles over to two of his partially-trained niggers and let them follow-up. Sometimes they would manage to finish off one of the wounded ones; but as there were frequently three, four or five they didn't bother about the others, being quite satisfied with the one. The only reason there weren't more deaths or injuries amongst the local coons was due to the fact that in good buffalo country you will nearly always find a pair of magnificent male lions following the herds. These mighty fellows are much bigger than "ordinary" hunting lions, and seldom lower themselves to kill lesser game than buffalo. They would undoubtedly have killed off a great number of these wounded beasts.

This fella was not using too much power; he was using too little and not using that properly. But the results could have been just the same had he been using too much.

The various calibers in the .470 group were only introduced when the .450 was barred in India. And the reason why there are so many of them is just that the gunsmiths raced to bring out the first acceptable caliber to replace the ever-popular .450. There is no earthly need for them all, and for all practical purposes there is no difference between them as far as actual killing is concerned: one is just as good as another—and no better. There is a slight difference between them all on paper; but you won't notice it when you come to use them in the Bush. I speak from my own experience. I have used every one in the .450–.500 group, with the exception of the .476. There is no question but that the .500 is more powerful than the others; but as far as the different calibers in the .450–.475 lot are concerned there's nothing to choose between them. However, the .450 N $\stackrel{\circ}{=}$ 2, .465 and .470 have lower chamber pressures than the others, and therefore are to be preferred. Look around the big game hunting worlds of Africa, India, Burma, Malay and Indo-China, that is, the countries wherein you find the really dangerous animals, and you will hardly find an experienced hunter who hasn't at least one of these calibers—the only exceptions are those who prefer the .400; but we will come to it later.

From the time of its introduction it has gradually and more and more emphatically been brought home to hunters that there is really no need for more power than the .450 can give you. It will satisfactorily answer any questions that you are ever likely to ask it; and when I say .450, I am referring equally to any of its contemporaries. The 480–500-gr. bullets thrown by this group hit a splendidly heavy punch; they can be relied upon to stop anything, even at very close quarters, if reasonably well-placed; whilst the weapons that fire them are of just nice weight, well-balanced, compact and easy to handle. And by "nice weight" I mean light enough to carry all day without tiring you, whilst having sufficient weight to cause them to settle down steadily in your hand when aiming—which is most important.

These weapons can be safely taken against all dangerous game in the thickest of cover without a qualm. The "shock" or punch inflicted is sufficient to stop any death-charge. There seems to be a lot of misunderstanding about this word "shock"; men seem to be under the impression that it implies killing power. But that is erroneous. "Shock," as applied to heavy, massive-boned animals such as elephant, rhino and buffalo, should read "Knock-Out Blow" or "Punch." Even Bell, the greatest exponent of the small bore, who killed 1,011 elephant with a .275 (7mm) Rigby-Mauser —at least he killed most of them with it—completely misses the point in this connection. In that excellent book of his, "*The Wanderings of an Elephant-Hunter*," he writes as follows:

". . . I have never been able to appreciate 'shock' as applied to killing game. It seems to me that you cannot hope to kill an elephant weighing six tons by 'shock' unless you hit him with a field-gun. And yet nearly all writers advocate the use of large bores as they 'shock' the animal so much more than small bores.

They undoubtedly 'shock' the firer more, but I fail to see the difference they are going to make to the recipient of the bullet. If you expect to produce upon him by the use of large bores the effect a handful of shot had upon the jumping frog of Calaveras County, you will be disappointed. Wounded non-vitally he will go just as far and be just as savage with 500 grains of lead as with 200. And 100 grains in the right place are as good as ten million."

Now all that is perfectly true—every word of it. But the point is that nobody *does* expect to kill an elephant by "shock"!

Both barrels from a .600 in the belly will have little more apparent effect on him than a single shot from a .275 (Bell's favorite rifle) in the same place. But the 900-gr. bullet in the head, even if it missed the brain by a considerable amount, would knock the elephant down and out—unconscious; whereas the 173-gr. bullet from the .275-bore in the same place would do nothing of the sort.

Bell shot by far the greater number of his elephant in flat open country in oceans of 10-ft. "elephant" grass. He used to sit up on a light bamboo ladder he brought around with him and pot the elephant in the brain whenever they exposed their heads over the tops of the grass. For this sort of shooting a small bore was undoubtedly preferable to a large bore; not only could more accurate shooting probably be made, but the little rifle would not make much noise as compared with a large bore. These elephant were comparatively unsophisticated and since they couldn't see their companions dropping on account of the grass, and since there was no general disturbance, they saw no cause for alarm in this strange new whip-like cracking noise. It was easy.

I know, because I had evolved an identical method myself more than a thousand miles away, long before I had ever heard of Bell and his methods. I also found a small bore preferable to a large bore, both for the reasons given and because I was scared my .600 might knock me flying from my perch on top of the ladder, which was somewhat wobbly, if the coons who were supposed to be steadying it got bored with the proceedings—as they inevitably would when things had gone on for half an hour or so and they unable to see what was happening. When you can pick your shot a small bore is every bit as deadly as a large bore. But the elephant are by no means so accommodating nowadays. In thick cover you cannot pick your shot; you must take what the gods offer you and be darned glad to get a shot at all. A small bore is no use for those conditions—it cannot be relied upon to smash massive shoulders and hips. It's no good drilling a neat little hole thru the shoulder-blade if you want to anchor your elephant with certainty; you've gotta bust it.

This is where the .450–.470 group comes in. You can slam a bullet from any one of them into an elephant's shoulder with the pleasing certainty that he won't be able to get away. I'm amazed that nobody seems to use this shot for elephant; or if they do, they seem to keep mighty quiet about it! Everybody who writes about such matters takes great pains to describe the various brain shots, heart and lung shots, and just occasionally may mention that if the elephant is quartering towards you you can give him a bullet on the point of the shoulder. But there is never any word of the shoulder-shot when the elephant is broadside. Why? All hunters know by this time that the shoulder-shot is the best where all other animals are concerned, since it's the biggest, steadiest, and most vulnerable target; then why not in the case of elephant? Anyway, I always use it when the conditions permit; and prefer it for elephant just as I do for any other beast. The 480 and 500-gr. slugs are fine for this.

I am not recommending any man to make mistakes when hunting dangerous game, nor am I suggesting that a thoroly experienced hunter can safely allow familiarity with the game to breed contempt for them; but what I do say is, that human nature being what it is, mistakes will be made from time to time even by the most experienced—unless, of course, he is one of those rare creatures nowadays, the natural, born hunter. Such may make mistakes in their early days thru lack of experience; but they do not forget the lessons learnt and do not twice make the same mistake. And the hunter who has armed himself with a rifle from this group can sometimes make foolish mistakes and get away with it, where the story would have had a very different ending had he been using a weapon that lacked power. Here is a case in point, the hunter in the yarn, Salmon, having had around 30 years experience and being credited with having shot his thousandth elephant some little while previously. He was on the Elephant Control staff in Uganda.

Not long before the recent war he went out to shoot-up a troop of marauding elephant. I don't know what rifles he had with him; but since he says he knocked one of them out for what must have been four or five minutes, it must have been something in the .450–.470 group. He came on two bulls and opened fire. The first he dropped with a head-shot which must have missed the brain, and then gave the second a heart-shot. The second bull ran 50 yards or so and dropped. Salmon was an experienced hunter, yet he foolishly went towards the second bull to make sure he was dead instead of first making sure of the other one. He ought to have known that the second one was dead or dying, since he had given him a bullet in the heart, and when an elephant drops from that sort of wound he's finished; but an elephant brought down with a head-shot is a different proposition. Anyway, when Salmon was examining the second bull the first one scrambled to his feet and came rushing past. He had but one tusk and disappeared before Salmon could get his sights on him.

Then the following-up business started. It went on for hours, and the going was not easy. Sometime after midday they caught up with the bull; but could only see his head looking towards them thru the grass from about 50 yards away. Salmon admitted that he was so tired he just couldn't take the shot at that range (the target is barely 3″ x 4″ on a big bull), and frankly didn't feel like closing-in. In other words he was a mite scared and had lost confidence owing to his fatigue. Finally, the elephant came towards him and he foolishly fired too soon. But the bullet must have been very badly placed, because, altho it knocked the animal down, in a moment he was up again and away.

Once more Salmon took up the chase, in which he was making another serious mistake. If he was so tired that he disliked the idea of approaching within 50 yards of a wounded elephant that had seen him and was almost certainly preparing to charge, then it was most unfair on his trackers and gun-bearers to continue on the spoor. He ought to have quit then and there and tried again next day. However, he didn't. Somewhere in the late afternoon or early evening, the spoor led him into an impossible tangle of old and tough elephant grass that had been trampled down in all directions by the big fellows and then had grown up again and hadn't been burnt for years. Utterly impenetrable stuff except along the tracks made by the elephant themselves. Shortly after entering this, the wounded bull's spoor turned off sharply, and Salmon's tracker grabbed him by the arm and whispered that the bull was waiting for them close by.

Next instant Salmon heard a movement in the grass alongside him, looked up, and saw a dim indistinct mass right beside him. He swung up his rifle and fired with the muzzles touching the elephant. The shot blinded the elephant on that side, but the angle was too acute to do any other damage. His trunk whipped round, grabbed the rifle out of the hunter's hands, and hurled it far away. He then took Salmon by the shoulders and deliberately used him as a flail to beat down the tough grass. When he had made a bit of a clearing round about, he placed Salmon on the ground with his feet between his own fore feet and attempted to bash the life out of him with his one immense tusk, which was much too long and too curved to permit him to use it otherwise. Salmon was able to save himself because the tusk was on the now blind side. This meant that the elephant had to twist his head sideways to see with his left eye where Salmon was, aim, and then bring down the tusk with a thud on to the ground, as Salmon rolled slightly sideways when he saw the tusk coming. The loose portions of his shorts and tunic on his left side were literally beaten to shreds where the tusk just missed his body each time it came down.

After some time Salmon noticed his gun-bearer creeping up on hands and knees pushing a rifle in front of him in the hope that Salmon might be able to get hold of it and perhaps do something to save himself. As it subsequently transpired, he had told the others that he was scared to approach on the side of the elephant's tusk and so approached on the side on which the wounded bull could see him. Poor devil! if only he had realized the bull was blind on the tusk side, he might be alive today! As it was, the elephant raised his head, coiled his trunk, waited until the man was nicely within range, then lashed out his trunk like a whip, shattering the plucky fellow's head like a pumpkin. He was killed instantly. The bull sniffed over him to satisfy himself that he was really dead; and then turned his attention once more to Salmon. In the meantime, Salmon's second gun-bearer, who knew little or nothing about shooting, but naturally knew how a rifle worked, crept around to the side and banged off a shot into the elephant's ribs. The bull thereupon moved slowly away, Salmon being lucky not to be trodden under foot, and died about half a mile further on, where he was found next day. The gun-bearer said he had been scared to fire any sooner for fear the elephant would fall on Salmon.

Incredible tho it may seem, the only damage Salmon suffered, apart from the destruction of his clothes, was a smashed wrist watch! But that chapter of mistakes on the part of a thoroly experienced hunter cost the life of a brave and faithful gun-bearer. There's many a plucky gun-bearer gone to the Happy Hunting Grounds thru mistakes on the part of the hunter whose rifle he was carrying. It's not good enough.

I said this was a case in point, but I'm afraid it isn't really; because Salmon's rifle had adequate power. But the yarn is a good one—and perfectly true—and will serve as an object lesson on what not to do. However, I can give you two other examples that are cases in point:

Palmer-Kerrison, also of the Elephant Control staff in Uganda, used a .318 and concentrated on brain-shots. He had a powerful double rifle with which to back up his medium bore, but I forget its caliber—either .450 or .577— anyway, it was either a large or ultra-large bore, and therefore had ample power. Now much of the elephant country in Uganda is what I would describe as delightfully easy open country, and it's quite possible for a man to specialize in brain-shots there. But there are parts where the grass is long, and when a herd has been trampling some of that down and leaving other parts standing, it's advisable to take over the heavy rifle when closing them because you may have some of them pretty close to you on the other side of a clump of long grass, and if they take a notion to rush towards you during the stampede you will want your heavy gun to make sure of stopping or turning them. Kerrison was tackling a large herd in this sort of stuff, and after shooting one or more with his .318 was just passing a clump of long grass when a group of elephant rushed from behind it. Whether they were charging or merely stampeding is immaterial and irrelevant; the fact remains that Kerrison just had time to fire a shot into the chest of the nearest bull. But it had no apparent effect, and the elephant picked up the hunter on one tusk and carried him like that for some considerable distance before he finally fell off, badly hurt in the stomach. The elephant died about 60 yards further along. Had Kerrison been using his heavy rifle he would have had a very much better chance of either dropping or at least turning the elephant.

There was a Lieutenant Commander Combe who was shooting lions up around the Okavanga swamp. It is, of course, open country and Combe had bagged a number of lions quite easily with his 7mm Mauser. He had a double .450 with which to back it up, and presumably for use when following-up any lions he happened to wound. After killing about a dozen, he wounded one. He made the mistake of shooting at a non-vital part, placing his little bullet on the thigh in the hope that it would rake forward into the heart or lungs as the lion was facing away from him at a slight angle. Had he been using his .450 all might have been well; but the little light 7mm slug got no farther than the paunch.

When Combe came to follow-up, he continued to carry his light rifle, altho the spoor led him into long reeds bordering the swamp. Surely if he was ever going to need the .450 it was now. When the lion charged, Combe fired and turned to grab the .450, only to find that the local coon who was carrying it had bolted. He now turned back to face the lion and naturally hadn't time to reload. His old farm boy, Chimoyra, seeing the local coon decamping with the .450, rushed after him, took the rifle from him and returned to rescue his master. A very stout effort. Combe was pretty badly chewed up, and lost a leg and a good deal of the use of one hand.

But what the hell is the good of having a second rifle if you never use the thing? Can any man really believe that a wounded lion charging thru thick reeds will politely wait and allow the hunter to exchange rifles with his gun-bearer if the first shot from the light rifle fails to kill? It seems incredible to me that any man outside the loony-bin could reason along those lines; yet how otherwise do they reason? Or is one to assume that they don't reason at all; that they just do things without thought because they have heard that other men do them? That if you like to shoot with a small bore, well and good; but it's customary to have a more powerful weapon in reserve. In reserve? Okay, then in reserve it must stay, of course; it wouldn't do to use it—would it?—if one used it it would be in action, not in reserve! . . .

By the way, I had a most interesting example of instantaneous killing one day when using a double .470 by Manton. I was out on reconnaissance to see if the elephant had commenced their seasonal migration, and spotting a sable bull decided we could do with some fresh meat. I was hunting in light open forest, and the sable was lying down facing me on the far side of a clearing or *dambo*. There was a slight depression that ran around the edge of the *dambo* like a U, and I dropped into this and stalked the sable. When I guessed I was about opposite him, I gathered my feet well under me so that when I stood up my shoulders would be well above the top of the depression, as I knew I would be mighty close to the bull and a quick shot would be called for. As I slowly stood up the bull rose to his feet barely ten yards away with a look of amazement on his face at this apparition rising out of the ground immediately in front of him. The 500-gr. solid bullet took him fairly in the centre of his chest just at the base of his throat. It was as tho all four legs had been simultaneously whipped from under him—never have I seen a more instantaneous collapse. He never moved, never struggled, never even kicked—there wasn't even a twitch. If ever an animal was pole-axed, that one was.

Now the velocity of the .470 is given as 2,125 f.s. But since all British standard ballistics are taken from 28″ barrels, and since my rifle was fitted with 26″ barrels, we can knock about 50 f.s. off and call it 2,075 f.s. As the sable certainly wasn't more than 10 yards away, we can take it that the striking velocity of the bullet was the same as at the muzzle. Which would seem to indicate that the critical striking velocity to which I referred in a previous chapter is appreciably less than the 2,350–2,400 f.s. at which we had tentatively placed it, *when the other necessary factors are present in a sufficient degree.* Those factors, you may remember, were weight and diameter of bullet combined with speed and depth of penetration. In this case there was a bullet of 500 grains with large diameter (actually the diameter of the unfired bullet for the .470 is .483″), and altho the speed was not particularly high, the penetration was complete—the bullet making its exit alongside the anus. There was no question of this animal being stunned; the bullet could have encountered no bone in its passage thru the body. Yet his entire nervous system must have been totally paralyzed to bring about such instantaneous collapse. So what do we learn from that? Surely that the "hydraulic wave of shock" theory contains the answer.

In the discussion to which I referred it was the .375 Magnum that was mostly mentioned, and we rather tended to lose sight of the central problem by considering the spot where the bullet took the animal—I'm afraid I was responsible for that by bringing in the shoulder-shot, forgetting that an animal so hit was actually brought down by concussion and killed by rapid internal hemorrhage, and not by total paralysis of the nervous system—an entirely different thing.

It is to be noted that the .470 will not paralyze an animal in this manner other than at point blank range on such a shot. Which would seem to indicate that it and its contemporaries require a minimum velocity on impact of, say, 2,000 f.s. It would be extremely interesting to experiment with the Jeffery .500-bore Mauser in this connection. With a bullet of that diameter weighing 535 grains and thrown at 2,400 f.s. it should be capable of bringing about this instantaneous death up to nearly 150 yards on a frontal chest shot—tho it must not be forgotten that the size of animal will probably have some say in the matter.

But don't let anything said about the paralyzing effect of any rifle mislead you into the belief that with one of these weapons in your hands you can become careless about aim and trigger squeeze; just point the muzzles more or less in the direction of the animal and heave on the trigger—far from it. Somewhere else in this book I have occasion to refer to the time a wounded lion brought Blaney Percival down—(I am constantly referring to this sportsman because he was for so many years Game Warden of Kenya and has written it all down in the most charming and delightful way, and has certainly had as much experience of general all-around African big game hunting as any man); and it will be noted that the muzzles of his double .450 were touching the lion's chest when he fired his left barrel. Yet altho the lion received the blast of 70 grains of cordite as well as the 480-gr. soft-nose bullet, he was still capable of grabbing one of the Masai spearmen who sprang to the attack and drove their long-bladed spears home—which means right thru the lion; and in spite of the blast and the bullet and the two spears, he was still busy with his teeth when at last Percival was able to blow out his brains. Percival's bullet probably took the lion diagonally thru the chest —I cannot conceive of a direct central shot not killing him instantly with such a rifle; but it illustrates my point that, no matter what the weapon, it must be held straight.

It's for this reason that I am always a mite chary of discussing this question of instantaneous killing power if there are any inexperienced men listening to me; because I have known of more than one who immediately jumped to the conclusion that now he had the answer; now the whole matter had been simplified into words of one syllable. And eminently suitable weapons of moderate velocity were discarded in favor of new ones with light bullets and ultra-high speeds. The deaths of other sportsmen who had done the same thing after the introduction of the .280 Ross, were conveniently forgotten.

Nevertheless, I have brought the matter up in this book, because I know that it holds great interest for many riflemen and hunters all over the world; and is a question that indubitably deserves airing. But I have not hesitated to repeat my warnings —even at the risk of becoming wearisome.

The rifles in this .450–.470 group are just about ideal for stopping a charge from any animal. For elephant the solid or full-patch bullet should be used; and for rhino either it or the soft-nose with the lead barely showing at the tip. For buffalo I like the plain soft-nose with plenty of lead showing. These always mushroom perfectly and remain in his body. I do not like bullets that whip clean thru. I have never had one of these soft-nose with the large blue nose break up—and the African buffalo is the heaviest and most massive of all buffalo. If you are following-up a wounded buffalo it might be advisable to load solids just in case you misplace your shot and hit that tremendous boss that forms the centre of his horns. Mind you, the plain soft-nose would bring him down, and I personally would not hesitate to use it; but I would rather recommend the solid if you are following-up. The plain soft-nose is perfectly satisfactory for a frontal shot at lion; but I prefer the soft-nose-split for side shots, and when hunting lions load nothing else. A lion does not offer great resistance on a side shot, and a 480 or 500-gr. slug is a pretty massive projectile; but the mighty muscles of the chest and surrounding parts offer great resistance. Given a reasonably well-placed bullet, and any one of these rifles will crumple a charging lion in the most satisfying way.

The rifles in this group have ever been found so eminently satisfactory that there just isn't a great deal to say about them. Arguments and discussions only arise when one man is pleased and another is not; but I've never heard anybody complaining about any of these weapons.

Those that we've been discussing are all doubles—the single-loader is seldom seen nowadays; but there are two big magazines that come into this group and which were only introduced during the twenties: the Jeffery .500 and the Gibbs .505. The Jeffery is the more powerful of the two, throwing a heavier bullet at a higher velocity; but they both have such a tremendous reserve that the difference is not noticeable. I never owned one of these great magazines; but used three different .500s and one .505. I have never used a magazine rifle that appealed to me to the extent that the .500 did—why I never bought one is one of those questions that I just can't answer. It's a truly magnificent weapon and a great killer.

Fletcher Jamieson, who was a real hunter and a country block ahead of all other professionals in the Rhodesias, had Jeffery build him up one of these .500-bore Mausers to special order and he did an immense amount of shooting with it. I kept no record of the animals I shot with those I used but I can well remember I killed everything I hit. I only used them on elephant, rhino and buffalo but would be inclined to think that they are altogether too powerful for lion. The British manufacturers used to load the .505 ammunition, but for some reason best known to themselves they did not load the rimless .500. Whether or not they will do so in future, I cannot say; but it would be a very great pity if this splendid cartridge was allowed to die out. Maybe the great American firms will turn out large bore stuff in days to come, and build rifles to handle it. There's an immense market awaiting the enterprising manufacturer who cares to cater for it. The demand for powerful rifles and ammunition is unprecedented; there was nothing like it after World War I. It is doubtful if the British will ever satisfy it; and Germany is out of the running for many a long day to come.

We can now separate these large bores in the .450–.500 group and talk about them individually.

.450 BLACK POWDER EXPRESS: Case 3¼"; Powder 120 grs. Black; Pressure 11 tons; Bullet 270-gr., lead copper-tubed; M.V. 1,975; M.E. 2,340.

310-gr. lead solid; M.V. 1,800; M.E. 2,240;

325-gr. lead copper-tubed; M.V. 1,775; M.E. 2,280;

365-gr. lead solid; M.V. 1,700; M.E. 2,340.

This was probably the most popular and widely-used of all the Expresses. The number of different loads show the great demand there was for it. I have used all four loads on different types of game and found them most satisfactory. But I am not keen on the copper-tubed slugs—they tend to break up too soon on all but the lightest animals. The plain *soft* lead bullet is much better.

I had a falling-block single-loader handling this cartridge and also a double hammerless rifle by Holland. I killed elephant, rhino and buffalo with the 365-gr. hardened lead bullet, and lion with the soft solid bullet of the same weight from both these rifles. In the dry season the smoke with modern black powder does not worry you unduly; but it is a decided liability during the rains. My Holland was sighted for 150 yards, with a folding leaf for 250 which I never used. For my work I found the 150-yd. sight entirely satisfactory. I was very fond of this little rifle, and only sold it because the stock was much too straight for me having apparently been built for a man who did practically all his shooting from the prone position. If a quick shot was called for, I almost invariably went high. But the rifle did great work for me, and was a real killer.

This was Selous' favorite cartridge. He had Gibbs of Bristol build him a Farquharson-actioned falling-block single-loader with Metford rifling to handle it and used it for close on 30 years for all types of African game. He generally used the 365-gr. bullet.

The modern edition of this cartridge firing 45 grains of cordite back of a 365-gr. metal-based lead bullet, to show a M.V. of 2,100 and M.E. 3,578 is a real killer but I only used it a few times. It's a mistake to fire cordite in a weapon built for black powder. The rifling in a black powder Express was deeper than in a nitro-firing weapon and the steel was softer. The result is that if you fire cordite in such a barrel the high temperatures generated by the nitro-glycerine powder cause erosion at the very moment of firing, and the deeper rifling grooves make it extremely difficult to clean the barrel properly after nitro powders have been fired thru it. But if you like a large caliber you can have it specially built today to handle the cordite load. Such a weapon in double-barreled form, with 26″ barrels, need not weigh more than from 9 to 9½ lbs.

The solid soft lead bullet is undoubtedly the best and most satisfactory expanding bullet that has even been designed. It invariably mushrooms perfectly and never breaks-up. With the metal base that is essential for velocities of 2,000 f.s. and upwards to protect the naked base, these metal-based soft lead bullets are splendid.

.450 NITRO-EXPRESS: Case 3¼″; Powder 70 grs. Cordite; Bullet 480-gr. Metal-covered; Pressure 17 tons; M.V. 2,150; M.E. 4,930.

This was easily the most popular and widely used caliber for all heavy and dangerous game thruout the world. John Rigby introduced it in 1898; up to which time the nearest equivalent had been the old 8-bore. It took the big game hunting world by storm, and immediately became a standard caliber in the British gun trade. Look thru the books and records of practically all experienced hunters, from the turn of the century up to the present day, and you will see where almost all of them carried a .450 with which to back up whatever lighter rifle they used. It was much lighter than an 8-bore and far more effective owing to the greater penetration of its metal-jacketed bullet.

The full-patch bullet is excellent for elephant and rhino; the soft nose, with lead barely showing at the nose, or Westley Richards' round capped, is preferred by some men for rhino; whilst there is nothing more effective than the plain soft nose, plenty lead showing, for buffalo or for frontal shots at lion. However, for broadside shots at lion and tiger, the soft-nose-split is preferable. The 480-gr. metal-covered bullet is too massive for non-dangerous, soft-skinned animals—it was never intended for such work. For such game use a lighter and less expensive cartridge.

500/.450 NITRO-EXPRESS: Case 3¼″; Powder 75 grs. Cordite; Bullet 480-gr. Metal-covered; Pressure 15½ tons; M.V. 2,175; M.E. 5,050.

Seeing the immense popularity of Rigby's straight .450, Holland & Holland decided to see if they couldn't improve upon it; so they took the old 500/.450 Magnum black powder Express shell and experimented with it. The reduction in chamber pressure that ensued was certainly an advantage, as these rifles were and still are used in some of the hottest parts of the world. However, from the point of view of the practical hunter, there is nothing whatever to choose between these cartridges—one is as deadly as the other. My friend, C. Fletcher Jamieson of Rhodesia, used one of these Holland rifles for some years; and most of his excellent photos which illustrate this book are of animals shot with it. I have used both of these shells considerably, as well as the third .450 which I shall presently discuss, with the greatest possible satisfaction. You may tackle the heaviest and most dangerous beast in existence, in the worst cover imaginable, with any one of these calibers without suffering a single qualm of nervousness—they will not let you down.

.450 N⁰ 2 NITRO-EXPRESS: Case 3½″; Powder 80 grs. Cordite; Bullet 480-gr. Metal-covered; Pressure 13 tons; M.V. 2,175; M.E. 5,050.

I'm not quite sure who introduced this cartridge, tho I have an idea it was Jeffery. It shows the lowest chamber pressure of any Nitro-Express: so much so in fact, that there would seem to have been no real need for such an exceptionally massive shell. However, the idea behind it was essentially sound. The other two .450s had been adapted from their black powder predecessors, and in the first instance it was not fully realized that much stronger brass was needed with cordite than with black powder. The result was that occasionally there was some difficulty in extraction with the earliest loadings. The .450 N⁰ 2 shell was specially designed for cordite. It is almost inconceivable that it could ever be expanded sufficiently to stick in the chamber (not that there is any likelihood of any of these modern cartridges giving any trouble of that kind).

I have had four different rifles handling this .450 N⁰ 2 shell, and have killed some hundreds of elephant with it besides scores of rhino and more hundreds of buffalo. Like many other hunters I used to think there was nothing to compare with it; but later reflection has convinced me that its peculiar appeal—apart from its natural excellence—is entirely psychological. I am quite sure that it's the "eager" look of that close on $4\frac{1}{2}''$ of brass and nickel that makes men think it so much better and deadlier than either of its contemporaries. Except for its lower chamber pressure, its ballistics are identical with those of Holland's 500/.450; and there is no practical difference between that and Rigby's original straight .450. But that this peculiar appeal does exist is indisputable; and it's almost certainly because of it that the .475 N $\stackrel{\circ}{=}$ 2 came into existence when the .450s were prohibited in India and the Sudan. When that order came into force, gunsmiths raced to bring out the first acceptable substitute; and amongst the various calibers that then appeared, sure enough there was another immense $3\frac{1}{2}''$ shell. But where the .450 N $\stackrel{\circ}{=}$ 2 had the justification of an appreciably lower chamber pressure to excuse its greater cost and weight, I cannot see that the .475 N $\stackrel{\circ}{=}$ 2 has any genuine excuse for its existence—other than the psychological appeal already referred to, and which it undoubtedly has for some men.

Practical experience has shown that theoretical energies running around 5,000 ft.lbs. are ample for the heaviest animals. The rifles that develop such energy *need* not weigh more than 10 lbs., altho they are generally built at various weights between that and 11 lbs. Such rifles can be handled and carried without undue fatigue, and used easily, quickly and effectively in an emergency. The immense popularity of these calibers in the .450–.470 group, speaks for itself. For all practical purposes there's nothing whatever to choose between any of them as far as killing power is concerned.

I've just been thumbing thru an old notebook in which I used to jot down anything of interest as soon as possible after it happened lest it slip my memory, and then later write it up more fully in my journal. The entries are mostly curt and much abbreviated, tho here and there there is one in red ink written a trifle more fully. I've just come across one that I'll show you, because it's appropriate here as showing something of the work these rifles do that we have been discussing. I said it's written in red ink, and I'm typing it in red right now, tho I doubt if my publisher will consider it worthy of printing that way! Anyway, here it is:

"Oct ? '33   *In camp, Lifumba, P.E.A.*

"Red ink today, brother! 9 buffalo with 7 shots from D.B. .450 N≗2. Good work. It was nice shootin, John; and good huntin too. But don't get cocky, son. 'Tain't goats or sheep you're huntin. Never forget these bhoyos can hit back, and hit hard. But I'll say again it was nice work, an will help to pull up your average of kills to cartridges. Keep acomin, son, keep acomin!"

It will be apparent that I was feeling pleased with myself. There are other entries in which I address myself in a very different manner! But on the above occasion I had reason to feel contented, because two double kills with buffalo on the same day is not common.

I'll run thru the hunt for you because, altho it happened a long while ago now, that little book brings it all back as clearly as tho it had happened but yesterday. I was camped in the heart of a magnificent district for buffalo at that season; so much so, in fact, that the buffalo are classed as varmints on account of the devastation they cause to the local Injuns' food crops and cotton gardens—to say nothing of the way they spread the tsetse fly. I found a large herd of maybe 300-odd all lying down on the edge of a wide plain on which the grass had long been burnt off. I had sneaked up to the very last of the bush, which in this part consisted of a palm forest with clumps of palmetto all over the place which afforded excellent stalking cover. There wasn't a stone within miles, so that movement was silent.

As I reached the last clump of palmetto, growing at the foot of a tall palm-tree, I was within about 20 paces of the nearest bull. I had a soft-nose slug in each barrel, plenty lead showing; but seeing a big cow lying immediately in line with the bull, I drew the soft-nose from the right barrel and substituted a solid. Then dropping to one knee to get the angle right, I whistled quietly to the bull to attract his attention. At the second attempt he turned his great head slowly in my direction and lifted his nose. That's what I wanted, so I slipped the full-patch slug into his forehead immediately under the immense boss of his horns. It killed him instantly, passed out of the back of his head, and smacked into the big cow's neck, breaking it. Neither of them budged. As the herd scrambled to their feet in alarm, I slammed the soft-nose from the left barrel into the shoulder of another bull, dropping him in his tracks.

Reloading both barrels with soft-nose as the herd stampeded, I stood up against the tree and waited. I knew they would pull up again after running 40 or 50 yards to see if the danger was following them out into the open. And so they did; cows and calves huddled together in a great black cluster and the bulls all facing outwards in all directions and about their own length out from the cluster of cows. I gave one big bull on the left a bullet thru the shoulder, and as the remainder swung around to go, I gave another that had been facing me a similar shot. Both dropped instantly. Five with the first two rights and lefts.

Reloading with soft-nose slugs again, I and my gun-bearer followed the stampeding herd at a jog trot, keeping in the dense black pall of dust and ashes of burnt grass kicked up by the herd. And was it hot! But I had found that these tactics paid handsomely, because when the herd halted and the dust cloud began to settle, I was in position within maybe 40 or 50 yards of them, and as I halted and remained motionless as soon as there was the first indication that the buffalo were thinking of pulling up, they weren't able to identify me soon enough thru the murk. Once more I got a right and left, dropping another two bulls; and then after the herd again. This time they ran some considerable distance—and so did we!

All this was taking place during those sweltering midday hours, and I was mighty glad I had long taken to wearing a turban instead of a hat or helmet, because the sweat was literally pouring down, but the turban prevented it from blinding me. Breathing, or rather, gulping, in that heavy black dust was hard on the lungs, and when at last the herd decided they had run far enough, I couldn't have held that rifle steady to save my life! It normally weighed exactly 11-lbs. but right now I could have sworn it would have turned any scales at 11-cwt at least! I couldn't steady it on my gun-bearer's shoulder, because he was gasping for breath nearly as badly as I was; so I told him to brace his left leg, and knelt down and steadied the barrels against the outside of his thigh. That worked splendidly. I was about 40 paces from the herd as the dust settled and gave me a clear view of them. They gazed unconcernedly at us not realizing that we could still be with them, and presumably taking us for some feature of the landscape. I was glad to see that they were also panting!

Getting another big bull and cow in line, shoulder to shoulder but facing in opposite directions, I again substituted a solid for the soft-nose in the right barrel. The cow moved slightly just before I was ready to fire, and I could see that my bullet would not break all four shoulders; but I figured I had them both dead to rights for all that. I let drive, and the bull collapsed instantly; but the cow pitched forward on her nose, leaving her hindquarters in the air, for an instant she remained like that, then scrambled groggily to her feet and lurched around in a small circle with one foreleg swinging. She pulled up, swaying, with the blood pouring from her mouth and nostrils, and then fell. The bullet had taken her behind the near shoulder, passing thru her lungs, and then smashed the off shoulder. There was no second barrel that time, as nothing was offering a fair chance for a kill and I didn't want to merely wound.

500/.465 NITRO-EXPRESS: Case 3¼"; Powder 75 grs. Smokeless;
                          Bullet 480-gr. Metal-covered;
                          Pressure 14 tons; M.V. 2,125;
                          M.E. 4,820.

This was Holland & Holland's answer when the .450 was barred in India. It is apparent that it is just their 500/.450 shell necked to .465. Everything said about their .450 can be equally applied here. The various .450s gained such a splendid reputation for themselves, that gunsmiths realized there was nothing to be gained by trying to improve upon them. Accordingly, as can be seen, all these new calibers that were introduced have, for all practical purposes, identical ballistics with the .450s they had to replace in India and the Sudan. As far as other parts of Africa are concerned, there has never been the slightest necessity for anything better than the ever-popular .450. Naturally, with the introduction of these .465s and .470s, they began to appear in various parts of Africa; but it's quite impossible to find anything different to say about them than about the .450s. Almost any good firm will build you a rifle for any caliber you fancy; but it's generally customary to choose a caliber that is a definite speciality of the firm whose rifles most appeal to you—unless, of course, there's some very good reason why you want a particular cartridge. For instance, if you had a Rigby .470 and wanted a second rifle to handle the same shell, but thought you'd like to try Westley Richards' action, well, you've only to say so and Westley Richards will build you up a .470 with pleasure. However, it's unlikely that a visiting sportsman will be wanting a pair of rifles to handle any particular cartridge.

THE .465 NITRO EXPRESS

I've done a great deal of shooting with this .465 cartridge, and have nothing but praise for it. For general all-around work amongst heavy and dangerous game you will go a long way to beat the 480-gr. bullet—and let it be clearly understood, to avoid needless repetition, that it matters not from which of all these rifles the bullet is fired or whether it's 480, 500 or 520 grains in weight, or whether the rifle is nominally of .450, .465, .470, .475 or .476 caliber: what applies to one can be applied to all of them.

Use full-patch bullets for elephant and, unless you are concentrating on them considerably, for rhino also—to avoid the nuisance of a multiplicity of different types of slug. But if you are hunting rhino regularly, you will find the soft-nose with the lead barely showing even better than the solid, other than for rear raking shots. However, I know of few men who have ever made a regular practice of rhino hunting in thick bush—other than myself. For buffalo, use the soft-nose with large blue nose. These bullets crumple buffalo in the most satisfying way. Even on a shot behind the shoulder, a lung shot, which will bulge the skin on the far side, that buff will not get far—maybe 15 to 20 paces—before collapsing. On a frontal chest shot it will bring him to his knees and

his nose with certainty. You can also use them perfectly satisfactorily for brain or neck shots. I cannot remember ever having
one of these bullets break up: they mushroom perfectly and stop in
the animal, so that he receives the full force of the 5,000-lb. punch.

It must not be imagined from this that you can just take a blind
shot at an animal and kill him instantly if you happen to be armed
with one of these rifles. Your bullet must be reasonably well
placed no matter what weapon you are using. I do not want to
give a wrong impression—no rifle under the sun can be relied upon
to knock down and instantly kill any animal if the bullet hits far
from a vital spot—even a .600 won't do it. But what I do say is,
that if the man behind the rifle is as good as his gun he will have
nothing to worry about if armed with any weapon in this group.

But I would slip in a word of warning right here—and an important one. It's this: *Don't use solids from any of these weapons when
tackling a herd of buffalo.* A full-patch will almost certainly go
clean thru the animal at which you are firing and maybe wound
several of his companions standing yards beyond. I knew a man
who was terribly mauled by a buffalo when returning to camp after
killing a good bull. He hadn't the remotest idea that there was a
wounded buffalo within a hundred square miles; but as it subsequently transpired the shot he fired to kill his beast had passed
thru and shattered the shoulder, low down, of this other bull.
The solid bullet (480-gr.) had smashed the joint and probably
knocked out the bull for a short time; but had struck too low to be
fatal. The wretched beast had an appalling wound, but was far
from dead. The hunter, satisfied that the herd had cleared off at
right angles to the route he would be following to get back to
camp, had handed his rifle, a double .450, to his gun-bearer and
was striding along without a care in the world. He was barely
300 yards from camp when he was charged from close quarters by
this wounded bull. He spent the next five months or so in hospital.

The penetration of these 480- and 500-gr. solid bullets is amazing, and must be experienced to be fully realized.

.470 NITRO-EXPRESS: Case 3¼"; Powder 75 grs. Smokeless;
Bullet 500-gr. Metal-covered; Pres-
sure 14 tons; M.V. 2,125; M.E. 5,030.

This and the .465 are the two most widely used shells in this
group nowadays. The .470 is a splendidly balanced cartridge in

every way. It was introduced by Grant & Lang, and has been adopted by Rigby and most other firms in place of the .450.

I've had two rifles handling this shell, one by Rigby and the other by Manton of Calcutta. I used the Manton exclusively for two or three years, it being the only rifle I possessed at that time. Both these weapons were fitted with 26″ barrels, and were, I think, the most perfectly balanced rifles I have ever owned, and the easiest to handle and shoot. The .470 is a killer—a real killer. But much and all as I like it, I cannot help feeling that in some loadings of this cartridge the full-patch bullet tapers a trifle too much towards the nose. I like a perfectly parallel-sided bullet with a round nose when tackling elephant.

Now I've killed more than a hundred elephant with this cartridge, so I guess I can claim to know something about it. Generally speaking I found it most excellent, and, I think, possessed of rather better penetration than any of its contemporaries—that is probably on account of that slight taper. But, by the same token, I found on three occasions that I had to give an elephant a second shot after bringing him down with a frontal brain shot, which I was, and am, quite sure would not have been necessary had I been using either the .465 or one of the .450s. I put it down to that taper. I figured that the bullet had not held quite such a straight course after entering the elephant's head as would the more parallel-sided bullets thrown by the .450s and .465. Now I frankly admit I may be wrong about this and be doing the .470 a grave injustice by mentioning it. It's a point of extreme nicety anyway, since I did not lose any of the three elephant in question. It is also but fair to add that I have on many occasions had to give an elephant a second shot after bringing him down with a frontal head shot that I reckoned ought to find the brain, when using both .465 and .450 caliber guns. I very much doubt if there is a man in existence who has done any quantity of elephant hunting who can honestly claim to have killed clean every time he took a frontal head shot. But it's just that I never considered it worthy of note to mention in my diaries or journals when these occasions occurred, simply because I *knew* there was no doubt about the shape of the bullets thrown by the other calibers; whereas I was looking for it in the case of the .470. I merely supposed that the fault was mine: too high, too low, or possibly the wrong angle. It's quite on the cards that it was just my fault in the three cases mentioned when using the .470. But as any gun crank or bug will readily appreciate, if for any reason you develop the slightest prejudice against a gun or its shells, it takes a hell of a lot to eradicate that bias from your mental make-up.

And there's no getting away from the fact that this .470 shell has given enormous satisfaction to thousands of users thruout the years that it has been on the market. In every other respect it gave

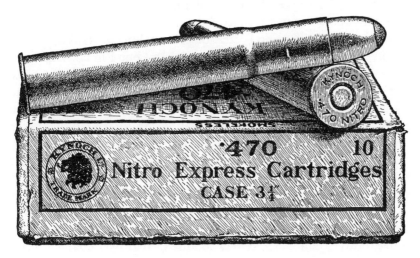

THE .470 NITRO EXPRESS

me intense satisfaction when I was using it; and I repeat, it may be entirely imagination on my part and in no way the fault of the bullet—if other hunters could either corroborate or quash this notion of mine, or rather, be persuaded to do so, then it would be a very simple matter to have a different shape of bullet cast for the full-patch .470.

It's but fair to the .470 to add that I killed many elephant with frontal brain shots when using it—the one shot being all that was necessary.

The question might legitimately be asked: Why didn't I trace these three slugs and see just what did happen to them, since it was a matter of considerable interest and importance? And the answer to that is easy: I certainly would have done so under normal circumstances; but candour compels me to admit that a great many of my elephant were poached, and an ivory-poacher cannot sit down and dissect elephants' heads at his leisure—a long and tedious process; he's got to chop out the ivory as quickly as possible and git!

.475 N $\stackrel{o}{=}$ 2 Nitro-Express: Case 3½"; Powder 85 grs. Smoke-less; Bullet 480-gr. Metal-cov-ered; Pressure 15½ tons; M.V. 2,200; M.E. 5,170.

Introduced to take the place of the .450 N $\stackrel{o}{=}$ 2 when all .450 caliber weapons were prohibited in India and the Sudan it is a splendid cartridge; but no better for practical purposes than any of its contemporaries. It's extremely popular; but I'm convinced its popularity is entirely due to the psychological effect of that close on 4½ inches of brass and nickel—just as in the case of the .450 N $\stackrel{o}{=}$ 2. I plead guilty to having felt this same thing in connection with the .450 N $\stackrel{o}{=}$ 2 before my German friend interested me in the study of ballistics, and I'm certain there are many other men who feel the same way about it. Actually, experience has shown that where killing is concerned there just isn't anything to choose be-tween any of these shells in the .450–.470 group.

But there is a real difference when it comes to building the rifles that fire them; for instance a .465 can be built about one-half a pound lighter than a .475 N $\stackrel{o}{=}$ 2, because of its lower chamber pres-sure and less immense cartridge. Accordingly, if you like a light rifle—and most men nowadays want their rifles built as light as re-coil permits—the .465 shows a very considerable advantage over the .475 N $\stackrel{o}{=}$ 2. The ammunition is also appreciably lighter. How-ever, this needn't dissuade you from buying a .475 N $\stackrel{o}{=}$ 2 if for any reason it appeals to you. You will find it an eminently satisfactory shell and a certain killer—but don't let yourself be hypnotized by that great long fat gleaming shell into the belief that you have something comparable with the atomic bomb to play with!

Jeffery, who used to build his rifles for the .450 N $\stackrel{o}{=}$ 2 shell, took to the .475 N $\stackrel{o}{=}$ 2, but gives it a different load. He used the same shell and loads 80 grs. of powder back of a 500-gr. bullet. This re-duced the pressure a bit, but not much—to about 15 tons, I think—and also reduces the velocity to 2,000 f.s. and the energy to 4,450 ft.lbs. This, I cannot help feeling, is a mistake. Because, altho the actual shells are interchangeable, a double rifle regulated for one of them could not be expected to group accurately with the other. Comparatively few sportsmen would realize this, and in the careless way they have of buying ammunition locally and quite casually, could easily take anything that was marked .475 N≗2 and fitted in the chambers of their rifle and try to use that, irrespective of whether or not it was the load for which their rifle was

.475 N≗2 NITRO-EXPRESS.

The illustration here shows clearly the massively strong cases these N≗2 shells are given. This originated with the Jeffery 3″ 450/.400 and then the .450 N≗2, owing to the trouble that was occasionally experienced in extraction with their earlier contemporaries which had been developed from their black powder predecessors. The idea behind these extra-strong cases is essentially sound but experience has shown that *all* these flanged shells are made so strong nowadays that there would seem no earthly need for the additional strength of the N≗2s. It spells additional weight and additional cost, without anything practical in the way of benefit to balance matters.

The bullet shown here is the ordinary nickel-jacketed soft-nose. Personally, I reckon it would be far better to put the extra cost of these cartridges into reinforced steel-covered solids instead of needlessly strengthening the base of the shell.

regulated. The ammunition makers are always most particular to mark Jeffery's load "For Jeffery Rifles" but from what I've seen of the ordinary casual hunter, that would have no effect on him whatever nor make the slightest impression. "This is a .475 N≗2, isn't it?" he'd say, buying a secondhand rifle locally. "And this is .475 N≗2 ammunition, isn't it? Well, it seems to fit all right; so what's the difference. It'll be all right." And off he goes to shoot with a rifle the two barrels of which probably won't be grouping within 6 inches or so of one another! I'm not exaggerating—I've seen it done, and I have little doubt it's being done all over Africa all the time.

As far as this special load of Jeffery's is concerned, I must say I found it entirely satisfactory, altho its ballistics are not so good as those of the standard load for this shell. I've seen a good many of these rifles of Jeffery's in use, and the owners of them are entirely satisfied—at least when they are using the correct load. I repeat, however, it's a mistake to have two loads in interchangeable shells for use in double rifles, only one of which loads is suitable for either rifle.

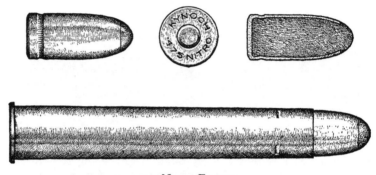

.475 NITRO EXPRESS.

Case 3¼″; Powder 75 grs. Smokeless; Bullet 480-gr. Metal-covered; Pressure 15 tons; M.V. 2,175 f.s.; M.E. 5,050 ft.lbs.

An excellent cartridge for general all-around work amongst heavy and dangerous game. It was one of those introduced when the .450 caliber was prohibited in India and the Sudan. There is nothing whatever to choose between any of the cartridges in this group from the point of view of killing power and effectiveness, whether the comparison is attempted on paper or in actual practice in the field. I speak from my own experience—at one time or another I think I have used each and every one of them. The bullet shown in this illustration is the plain soft-nose, plenty lead showing. It's my favorite for buffalo. For frontal shots at lion it is also entirely satisfactory but is all too liable to smash clean thru on a broadside shot, not meeting with sufficient resistance to stop it.

As I said before, this .475 N⁰2 is a rifle that has been widely touted, but let me repeat that it is really no better than any of its contemporaries. There is a hunter of very considerable experience in the French Cameroons who used it extensively; but he recently wrote that in his experience the .465 is every bit as good. That exactly bears out my own opinion. I did not use it to anything like the extent that I used the .470, .465 and .450 N⁰2; but I used it sufficiently to see that it was in no way to be preferred—any more than the .450 N⁰2 is really any better than the 500/.450.

But as I have mentioned elsewhere, it did at least have a lower chamber pressure to justify its existence. But the .475 N $\underline{o}$ 2 cannot even claim that; and it has the disadvantage that it must weigh about 8-ozs more than the .465.

.476 NITRO-EXPRESS

Case 3¼"; Powder 75 grs. Smokeless; Bullet 520 grs. Metal-covered; Pressure 16 tons; M.V. 2100; M.E. 5100.

This is the only caliber in this group with which I've had no personal experience. But I don't really need to have used it to know how it would behave. In point of actual fact, it's a .500-caliber, because the diameter of the unfired bullet is .510″. The only real advantage it possesses over its contemporaries is that Westley Richards' "L.T." hollow pointed capped bullet is available for it, and such a bullet in this weight would be more generally suitable for lion or tiger than any of the various soft nose and split bullets. Nevertheless, there's no reason under the sun why such bullets couldn't be supplied for the .465 and .470 calibers. In these weights—480, 500 and 520 grs.—you need a slug that will always expand to its maximum extent on critters that can only offer but a limited amount of resistance to such comparatively massive projectiles.

Westley Richards also supply a lighter bullet, 385 grs, with a special round-nose hollow-cap. I know nothing about this bullet, and have not met up with any one who had used it. I know nothing about its velocity either; but doubt very much if it could be used in a double regulated for the heavier slug.

THE B.P. .500 EXPRESS never had a very wide vogue in Africa, tho it was and is—in its more modern form, firing a reduced cordite charge to obviate the smoke nuisance—extremely popular amongst certain officers of the Forest Service in India; men who expected to be encountering a considerable number of tiger, but did not seem likely to be tackling elephant or buffalo. In its Nitro Express guise it was usually built far too heavy—12-lbs and up—so that most men passed it by. But in its modern dress, weighing but 10½ lbs, it is one of my favorites for elephant and rhino. It's a real killer.

.500 B.P. EXPRESS.

There were two of these cartridges, 3″ and 3¼″, the following are the ballistics:—

Case 3″; Powder 136 grs. Black; Bullet 340-gr. Lead copper-tubed; M.V. 1,925; M.E. 2,800.

Case 3″; Powder 136 grs. Black; Bullet 380-gr. Lead solid; M.V. 1,850; M.E. 2,890.

Case 3¼″; Powder 142 grs. Black; Bullet 440-gr. Lead copper-tubed; M.V. 1,775; M.E. 3,080.

Case 3¼″; Powder 142 grs. Black; Bullet 480-gr. Lead solid; M.V. 1,700; M.E. 3,080.

The black powder .500 was never very widely used in Africa but was, and still is, very popular with forest officers in India whose work brings them into contact with a fair number of man-eating tigers, but who do not expect to be tackling elephant or bison. The .500 was light to carry and a powerful weapon against soft-skinned game when properly handled. The copper-tubed bullets should never be used against dangerous game—they tend to break up much too quickly; but the solid *soft* lead bullet is excellent—it invariably mushrooms perfectly and never breaks up.

I shot quite a few man-eating and cattle-killing lions with a double hammerless .500 B.P. Express using the solid soft-lead bullet, and a few buffalo with the solid hardened-lead slug. With the buffalo it was necessary to take heart and lung shots, and it would not have been pleasant to have to face a charge with only a lead bullet. In the dry season I did not find the smoke a nuisance but during the rains, particularly in the early morning when the atmosphere was saturated with moisture and there was no breeze at all, it lay like a dense gray pall in front of me and seemed to take a hell of a time to clear.

Another disadvantage of those old black powder shells was the paper patch around the bullet. On several occasions I found that a small bit of this paper has remained on the lip of the shell, and as I removed the shell from the breech to reload the little bit of paper would sometimes drop down behind the extractors, which was quite sufficient to prevent a well-made weapon from closing until the obstruction had been removed. This besides being a nuisance might well have been dangerous owing to the delay it caused in reloading. Nevertheless, I must confess to a weakness for black powder and the weapons that fire it.

But when using it for buffalo, you got to be very careful. Even with plenty lead showing, that 570-gr. slug takes a lot of stopping. But if you are careful to always hit bones, then you won't get a better buffalo gun. But I wouldn't recommend it for lion. Its bullet is altogether too massive for any soft-skinned critter. True, on a frontal shot, the split slug will do its stuff nicely; but then you don't always get frontal shots. I've a notion that this also was one of the things that counted against the .500's popularity.

Nevertheless, there were some men who swore by it. The late Dr. Cristy, the greatest authority on the little forest buffalo of the Congo and across to West Africa, used nothing else, both for them and also for the rare and elusive okapi. The latter is not dangerous, but Cristy always recommended some such weapon of plenty power, such as the double .500, for them because of the general density of the undergrowth in which they were mostly found. Lighter bullets would be all-too-easily deflected. It was one of those same little forest buffalo, renowned for their aggressiveness, that finally killed the doctor.

. His book—I forget its name—dealing with these little buffalo, is a mass of information; but like all too many of these knowledge-able folks, he *will* try to split hairs. Lydekker was another, who tried to divide the African elephant into a dozen different races, basing his theories on single specimens of their ears taken from elephant from all over the continent. Blunt lets himself go a mite when speaking of this, and describes it as worse than splitting hairs. He says he would be willing to hunt for and find all Lydekker's new races in the Lindi province of Tanganyika alone. I would be willing to do likewise; and also hunt for and find all the different shapes of buffalo's horns in the Lifumba area of Portuguese East. It's true that the little forest buffalo is a different critter from the big Cape buffalo, as he's generally called, that's found thruout the rest of the continent, and which invariably comes to mind when African buffalo are mentioned; but Cristy spends the greater part of his most learned book in an attempt to divide the forest buffalo into numerous races just because of slight variations in the shape of their horns. Much the same sort of thing has been attempted with the ordinary buffalo. But I consider all such attempts as evidence that the scientist concerned has nothing better to do to pass the time, and is merely filling in an otherwise idle

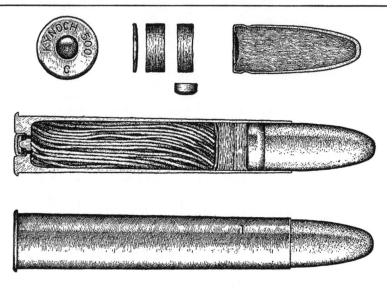

.500 NITRO EXPRESS.

Case 3″; Powder 80 grs. Smokeless; Bullet 570-gr. Metal-covered; Pressure 16 tons; M.V. 2,150; M.E. 5,850.

There are two of these .500s—the other has a 3¼″ shell; but the same load is used. This gives it a reduction of half a ton in pressure and a drop of 25 f.s. in velocity. The difference between them is so slight that I'm not concerned with it, and the remarks made with regard to one can be equally applied to the other. It must be remembered, however, that the shells are not interchangeable on account of their difference in length.

Both these cartridges were evolved from their black powder predecessors. The .500 has tended to be overlooked because in the past they were almost invariably built far heavier than they need have been. The usual weight ran in the vicinity of 12 lbs. or so. The result was that if a man felt he wanted something more powerful than a .450, he usually went the whole hog and got himself a .577. But nowadays you can get a double .500 built to weigh but 10½ lbs. It's a really powerful cartridge and a great killer. I'm very fond of it for elephant.

I remember bowling a rhino over for all the world like a rabbit with a soft-nose bullet from a double .500, lead barely showing at the nose. He was galloping across my front at a range of about 15 paces and descending a slight slope. I slammed the 570-gr. slug into his near shoulder and he turned two complete somersaults, his heels over his head, and looked like throwing several more if he hadn't been pulled up by a tree into which he crashed. My heart was in my mouth for fear he would smash his horns—they were good ones—but fortunately he didn't. He was as dead as a canned lobster on receipt of that bullet. The plain soft-nose bullet, large blue nose, crumples buffalo in the most satisfying manner, but is too massive for good results on lion.

The cartridge illustrated here is most interesting and shows something I have never previously seen. It will be noticed that the neck of the shell has not been swedged or crimped into the cannelure of the bullet, but below the base of the hour or two. Or else reckons it's time he got his name before the public again before they forget him. For instance, Lydekker stated that one mounted elephant's ear he had examined showed no evidence of having had a turn-over flap at the top. The inference being that he had discovered a new breed of elephant that didn't have this flap. But no elephant's ear shows that flap when mounted in the ordinary way as a card table or occasional table; yet every African elephant with normal ears has that flap in life.

I'm not gonna say a great deal about the .500 because Holland & Holland, with whom I've been in communication, told me recently that they very much doubt if Kynoch will continue to turn out shells of that caliber, as there had been such a very small demand for them prior to the war. So, altho the .500 is a magnificent gun for elephant, rhino, and possibly buffalo, make all due enquiries from the makers of the shells anent future supplies of ammunition before investing in a weapon of this caliber. If they give you the all-clear, then you needn't hesitate to buy if your fancy runs in this direction. The difference between the two shells, 3″ and 3¼, is not worth considering.

.505 RIMLESS (GIBBS): Powder 90 gr. Smokeless; Bullet 525-gr. Metal-covered; Pressure 15 tons; M.V. 2,300; M.E. 6,180.

One of the two most powerful Mauser-actioned magazine sporting rifles in existence—only surpassed by the Jeffery .500, the ammunition for which was only obtainable in Germany. I never possessed one of these rifles; but used one belonging to another fella who wanted my opinion of it. I had no difficulty in giving

---

bullet. I am very glad that my publisher has managed to get hold of an example like that, because it just shows how very necessary it is to examine every darn thing you take out with you when after animals that can hit back. I am quite sure that this is exceptional and was due to some mal-adjustment of the loading machine. After all, what other explanation can there be? There can be no earthly reason for crimping the case below the bullet. But it's certainly going to make me even more particular than I have been to look to all details. It naturally raises the question: Have you ever had the bullets in these big shells "jump forward" when kept in the left barrel whilst a few shots were fired thru the right? To that I can definitely answer "No." And assuming a weapon that was properly chambered and in which the bores have been kept in good condition, I do not think it would be possible for the bullet to get far forward without coming in contact with the rifling which would prevent it coming right out of the shell.

him that. It's a magnificent weapon, if you like a magazine, and has adequate power for all emergencies; so much so, in fact, that it would comfortably stand a reduction in barrel length to around 22″, which would make it a much handier weapon in thick cover.

I had expected considerable recoil; but was most agreeably surprised to find how little there was. This is undoubtedly due to the solidity with which these great magazines are built. They are very pleasant to shoot, and very accurate. I did not do as much shooting with this weapon as I would have liked to have done, because the owner was hanging about waiting for it and I could not think of a good enough excuse to delay returning it! However, I recollect one buffalo bull deliberately shot at very long range—196 very long strides—just to see how the rifle behaved. The 525-gr. slug took him fairly on the shoulder and he dropped as instantaneously as tho the range had been but 19 strides. Except for a slight lift and fall of his head, which showed that rapid internal hemorrhage was at work, he never budged after receiving the bullet and was dead within less than a minute.

Various other buffalo and a couple of rhino were shot, but there was nothing remarkable to mention. If you think you would prefer a powerful magazine to a double for dangerous game, then this .505 of George Gibbs' can be strongly recommended.

.500 RIMLESS (JEFFERY): Powder 95(?) grs. Smokeless; Bullet 535-gr. Metal-covered; Pressure 16 tons; M.V. 2,400; M.E. 6,800.

This is the most powerful sporting magazine rifle that has ever been placed on the market. It's a glorious weapon, and very easy and pleasant to handle and shoot. I used three of these rifles at different times, trying them out for their owners, and each time told myself that I simply must get one for myself. This is the only magazine rifle that has ever had that effect on me. I preferred it to the .505, but it's not easy to say why; I think the answer is to be found in the fatter fore-arm with which Jeffery fitted his weapons and which gave me a much better and more comfortable grip. These were, I think, the most perfectly balanced magazine rifles I ever used. If I was having one built, however, I should certainly insist on a 22″ barrel instead of the 24″ that is normally fitted. The cartridge has an ample reserve of power to permit of this reduction in barrel length, whilst still leaving an adequate reserve. As with

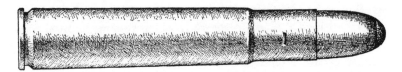

UPPER CARTRIDGE IS .500 JEFFERY RIMLESS.
LOWER CARTRIDGE IS .505 GIBBS.

As in these two illustrations, you will find varying amounts of lead showing at the nose of British soft-nose bullets. This is not accidental, neither is it carelessness on the part of the illustrator. On the contrary he has taken the greatest care to get all such matters as exposed lead points, and thickness of bullet jacket in the case of solids, absolutely accurate and to scale. All these cartridge illustrations are exactly life-size. The varying amounts of lead exposed are the British method of controlling expansion—the more lead showing, the more rapid the expansion. In rifles like these two large bore magazines that would only be used against heavy animals, and in view of their comparatively high velocity for such calibers, it would be inadvisable to have too much lead exposed for fear of the bullet breaking up too soon. There are some men who like to use soft-nose bullets with the lead barely showing for heart, lung and body shots at elephant and rhino. If too much lead was exposed they might fail to penetrate sufficiently. This method of controlling expansion is very effective. The pattern with a larger "blue nose," as we call it, is my favorite for buffalo.

the .505, I was most pleasantly surprised at the lightness of the recoil—no normally constituted hunter would be worried by it in the slightest. I found it a most accurate cartridge and killed several elephant, rhino and buffalo with it, but cannot find any record of the numbers shot; all I can remember is, that no beast got away from me when I was using any one of these three .500s—I killed all I shot. It's an immensely powerful weapon.

My friend, C. Fletcher Jamieson, the Rhodesian professional, had Jeffery build him up one of these rifles to special order with a

26″ barrel. He was a tall man of fine physique and owing to the way he held his rifles he reckoned he got better handling with a fairly long barrel. Since he had that weapon built, some ten or twelve years ago, he used it exclusively, and did a great deal of shooting with it. I'm not quite sure of the extent of his bag, but it cannot be far short of 300 elephant with this .500-bore Jeffery-Mauser—maybe more. The very last thing in the world he thought of was changing it for anything else—tho if he cannot persuade one of the great American concerns to load shells for it he may be compelled to, when he has exhausted what ammunition he has left for it. Still, there seems no very good reason why he could not have it rebarreled to handle Gibbs .505 cartridge, which the British manufacturers do load. He told me that when testing it on the range he fired a number of groups at 100, 200 and 300 yards, and found it the most accurate rifle of any caliber he had ever tested; it consistently shot into 1½″ groups at 100 yards. I happened to mention that I wouldn't have cared to have done so much shooting with so powerful a weapon from the prone position, to which he replied that he hardly noticed the recoil, it in no way upset him, and didn't appear to interfere in any way with the grouping of the rifle. Jeffery fitted splendidly massive barrels to these weapons, which no doubt has a lot to do with their consistent accuracy. Yet they weighed but from 10¼ lbs. to 10½ lbs.

If you can get the shells for it, you won't find a better magazine rifle for dangerous game than this .500-bore Mauser.

12-BORE "PARADOX," "EXPLORA." The Paradox was originally brought out by Holland & Holland, but I think any gunsmith will build you such a weapon nowadays. They mostly have their own names for them, such as Westley Richards' "Explora" and somebody else's "Jungle Gun," and so on. The principle of all is the same; there is some broad and shallow rifling at the muzzle end of the barrels—actually in what would normally be the choke. The result is that the heavy conical bullet is thrown as accurately up to 100 or 150 yards as it would have been from a rifle. The 8 and 10-bores were very popular in days gone by, particularly the latter, when used as a stand-by to back up a light rifle for lion-shooting. However, they are rarely seen now. But the 12-bore is widely used. The 2¾″ shell illustrated is considerably more powerful than the regular 2½″ British cartridge. It fires the cordite equiv-

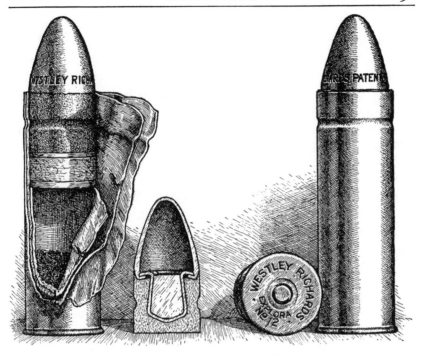

THE 12-BORE "EXPLORA."

As loaded by Westley Richards with the patent "L-T" capped projectile.

alent of 4½ to 5 drams of black powder, which makes it a really powerful weapon for soft-skinned game at close ranges.

The original Paradox bullet was a plain lead affair of 750-gr. The bullet illustrated here is Westley Richards' patent L-T capped, weighing 735-gr. and unless memory fails, it develops a M.V. of slightly better than 1,300 f.s. For non-dangerous animals it is probably better than the Paradox bullet, because owing to its design it *must* set-up on impact; but if it's to be used against lion, I would strongly recommend that the original 750-gr. solid soft-lead bullet be chosen. The mighty chest and shoulder muscles of a lion offer tremendous resistance to a bullet, and the capped bullet here shown may sometimes fail to penetrate sufficiently. I knew one sportsman who had to give a charging lion three of them before he succeeded in killing him. The first was fired when the lion was about 25 yards or so away from the gun; he swerved slightly, but came on; the second was fired when he was some 12 paces away, and knocked him down; he was up again almost immediately, but was obviously dazed and sick, and gave the gun time to reload and fire a third time, which finished matters. Both the first two shots took the lion in the chest; the third was placed just under the eye. I consider that fella would have done very much better had he been using the plain soft lead Paradox slug.

However, if you are merely wandering around with one of these weapons looking for something for your own pot, then you will probably find the hollow-capped bullet preferable. It has completely taken the place of the old copper-tubed bullet that was originally obtainable along with the solid. Personally, I used my Paradox chiefly for leopard, loading 1¼ ozs. of buckshot in one barrel, and the 750-gr. solid soft-lead bullet in the other in case of a longer shot being offered. The British shot size preferred to all others for this work is SSG (15 slugs to the ounce) which gives about 19 pellets to the 1¼-oz. load—unless I'm mistaken, this is roughly the same as the American AAA.

Men who don't know are inclined to imagine that a full-choked duck gun would be better with slugs than a Paradox, since the latter's boring is equivalent to true cylinder; but the curious fact is that buckshot seems to give far better and closer patterns with open boring than it ever does with choke. I can't explain it, but there it is. I killed quite a few leopards at ranges varying between 30 and 40 yards with 1¼ ozs. of SSG from my Paradox, tho usually I shot them at much closer distances than that. The capped bullet is perfectly satisfactory on leopard; but since my gun had been regulated for the 750-gr. bullet, I preferred to use it. I can strongly recommend one of these weapons; they are most useful, and a splendid thing to have handy, loaded, in case of an attack on the camp at night.

CHAPTER IV

The Large Medium Bores

IN THIS GROUP WE HAVE SOME OF THE MOST WIDELY USED CALIBERS IN the big game hunting world.

The .440 (11.2MM) MAUSER is so generally useless that I'm going to dismiss it at once. The diameter-to-weight ratio, or sectional density, of its bullet is so poor that it fails badly in penetration. It and its ammunition were only obtainable from Germany, and it's extremely improbable that it will ever again be made.

Next in the list comes the .425 WESTLEY RICHARDS. When this weapon was first introduced, back in '08 I think it was, it was the most powerful magazine rifle in the world and met with a great reception thruout Africa. There is no question, it is a most excellent cartridge and a real killer. It was specially designed for heavy and dangerous game; but the makers, who patented the cartridge, made the mistake of fitting absurdly long 28″ barrels to their rifles for stock and also of building a cheap model for the colonial trade. The result was that the weapons got themselves a bad name; the most usual complaints being the unnecessary length which made them very clumsy and ungainly in thick cover, and the fact that the magazine springs were not always up to their work. Five-shot magazines were customary, and it was found that the springs had a habit of weakening and were unable to press up the last shell sufficiently for the bolt to get hold of it. They were also known to kick like mules, because they were really too light for their power.

I knew a man who was very nearly killed by a wounded buffalo when using one of these rifles. He had wounded the buff and when following him up saw a small patch of bush on his half-left front and foolishly jumped to the conclusion that his beast would be in there. He ignored a little clump of grass on his half-right front;

93

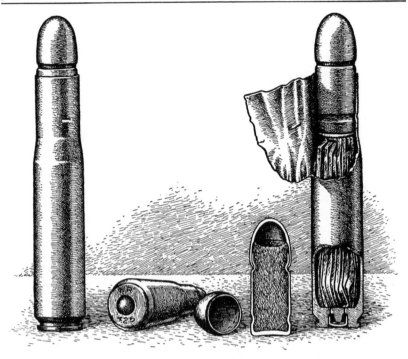

.425 (Westley Richards).

Powder ? grs. Smokeless; Bullet 410-gr. Metal-covered; Pressure 18½ tons; M.V. 2,350; M.E. 5,010.

In the accompanying illustration you can see the round copper-capped bullet in section. This bullet is specially designed for penetration combined with expansion—in other words, for very slow expansion. I have ever found it most satisfactory on the heavy animals for which it was intended. It was available for all the .450s, .500s, and .577s, and, I believe, also as a 300-gr. slug for the .375 Magnum, as well as for Westley Richards' own special calibers: .318 and .425.

The cap, which is of tough copper, protects the lead core on initial impact, and then, when expansion commences, it prevents the bullet setting up too quickly, and, in my experience, stops all tendency of the bullet to break up. If Westley Richards hadn't patented both his capped bullets, I have a notion that they would have been much more widely used than they are. They are the only expanding bullets you can get for the .425.

Then if you compare the "L.T." hollow-pointed-capped slug, you will see that it is of entirely different design, and obviously, therefore, intended for an entirely different purpose. From its very design, it *MUST* expand almost to its maximum on impact. But, and here's where the beauty of this bullet shows itself, when the cap expands it forms the "mushroom" and its edges turn back and so protect the remainder of the bullet from breaking up. I have never known one of these bullets to disintegrate. But it's quite clear that they were never intended to be used on any of the heavier animals; if they are, they may fail to but just as he passed it, with all his attention concentrated on the bush on his half-left, the buffalo charged him from behind the grass. His tracker shouted a warning, and in wheeling around to face the charge, the muzzle of the hunter's long 28″ barrel caught in something and he only just managed to clear it in time. He told me that the buff's forehead almost bumped the muzzle of the rifle as he fired. That sort of thing is altogether too close. The man who consistently hunts dangerous game will get all the narrow escapes any man in his right mind could want without deliberately asking for them—and fitting a stupidly long barrel on a magazine rifle of this caliber is certainly asking for trouble.

The makers, of course, will give you any length of barrel you want if you are having the weapon built to order; but many men want a gun in a hurry and don't want to wait while the makers in far away Britain build it up. You can also have a 3-shot magazine if you ask for it, and really it's ample.

But altho the rifles got themselves bad names, there was nothing wrong with the cartridge and I heard no complaints about it. On the contrary, all those who used it, and they were many, spoke highly of its killing power. I used it myself with considerable success, but quickly got rid of the rifle because of its unhandiness. I didn't own it, but had borrowed it to see for myself just how it behaved. Given a reasonable length of barrel it's undoubtedly one of the finest lion-stoppers in existence. I consider both it and the .416 in every way preferable for lion than any of the .450–.470 group, because the bullets thrown by the large bores are really too heavy for broadside shots at any soft-skinned animal. But the

---

penetrate sufficiently. But that in no way reflects on the bullet. Expanding as it does to its maximum extent on impact, it naturally meets with considerable resistance from that very moment. You will remember it does not have to encounter a bone to set up—that hollow-cap packs up the instant it hits anything. The only complaints I have ever come across about this pattern of bullet were from men who had tried using it on animals much heavier than those for which it was intended. Under such circumstances, it is a poor show to blame the bullet.

I consider these capped bullets of Westley Richards' the best expanding bullets extant.

(Incidentally, the theorists who have never used them are sometimes heard to suggest that the "L-T" pattern might start setting up in the magazine box if the rifle had much recoil. I have used them in the stock .425 magazine in which the recoil was considerable, and never had the slightest trouble with them, nor did I find that there was any inclination for them to set up in the box.)

410-gr. is excellent. I'd very much like to try a double rifle firing this shell, but have never as yet had an opportunity of doing so.

The extensively-trained native hunters employed by the Elephant Control section of the Game Department of Uganda are all armed with .425-bore magazine rifles, and some of these men have put up quite remarkable performances. For instance, a few years ago three of them were specially commended for killing no less than 300 marauding elephant between them in the space of seven months, and another killed 90 in nine months. It's the considered opinion of the Game Warden that their efficiency has been considerably increased since they were armed with these rifles. Provided it's fitted with a sensible length of barrel, this rifle can certainly be recommended for general all-around work amongst heavy and dangerous game if you like a magazine—or, of course, you can have it built to order as a double by Westley Richards.

Apart from the full-patch, or solid, the only bullets obtainable are Westley Richards' patent-capped, the "L-T" pointed hollow-capped, and the round-capped. These are a most excellent pattern of bullet. The L-T is intended for rapid expansion, and behaves most satisfactorily on all soft-skinned animals, including lion; whilst I have killed a few buffalo with it also. But the round-capped is generally preferred for buff as it is designed for penetration combined with expansion. I have cut the L-T-capped out of various animals and found it expanded to an enormous extent—so much so that wouldn't go down an 8-bore; but I can't remember ever having it break up.

After trying one of these rifles Selous reckoned that if only he had been armed with one of them in his old elephant-hunting days he would have killed four or five times as many elephant as he actually did.

The .423 (10.75MM) MAUSER is undoubtedly one of the most widely used calibers in Africa; but in my humble opinion it in no way deserves its popularity. I'm quite sure that the reason it's so widely used is to be found in the fact that it's light—7¼–7½ lbs—thanks to its low chamber pressure, and because these German Mausers could be bought fairly cheaply. But the 10.75mm lacks penetration. It's better than the 11.2mm; but that's about all you can say for it. It won't kill an elephant on a frontal head shot, there's plenty of evidence on that point; and is incapable of driving even a full-patch bullet thru a buffalo's shoulder. Well, that's no good to me. In the same way, it's unable to drive an expanding bullet deep enough to kill with certainty on eland or lion. Now I could never recommend a rifle that needed full-patch slugs for lion; because even if the lion does stop the bullet, it does so little damage as compared with an expanding slug that it cannot inflict the requisite shock to the lion's nervous system and therefore cannot be relied upon to stop him so quickly if he is coming. The lion's vitality and tenacity-to-life is incredible. There is an authentic case of a party of men putting no less than 17 bullets from modern high power rifles into a lion before they succeeded in killing him. I've seen a lion come on for 8 or 10 paces with a gaping hole where his heart should have been.

The sectional density of the 10.75's bullet is poor, hence its lack of penetration and general unreliability. I once had a full-patch bullet from one of these rifles blow to bits on the boss of a wounded buffalo's horns without having the slightest effect on him—I might as well have fired a revolver at him. There was just a leaden blotch to show where the bullet hit him.

Then there was a Russian hunter who was a great believer in the 10.75mm. Whether it was lack of power or that his cheap rifle let him down, I can't answer; because the elephant that killed him smashed his rifle to smithereens also. His boys came running in to my camp one day in a great state to tell me that he had been killed by an elephant. But there was nothing I could do when I went along with them. There was nothing to pick up but his boots—with his feet still in them—his belt and his hat. He, himself, had literally been wiped out of existence—just as a native will wipe out, with a twist of his foot, the mark where he has expectorated. There was merely a stain on the ground where the bull had trampled him into jelly.

However, it's but fair to mention that there are many hunters who are very fond of the 10.75mm. It can, of course, be used with a fair degree of safety, if not too much satisfaction, against almost anything provided you have a decent weapon built to handle it and eschew those cheap, mass-production rifles that once flooded Africa. You never know when they are going to let you down. As a correspondent once wrote: "You can try to make them jam a thousand times without success, and then they will let you down

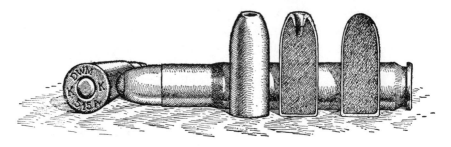

THE 10.75MM MAUSER

Powder 68 grs. Smokeless; Bullet 347-gr. Metal-covered; Pressure 14½ tons; M.V. 2,200; M.E. 3,750.

The wide popularity this cartridge enjoys is undoubtedly due to the light weight at which the rifle can be built—from 7¼–7½ lbs., and this in turn is due to the low chamber pressure generated by the cartridge. Also, these weapons as supplied from Germany could be sold at a comparatively low price in Africa. There are many men who declare that it makes a perfect all-around cartridge but I certainly don't agree with them. Its staunchest upholders have to admit that it lacks penetration both when used with full-patch bullets as well as with soft-nose.

Daly, who is a great admirer of it, states in his book that out of more than a hundred elephant shot with it, he never once succeeded in finding the brain with a frontal head shot, and invariably had to finish off the elephant with another shot somewhere else. He also mentions that he generally had to use full-patch bullets for lion because he found that the soft-nose failed to penetrate sufficiently on frontal chest shots.

A Col. Henderson, also of Kenya, who thinks so highly of the 10.75mm that he had a costly double rifle specially built to handle it, has admitted that in his experience the soft-nose bullet has insufficient penetration for eland—a soft-skinned animal—and the full-patch bullet, altho capable of knocking down buffalo on a shoulder shot at close range, is incapable of driving thru the shoulder to kill. The result being that unless finished off at once the buffalo will get up and clear off with a broken shoulder—a horribly dangerous proposition in long grass. And then when you follow him up you may find that your 10.75mm full-patch bullet disintegrates on the boss of his horns without even dropping him, much less killing or at least stopping him. I have mentioned elsewhere in this book how I had a full-patch bullet from one of these rifles blow to pieces on the boss of a wounded buffalo bull's horns without having the slightest effect on him.

The reason for all this is, of course, the very poor sectional density of the bullet. I certainly, and very emphatically, can *not* recommend this cartridge.

It was owing to the many complaints that must have been received by the manufacturers; complaints concerning lack of penetration of the ordinary soft-nose expanding bullets for this caliber, that the Germans brought out this metal-cased hollow-nosed bullet. This was the *only* expanding bullet for the 10-75mm I ever used that gave even reasonably satisfactory results. But even it was a hell of a long way from being perfect; if it failed to strike a bone, it would usually whip clean thru like a hard-nose without expanding at all—I remember driving one right thru an eland bull on a shot behind the shoulder; the exit hole was no larger at the worst possible moment. A fellow hunter used one for some months without any trouble, he then sold it to a friend who wounded a lion, had a jam, and his body was brought in by his hunting boys."

A 10.75mm, said to be of rather better quality than the ordinary run of these low-priced German weapons, once let me down badly when in the centre of a large herd of elephant in a sea of 10-foot grass. The herd had spread out in a rough horseshoe formation—there were about 80 of them—and I had entered between the prongs of the horseshoe, as it were, and consequently had elephant on both sides of me as well as in front but could only see shadowy shapes in the grass here and there. They were just standing around doing nothing.

I moved quietly up to the head of the horseshoe, as I knew the big bulls would be up there. I came on a fine tusker and closed to within some 20 or 30 feet of him. I raised the rifle and squeezed the trigger, only to be rewarded with a dull "click." Careless of noise, for I badly wanted that big fella, I whipped back the bolt and slammed it forward again. Subconsciously, I seemed to feel that it moved forward suspiciously easily; but at the time I did not really grasp the significance. The bull had heard me, of course, and moved away, only to pull up again when he had gone some 10 or 15 paces. Again I tried for him, and again my wretched rifle only clicked. The remainder of the herd were now on the alert and were moving about restlessly, not sure whether to run or not. I was right in amongst them.

The big fellow that I wanted so badly now moved off and disappeared in the grass, and another with good teeth, but smaller, took his place. I took a fresh shell from my pocket and slipped it up the spout. This went off all right and dropped the bull. On the heels of the shot there was the usual pandemonium, and I saw the first big bull run up to my right and join a small group of elephant up there, whilst the main body of the herd cleared off to my left.

I raced after the big tusker in the hope of getting a smack at

---

than that of entrance. If it hit a bone like that of the shoulder on one of the heavier varieties of soft-skinned game, you had no guarantee that it would get in far enough to kill. However, it was undoubtedly the best of the bullets I ever saw for this caliber. For some reason best-known to themselves, the Germans did not bring out the reinforced-jacketed bullet for the 10.75mm.

him before he realized that he and his companions were being deserted by the remainder of the herd. I came on him standing facing me, ears out and trunk down, offering a perfect frontal brain shot at a range of about 20–25 paces. He had obviously heard me coming thru the grass, but could not see me. But that elephant's luck was in that day; for my so-and-so rifle again only clicked and, on my manipulating the bolt, did the same thing again. Fortunately for me the bull then swung around and cleared off. I was so disgusted that I hurled the rifle after him, together with some suggestions as to what he should do with it. . . .

On examining it later, I discovered that the magazine spring had broken. And there was I clicking and snapping what was for all practical purposes an unloaded rifle in the midst of a large herd of elephant in long grass! The first shot had, of course, been a genuine misfire, and thereafter the manipulation of the bolt had been unable to reload the rifle as the broken magazine spring had failed to push the shells up sufficiently to enable the bolt to get hold of the uppermost one and carry it into the chamber.

Altho I killed a fair quantity of game with it I found it a most unsatisfactory cartridge. I have already mentioned how I had a full-patch bullet disintegrate on the boss of a buffalo bull's horns; and apart from that I found the various types of expanding bullets very unreliable; usually they lacked penetration on all but the lighter varieties of game, and yet I had expanding bullets whip clean thru eland without setting up at all on body shots—the exit hole was no larger than the entrance wound. How those particular bullets would have behaved had they encountered a bone I am not in a position to say.

All the same, one Assistant Game Warden in Kenya killed 300 elephant with one of these rifles; and I know of many men who prefer it to anything else and won't hear a word against it. However, I prefer to go by my own experience; and that has been such that I cannot recommend this rifle. It's been so widely used that I dare say the British manufacturers will continue to turn out shells for it as they did before the recent war.

Now, let's take up a really good cartridge; the .416 Rigby.

Auctor: Just a moment, ole timer, before you get launched on the .416. You told us a few minutes ago how you lost a big tusker owing to the magazine follower-spring of your 10.75mm

Mauser breaking. Well, you know, that's certainly gonna cause a question to be asked which I reckon you'd do well to answer right here. The experienced hunter will know the answer; but you are writing principally for the benefit of the inexperienced, and I can already hear some of those fellas beginning to bawl: "But why the hell didn't the fool look down at his rifle and see what was the matter when, as he says, he seemed to feel that the bolt moved forward suspiciously easily? If he'd been looking at his rifle and watching what he was doing, he could have slipped another shell up the spout by hand and bagged his big tusker just the same as he did the smaller one." Okay; you tellem now.

Lector: I'm glad you've brought that up, because I must admit that it didn't occur to me: tho I can quite see that it needs explaining. Well, the answer is easy; it's this:

You have finished your stalk and are now about to open fire. From the moment you first squeeze trigger against any animal, but particularly dangerous game, *you should not take your eyes off the beast* at which you are firing until you are absolutely sure of him. It applies anywhere, but naturally is especially important in thick cover, and doubly so in the case of dangerous game. Remember, one pace can take your animal out of sight, and one pace can place another in almost the same spot. If you have looked down at your rifle whilst reloading, you may not notice the difference when you again look up, and may place a bullet in an animal you had no wish to kill, under the impression that it was the same beast at which you had previously fired.

Not long ago I was reading a book in which a fella mentioned doing just that—tho he missed the point and failed to see that the fault was his for not keeping his eyes on the animal at which he had first fired. He was tackling a troop of elephant with one good bull amongst them. His license permitted him to shoot four bulls; cows were prohibited, and if one was shot, accidentally or otherwise, it would count as two elephant on the license and the ivory would be confiscated. He took a shot at the bull and then looked down as he reloaded (he didn't say he looked down; but he said that when he "looked up again," which implies the same thing) he saw what he thought was the same elephant and fired again.

Once more he looked down as he reloaded—he was using a double .450 non-ejector—and when he again looked up he found that the elephant had moved somewhat but that there was the same big bull partially concealed by a tree. He again fired as he thought at the self-same animal. It was only after the troop had finally cleared off that this hero found that he had shot two big cows as well as the bull! The result was that *all* the ivory was confiscated and he was heavily fined for shooting one elephant more than the number permitted on his license!

There was another fella whom I knew who is recorded as having shot five elephant one day under the impression that he had only shot one. Following an elephant path towards a small, more or less dry, river bed thru fairly high grass he suddenly saw an elephant's head looking straight at him down the path about 20 yards away. He fired, the elephant disappeared, and when he looked up again after reloading there was what he thought was the same elephant still looking at him from the same place. Again he fired and again the elephant disappeared; and in the same way this fella again looked down to reload just as a beginner looks down to shift his gear lever when learning to drive a car. When he looked up once more there was the same elephant still looking at him.

Finally, after he had fired five times, he recharged his magazine and then, as nothing further happened, he moved forward to see what had caused the elephant to keep on returning for another bullet. He expected to find one dead bull, but found no less than five lying across the river bed. Apparently, on each elephant receiving a not-too-well-placed frontal brain-shot he had reeled back and fallen and another had taken his place to see what all the commotion was about (these elephant had not been shot-up for some years). Being a big-shot police cop he was able to get away with it by claiming that the elephant were marauders.

A thoroly experienced hunter who is also a rifleman and can tell with certainty where his bullet has taken the animal can take his eyes off it immediately after the shot if he wants a crack at another; but the inexperienced sportsman cannot be so certain of his shot; nervousness, "buck-fever," fatigue, wrong angles, twigs in the line of fire that he didn't notice, all are weighed against him.

Accordingly, you must learn to reload your rifle, or manipulate the safety, or anything else, irrespective of whether it's a double, single, or magazine, without having to look down at it. It's very easy; even easier than shifting the gears of your automobile. You can give yourself as much "dry-practice" as you like in your own bedroom, sitting room, or in camp, or anywhere else you like. You should be able to manipulate your weapons entirely automatically, without conscious thought.

And now to return to the .416 RIGBY.

This is also a magazine weapon; but I've never heard of the magazine, or any other, spring breaking on a Rigby rifle. I have never handled any magazine rifle, with the possible exception of the .500-bore Jeffery-Mauser, in which the feed from magazine platform to chamber was quite so smooth or required quite so little effort as it did on my Rigby .416. This was Blunt's favorite rifle, and the weapon with which Daly shot most of his elephant. You certainly could not get a better or more reliable magazine rifle for general work amongst dangerous animals. It's tremendously popular thruout Africa, and deservedly so. It's a great killer. Its plain soft-nose bullets crumple a charging lion as few other weapons are capable of doing. There is a certainty about it that gives one great confidence. I've subjected this rifle to some very hard usage both against lions and when on ivory-poaching expeditions. Time and again have I slammed that bolt back and forth when shooting rapidly; yet never once did it show the slightest tendency to jam.

One of the great points about this rifle is the fact that Rigby's splendid steel-covered solids are available for it—just as they are for his special .350 Magnums. These bullets have three of four times the thickness of solid metal at the nose that you find with the ordinary full-patch slug, and the result is that I have never known one to be even marked much less distorted. This is a very real asset when you are tackling massive-boned animals like elephant or rhino at very close quarters, because if a bullet is at all distorted at the nose it may tend to be deflected and lose its direction after entry. So that, altho perfectly placed and fired at the right angle, it may fail to kill thru failing to reach a vital spot. You do not get that trouble with Rigby's bullets. And you certainly do not get the trouble that I shall be mentioning presently in connection with the .404, of full-patch bullets breaking up. I just cannot speak too highly of the .416.

But I have never been able to understand why John Rigby

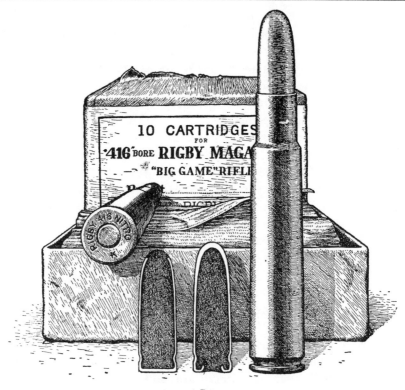

.416 RIGBY.

Powder 69 grs. Smokeless; Bullet 410-gr. Metal-covered; Pressure 17 tons; M.V. 2,350; M.E. 5,010.

John Rigby clinched his reputation as African gunsmith when he placed his .416 Mauser on the market for heavy and dangerous game. If for any reason you prefer a magazine rifle to a double, there is no finer or more satisfactory weapon for all-around use against dangerous animals than this .416. Since a really good magazine rifle can be used safely and satisfactorily for almost all kinds of African hunting, if you prefer that kind of weapon, and since they cost very much less than doubles, magazines are widely used thruout Africa. Rigby's .416 was just exactly what had been wanted—it's an essentially African weapon. Some of the most experienced hunters use, recommend and swear by the .416. Rigby, very wisely, does not cater for the cheap, colonial market; you can absolutely rely upon his rifles, whether they're double, single or magazine. They're expensive, surely, if you merely consider the cash side of it but the certainty of absolute reliability is well worth paying for if you are hunting animals that can hit back. Further, that reliability does not deteriorate with age provided they are looked after as such weapons deserve to be looked after.

Take particular note of the solid bullet shown here. See the quite exceptional thickness of *steel* at the nose. This is what we want in Africa. Not only is the jacket of steel, but the quantity of metal used to reinforce the nose is greater hasn't brought out a double-barreled edition of his .416, which he could have called a .416 N º 2 and which could have had the same ballistics as the Mauser—just as he has done in the case of his .350 and .275 calibers. For all-around work amongst heavy and dangerous game in any part of the world such a rifle would be just about ideal. Fitted with 26″ barrels it need not weigh an ounce over 10-lbs.; and there are many men who would prefer such a weapon to anything in the .450–.470 group, the average weights of which run close on a pound heavier. I myself would very much prefer it for lion or tiger as there is less likelihood of its bullet driving clean thru than in the case of the larger calibers. I know that I would never be happy until he had built me a pair if only he could be persuaded to do so.

By the way, it will have been noticed that I have spoken of the "steel-covered" solid bullets that Rigby supplies for use with this weapon (and also, incidentally, for his .350 Magnum and .350 N º 2). I do not know if these bullets are still steel-covered; but they certainly were originally, and I see no reason to suppose that Rigby has changed them for ordinary nickel jackets. At any rate, in his most recent catalog, published shortly before the last war, he was still emphasizing his steel jackets by printing the word "steel" in italics. In one of his catalogs, that dealing with the .416, he shows one of these bullets in section so that the amazing thickness of solid steel at the nose may be seen. This was undoubtedly one of the principal selling points of these special calibers of his; because I have seen many full-patch nickel-jacketed bullets considerably distorted and with deep grooves cut in their noses after encountering massive bones, and on one occasion had a full-patch 300-gr. slug from a .375 Magnum rivet quite considerably, but without breaking the envelope, after being slammed into a buffalo's spine at point-blank range. I have experienced the same

than on any other bullet. These bullets do *not* break up or become distorted. Also note how well the jacket is turned into the lead core. You will find this in all Rigby's solid bullets—even his original old .350. I have had solid bullets of practically every caliber distorted to a greater or lesser extent after smashing their way into an elephant. I've had them buckled at the nose, bent lengthways, and a few with the nose buckled and the whole body of the bullet bent, whilst the nickel jacket was split for about three-fifths of its length from the base up. Admittedly, in no case had the envelope broken open at the nose and it's true the bullets all killed but they ought not to have behaved like that. Rigby's don't.

thing with full-patch 480-gr. bullets from various rifles. It's true they never broke open; but in my opinion they ought not to have been even marked, much less distorted. I have never seen a solid from one of Rigby's rifles in any way deformed. I don't know of anybody else who supplies bullets of this type, but they're sure tops in my opinion.

I cannot say off-hand how many elephant I killed with mine but it was quite a few. It would have been very many more, but I generally used it only for those occasional longish or difficult shots, because of its peep sight.

Firing its plain soft-nose slug it crumples a charging lion as few other weapons are capable of doing. I consider this 410-gr. bullet better than anything heavier where lion and tiger are concerned, because it can be relied upon to mushroom perfectly and remain in the animal's body; which not only means that he has received the full force of the 5,000-lb. punch, but also that there is no fear of another of the lion's companions being wounded.

The .416 Rigby shows almost identical ballistics with the .425 Westley Richards, but a lower chamber pressure. Let me say right away, it's a perfect weapon for all-around use against heavy and dangerous game if you like a magazine rifle. Rigby normally fits it with a 24″ barrel and a 4-shot magazine.

If you like a magazine rifle for dangerous game, I can strongly recommend this cartridge. It's essentially an African caliber.

.405 WINCHESTER. This rifle's caliber compels it to be included in this group, tho it does not otherwise deserve to be. It was sufficiently widely used once upon a time to induce the British manufacturers to load its ammunition. It is seldom seen nowadays, however. The sectional density of its bullet was none too good, with the result that it lacked penetration on all the larger species. I never used it to any great extent.

It got a great boost after the ex-president, the late Theodore Roosevelt, was known to have preferred it for his lion shooting. But nobody thought to ask, to what did he prefer it? If he preferred it to his .30–06, that would be quite understandable. It is not usually known, perhaps, that Holland & Holland supplied at least two of their 500/.450 bore nitro express rifles to the Roosevelt expedition. I do not know if the ex-president himself had one, but some of his party certainly had. In addition, Roosevelt had the late R. J. Cunninghame as his professional; and it's a positive certainty that Cunninghame would have had some such weapon handy when Roosevelt was shooting-up his lions with the Winchester.

The .405 Winchester is perfectly capable of killing lions; but an experienced man would prefer something more powerful if it came to stopping a charge. I know a very good native elephant-hunter who was employed by a Britisher to shoot elephant for him, and this lad chose a .405 Winchester out of his master's battery in preference to anything else for the elephant. But then, there wasn't a great selection from which to make the choice—a 28″-barreled .425 magazine; a double .577 B.P. Express; a 7.9mm Mauser; and the .405. The man chose the .405 because it was light and much handier than the long .425. He shot a good many elephant with it but, of course, not with frontal head shots. Further, he relied upon his natural agility to get him out of tight corners rather than the rifle.

I would not advise anybody to invest in a .405 if they can get anything else for African hunting. Nevertheless, if you have an old favorite and would like to try it—why, bring it along by all means. There's one sure thing, and that is that you will never go hungry out here so long as you have any shells left for your .405. But I see in a recent copy of that so authoritative journal, the AMERICAN RIFLEMAN, that Winchester have decided to discontinue loading .405 ammunition, and I have a notion that the British ammunition manufacturers will follow their lead. I have it on good authority that they are considering which calibers to drop, and will cease turning out all shells for which there is little demand. I have long advocated this, as there has been an absurd multiplicity of calibers in the past, many of which were entirely obsolete.

.404 RIMLESS NITRO EXPRESS: Powder 60 grs. Smokeless; Bullet 400-gr. Metal-covered; Pressure 16 tons; M.V. 2,125; M.E. 4,020.

Powder 70 grs. Smokeless; Bullet 300-gr. Metal-covered; Pressure 16 tons; M.V. 2,600; M.E. 4,500.

It was Jeffery who originally introduced this cartridge and Mauser-actioned rifle to take the place of the single-loader 450/.400 that had been so widely used by those men who didn't think they could afford a double—its ballistics are identical when firing the original 400-gr. bullet. I can say at once that it is one of the most popular and most widely-used calibers thruout the big game hunting world. Altho I have only mentioned two firm's names in connection with it, most gunsmiths, including the Germans, listed rifles of this caliber in their catalogs—which speaks for itself.

The Game Warden of Tanganyika, who started his hunting career shooting buffalo for their hides in Portuguese East with a rifle of this caliber, found it so entirely satisfactory that he has armed all his native game scouts in the Elephant Control Department with Vickers' .404 magazine rifles. His answer when asked why he didn't choose a more powerful cartridge is, that the .404 has all the power necessary to render it a perfectly safe weapon and at the same time it is light and handy and his men can use their weapons with ease and certainty. The weight of these rifles runs around 8½ lbs.

Now that's sound reasoning, and is borne out by the great numbers of these weapons that one sees on all sides. However, I have heard complaints concerning its full-patch bullets. One professional hunter in Tanganyika, who has used this rifle extensively, says that on many occasions he has had the full-patch slug break up in an elephant's head, and therefore fail to kill. He traced the course of a number of these failures and they certainly behaved in the most curious manner. One, for instance, which wasn't too well-placed, split a tusk, broke in two pieces, and then, instead of traveling straight into the head, turned around and the two pieces of the bullet made their way *down* the tusk. Another, which became badly deformed but didn't actually break open, also failed to make its way into the brain; it turned thru an angle of some 65° and lodged in the cheek altho fired from directly in front. Many others just broke up. Now this is bad; but I am assured that the ammunition was both British as well as German—it just didn't seem to matter who made it. Let me add, that all these elephant were knocked down and there was little trouble in finishing them off. Still, those full-patch slugs ought not to have behaved like that. The hunter in question has had considerable experience and

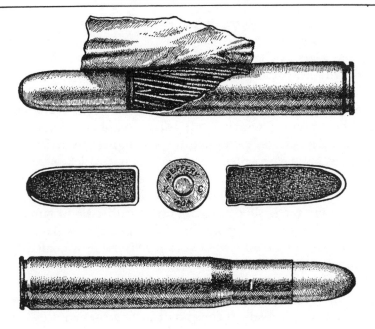

.404 Jeffery.

Note the solid bullet shown in this illustration, and its excellent reinforcement at the nose. Harking back to the complaints that reached me from Tanganyika concerning full-patch .404 bullets, and which I have mentioned in the chapter dealing with this rifle, it is difficult to see how such a bullet as that illustrated here could break up entirely. Any of these nickel-jacketed bullets can become distorted but distortion is a very different thing from disintegration. As I said when discussing the rifle, I can't help thinking that that fella was exceptionally unlucky in striking a bad batch of ammunition both from Britain as well as from Germany. In view of the immense popularity of the .404, I find it difficult to believe that its solid slugs could habitually misbehave. After all, why should they be so much less excellent than their brothers, the .400? Nobody has ever complained about them—their reliability is taken for granted.

is something of a rifleman, shooting for one of the East African territories at Bisley. In other words, he should know where he is putting his bullets. I must admit I never had any trouble when using a .404; but then it's only right to add that I didn't use it much, because of my preference for doubles. Personally, I cannot help thinking that that man's experiences were unusual; that maybe he was unlucky enough to strike a bad batch of shells. I cannot see that the .404 would have become so popular if its slugs habitually behaved so badly.

Firing the plain soft-nose bullet it's one of the favorite lion rifles.

Some years ago Jeffery brought out a H.V. load that brings it within the Magnum group. This 300-gr. slug, thrown at 2,600 f.s., would be wonderfully deadly for all soft-skinned African game, including lion, if only other patterns were available than the copper-pointed which is all Jeffery supplies. These copper-pointed slugs are only suitable for the lighter varieties of non-dangerous animals. When I pointed this out to Jeffery and asked if he couldn't be persuaded to supply semi-pointed soft-nose also for the heavier beasts, he replied that he only intended his H.V. load for long range shooting, and really had India in mind rather than Africa when designing it. His .404s are widely used in India and Ceylon, and he wanted to give those men a suitable load for Himalayan *shikar* should any of them feel like climbing those high hills for a breath of cool air and a bit of sport as well, and that the regular load with its 400-gr. bullet should be used for general African hunting. Well, there's no disputing that advice; but men being what they are, the 300-gr. copper-pointed slug is used by quite a few of them for general African purposes by those who do not go after the thick-skinned game and the net result is that they are not too pleased with their .404s. I tried to point out to two or three of them that they should have been using the regular slug; but their attitude was that 300 grains was a more suitable weight than 400 for non-dangerous animals, whilst the trajectory was considerably flatter. That also is indisputable; but the pattern of bullet must be taken into consideration, and no copper-pointed slug is suitable for heavy animals even if they do come within the soft-skinned group—witness the fact that John Rigby has discontinued supplying copper-pointed slugs for his .350 Magnum.

It was chiefly in connection with this H.V. load that I used the .404. I had had so much experience with the double 450/.400 that I did not bother to take much note of the rifle's behavior when firing the regular load—I took it for granted that the performance would be the same as that of the .400, since the ballistics were identical—but I was very anxious to try the H.V. 300-gr. bullet. There's no question but that it's most deadly when it can get in; but the trouble is that it usually disintegrates on the surface, causing a terrible surface wound but failing to do anything like

the damage inside that it ought to do.   It is, of course, a mistake
to use it on any but the smaller animals; but even where they are
concerned in Africa the range is usually too close.   The very high
striking velocity of the bullet causes it to break up immediately.
It's true that it kills instantly; but what I fear is that some inexperienced men may be tempted to use it for lion on the strength of
seeing its power on lighter animals.   It would be a grave mistake
to do so.   Where lion are concerned you *must* use a bullet that will
hold together.   The regular 400-gr. soft-nose slug is a peach here,
plenty lead showing at the nose; but not the soft-nose-split; this
latter is only suitable for non-dangerous beasts as it is apt to lose
too much weight when it encounters the massive chest muscles of a
lion.

In Jeffery's catalog there is a testimonial from a fella in Ceylon
who had just shot a leopard or a small bear or something and he
states that the penetration was so good, altho the bullet blew to
bits, that he wouldn't hesitate to use it on buffalo.   We can only
hope for his sake that he didn't!   Maybe he did, and that's why
there is no second letter from him!   I consider gunsmiths are
gravely at fault for printing and disseminating this sort of thing
thru the medium of their catalogs and advertizements.   Jeffery
knows perfectly well that this high-velocity 300-gr. copper-
pointed bullet is totally unsuitable for such animals as buffalo or
bison, and will tell you so if you write to him.   He will tell you
that he only intended it for use against non-dangerous soft-skinned
animals at long range; and yet he includes a letter like that in his
catalog!   Don't get me wrong.   Jeffery is by no means the only
firm known to publish grotesque testimonials.

450/.400 Nitro-Express: Case 3¼"; Powder 60 grs. Smokeless;
            Bullet 400-gr. Metal-covered; Pres-
            sure 16½ tons; M.V. 2,150; M.E.
            4,110.
            Case 3"; Powder 60 grs. Smokeless;
            Bullet 400-gr. Metal-covered; Pres-
            sure 16 tons; M.V. 2,125; M.E.
            4,010.

Jeffery designed his 3" .400 specially for cordite when it was
found in the early days of the transition from black powder to
smokeless that the 3¼" shell was inclined to stick in single-loaders

after firing. It's a very much stronger shell in every way and shows a slightly lower chamber pressure. Nevertheless, both cases are made so strong nowadays, that there is really nothing to choose between them. Accordingly, I am not going to discuss them separately; the difference in their ballistics is so slight that it's not worth considering. It must be remembered, however, that the two shells are not interchangeable.

With the possible exception of the .450 only, this is certainly the most popular caliber that has ever been placed on the African, and Asian, market. For many years, prior to the introduction of Holland's .375 Magnum, it was *the* all-around caliber. Doubles and singles were seen all over the place until Jeffery brought out his .404 Mauser in place of the single-loader. It's one of the grandest weapons imaginable for all big game hunting. It became a standard caliber thruout the British gun trade, just as the .450 did. I can hardly think of a single British gunsmith's name that I haven't seen at some time or another engraved on a rifle handling this shell. It has ever been one of my favorites. I have used it extensively on all kinds of African game from elephant down with the greatest possible satisfaction. In its new 9½-lb. guise it's one of the best weapons you could possibly choose.

I'm not alone in saying so. Let me give you the opinion of other keen hunters on this caliber. Major Evans, who spent the best part of his life hunting in Burma, says:

"As to rifles, the writer believes implicitly in a D.B. 450/.400 high-velocity rifle taking the equivalent of 60 grains of cordite in Axite, and a 400-gr. bullet. With this rifle elephant, bison, and tsine have been shot in the densest cover and in the open alike. It has now been in use several years and during that time it has not lost its owner a single beast shot at. Generally one, or at most two, bullets have been sufficient to account for the biggest animals; but I have had occasionally to give a beast as many as half a dozen shots before securing him. This, however, has been under exceptional circumstances when either the denseness of the jungle or the failing light has prevented an accurate aim being taken . . . it will suffice to state that it has accounted for close on eighty head of game both in India and Burma, from goral to elephant, and has never yet failed me."

Then Major Powell-Cotton has written:

"The Jeffery double .400 ejector express rifle I first carried in my Abyssinian expedition is my favorite weapon for dangerous game. With all nickel-covered bullets it is excellent for head or heart shots at elephant. With the lead just showing at the nose they do good work on rhino and buffalo; whilst with half the lead exposed I do not think you can get a better weapon for lion."

Wilfred Robertson in his book says:

"The finest rifle I have ever used was a 450/.400 bore, double-barreled ejector express rifle by Jeffery of London. This rifle was absolutely accurate, flat in its trajectory, and possessed wonderful killing power. With this bore I have shot all sizes of African game from elephant downwards."

One of the Game Rangers of Tanganyika, whose work is spent chiefly amongst elephant, uses nothing else.

I can fully corroborate those opinions from my own experience. I have had three different rifles handling this shell, two doubles and a single-loader, and have no complaint to make. I have never heard any African hunter complain about the .400; on the contrary, they are all enthusiastic who have used it. There were some of the old large bore diehards in India who claimed that it lacked power; but there are many others who think of it as Major Evans above does. I have only brought that example of Asiatic hunting in because you sometimes hear the other opinion expressed—frequently by those who are all too inclined to rely upon theory, but have not had much practical experience.

Just because a .400 looks small when compared with an 8-bore, or even a .577, is no argument. Sure, it's small by comparison; but practical experience has shown that it's a simply splendid weapon for all heavy and dangerous game *anywhere*—particularly when in the hands of an experienced hunter.

It must not be forgotten that the great majority of books written on Indian hunting are written by amateurs. There are no professionals in India as there are in Africa. And altho these men may be including the experiences of a "life-time" in their books the fact that they are so often military men means that they have only been able to get out into the jungle for a couple of weeks a year, with possibly a somewhat longer stretch at intervals of four or five years when long leave comes around and they choose to spend some of it in the jungles on their way back "home." Men

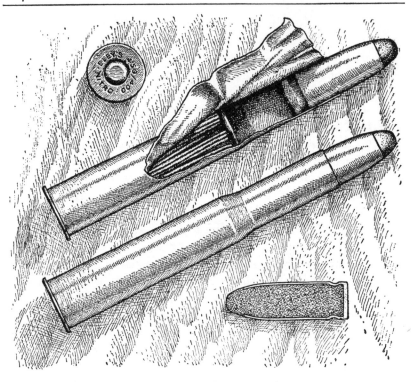

THE 450/.400

This is the original 3¼″ 450/.400, evolved from its black powder predecessor. It was this shell in its original guise that gave the caliber a bad name thru sometimes sticking in the chambers of falling-block single-loaders. Naturally, nobody thought of blaming the criminals who allowed their chambers to become pitted; the blame was dumped solely on the cartridge. It was then that Jeffery came to light with his 3″ shell, specially designed for cordite. If you want to see what it looks like, again turn to the .475 N ≗ 2 shown in section on page 81. But as in the case of the .450s, both these .400-caliber shells are made so strong nowadays, that you can use either, as I did, with the utmost satisfaction. I never had one stick in either double or single-loader.

Until Holland & Holland introduced their .375 Magnum, in 1913 I think it was, the .400 was the weapon that was generally reckoned to be the nearest approach to an "all-around" rifle on the market—and there are many hunters who still describe it as such. My own opinion is that it depends entirely on the extent to which you intend to hunt heavy and dangerous game in the thick stuff. There is no getting away from the fact that the 400-gr. bullet thrown by the .400 hits a heavier punch at close quarters than does a lighter bullet, irrespective of the latter's velocity—and especially is this true if for any reason an immediately vital spot is missed.

who are not constantly hunting dangerous game cannot have the same confidence as those who are, and therefore it is but the part of wisdom to arm themselves with weapons that they know are sufficiently powerful. There is no doubt about the various calibers in the .450–.470 group but if a man is not too sure of the .400, or rather of his own ability to put the bullet where it's wanted, then he is quite right to choose a more powerful weapon on the assumption that if the bullet isn't too well-placed it should have more stopping power than the smaller caliber. But just because these men who write are not too certain of their own ability is no argument against the .400. There are many officers in the Forest Service in India and Burma whose work takes them continually into the jungles, and who prefer the double .400 to any other caliber.

There certainly is no question of its suitability for African use and I had no hesitation in using it in India, nor did I see any reason to regret doing so. However, maybe I'd better confine myself to Africa.

I have never heard similar complaints concerning the bullets thrown by the .400 that I mentioned when talking about the .404, and certainly had no complaints of their behavior myself when using these rifles. For some reason that I find difficult to explain I derived greater pleasure from using the .400 than any other caliber; and no weapon behaved more successfully in my hands. There is something about the double .400 that just seems to suit me. I would happily finish the remainder of my career with a pair of them and nothing else—unless it was a third, just to give me a set of three!

A lot of what should have been most interesting discussions have taken place with the .400-bore in the centre of the picture, but they failed to hold one's interest because those who have attempted to run it down and claimed that it lacked power had

I've done a lot of shooting with the .400—both of them—and am very, very fond of it. I had two doubles and a falling-block single-loader; one of the doubles was a Purdey, the other a Jeffery; the single-loader was a Westley Richards. With one or other of these rifles I killed practically all species of African game and my experience was such that I would not hesitate to follow any dangerous animal into any sort of cover if armed with a double .400. Naturally, it will be understood that I speak as a hunter and there are certain types of thicket into which no hunter in his right mind would attempt to follow any wounded and potentially savage beast; if he gets in there, well and good—he wins.

either never used it or else had only done so to a very limited extent. They said that in their experience it lacked power, but they were unable to give details, or at any rate failed to do so. Naturally, it would seem to lack power if you used the split bullet on animals like lion or tiger but that is a very poor base from which to build an argument against the rifle. Those men were staunch upholders of nothing smaller than .450. But to speak like that is merely to expose one's ignorance and lack of experience. It's merely absurd to state categorically that an animal like a lion or tiger cannot be stopped with certainty with less than 5,000 ft.-lbs. energy. Experience has shown that 4,000 ft.-lbs. can safely be taken against any animal anywhere. Those who answered the argument contented themselves with saying that they had used the .400 with the greatest possible satisfaction for so many years, and utterly failed to see what reason the other fellas had for saying that it lacked power. They had never noticed any lack of power; and that was that. But the whole discussion could have been made much more interesting and instructive if actual instances had been given. I've never yet succeeded in pinning down one of the .400's detractors to actual details of where and when the .400 let him down. I repeat, these detractors are all men with Indian experience —some with not much; I have never heard a word against the .400 from men with African experience.

And right here I'm strongly recommending the double .400 for African big game hunting. In the light of my own experience, I'm perfectly convinced that you will not find a more generally satisfactory weapon. But let it be clearly understood that the .400 is not a small game rifle, and it's unreasonable to expect satisfactory results when using a 400-gr. slug against little light thin-skinned animals. However, it's very much better to use too much power than too little.

But if those fellas who try to decry the .400 can't give us actual details of how it failed them I can give you actual details of just one or two occasions when it did its duty nobly by me. For instance:

I had been following a mixed troop of elephant one day with the pad marks of two good bulls, one of them a monster, tho it was only later that I found the brute had no tusks. The wind had been contrary, little fitful puffs coming from all points of the compass in succession. Time and again we came to where the elephant had halted and then moved on. They hadn't stampeded; the little puffs of wind not being sufficiently strong to alarm them, but just warn them that man was coming. So it had gone on all day. It was near sundown before I finally caught up with them. But altho the country had been fairly open, permitting us to follow as fast as we could walk, it had been hard going—very rough under foot and intensely hot. Spooring having been easy, we must have covered fully 30 miles, maybe more, and I was tired. As I closed the herd I saw a good bull, but not the big one, offering a clear shot. As the animals were very much on the alert and moving about restlessly, I decided to take what the gods offered. Accordingly, I let drive at the bull I could see with my Purdey double .400, and dropped him in his tracks. I was quite confident of the shot, and looked around to see if I couldn't spot the second bull as I reloaded that barrel. I had just closed the breech when I heard a series of deep throaty roars coming from my right front; there is no mistaking that sound if you have ever heard it, and it spells a charging bull elephant and one that means business. I turned to face it, and then saw a monstrous tuskless bull coming under full throttle.

Now I was shooting under license at the time, and my license limited me to five bulls. Altho this brute would be of no use to me if I shot him, he would count as one elephant on my permit. Accordingly, I did not want to shoot him as I was a newcomer in the district and was not yet ready to attempt any poaching. So I and my tracker dodged downwind and took up a position behind a convenient tree whence we could see what was happening. The bull dashed up to the very spot on which I had been standing—one of his immense forefeet actually trod into the ground the empty shell I had dropped when reloading. He stopped there and, ears out and trunk up to test the breeze, he twisted around to try and find us. Failing to do so, he moved off and in the most deliberate way picked up the wind and circled around until he scented us. Once more he charged, as furiously as before, the instant he picked up our wind. We, however, had seen what was coming when he started circling around, and had spotted another small bush downwind that would serve our purpose. We dodged behind that and waited. He again rushed to the very spot where we had been, his trunk telling him where it was, and once more went thru the same performance.

He now knew we were still in the vicinity, and the deliberate and cold-blooded manner in which he set out once more to find us would have been alarming had I not had complete confidence in my rifle. When it was apparent that he was going to charge again, I decided that I had had enough of it: I was tired, the sun was dropping, and we still had to find water. Consequently, I made up my mind to finish matters and stepped out from behind the little bush that had concealed us and shouted to him just as he caught our wind and wheeled towards us. "All right, damn you!" I yelled, "come and get it!" And he sure came! But when he was within about 20 yards the 400-gr. bullet took him between the eyes and killed him instantly.

Now this was comparatively easy on account of the light open timber in which it all took place—it could hardly be called forest— and doubtless I could have killed the brute just as easily with a small bore, provided I could have held it steadily; and remember I was very tired.

But another occasion that stands out very clearly in my memory shows better what the .400 can do, and how it upholds my contention that it is a perfectly safe weapon to take against dangerous game. I was canoeing up the Zambezi one time, and stopped off on one of the large sandy islands where some of my men's folks lived. Their villages here are mostly only temporary reed structures which they build when the annual floods subside and they make their seasonal migration to get a crop off the rich alluvial mud left by the flood. These islands are partially covered with "matetti," tough cane-like stuff 10–12 feet high and covered with spikey leaves the points of which are as hard and sharp as needles. Many of these coons have a few sheep and goats, and there are also hogs running around. Lions come across to the islands and live on these animals, killing a man or a woman now and then. They find good and cool lying-up in the seas of matetti.

I had promised to shoot a hippo that had been playing havoc with the crops, and was just making my way down to look for him, around 9 or 10 o'clock in the morning, when I heard a great hulla-balloo behind me. It appeared that lions had killed a woman and were eating her close by. So I retraced my steps and sure enough there were three lions busy on the body of a woman which they had killed right beside her hut and dragged a short distance towards the surrounding matetti. I was again armed with a double .400, a Jeffery this time, and took a quick right and left from a range of about 12 paces, killing a lion and lioness. The third beast, also a lioness, sprang back and wheeled around to stand broadside on at the very edge of the matetti and look back to see what her companions were doing. I reloaded the right barrel only, snapped-to the breech, and swung up the rifle for a quick shot before she got away.

My sights had just lined up nicely on her shoulder and I was in the act of squeezing the trigger when some fool of a half-breed let drive at her with an old shotgun. The reports of the two weapons blended into one, but the gun had been fired just a split second before the rifle. Well, some men's reactions are quicker than others, and possibly there are some who could have countermanded the brain's order to the trigger-finger in time to refrain from finishing its squeeze; but if so I'm not one of them. The whole thing took place so suddenly and so totally unexpectedly that my bullet had gone before I fully realized that another weapon had been fired. And then was I mad! Here now, instead of a clean and certain kill on the edge of the reeds, I had the extremely unpleasant business in front of me of following a wounded man-eating lioness into that sea of matetti because on feeling the sting of the slugs from the gun the lioness had wheeled around and bounded into the cover. My bullet, instead of taking her thru the shoulder, had entered her ribs on the left side, raked forward thru her liver, and was later found bulging the skin immediately behind her off shoulder.

Now it's customary to allow an animal half an hour or so in which to stiffen before attempting to follow-up but personally I doubt if it does any good. Anyhow, on this occasion, in view of the general noise that was taking place—I bawling-out the fool with the shotgun; all the relatives of the dead woman yelling their heads off; and the young bucks prancing and jabbering and singing around the two dead lions—I figured the wounded lioness would not remain long in the immediate vicinity, and that it was better to get after her at once. So I took up the spoor.

Tracking on the soft white sand was easy but it was impossible

to move quietly thru the reeds: she would certainly hear me
coming. After about ten minutes I came to a little clear patch
—only a short four paces across—and as I straightened up on it
I halted; because there was a very good chance that the lioness
had given herself the advantage of that little clearing to ambush
me. And so it was. Even as I stepped out of the reeds on my side,
she hurled herself towards me from my half-left front. Now I'm a
firm believer in letting a charging lion get close before attempting
to fire but there's a big difference between 12 yards and 12 feet!
If your first shot at 10 or 12 yards fails of immediate effect, then
by all means let him come really close before giving him the second barrel; but since I've seen a lion come on for another couple of
lengths after receiving a 500-gr. slug thru the heart, it's obviously
advisable not to over-do things. On this occasion, however, I
had no alternative; the only advantage I had was that I was expecting her. I dropped to one knee and gave her a bullet in the
open mouth. She bit the dust a bare five or six feet in front of me
just as I stood up and gave her the left barrel down thru the top
of her head.

After that, no man could tell me that the .400 lacked power.
Another adventure, when I was again using the Purdey, clinched
matters for me and definitely cemented my love for this weapon.
But before I tell you about it, let me slip in a word: The reason
why I have always disliked relating adventures of this description
is that one leads to another and the inexperienced listener or reader
not unnaturally gets the impression that big game hunting consists of constantly and incessantly saving one's own life or that of
someone else. It's not so at all. These sort of adventures are
high-lights in the hunter's life and there may be years of more or
less uneventful hunting between them. This incident also concerned elephant.

I had followed three mighty bulls into a hideous tangle of
bush. I eventually got a shot at one of them and killed him without difficulty. I had barely reloaded that barrel when I heard
what sounded like a couple of tanks gone mad and making their
way thru the bush straight for me. It was the other two bulls
who had mistaken the direction from which I had fired; there was
no evil intention on their part, but since I couldn't get out of their
way, the result might be the same as if there had been. I saw a

dim something loom up in a welter of flying bamboo and smashing branches but dared not fire until he had broken thru most of them, as it would have been madness to expect any bullet to plough thru that stuff and maintain a straight course. This delay brought him almost on to me, and I knew he would be much too close for a brain shot—the angle would be all wrong. Accordingly, all I could do was to slam a bullet into his face and swing on the second who was coming almost shoulder to shoulder with him. My first bullet checked the first elephant; he flung his trunk up over his head and squatted on his haunches and I fired for the second one. I would have liked to let him rush past and give him a shoulder shot but he was altogether too close, and might have converted his stampede into a charge and run me down. So I slammed the slug into his head above the eye. I knew it couldn't be expected to kill but I guessed it would knock him down or at least turn him. He fell with a splintering crash of bush and sticks, and felled a small tree which knocked me down. However, my gun-bearer, who was standing a little way behind me, helped me up and I was able to reload and kill both bulls before they could get away. The first one heaved to his feet as I completed reloading, but his head hanging down made it possible for me to get a brain shot altho so close. The second was struggling to his feet, so I gave him a shot thru the shoulder as his head was moving too violently to make a brain shot certain.

Well, that day's work satisfied me concerning the suitability of the .400.

When I mentioned a few moments ago that experience had shown that 4,000 ft.-lbs energy was sufficient to make a weapon safe to take against dangerous game, I was, of course, implying a suitable weight of bullet. If the velocity was boosted enough a light bullet could doubtless be made to show energy figures of around 4,000 ft.-lbs; but that would be the wrong combination entirely. A reasonably heavy bullet is essential when it's a case of knocking down some big beast at close quarters. The 400-gr. bullet thrown by the 450/.400 does so, tho naturally it won't keep the animal down so long as would a heavier slug; but the fact that it can be relied upon to bring him down makes this a safe weapon to use for such work.

I have not had anything like the opportunities in India that

I have had in Africa, but personally I should use the .400 with every confidence in India or anywhere else. I have used it in the densest of African cover against all kinds of dangerous African game, and it never showed the slightest signs of letting me down. With the sole exception of the .450, and corresponding bores, I can safely state without fear of contradiction that the .400 has been, and is, the most widely used caliber for African big game.

The full-patch bullet is excellent for elephant and rhino; the soft-nose with lead barely showing is very effective on rhino and splendid for buffalo; the plain soft-nose with large blue-nose is one of the most certain lion killers obtainable and very deadly on all the heavier varieties of soft-skinned game—they mighty seldom need a second; the soft-nose-split behaves well on the lighter animals. In fact, you will go far to find a better all-around rifle than the .400.

My old friend, Mussa Issa, an Indian-African half-breed, who hunted for some 40 years or more until the tsetse fly got him, was a great lover of the 3¼" 450/.400, and whether or not he had a rifle to fire it, invariably carried a loaded shell of that caliber in his pocket. On the slightest excuse, or without any at all, he would produce this from his pocket, hold it up for all to see, and repeat like a formula: "Now that's a *good* cartridge, that's a *really* good cartridge for elephant; oh! I *like* that cartridge." And he would gaze at it fondly for a while and then return it carefully to his pocket, where it would remain as his talisman.

CHAPTER V

The Medium Bores

It's this group that gives rise to most controversies and arguments amongst big game hunters, one man claiming that there is nothing to touch his pet caliber, whilst another is equally emphatic that his choice beats them all. But what they all are inclined to overlook is whether the rifle is to be used alone, or in conjunction with a more powerful weapon. As I think I have said before, the usual battery in Africa consists of a medium bore for general use, and a large bore for the big fellows. Accordingly, since the medium bore would only be used against dangerous animals when they are encountered in the open and the hunter knows that he will have plenty of time in which to take over his heavier weapon in the event of a charge, the actual power of the medium bore does not matter a whole lot provided it throws a suitable bullet and has adequate penetration to find a vital spot. This is borne out by the fact that all the better medium bores have been used with satisfaction and success thruout the years. Yet some of the most widely used and popular have been denounced as obsolete—completely superseded by their more modern counterparts. But in many cases, experience does not support this view; some of the older weapons in this group are fully capable of holding their own today against any of the super-hotter-up moderns—and in some cases even surpassing them when used without the support of the larger caliber. But we'll come to that presently.

In the ballistic tables I have only included those calibers that have proved generally satisfactory for African hunting. There were many others that I used at different times, but since they proved disappointing I have omitted them and will not clutter up this chapter with a discussion of them. Let us see what we can find to say about the others:

.375 MAGNUM HOLLAND & HOLLAND. Undoubtedly one of the deadliest weapons in existence. It heads the list from the point of view of its caliber, and in the opinion of many hunters ought to easily head it from the point of view of its power also. I've had five of these rifles—two doubles and three magazines—and have fired more than 5,000 rounds of .375 Magnum ammunition at game. The animals included most species from elephant down. One of them accounted for more than 100 elephant and some 411 buffalo, besides rhino, lions and lesser game, so that both it and I well knew each other's little ways. The others had similar animals to their credit, if not so many.

Now if you can put a list of animals like that at the head of a medium bore, it speaks pretty well of its killing power. But more is needed. It must be shown how at least some of the beasts were killed; had the shooting all taken place in very open country there would be nothing very remarkable about it—a small bore in the hands of a steady shot would probably have done just as well. But few of these beasts were shot in the open. The type of country varied from heavy forest and thick bush thru long grass to semi-open scrub.

Altho my formula gives this rifle a Knock-Out value of 40 points, I must regretfully admit that does not really do full justice to it. In actual practice the stopping power of the .375 Magnum would seem to warrant a higher classification. As I have mentioned in a previous chapter, when a bullet of reasonable diameter and weight possesses a sufficiently high striking-velocity it appears to develop a peculiar property of "shock" which is not seen when the velocity is lower. And it is the considered opinion of the majority of experienced hunters who have used this rifle, that the .375 Magnum possesses this power to a greater extent than any other weapon of its class. But if the effect is to be obtained it is to be noted that the bullet *must* hold together. Let me give you two instances, one showing this instantaneous stopping and killing power at its best, and the other showing how the power is dissipated if the bullet breaks up.

I was following-up a wounded buffalo bull, a big brute, that had killed a woman and two kiddies the previous day and badly injured a native hunter the morning of which I write. He had been wounded by a self-styled hunter who had been wounding many of them in this district, but hadn't the guts to follow them up and finish them off. So far as I knew the animal had a bullet in the belly and a broken foreleg, and was in a very savage and dangerous mood. He had taken refuge in a heavy forest with very dense undergrowth that grew around one side of a small lake, and extended over some thousands of acres. He might be just within the fringe of the forest, or he might have plodded right away into the heart of it. This forest had long been looked upon as a sanctuary—the pseudo hunters that frequented the district from time to time were scared to tackle it—and quite a few old bulls that had been wounded in previous years lived all the year around in the forest, only coming out by night to feed and water around the margin of the lake.

I'd worked this place in the past and knew something of it, and also of the old bulls who inhabited it. I had found that they were not on the alert when the forest closed behind them as they apparently considered themselves quite safe in here. But the bull I was following was a very different proposition; he had only recently been wounded and had to abandon his harem; his wounds, at any rate the broken foreleg, would still be painful; he would still be in a savage and vengeful temper which would only have been augmented by his successful attack on the wretched native hunter that morning on the outskirts of the forest. The one advantage the hunter has in this forest is that it's sandy underfoot, permitting silent movement but limiting visibility to about 30 feet.

It might be imagined that an animal weighing a ton or more would be seriously incapacitated with a broken foreleg, and that his charge could not be very fast or difficult to stop. That sounds reasonable, but it does not apply to African buffalo. Altho a broken foreleg will make him limp badly when walking, it appears to in no way to interfere with his speed when charging; on the contrary, if anything it seems to make it worse than ever, because the leg swinging causes the ends of the broken bone to scrape together, which must hurt like hell, and literally drives him crazy—bloodmad. I've seen a big bull so wounded charge his companions again and again, roaring like fury, and bowl them over like nine-pins. So you will readily appreciate that a beast like that, coming at maybe 25 miles an hour and less than 10 yards away when you see him, takes a deal of stopping.

I was carrying a double .375 Magnum loaded with bluff-nose solid 300-gr. slugs. The first intimation I had of the bull's presence was the twitch of his ear as he flicked a fly off it. He was standing behind a dense clump of undergrowth with a little clear patch in the centre of it, and there was a clear space about 11 paces wide between me and the clump. He must have seen some movement, for he was looking straight at me. I let drive immediately but my bullet had to find its way thru a tangle of twigs, and must have been deflected slightly. These 300-gr. bullets are excellent for this sort of thing but there are limits to what you can reasonably expect. The bull dropped to the shot but in an instant was up again and coming. I sank to one knee and waited for him to break thru the bush. When he did, I gave him the left barrel fairly in the centre of his great chest. Well, the effect of that shot was exactly as tho there had been a steel hawser stretched across his path just the right height above the ground to whip the two forelegs from under him. He crashed on his nose and his knees and remained like that with his hindquarters in the air whilst I reloaded. I was about to give him a bullet in the spine when he keeled over—stone dead.

If that's not stopping-power, I should very much like to know what you would call it. It was more than mere stopping-power; I'm convinced that bull was dead on receipt of the bullet, even altho it took a few moments for his back-side to collapse.

The reason why I fired so soon in the first place was that animals know very well if the hunter is scared of them or not and, if not, they are quite likely to clear off without offering a shot at all instead of charging. It does not always pan out like that, but sometimes does and I had no wish to follow the brute any further into that forest at that hour of the day with the knowledge that if I failed to finish him I would have to make my way out in the dark, for the tops of the trees met overhead and it would have been pitch dark as soon as the sun went down; and it would not have been pleasant to encounter the wounded bull under such conditions should he have managed to get ahead of me.

In support of that statement that animals know if the hunter is scared of them or not, of which I have had ample evidence in my own experience, I might mention that Blunt described an occasion when he was hunting a rogue elephant which had made a custom of ambushing natives along a small path and chasing and killing all whom he could catch; but that when an eddy of wind carried the scent of Blunt to him, he tucked in his tail and went for his life. There was no question of him attacking Blunt. I had an almost identical experience myself.

The other example occurred when I was hunting for meat for my men. There wasn't much game about, so I had loaded the .375 Magnum magazine with 235-gr. copper-pointed loads, intending to knock over two or three smaller animals for which it would be suitable. It was loaded to 2,850 f.s. However, when I put up a water-buck bull at about 40 yards I let rip, placing the bullet well up on his hip as he was quartering away from me. He dropped to the shot and disappeared in the grass. Quite certain that his hip and spine would have been shattered—as either the 270 or 300-gr. slugs would have done—I took no notice of a rush thru the grass when I closed in to finish him off. I guessed that it was maybe a companion but to my astonishment my bull wasn't there when I arrived at the spot where he had dropped. There was plenty of blood scattered around, however, and there was no difficulty in spooring him. But he was still very much alive when I finally got another shot at him a quarter of a mile farther along.

I found that the copper-pointed bullet with its tremendously high striking-velocity at such close range had literally disintegrated against the spine. Hitting the sloping bones of the hip, it had opened up, skidded along the bone, and crashed into the spine, making an appalling surface wound but smashing itself to pieces instead of breaking the spine. You can readily see how hideously dangerous it could have been had it been a good-maned lion that tempted me into having a smack at him without giving me time to change to a more suitable bullet. You will inevitably meet with these temptations from time to time, and my advice is don't succumb to them. However, I am aware that the best of advice usually goes by the board when the chance of a lifetime occurs and it is only after the tyro has been taught a bitter lesson or two by personal experience that he will realize that the old-timer was probably right after all!

But it's worth bearing in mind that, where non-dangerous game are concerned a "bitter lesson" may merely mean a bitter disappointment; but if the lesson is to be taught by a lion whom you have rudely (and very foolishly) clouted in the ribs with an unsuitable slug, things can have a very different ending.

A Colonel Stockley, a keen sportsman with considerable experience who doesn't like large bores, relates an adventure of his that is very much to the point altho it don't actually relate to the .375 Magnum. Stockley had ordered some soft-nose slugs for his medium bore, but the gunsmith from whom he ordered them sent him hollow-nose bullets instead. As Stockley was away out in the "blue" he had no opportunity of changing them. The yarn deals with a tiger; but for the purposes of this discussion a tiger can be reckoned the same as a lion. Stockley met up with an immense tiger in 3-foot grass on the edge of a swamp and fired when the tiger was facing slightly away from him. The bullet took him much as mine had taken the water-buck and he dropped into the grass. Stockley, forgetting all about the wrong type of bullet, thinking he had broken the beast's spine, closed in to finish him. But when he arrived within some ten yards or so of the spot, he found the tiger coming for him hard. The hunter fired again, breaking a leg but the light was so bad that he couldn't see his sights properly. He put in another shot or two but was compelled to leave the wretched beast there until morning when he came out and finished him. Now had the grass been somewhat longer, Stockley would probably have run right into the tiger's jaws as he was quite sure the beast's back was broken.

But to return to the killing power of bullets that don't break up. I have killed numerous buffalo with other rifles in this group and when for any reason the bullet has to be placed behind the shoulder, they have run anything from 40 to 140 yards and in many cases have still been potentially dangerous when I caught up with them; but on a similar shot with the .375 Magnum, using either the 270 or 300-gr. bullet, I cannot remember ever having one go more than from about 15 to 25 paces, and frequently not more than once or twice their own length, and invariably they have been dead when found. It was very, very rarely I had to give a buffalo, or for that matter any other animal, a second shot when using the .375 Magnum. Except, of course, those occasions when I could clearly see that it was impossible to hope for a clean kill from the first shot.

And altho I've been speaking of heavy and dangerous animals, it must not be imagined that the .375 Magnum is only suitable for them. This is where the .375 Magnum's great beauty comes in—it is equally effective on all the non-dangerous list, both the heavier as well as the lighter varieties. For the former, the 270 and 300-gr. slugs are pretty nearly ideal. In some of the more open parts of the country, where slightly longer shots are called for, the 270-gr. semi-pointed soft-nose is indicated but personally I have come to prefer the round-nose soft-nose 300-gr. for my stamping grounds. And the reason is that there is such a very much smaller percentage of lead showing on the 270-gr. that if for any reason you have to place it behind some beast's shoulder, it will often go clean thru. It will always expand, and never fail to kill if at all well placed but I like my bullets to remain in the animal's body. Not only is there then no fear of needlessly wounding others standing beyond the one at which you have fired, but in my experience the animal will be killed much sooner if the bullet remains in him—in other words, if he stops it.

I had this very forcibly brought home to me when bagging two water-buck bulls one day for the pots, and two kudu bulls on another occasion also for meat. Both times I was armed with a double .375 Magnum, and had loaded a 300-gr. soft-nose slug in the right barrel and a 270-gr. semi-pointed soft-nose in the left in case of a longer shot being offered. But on the two occasions in question the animals were standing together. Each time I had to place the bullets behind the shoulder on account of the angle at which the beasts were standing. On each occasion I took a quick right and left at about 80 yards. The 270-gr. bullet on each occasion set-up but went thru whereas each of the 300-gr. slugs mushroomed perfectly and were found bulging the skin on the far side. The two beasts that had received the 300-gr. slugs didn't go ten yards before dropping but the other two that got the 270-gr. ones ran about 25–30 paces before collapsing. From this it was quite apparent to me that a bullet that remains in the animal's body kills quicker than one that goes right thru. On each occasion the animals might have been twin brothers and were shot at almost exactly the same range and hit in, for all practical purposes, the identical spot. So that the comparison was as fair as was humanly possible where life is concerned—and death.

Since you have three different weights of bullet to choose from, and since they can all be fired from the same weapon irrespective of whether it's double, single or magazine, it would be difficult to see how the .375 Magnum could fail to give satisfaction for any kind of big game hunting. For instance, a man would need to be certified who would try to kill a rhino with the 235-gr. copper-pointed bullet. Yet I have known this done—and the moron actually had the gall to grumble afterwards that the .375 Magnum was nowhere near such a deadly weapon as he had been given to understand!

Here is a bit of added discussion about this fine cartridge and its various loads.

.375 MAGNUM FLANGED: Powder 58 grs. Smokeless; Bullet 235-gr. Metal-covered; Pressure 16(?) tons;M.V. 2,750, M.E. 3,950.

Powder 58 grs. Smokeless; Bullet 270-gr. Metal-covered; Pressure 17(?) tons;M.V. 2,600;M.E. 4,060.

Powder 58 grs. Smokeless; Bullet 300-gr. Metal-covered; Pressure 17(?) tons;M.V. 2,450;M.E. 4,010.

.375 MAGNUM BELTED RIMLESS: Powder 60 grs. Smokeless; Bullet 235-gr. Metal-covered; Pressure 17 tons; M.V. 2,800; M.E. 4,100.

Powder 60 grs. Smokeless; Bullet 270-gr. Metal-covered; Pressure 18 tons; M.V. 2,650; M.E. 4,220.

Powder 60 grs. Smokeless; Bullet 300-gr. Metal-covered; Pressure 18 tons; M.V. 2,500; M.E. 4,160.

The above are the standard ballistics for the British loading of these two cartridges but Holland & Holland, the designers of them, have recently boosted the velocity of the 235-gr. bullet to 2,900 f.s. in the belted-rimless shell. This was quite permissible since it showed a lower chamber pressure than either of the two heavier bullets but I do not know whether or not a different aim would be necessary when it is used at this new velocity. Probably it would, tho the difference should not be very great; nevertheless, it's a pity, because one of the great selling points of this rifle was the fact that all its three loads could be fired at the ranges for which they were primarily intended without any alteration in sighting or aim being necessary.

As usual, it will be noticed that the flanged shell for use in doubles has a slightly reduced loading so as to bring about a lower chamber pressure. However, the difference in ballistics is so slight that it can be ignored. This cartridge and rifle was definitely designed for the "one-rifle" man; it's the only weapon that has ever been definitely designed as an "all-around" rifle for the man who cannot afford or does not want to be bothered with a number of different weapons, and yet who wants to shoot a wide variety of animals. There is no other rifle on the market with which such a wide variety of different species of big game, from the largest to the smallest, can be killed equally satisfactorily. Its three different weights of bullet are all most deadly *on the type game for which they were intended*, and at the ranges at which such animals are normally shot.

The trajectories of all three bullets are flatter than those of any of their contemporaries and they all three have a higher striking-velocity at any given range than any similar weights of bullet. Still, I do not like that copper-pointed 235-gr. slug—I do not like any copper-pointed bullet—I do not consider them reliable. In my experience they tend to fly to pieces all too readily if they encounter a bone and if they don't they will frequently snick thru like solids without setting-up at all.

The semi-pointed soft-nose 270-gr. is a wonderfully deadly projectile. I know a half-breed who has claimed to have killed an elephant with a lung shot with it, and see no reason to disbelieve him. I have never known this bullet to break up, and I have slammed it into many and many a buffalo. I have also killed a big hippo bull instantly with a head shot with it—and a hippo has a pretty massive skull. Accordingly, I fail to see why it should be unable to find an elephant's lungs. I have found it an excellent lion-stopper, undoubtedly due to its high striking-velocity and the fact that, altho it can always be relied upon to mushroom, it does not lose weight. Its weight and diameter, combined with its speed and depth of penetration, would seem to be the factors that are

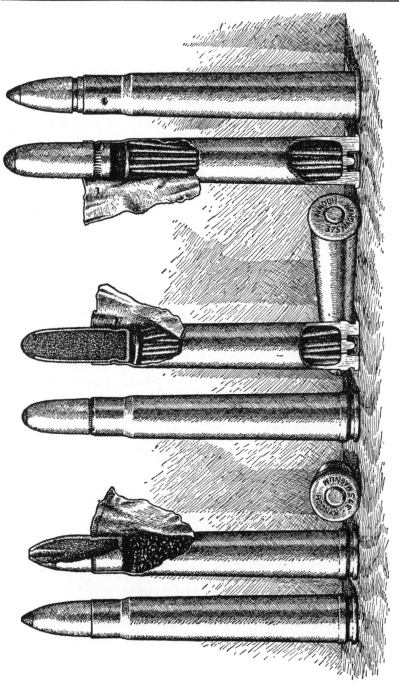

.375 Magnum.

responsible for its amazing killing power. And when I say "amazing killing power," that's just what I mean—it's not mere hyperbole. Only those who have actually used this cartridge on a wide variety of different animals, having previously used "ordinary" rifles on those same species, are in a position to thoroly appreciate the .375 Magnum's deadliness. I find it difficult right here to remember a single animal that required a second shot from this rifle—other, of course, than those that were deliberately crippled with the first shot when I could clearly see that it was impossible to hope for a clean kill from the first bullet.

The only exception that comes to mind was a magnificent black-maned lion that cut across my bows when I was returning from a buffalo hunt. But even he is not really a fair case to mention because of the peculiar manner in which he was shot. My first shot, intended to take him at the base of the ear, was not well-placed; it hit him a glancing blow along the base of the skull and smashed one of the projections of the first curvicle vertebra, which knocked him out. He disappeared in the grass, but I was by no means certain of him. It had been a difficult shot owing to obstructions, altho the range was only eleven paces and I well knew the lion's remarkable ability for "coming to life" again after dropping so instantaneously to a bullet. Accordingly, I did not advance straight towards him, but moved around so as to get behind him. As I did so I saw his tail lashing up and down and heard a series of grating roars, but he didn't appear to be otherwise moving or turning around to keep facing me. When well behind him I closed in towards those unceasing roars and flailing tail. I saw him lying on his side, and altho he appeared to be unable to move that didn't appear to make sense in view of that tail lashing the ground and his exposed flank, whilst there was no diminishing in the volume of the roaring. I put a bullet into him behind the shoulder, raking forward, but it had absolutely no effect—I guess it passed alongside the heart. So I then gave him another which, on account of the angle at which I was firing, tore a hole in him into which I could

In the illustration here the two outer belted-rimless shells are British loaded and the two inner ones American. You will note that the British still load cordite. Cordite is a very sure-fire powder and easy of ignition. The copper-pointed 235-gr. bullet shown in the flanged shell is steel-jacketed. I think that must be an old shell. All mine were Nobeloy-jacketed.

easily have stuffed both my fists; but that had no more effect than
the other—the tail continued to lash first the ground and then his
side, whilst his short grating roars were unceasing. I then moved
around in front of him as various obstacles prevented my taking up
any other position. Here I knelt down and put a bullet into the
centre of his chest. That finished him. I repeat, however, this
is hardly a fair case but I mention it because it is the only one that
occurs to me.

But do not get me wrong about all this—I'm not suggesting
that all you have to do is to just point your .375 Magnum at some
animal, pull the trigger, and then stroll along and collect your
trophy. When I speak of the extraordinary killing power of this
rifle, I am, naturally, implying reasonably well-placed shots. The
lion, like all members of the cat family, possesses remarkable
tenacity-to-life, and no weapon that any man living could handle
under normal hunting conditions can be relied upon to kill him
instantly if the shot is badly placed.

The soft-nose 300-gr. slug is a beauty. Its penetration may not
be quite so deep as that of the 270-gr., owing to the fact that a
much larger proportion of lead is exposed but it is ample for all
purposes for which you would normally be wanting a soft-nose
bullet. I have never seen one that showed the slightest indication
of wanting to break up or lose any of its original weight. It invariably mushrooms perfectly and will usually be found bulging the
skin on the far side. For general use I prefer it to the 270-gr. because I have never had it go right thru any decent-sized animal;
whereas, when it may be necessary to place a bullet behind an
animal's shoulder, the 270-gr. will occasionally do so. It's true
that the 270-gr. will kill on such a shot but as I have frequently
stated thruout this book, I like my bullets to remain in the animal's
body.

The full-patch 300-gr. has, I think, deeper penetration than any
other bullet I have ever used. Nevertheless, there is room for
improvement in it, as I look at it, a full-patch—or "solid," as the
British call it—should have a sufficiently hard-nose to preclude
any possibility of it breaking or riveting no matter what it hits,
short of a battleship's hull. I have had several full-patch bullets
from this rifle become somewhat distorted, and had one rivet quite
considerably when slammed into a buffalo's spine at point-blank

range. Admittedly, in no case did the envelope break open; still, in my opinion, they ought not to have been even marked. A Col. Alexander used a double .375 Magnum for buffalo in Assam and bison (gaur) in India. He described killing one gaur at a range of about 6 feet after side-stepping a charge, driving the 300-gr. full-patch bullet in behind the near shoulder as the gaur passed him. He recovered the bullet and mentioned that its nose had been buckled up on a rib or something. It's true that the bison was killed instantly but, I contend, that bullet should not have lost its shape. The steel-covered solids Rigby supplies for use with his special calibers do not do so. I think it would be an excellent thing if similar bullets were available for the .375 Magnum; they should improve even this splendid cartridge.

This weapon can most certainly be recommended for African hunting.

Auctor: I know you said you weren't going to "clutter up" this chapter with a discussion of the various old calibers that had failed to give you satisfaction but don't you think you might make some mention of them. Some of them at any rate were quite widely used once upon a time, and one occasionally comes across a reference to one of them in some old book.

Lector: Okeh; have it your own way. But there isn't a great deal to say about most of them.

400/.375 HOLLAND AND .375 (9.5MM) MANNLICHER-SCHOEN-AUER. The 400/.375 was introduced to compare with the 9.5mm Mannlicher-Schoenauer for those who prefer doubles and single-loaders. It was a trifle less powerful than the 9.5mm, the energy of which was just over 3,000 ft.-lbs. The .375 caliber has always been a Holland specialty, just as the .350 has with Rigby.

I cannot say I ever cared much for any of these old .375s. They all three lacked penetration and could not be compared with the .350, .360 N $\stackrel{o}{=}$ 2 or .366 (9.3mm). I am aware that a great deal of game must have been killed with both the 400/.375 and the 9.5mm but I have heard many complaints concerning both, in which they failed in penetration. It must never be forgotten that the general run of animals shot in Africa is appreciably larger than in other countries; further, the vitality of African game is such that it cannot be appreciated by those unacquainted with it. Accordingly, a weapon which may prove perfectly satisfactory in other parts of the world, need not prove anywhere near so satisfactory when used against African game.

Selous had Holland build him a falling-block single-loader to handle presumably this 400/.375 shell. But he wrote to a friend of his that he didn't think much of it and reckoned that he would have done just as well with his old falling-block .303. That was in connection with one of his Canadian or Alaskan trips.

.375 FLANGED NITRO-EXPRESS: Powder 40 grs. Smokeless; Bullet 270-gr. Metal-covered; Pressure 14½ tons; M.V. 1,975; M.E. 2,340.

The B.S.A. concern used to build a Lee-actioned magazine rifle to handle this shell; not a very powerful one, as evidenced by the fact that the Lee action could stand it. It was not suitable for general African use, as it lacked power and penetration. I only heard of one man who appeared to be satisfied with it—he must have been easily pleased! He wrote a book describing his experiences in North-Eastern Rhodesia, and amongst other things said that he never wished to use a better or more accurate weapon. Well, to that I can but add that he could not have had much experience with other calibers.

.375 RIMLESS WESTLEY RICHARDS. It's one of life's little mysteries to me how this cartridge ever came into existance. Westley Richards built a Mannlicher-Schoenauer-actioned rifle to handle it which seems rather fatuous since the regular 9.5mm was available and a somewhat more powerful weapon. One gathers that this cartridge was intended to be the rimless edition of the flanged .375 B.S.A. I never used it and cannot imagine that I lost anything by not doing so.

.375 (9.5MM) MANNLICHER-SCHOENAUER: Powder 45 grs. Smokeless; Bullet 270-gr. Metal-covered; Pressure 17 tons; M.V. 2,250; M.E. 3,030.

This cartridge had a considerable vogue once upon a time, principally because these rifles could be obtained very cheaply from Austria, and for a mere $25 extra could have a cheap scope fitted. Also, men liked the revolving magazine which became so popular in the 6.5mm caliber.

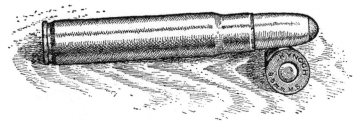

THE 9.5MM MANNLICHER-SCHOENAUER.

I did not like this shell. I found that the penetration was none too good, and heard many similar complaints from other hunters. I do not know of any professional hunter who ever used it to any extent, altho, as I say, it was popular with amateurs and occasional hunters. I cannot recommend it, and have nothing more to say about it.

.369 PURDEY. Purdey builds his .369 as a double only. Firing its 270-gr. bullet it is identical with the .375 Magnum when the latter is firing the same weight. The .369, however, only fires the one bullet, and altho it will surely kill anything its bullet will penetrate, you are liable to get rather better results when you can use a variety of different bullets for the different weights of game. You would need to go a very long way to get a better general purpose weapon.

.366 (9.3MM) BRENNEKE. This was the German attempt to compete with the Holland .375 Magnum. As far as I can remember it threw a bullet of about 275-grs. at slightly better than 2,600 f.s. It was easily comparable with the .375 Magnum, but just a mite less powerful. However, it was an excellent weapon and a great killer. I saw a kongoni or haartebeaste killed with it one day. The bullet took the animal on the shoulder, killing him instantly and the jolt had been so severe that his neck was broken. I had a similar experience myself with a .375 Magnum. I forget what the animal was now, but the bullet taking him on the point of the shoulder when he was facing me diagonally, broke the neck about half way along its length. My friend, the German hunter to whom I frequently refer, used one of these rifles fitted with a Zeiss scope and killed most of his elephant with it. It is strongly recommended if you can get the shells for it, but it may be that this cartridge will not be loaded again.

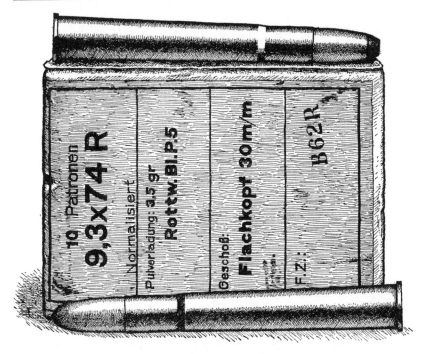

.366 (9.3 x 74MM R).

This is a shell I have never previously seen, tho I have heard that it is powerful fodder. [I'm quite prepared to believe that. I take it that it is the flanged edition of the 9.3mm Brenneke. The Germans were very keen to bring out something that would compare with Holland's .375 Magnum. Their 9.3mm Brenneke did that as a magazine; and this shell, I think, was intended to compare with the flanged .375 Magnum for use in doubles. Judging by my German friend's performance with his magazine, if this is indeed the shell I guess it to be, then it must be a peach.

.366 (9.3MM) MAUSER: Powder 54 grs. Smokeless; Bullet 285-gr. Metal-covered; Pressure 16½ tons; M.V. 2,175; M.E. 3,000.

This was the German answer to the demand of their folks in Tanganyika for something better than the 9mm and comparable with the British 400/.350 and .360 N⁰2. It was immediately acceptable and has ever since been the most widely used medium bore in Africa. This, of course, was because being German, it could be sold very much more cheaply than could a similar Mauser-actioned weapon of British manufacture. It's a simply splendid general purpose cartridge, and its shells could be bought in almost any store thruout the length and breadth of Africa; this being a most definite recommendation for any cartridge.

Its bullet of 285-gr. and energy of 3,000 ft.-lbs nicely met all requirements. This has always been reckoned the minimum energy for general African hunting, and the bullet must have good sectional density. It is in this connection that the 9.3mm proved itself so very much better than the 9.5mm. I have never heard any complaints about the 9.3mm. Its penetration is adequate for anything. It has never had the write-up that certain other calibers receive from time to time. Men just take it for granted and it goes steadily on its way like some honest old farm horse. In spite of all the more modern magnums and "supers," the 9.3mm still remains the favorite medium bore of many experienced hunters. It's a big asset to the professional hunter when he knows that no matter in what part of the continent he may be roaming, he can find shells for his rifles. Because, altho I always advocate ordering ammunition direct from the factory, soldered up in airtight packages of 50 or 100 depending on the extent to which you expect to be using them so that they are always fresh, there are times when a consignment can go astray or the hunter may have shifted operations to some distant part of the big game hunting world so that they take a long time to reach him, and then he may find that he can't get any shells locally with which to continue hunting. But there would be no fear of that happening if he was armed with a 9.3mm.

Having said that it's the most popular and most widely used medium bore in Africa, there isn't a great deal more that one can say about it—that just about covers everything. But it brings up a point concerning various other calibers that deserves noticing, and that is in connection with high velocities and flat trajectories, and the average ranges at which African game is shot. Some gunsmiths and arm-chair theorists would like to insist that the general run of the original medium bores has been rendered obsolete by their more modern counterparts, and that nowadays a high speed bullet and a flat trajectory are essential. Well, in answer to that one has only to point to the 9.3mm and refer to its wide popularity. Its velocity is very moderate, whilst its trajectory is anything from 50 to 70 yards shorter than that of some of its more modern high speed contemporaries—yet it's still the most popular of all medium bores in Africa!

This would seem to indicate that there is some truth in the contention that I have always held, that there is nothing to be gained by boosting velocities for the purpose of flattening trajectories, and thereby needlessly increasing chamber pressures, for the excellent reason that the increased flatness of the trajectory only begins to become noticeable beyond the range at which you would normally be using the rifle. And since the 9.3mm is so satisfactory there can be no real need for a flatter trajectory than it gives you as far as African hunting is concerned. A whole lot of this hooey about trajectories was brought out by gunsmiths, or those with a financial interest in the gun trade, at a time when competition was very keen, or else by those who had only shot in very open countries in other parts of the world where very long shots were quite customary. But the story of the 9.3mm puts it in its right place where Africa is concerned. The only genuine advantage of a high velocity in a medium bore rifle for African use is when it is to be used alone without the support of a more powerful weapon when tackling dangerous game at close quarters, but since the vast majority of hunters who intend to go after the big fellas include a large bore in their battery, the desirability of a high velocity does not arise.

There is nothing spectacular about it: it's just a sound, reliable, general purpose cartridge. That well-known and experienced American big game hunter, Dr. Sutton, in a letter to the *AMERICAN RIFLEMAN* quite recently, stated that if he was returning to Africa, India or Indo-China to hunt he would take a 9.3mm Mauser and a good British double such as a .450, .465 or .470, and nothing else. Banks, one of the most experienced professional elephant hunters in Africa, after using most calibers from .256 to .577, took to and became very fond of a 9.3mm Mauser, tho he usually carried a double in the .450–.470 group in thick cover. I have not heard of anybody with a complaint to make concerning the 9.3mm cartridge. I did a fair amount of shooting with it, and gave it up simply because I don't care for magazine rifles but if somebody was to present me with a Westley Richards double built to handle it, I should willingly use it for the remainder of my life.

There isn't really a great deal to say about it. Everybody found

THE 9.3MM MAUSER, OR .366.

This is the strong-jacketed "H" type bullet brought out by the Germans, and as you see is plain soft-nose. I never saw one of this pattern used, but strongly recommended such. I only saw the copper-tubed bullet in this pattern and caliber. It used to lose far too much weight; tho I never saw or heard of the jacket disintegrating. But you want more than the weight of the jacket, no matter how strong it is. I do not think these bullets were ever available for the regular velocity, only for the stepped-up edition of this grand cartridge. Unless I'm mistaken the Germans got somewhere around 2400 f.s. out of it, instead of the original 2175. But I cannot see that there was any real need to boost its ballistics, nor any demand. I've a hunch it was merely following fashion—which is not always a wise policy. At any rate, I never heard a single solitary complaint concerning the 9.3mm in its regular original guise. It was, and is, one of the very best-designed medium-bore shells that has ever been placed on the African market.

it so generally satisfactory that there wasn't anything to start a discussion. About the only time it was ever brought into an argument was when it and the 10.75mm were being compared from the point of view of all-around utility. The vast majority of us preferred the 9.3mm but there were and still are many who prefer the 10.75mm. Personally, I consider the 9.3mm an infinitely more satisfactory and better balanced cartridge. The full-patch bullet has adequate penetration to kill an elephant from any reasonable angle; it will also kill rhino and buffalo on the shoulder shot. The plain soft-nose bullet can be used on everything else—it will not break up and yet will have ample penetration to enable it to reach a vital spot. It is, of course, its much better sectional density that gives it this great advantage over the 10.75mm.

The strong-jacketed bullet brought out by the Germans for their high velocity cartridge somewhere in the '30s would have been most excellent had it been a plain soft-nose instead of the copper-pointed which was the only pattern I saw or heard of. But I cannot see that there was any necessity for boosting the velocity of this cartridge; on the contrary, without widely advertising the fact they intended to do so, I reckoned it unfair on, and even dangerous for, the thousands of users of this shell, most of whom could not read German even if the new ballistics were quoted on the boxes of shells. The British loaders did not alter their ballistics. There are so many of these rifles about, that I should think the British will again load 9.3mm ammunition when they get around to making sporting ammo once more.

The 9.3mm can certainly be recommended for Africa for general use.

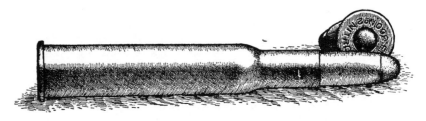

.360 N⁰ 2.

This was a very fine cartridge. Its 320-gr. bullet starts at 2,200 f.s. showing energy of 3,450 ft.lbs. for a chamber pressure of a mere 14.7 tons. It was, therefore, ideally suited for use in doubles and single-loaders. It never got the chance to win the popularity it undoubtedly deserved, because the .375 Magnum appeared too soon after its introduction. It was an extremely satisfactory cartridge, and a splendid killer.

You will note the extreme exposure of lead in many of these older soft-nose bullets. It has been very difficult to get hold of some of these older patterns to use as illustrations. As you can see it was manufactured by Eley Bros.—that means it was prior to the amalgamation of the British ammunition firms. Eley was fond of this type of expanding bullet, and generally I found it most excellent. However, he rather over-did it occasionally, and it was not unknown for the lead to catch the rifling on a new rifle, or if the rifle had unusually deep rifling, and so give rise to lead fouling in the bore. But this only happened in one or two calibers, notably the 450/.400, where it was possible to get a bullet with half the lead exposed. This pattern later disappeared, to be replaced by the modern "soft-nose-split" in which there is only a small amount of lead showing at the nose, but three or four cuts lengthways in the envelope down the shoulders of the bullet. Personally, I don't care too much for these soft-nose-split bullets, as they tend to break up too quickly and lose too much of their weight. Provided the exposure of lead was not too exaggerated, I prefer the older type with a really large blue nose, like that illustrated here.

.360 N⁰ 2. This was a splendid cartridge. Its 320-gr. bullet thrown at 2,200 f.s. showed energy of 3,450 ft.-lbs. for a chamber pressure of a mere 14.7 tons. It was, therefore, ideally suited for use in doubles and single-loaders. It never got the chance to win the popularity it undoubtedly deserved, because the .375 Magnum appeared too soon after its introduction. It was an extremely satisfactory cartridge, and a splendid killer. I used a falling-block single-loader firing it but was compelled to discard it because of the difficulty in obtaining shells for it. I would very much like to have a double handling it.

400/.360.

Here again you see the older type of bullet made by Eley with a very large blue nose. These were low velocity bullets of good weight, and needed every help if they were to expand properly on the lighter animals.

400/.360 AND .360 WESTLEY RICHARDS. These two rifles were much the same as the 9mm Mauser. All three showed M.E. of slightly over 2,500 ft.-lbs. They all three killed game, but failed to satisfy.

.355 (9MM) MAUSER: Powder 45 grs. Smokeless; Bullet 245-gr. Metal-covered; Pressure 17 tons; M.V. 2,150; M.E. 2,520.

Quite a useful general purpose cartridge provided it was backed up by something more powerful. Churchill supplied me with a very nice little sporter to handle this shell, and it was a participant in one of the most curious incidents I have ever witnessed in the Bush. I intended to work an area to which I was a complete stranger, and took along an Indian-African half-breed who claimed to know it, as I figured it would save me a lot of time to have someone along who knew the district. This fella had been hunting all his life, and amongst other things possessed a 7.9mm Mauser—a caliber he was never happy without.

We were hunting for meat for the men and came on an enormous eland bull—he must have run close to a ton on the hoof—standing under a small tree. The tree covered his shoulders but his head and neck were exposed, as also was his body. He was barely fifteen paces away, so I signed to my companion to take the shot as he was more or less between me and the eland. He swung up his 7.9mm, steadied, and fired. Absolutely nothing happened; the bull took not the slightest notice, did not even twitch an ear. Again my companion fired and again nothing happened, except that the eland took a half pace forward and leaned against the tree. My companion whispered urgently to me to shoot, but I was so convulsed with inward laughter that I simply couldn't. He then signed to me to let him have my brand-new 9mm, so I handed it across. Once more he fired. The big bull took a leisurely pace forward and just lay down.

When we examined him the only bullet wound we could find was that in his neck caused by my 9mm; what had happened to the first two from the 7.9mm I have no idea. To this day I am certain that that old bull died of sheer old age! He must have been stone deaf not to have heard the first two shots and his actual death was quite unlike what you would expect from a bullet in the neck—it wasn't an instantaneous collapse; he first took that leisurely step forwards before lying down—not falling.

The 9mm was never very widely used, tho some men were fond of it. An American friend of mine once had one which he used for years and swears there was never another rifle to compare with it but I can't help feeling that time has lent enchantment to his memories of it. After all, you can't get away from ballistics, and the ballistics of the 9mm have never been anything to write home about. I figure that it was just that he happened to get hold of a well-made weapon that fitted him like a glove, and consequently was really able to use it. I am quite sure that the majority of disappointments are caused thru badly-fitting weapons and not lack of power. Few men take the trouble to go along to a gunsmith and have their measurements taken, yet they know perfectly well that not one man in ten can enter a tailor's shop, have a suit reached down, don it, and feel well-dressed. A gun or rifle is just the same—it must fit you if you're to get the best out of it. Your ability to use a gun or rifle will improve out of all recognition if it has been built to your measurements; you'll be able to do things with it that you wouldn't have believed possible before.

As well as I remember I only killed one elephant with the 9mm but used it chiefly for the pot. Any of these weapons will keep your pot filled; the trouble is that men try to use them for all purposes. In the hands of a thoroly experienced hunter, well and good, but the casual sportsman cannot expect to get the same results. To get satisfactory results from such weapons, the bullet must be perfectly placed every time—few "occasional" hunters can hope to do that.

THE 9MM MANNLICHER.

There is very little difference between this and the 9mm Mauser cartridge, both having been brought out when the demand for something better than the 7mm, 8mm and .303 cartridges became insistent. They are comparable to the .35 Winchester cartridge, but both fall far short of Rigby's .350.

.355 (9MM) MAUSER AND MANNLICHER. The difference in the ballistics of these two weapons is very slight. They were both brought out when the demand for something better than the military calibers became insistent. They were comparable with the .35 Winchester, but fell far short of the .350 Rigby. I never owned the Mannlicher but had a very nice little 9mm Mauser one time. I seldom used it other than for the pot, which it had no difficulty in keeping filled.

.35 WHELEN; .35 NEWTON; .350 GRIFFIN & HOWE MAGNUM. I have had no personal experience of these three American weapons but have heard of a family in Kenya using one of them, the .35 Newton, I think it was. They reckoned it was a great cartridge for everything except elephant and rhino but complained that the rifle had an infuriating habit of shedding its cartridges from the magazine whenever the weapon was fired.

There is no question that, ballistically, any one of these three weapons would be just about ideal for general African use. *If the pressure is all right and if* suitable bullets are available for close range work, I personally would prefer the G & H Magnum to the H & H .375 Magnum. With its 275-gr. bullet of that caliber and velocity of 2,600 f.s. it would undoubtedly be an astounding killer. However, I repeat, I have never as yet had an opportunity of using it but if you possess one of these three rifles I would certainly advise you to bring it along when you come out here.

.350 N⁰2 RIGBY. This is merely the flanged edition of the .350 Rigby Magnum for use in doubles. The bullet weight and ballistics are the same, and everything said about the .350 Magnum applies equally here. I have never owned one of these doubles but would very much like to do so, because I have had such great pleasure and satisfaction from the Mauser-actioned edition which comes next.

.350 MAGNUM RIGBY. John Rigby was practically forced to introduce this cartridge and rifle owing to the incessant demand for higher velocity and flatter trajectory after the introduction of Holland's .375 Magnum. Some folks don't study things very closely or don't get much practical experience and are in all too great a hurry to jump to conclusions, just as they are all too ready to jump to velocity whilst ignoring bullet weight—as in the case of the .330 B.S.A.

Rigby's reaction was to reduce the weight of his bullet to 225 grains and load an increased powder charge behind it in a rimless shell. It produces a M.V. of 2,600 f.s. and is very effective on all soft-skinned game. With the sole exception of the .318, which is lighter and cheaper, Rigby's .350 Magnum is easily the most widely used British medium bore thruout Africa. It has taken the place of its predecessor, the 400/.350.

For long I reckoned that so light a bullet could never prove really satisfactory or as useful as the 310-gr. bullet thrown by the 400/.350; however, when I at last persuaded myself to get one, I was most agreeably surprised. Its 225-gr. semi-pointed soft-nose bullet behaves perfectly on all soft-skinned African game whilst the round-nose steel-covered solid has adequate penetration for elephant or rhino. It's an intensely satisfactory weapon and very pleasant to shoot. I've never heard a single complaint concerning it—in fact I've never heard a single complaint concerning any of Rigby's rifles or cartridges. I've never seen one of these bullets blow up or disintegrate.

An incident or two showed me that I need not have worried about the seeming lightness of the bullet. I remember I was stalking a herd of eland one day. Eland are the biggest of all the antelopes, a big bull running close to a ton on the hoof.' These big beasts are usually on the alert, and if anything goes wrong with your first stalk and they get wise to your presence, you will be very lucky to get a shot and you will not get it without an immense amount of very hard hunting. It was a pretty big herd I was after —I judged there must have been 40 or 50 of them—and as they got a wee eddy of wind before I was in position for a shot, I knew I was in for a long hard hunt, as there would now be plenty of very keen eyes on the look-out for me.

And so it proved. A coupla times I was spotted when they had halted and were looking back, and I was endeavoring to make a detour so as to get ahead of them (eland like fairly open scrub without too much long grass; it's easy enough to stalk a lone bull if you have been hunting with your eyes open and spot him first but it's very much more difficult when you have maybe 80 or 100 keen eyes looking in all directions and well spread out so that some at least will have a clear view no matter how you try to approach).

Eventually they led me to two fairly high kopjes, passing up over the shoulder of one and then dropping down into the low ground between them and commencing to climb the other. As I came over the shoulder of the nearer hill I saw the herd stretching out in single-file as they climbed up the side of the other kopje. It was a long shot for me—I figured it was all of 225 yards —and I wondered how my little 225-gr. semi-pointed soft-nose slug would behave at that range on such mighty animals. On account of the angle at which the herd was climbing the opposite slope I was unable to place the bullet on the shoulder, but aimed just behind the shoulder and about half-way between the centre of the body and the line of the back, to allow for the bullet-drop. I hoped the bullet would drive thru lungs and heart and bring up against the opposite shoulder as it raked diagonally thru. As the eland were climbing slowly, not having sighted me, I took my time and made sure of the shot. On receipt of the bullet, the big leading bull at which I had fired gave a convulsive leap forward and then put up the grandest fight I have ever seen to retain his feet. It was like a fine boxer out on his feet but refusing to go down. The bull was unable to hold his altitude, and he struggled and scrambled and lurched down the side of the kopje to finally sink to his knees and roll over.

The report of the rifle echoed and re-echoed between the two hills so as to completely maze the rest of the troop. They could see that their big leader was in trouble, but were unable to decide where the danger was. Rapidly reloading, I aimed for the second big bull just as he made up his mind that he knew of a healthier spot and started a lumbering gallop up the side of the hill and the rest of the herd streamed after him. Taking the same aim, but holding forward, I let him have it. He pitched forward on his nose, rolled over sideways, scrabbled to his feet, staggered, fell, and came rolling down the hillside. I let the rest go.

I traced both of these bullets to see what had happened to them. They had both been perfectly placed, and as I had hoped had driven in thru lungs and heart to pull up against the inside of the off shoulder. In the case of the first bull, the nicely-mushroomed slug was found against the inner side of the shoulder, but in the case of the second one, it had smashed the bone. I take it that the fact that this animal had been galloping had something to say in the matter—probably had something to do with muscle-tension and weight-distribution. Anyhow, it was undoubtedly owing to the shoulder being broken that he pitched forward on his nose on receipt of the bullet. Well, now, I reckoned that was mighty fine work for two such light bullets, and was correspondingly pleased with my rifle. A subsequent experience did nothing to disillusion me.

I had a base camp on a small island in the centre of a lake for some years, one time; a truly delightful place for a camp and vegetable garden, as there was nothing to worry the hunter and force him to sleep with one eye and one ear open—as is so very necessary in a man-eater's area, and there was no raiding of the precious vegetables by wild hogs or small buck—the only raiders were hippo, and I soon discouraged them! I had paddled across in my canoe to the mainland one day, and was following the small native path that ran along between the margin of the lake and the

.350 RIGBY MAGNUM.

Powder 62 grs. Smokeless; Bullet 225-gr. Metal-covered; Pressure 17 tons; M.V. 2,600; M.E. 3,380.

Originally Rigby supplied copper-pointed bullets as well as the soft-nose semi-pointed but I rather think he has discontinued them for some years now—and wisely so. The semi-pointed soft-nose bullet illustrated is undoubtedly one of the most effective on the market for all soft-skinned African game—it always sets up well, whilst I have never known it break up. There is nothing spectacular about this cartridge; it has never had the write-up that the .318 and .375 Magnum get from time to time; nevertheless, it is a splendidly effective shell and at ranges up to at least 150 yards kills just as instantaneously as the .375 Magnum. In addition, it has an appreciably lighter recoil. It is a typical Rigby rifle and cartridge, especially designed for African use. John Rigby has always concentrated on Africa tho his rifles are used all over the world with the greatest possible satisfaction to their owners, still they are each and all designed with particular reference to African requirements in the first place.

Rigby supplies his special steel-covered round-nose solids for this weapon as well as for his .416. They have great depth of penetration because the solid metal at the nose is about 3 or 4 times as thick as it is on the ordinary nickel-jacketed solid. The result is that these bullets of Rigby's never become distorted and so maintain a straight course after entering, no matter how massive a bone they may have encountered. Naturally, they do not retain their initial velocity as well as do the semi-pointed bullets, so that their trajectory would not be quite so flat at long range but then animals that require solids are not shot at long range, so what does it matter? With the original sighting, giving the rifle a 2″ bullet-rise at 100 yds., either bullet will carry as far as ever you are likely to want to use them without any alteration in sighting or aim being necessary.

No man in his right mind could possibly wish for a better medium bore rifle than this for general African hunting.

heavy forest that grew along that side. Coming to the top end of the lake, where the country opened out, I encountered two lions, a male and a female, the male being practically maneless. As these were ordinary hunting lions, and not the big buffalo-killers, and were very apt to turn man-eaters in this district, I decided to open fire. They were standing, at least one was, the other was lying, in the shade of a small tree that grew out of the top of an ant-hill. The range was about 90 paces. It was not easy to distinguish male from female, and I wanted to shoot the male first as that might well provoke a charge from the lioness and thereby ensure me a shot at her too. I finally let rip at the one lying down, placing my bullet on his shoulder. He never budged. At the shot the lioness spun around in a circle and stood broadside-on to me, obviously wondering why her mate wasn't taking any interest in the goings-on. She looked down at him and then towards me, and as she did so I let her have it thru the shoulder. She collapsed instantly. It was as clean killing as I have ever seen. The striking-velocity of the bullets would have been about 2,350 f.s. at the moment of impact; both had mushroomed perfectly, but neither had lost any weight.

This rifle has never had the press that the .375 Magnum and .318 not infrequently get but it sure deserves every bit as much. Of course, it's not so powerful as the .375 Magnum but then what men are apt to forget is that it was never designed or intended as a big game weapon—as we reckon big game in Africa. The maker himself would be the first to try and dissuade you from taking it alone against dangerous game in thick cover. But when used as it was always intended that it should be used, that is, as a general purpose medium bore, you could not find a more satisfactory weapon. If the dangerous animals are in the open you can safely use the .350 Magnum against them but take a more powerful weapon with you into thick cover.

This rifle shows the same phenomenon of "shock" that the .375 Magnum shows, but to a somewhat lesser extent—as is only to be expected—but the reason why it cannot be used alone against heavy and dangerous animals is to be found in its considerably lighter bullet. I knew a man who was very fond of his .350 Rigby Magnum and had shot a few elephant with it but when he was suddenly and unexpectedly attacked by a peevish cow elephant in very thick bush and found that the 225-gr. bullet fired upwards at the under side of her face was incapable of turning her, so that she got to him and considerably injured him, he had the sense not to blame the rifle but himself.

I can strongly recommend this rifle for African use. It is one of the best of the "mediums."

.350 Rigby (400/.350): Powder 43 grs. Smokeless; Bullet 310-
gr. Metal-covered; Pressure 16 tons;
M.V. 2,150; M.E. 3,190.

Having established his name with the .450, Rigby boosted his reputation thruout Africa by introducing his .350. He produced a magazine rifle to handle it, as well as doubles and single-loaders. It was an ideal cartridge for general African use, and for many years was the most popular and widely used medium bore thruout the continent. It's fully capable of holding its own today against any of the more modern magnums—there are plenty of hunters who still use it. Its long parallel-sided bullet of generous weight has an excellent diameter-to-weight ratio, retains its velocity well, can plow thru an immense amount of obstructions and still remain head-on, and has deep penetration both as a soft-nose as well as full-patched. The fact that it became a standard caliber in the British gun trade, just as the .450 did, and that practically all firms built rifles to handle it, speaks, I think, for itself.

I had a Farquharson-actioned single-loader built by Greener to handle this shell, and can truthfully state that I have never owned a more generally satisfactory medium bore. I killed a lot of lions with it, shooting them off a large cattle ranch where they had been doing great mischief. My one regret was that it wasn't a double. Apart from the lions, I killed most varieties of African game with it and have nothing but praise for it. I have never heard of anybody who did otherwise than praise it. John Rigby has always had Africa in the forefront of his mind when designing any new rifle or cartridge.

I have a very soft spot in my heart for this cartridge, because when shooting it I secured some of my very best specimens; lion, buffalo, and my very best rhino—27-inch, which is exceptionally good for this neck of the woods—and one or two very big elephant. Frank Melland, who holds the record for ivory shot south of Tanganyika—119 lbs. the heaviest tusk, shot in Northern Rhodesia —and who had a quite considerable experience of elephant hunting both there and in Tanganyika, used a pair of double .350 Rigby rifles in preference to anything else. He had previously used one with a double .450 Rigby to back it up, but eventually discarded the .450 to avoid the nuisance of a multiplicity of different shells for all of which he would be wanting at least two different kinds of bullet, and because, as he says in his book: "I found that the .350 besides being unrivaled for smaller game would do all that the .450 would do with the bigger."

I entirely agree with him, always excepting, of course, very dense bush and an inexperienced man. I consider this .350 one of the best all-around cartridges in existence for the experienced hunter, if for no other reason than because it was so widely stocked in Africa. This is the snag where so many of the best flanged shells are concerned. Magazines being so much more widely used than doubles in the medium bores in Africa, that some of them, such as the flanged .375 Magnum and .350 N ≗ 2, for instance, can rarely be bought locally, tho their rimless counterparts can. Accordingly, if the consignment you ordered from the factory gets delayed or misdirected—as happened to me once, and it took 12 months to reach me!—you may find yourself without any ammunition for your pet rifles. But at any rate up to the outbreak of the recent war, you could always find sufficient 400/.350 ammo to keep you going until your own order arrived. Altho the velocity is but moderate, these cartridges have as flat a trajectory as you are ever likely to be wanting in general African hunting. The rifle will comfortably stand sighting for 150 yards, which will give you a bullet drop of a mere 5 inches at 200 yards. You do not need better than that out here. I have never known one of these bullets to break up.

It was when using this rifle I once killed two lions with a single shot. I was returning from a successful elephant hunt and still had a solid bullet in the chamber because there were rhino about. I was not thinking about lions at all, when I suddenly saw two of them standing broadside-on, shoulder to shoulder, but facing in opposite directions, and gazing at me. I would have substituted a soft-nose for the full-patch bullet, but could see that I had a splendid chance to bag them both with the one shot as they stood, using the solid bullet to ensure enough penetration to kill both and not merely wound the second one. So I let drive before they had made up their minds as to what we were. The full-patch 310-gr. bullet went clean thru all four shoulders. They both reacted in an identical manner; their tails and hindquarters arched up over their backs, they lurched forward, and collapsed alongside one another, still facing in opposite directions.

Another occasion when I was using this cartridge stands out very clearly in my memory, if only because the conditions were so very, well, shall we say "unconventional." I was hunting for meat for my men in palmetto scrub that was rather sharply undulating just where I happened to be. I dropped out of the hunt for a few moments, leaned my rifle against a convenient tree, and squatted down within reach of it. My men politely moved on across a small depression and up and over the rise on the far side, where I knew they would wait for me.

Scarcely were they out of sight when two enormous eland bulls apparently materialized out of the air and started slowly up along the depression across which the men had just passed. These were the tufted eland, with a thick black tuft of hair growing out of the top of their foreheads between and in front of the base of the horns. Big and all as the ordinary eland are, these Lord Derby's eland, as I think they are called, are considerably larger. They are simply enormous, and you can only truly appreciate their size when you get one down and are standing beside him. The two bulls were separated by about 40 yards, one following the other at a slow deliberate walk, quite unaware that danger lurked so close.

I slowly reached out a hand and got hold of my rifle, mighty glad that I had long made it an unbreakable rule never to allow it to be beyond arm's reach no matter what the circumstances. As I brought it to my shoulder the movement must have caught the nearer bull's eye—he wasn't more than ten paces away. One startled look he gave in my direction, his eyes staring straight into mine, then slewed around to go. The 310-gr soft-nose bullet took him about four inches below the anus as he was getting into his stride directly away from me. He lurched forward, and with his hind legs wide apart he stumbled along for possibly two and a half times his own length, and then fell. Reloading the instant I had fired, I stood up and swung on the second bull. My pants around my ankles pretty well anchored me, but the second bull galloped up the rise opposite and then halted when he reached the crest and stood broadside-on as he looked back to see why his companion wasn't following. My bullet took him thru the shoulder at a range of about 35 yards and brought him down in his tracks. He scrabbled around for a moment, but was unable to get to his feet again, and was dead before I was ready to close in.

These were both similar soft-nose bullets. And I would like to draw the reader's attention to the fact that both these immense bulls were killed with the one shot apiece, one being placed in the stern and the other thru the shoulder-blade. In neither case did the bullet pass clean thru the animal; both bullets were perfectly mushroomed, neither had lost any weight.

Personally, I consider that Rigby's original .350 makes a better all-around rifle than his modern Magnum for African use. There is no getting away from the fact that its 310-gr. bullet hits a heavier punch on a head-shot than does the 225-gr. bullet thrown by the Magnum, whilst its trajectory is as flat as you could possibly want in Africa. It's true that I am principally thinking of elephant and possibly rhino in very thick cover when I speak of its heavier bullet being preferable. For all other purposes the Magnum will doubtless prove just as satisfactory. Countless elephant, buffalo and lion have been killed with Rigby's .350 Magnums but not in the densest of cover. Actually, of course, for such work a heavier bullet than that thrown by any medium bore should be used. But in the hands of a steady and experienced hunter, the .350 could be used with great satisfaction and success. Melland, after a certain amount of experimenting with various calibers, including the .450, settled to use a pair of Rigby's double .350s and nothing else. I would be perfectly happy with a similar battery in all but the closest of bush and forest.

However, I cannot recommend any man to invest in such a battery because I fear the original .350 will be allowed to die out. I may be wrong, but I have an idea that the makers have long discontinued building rifles to handle it, and are concentrating on the Magnums. There are still a number of the old .350s in use thruout Africa but they cannot last indefinitely, and if you were to have a battery of this caliber built up for you, you might find difficulty in getting shells for them sooner or later. It would be very necessary to first find out whether or not the ammunition manufacturers will continue to turn out the 400/.350 shells in future. But I'm afraid you'll be disappointed.

Personally I much prefer it to the 9.3mm although I was never so fortunate as to possess a double rifle handling this shell. I killed more lions with this rifle than any other, not excepting that grand little gold-inlaid short sporting Martini-Henry I was so fond of. (It's a curious thing that each time I was concentrating on lions almost to the exclusion of everything else, I was armed with a single-loader.)

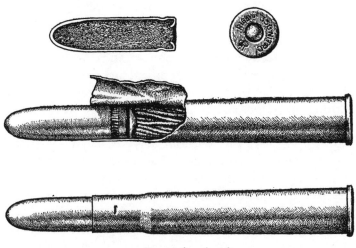

.350 RIGBY (400/.350).

This was a flanged shell for which Rigby produced a magazine rifle for those who preferred that type of weapon to either doubles or single-loaders. It proved an instant success. It's 310-gr. bullet had a splendid diameter-to-weight ratio which made it very effective either as solid or soft-nose. With energy of 3,190 ft.lbs. it was what everybody had been waiting for. It became the most popular medium bore of its day and well deserved its reputation. It's fully capable of holding its own even today. I was never so fortunate as to possess a double-rifle handling this shell but for years I used a Farquharson-actioned falling-block single-loader by W. W. Greener and swore by it. With it I killed practically all species of African game from elephant down. I killed more lions with this rifle than with any other, not excepting that grand little gold-inlaid short sporting Martini-Henry I was so fond of. (I have told elsewhere of how I lost this splendid little single-shot 577/.450 rifle when a cow hippo, a mite worried about her newborn calf, upset our canoe in the Zambezi, and everything we had went to the bottom of the river.)

Here again you will see the excellence of the shells John Rigby designed. Look at that solid bullet! Is there another medium caliber bullet in existence to compare with it? Only the solids supplied by Rigby for his more modern .350 Magnum and .350 N $\underline{\underline{o}}$ 2. The envelope is of *steel*, and there is grand thickness of metal at the nose. This is undoubtedly in large part the reason for this shell's great popularity and why it always proved so intensely satisfactory when used against elephant and rhino by those hunters who preferred to use their medium bore whenever possible. You will see that it has the characteristically good turn-in at the base, whilst the lead at the bottom is well swaged over the turn-in.

If I saw the chance of getting hold of a 400/.350 in good condition I would be quite prepared to use it as my only medium bore for the rest of my life.

The first time I was ever charged by a lion I was armed with this rifle. I was shooting lions off a big cattle ranch and was very new to the game but I was ever a good listener and had picked up a little hunting lore here and there. Since it had been my ambition to become an elephant-hunter almost as far back as I can remember I figured I was getting a good blooding, as it were, by taking on this job, tho as yet I had never even seen an African elephant. On the occasion in question I had stalked up to where a lion and lioness were feeding on the carcass of a big steer they had killed. I had killed a few lions at this time, but had never yet been charged.

I took a steady aim, waited for the lion to give me the shot I wanted, and killed him without any difficulty. Instantly reloading, I swung on the lioness. But, as is quite usual in the circumstances, she decided to have a say in the matter. One glance she gave at her fallen mate, which gave me time to reload, and then she came. Altho I've been charged many times since, that first time remains fixed in my memory. It didn't seem possible that any animal could possess so many teeth! She looked the very embodiment of vindictive fury as she came, ears back and mouth open, at an altogether incredible speed. Having but the one available shot, I waited until I was sure, then let her have the 310-gr. soft-nose slug fairly in the open mouth when she was about 12 paces away. It blew the base of her skull off and shattered her spine just where it joins the skull, killing her instantly. But the momentum of her rush carried her nearly half way to where I was kneeling. Reloading, I waited for a moment to see if there was any movement, then advanced towards her with the rifle ready for instant action. But she was as dead as a canned lobster and naturally I felt very proud of myself and my fine rifle. But I'm glad to be able to say that the successful manner in which I had stopped my first charge did not make me cocksure or careless in the future. I have only contempt for the man who permits familiarity with these animals to make him contemptuous of them.

It would be a real pity if this fine cartridge was allowed to die out but I'm afraid that's just what's happening, as I don't think Rigby or anyone else is building rifles to handle it. There are a good many still in use, but naturally they can't be expected to last indefinitely. Of course, as I said when discussing the .350 Magnum, the average hunter in Africa uses a large bore as well as

his medium but there are others who would like to be able to use
their favorite medium bore for everything, and there is no doubt
that they would be better armed with the 400/.350 than they
would with the more modern magnum, on account of the former's
much heavier bullet. It's true that in very thick cover you would
need something more powerful than the .350 but there are parts
of Africa where you can get all the big game hunting you could
possibly want in comparatively open scrub wherein a really good
medium bore would be perfectly satisfactory.

I would happily finish the remainder of my career with a
400/.350 as my only medium bore.

.35 Winchester. This was quite a good little weapon in its
day and sufficiently popular to induce the British manufacturers
to load shells for it. However, I have not seen it in use now for
many years. Experience has shown that for satisfactory results
in a medium bore rifle of medium velocity for general African
hunting a M.E. of around 3,000 ft.lbs is needed with a bullet of
somewhere between 250 and 300 grains. As can be seen as we work
thru the list of medium bores and hunters and sportsmen gradually
found out what was needed, their gunsmiths had to bring out
weapons that fulfilled the requirements. Not being hunters themselves, they could only obtain this information from those who
were and were also sufficiently keen riflemen to be able to suggest
what was likely to meet their needs.

.333 Flanged Nitro-Express: Powder 49 grs. Smokeless;
Bullet 300-gr. Metal-cov-
ered; Pressure 17½(?) tons;
M.V. 2,150; M.E. 3,090.
Powder 53 grs. Smokeless;
Bullet 250-gr. Metal-cov-
ered; Pressure 17 tons; M.V.
2,400; M.E. 3,200.

.333 Rimless Nitro-Express: Powder 50 grs. Smokeless; Bullet
300-gr. Metal-covered; Pres-
sure 18½ tons; M.V. 2,200;
M.E. 3,240.
Powder 54 grs. Smokeless; Bullet
250-gr. M.C.; Pressure 18 tons;
M.V. 2,500; M.E. 3,480.

This shell was introduced by Jeffery in 1911. As usual, the flanged cartridge has a slightly lighter load so as to allow a larger margin for excess pressure when the rifle is taken to the tropics. However, the difference in ballistics is so slight that it can be ignored—you will not notice it in practical hunting.

The Mauser edition of this rifle has been widely used thruout Africa and both double and magazine farther East. Its long, heavy 300-gr. bullet is a splendid killer and holds its velocity extremely well. It has great depth of penetration, and is one of my favorite bullets. Time and again have I driven it the length of an animal's body, and cut the perfectly mushroomed bullet out of his hindquarters. I have never had one break-up.

The foregoing applies to the 300-gr. load. I wish I could speak as highly of the 250-gr. bullet but it's one of those infernal copper-pointed affairs which I dislike so intensely. Why, oh why, must Jeffery be so fond of them? And anyway, why won't he supply other types for men who want them? If other patterns of bullet were available this would undoubtedly be a most satisfactory general purpose load. However, the 300-gr. load is so excellent that comparatively few men bother with the lighter one —except perhaps for those who shoot in very open country. In spite of its good weight, this copper-pointed bullet tends to break-up all too readily on all but the lighter animals—of course, it was for them that Jeffery designed it, so maybe I ought not to be grumbling. Nevertheless, I know two or three men who were disappointed with their .333s, and found on questioning them that they had been using the 250-gr. slug because its weight seemed to indicate that it should be perfectly satisfactory for all African soft-skinned game. The result was that the .333 got itself a bad name which it in no way deserved—the fault lay entirely with the design of the bullet. But that's the way things go.

This has always been a deservedly popular medium bore. Its 300-gr. bullet has splendid sectional density, which makes for very accurate shooting, retention of velocity, deep penetration either as solid or soft-nose, and gives it an exceptionally fine ability to plough thru intervening obstacles such as tough grass, branches, leaves and so on, and still remain head-on.

I never saw the double-barreled edition of this rifle in Africa, tho doubtless there are some and the reason almost certainly is that originally, and for many years, Jeffery only regulated his double for his 250-gr. bullet. The only bullet of this weight he supplied was pointed—either copper-pointed, or solid-pointed, neither of which is suitable for general African shooting. In more recent catalogs he states that he is prepared to regulate the double for the 300-gr. slug. But since the vast majority of men in Africa use a magazine for their medium bore because it's perfectly satisfactory and very much cheaper than the double, those few who prefer the double usually get a .375 Magnum as there is no difference in the cost of the rifle or the shells and where the double .333 could only handle the bullet and load for which it was regulated, the .375 Magnum has the enormous advantage of being able to handle any or all of its three loads.

But the magazine edition of the .333 earned considerable popularity for itself. Except that it shows a somewhat higher chamber pressure, it is very similar to Rigby's 400/.350, and is a sure killer. I grew very fond of a little 3-shot .333 of Jeffery's and reckoned it the easiest to handle of any magazine rifle I ever owned. I like these 3-shot weapons of Jeffery's. They seem to give me a very much better and more comfortable grip than when the stock is brought out to accommodate a flush 4- or 5-shot magazine, which means that it must taper considerably towards the fore-end. I like the 3-shot because it gives a decent fat forearm the under run of which is roughly parallel with the barrel. But this may just be a personal preference. I would have used this rifle very much more than I did, had it not been for my preference for doubles, but I did some good shooting with it, including, as usual, most species from the heaviest downwards. I only fired 11 shots at elephant with it; but those 11 shots killed 11 good bulls. Maybe it was just coincidence; maybe it was just that my luck was well in when I was using the .333 and found the elephant under easy conditions and offering easy shots; I dunno. But as I said before, I found the .333 exceptionally easy to handle for a weapon of its type. There was a fella in the Congo who used nothing else for elephant.

But those remarks must not be taken as a recommendation of the .333 as an elephant rifle. It's essentially a medium bore, and should be used as such. But it will be found as satisfactory a medium bore as you could possibly wish. Mind you, with all these rifles you *must* place your bullets within reasonable distance of a vital spot. I'm a firm believer in never pressing trigger against any animal until I am quite sure of my shot. I have no sort of use for those men who let drive the instant they see anything moving.

And there is another little point that might be mentioned in connection with all medium bores: These rifles, when loaded with suitable bullets, prove such splendid killers in the general run of your hunting that many men with not too much experience are apt to become over-confident and attribute to their medium bores powers that they simply do not possess. They take them against dangerous game forgetting that they may become excited and omit to place their bullets in exactly the right spot. When they are charged they blaze off wildly and consequently fail to stop the charge, tho no blame can attach to the rifle.

As an example of this I might just mention two young fellas who went out after their first elephant armed with a .333 and a .318 with which they had shot a fair quantity of non-dangerous game, and because of their success had exalted their rifles to quite ridiculous heights. I heard their shooting spasmodically thruout the morning, and it was apparent to me that they were firing together, presumably at the same elephant, as they had told me they intended to do. They quite casually mentioned at the time that of course either weapon was quite capable of doing the work on its own, but that since they were new to the game they would both fire together; and no elephant could stand up to both weapons simultaneously—why, the combined power of the two would far surpass a .500!

As it subsequently transpired, they put a volley into the bull each time they caught up with him in the light open forest in which they found him. Finally, he had enough of it and ambushed them. When he charged they blazed away from their magazines without taking time out to aim with certainty, and so were unable to stop him. He killed one and seriously injured the other before moving off a short distance to lean against a tree. He died there in a kneeling position, so that I could count the bullet wounds in him; there were 42 of them. Now that in no way reflects on either of these rifles; either of them could have killed that elephant with a single well-placed bullet at the very commencement of the hunt; either could have dropped him stone dead in his tracks as he charged. But the two unfortunate youths were quite excusably nervous and rushed things. The whole and sole reason why some men prefer medium bores to large bores is because such weapons are considerably lighter and handier and they reckon they can use them with greater precision than they could more powerful weapons. *Greater precision*. That is the important thing to remember; but it's all too often forgotten.

This rifle would have been even more popular if Jeffery had supplied other types of bullet for his 250-gr. load than the copper-pointed one which is all you can get. There are many men who do a lot of hunting but who never attempt to tackle dangerous animals other than an occasional lion. For these the 250-gr. bullet might have been even preferable to the 300 had it been obtainable in other patterns than the rapidly-expanding copper-pointed. I can't think why he is so fond of this bullet; it is the only pattern he supplies for all his special high velocity cartridges—.280 and .404 as well as this 250-gr. .333.

I had a most unusual "right and left" on one occasion when using this rifle. ("Right and left" is an obvious misnomer where a magazine rifle is concerned; but you will doubtless get my meaning: two quick consecutive shots, with or without lowering the butt from the shoulder.) The animals were a very fine kudu and one of the best sable I have ever shot. The kudu was about 35 yards away, and almost directly beyond him there was a black lump which I thought was a rock or something. It was probably as far away again, and I scarcely noticed it as my attention was entirely concentrated on the kudu. But when the 300-gr. soft-nose on the shoulder brought the kudu down, my "rock" suddenly jumped to its feet and showed itself to be a magnificent sable bull. For an instant he stood there as only a sable can; head held high and proudly, the great scimitar-shaped horns sweeping back over his shoulders, one fore-foot raised after pawing the ground. It seemed almost a crime to kill such a splendid beast; but "the troops must be fed," so I had no alternative. A similar bullet took him also thru the shoulder, and he sank down in his tracks. It was most unusual to find these two species so close together, as they normally like rather different types of bush; but just there where I shot them there was a merging of their more favored pastures.

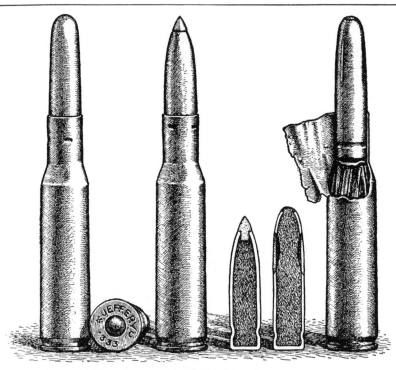

.333 JEFFERY.

Is it any wonder this rifle is known for its great depth of penetration? Look at the length of that bullet, and reckon its sectional density. The nickel-jacketed solid behaves very well indeed but, like all similar bullets, it's far from perfect. I never had one break open, but have known them bent and somewhat distorted. Now altho these bullets kill, it stands to reason that if a bullet becomes distorted it may very likely lose its direction and so fail to find a vital spot, altho perfectly placed. I'm aware that such things do not frequently happen—but they *can*, and occasionally *do*, happen. The result being that the animal has to be given another shot or may even manage to get away altogether. If no other pattern of bullet was obtainable, well and good but I can't see why *all* solids are not made like Rigby's. I certainly can't believe that Rigby has patented his steel-covered bullets. Actually, it's up to sportsmen and hunters to keep on squealing about the nickel-jacketed solids and demand steel-covered bullets instead.

The soft-nose-split bullet illustrated is designed for rapid expansion. If used on one of the heavier varieties of soft-skinned animals, it tends to break up altogether too quickly. It's quite understandable, of course, that some quickly expanding bullet was desirable in case the hunter wanted to shoot one of the smaller beasts that could not be expected to offer sufficient resistance to cause the 300-gr. plain soft-nose bullet to set up but personally, I would have much preferred the older type that was used in other calibers prior to the introduction of the soft-nose-split. The plain soft-nose slug for the .333 is excellent for all the heavier types of soft-skinned African game.

There were many occasions that convinced me of the excellence of these long heavy bullets of moderate velocity thrown by the .333 and .350. For instance, there was an exceptionally big water-buck bull I killed one day. These are big tough heavy animals covered with long coarse hair and can take a lot of punishment without falling if the bullets are not accurately placed. I spotted this fella's horns just showing above the grass in the vlei, and proceeded to stalk him along a dry water-course. He was lying down, and as I got to my feet to take the shot from about 15 paces range, he also rose and for just an instant stood looking at me. My bullet took him at the base of the throat and I later cut the perfect mushroom out of the hindquarter. It was the certainty and regularity of behavior of these bullets that made such a great appeal; you find the same thing with the 9.3mm Mauser. It would seem that it is easier to design a satisfactory expanding bullet if the velocity is to be kept moderate, than is the case where the speed has been boosted to the skies. This is, of course, quite understandable; since there will be nothing like the great variation of striking velocities that are inevitable with the light, high speed bullet. The latter must be designed to stand up to the tremendous impact it encounters if used at close quarters; and then since velocities drop very quickly, it is difficult for it to expand properly at longer ranges. These conditions do not apply to anything like the same extent with the heavier and lower initial-velocity bullets.

.330 B.S.A. In spite of its caliber this is not a satisfactory weapon for general African hunting. It throws a bullet of a mere 165 grains at 3,000 f.s. Such a bullet lacks penetration on all but the lighter varieties. As far as they are concerned, it is a killer; but we want more than that from a medium bore in Africa.

.318 WESTLEY RICHARDS. This is undoubtedly the most popular and most widely-used British medium bore. When it was first

---

The copper-pointed bullet shown is the 250-gr. load. It has a steel jacket with a heavy coating of copper. But as I have frequently stated, I dislike *all* these tubed bullets. It's merely a modern adaptation of the old hollow-nosed lead bullet and it matters not if that hollow is left open or plugged with wax, wood, or a copper, bronze, or "silver" plug—the result in each case is equally bad—the bullet breaks up too soon. These modern tubed bullets merely have a point on the tube for the sake of its better ballistic coefficient but they retain all the faults of the old copper-tubed slugs. My advice is, don't use them.

introduced there was nothing to compare with it, and it still holds pride of place owing to the fact that it can be made appreciably lighter than various of its competitors. It is a splendid little weapon. The sectional density of its 250-gr. bullet is very good indeed. The result is that it shoots extremely accurately and maintains its velocity well at the longer ranges. It has quite remarkably deep penetration—fully capable of driving its bullet the length of a big elephant's body. With expanding bullets it also has adequate penetration for anything on which you would be wanting to use that type of slug. It makes a splendid killer.

When other folks started boosting their velocities, somewhere in the middle twenties, I think it was, Westley Richards brought out a catalog wherein they claimed that they had stepped up the speed of their .318 to 2,500 f.s. However, I see in their later catalogs that they have apparently reverted to the original velocity of 2,400. Since this showed a pressure of 19.5 tons, I consider they were well advised not to try to be too clever. As the rifle is used in the hottest parts of the world any increase in pressure is to be deprecated; especially as it has always proved so extirely satisfactory. For general African use there is no real need to squeeze the very last foot-second out of your rifle in view of the comparatively short ranges at which most animals are shot.

Auctor: Hey! This won't do! Surely you can find more to say about it than that. Umpteen men positively swear by the .318; reckon there's nothing like it under the sun; but you don't appear to be particularly enamored. Why?

Lector: I see your point and am glad you raised it; but don't run away with the notion that I have no use for the .318. On the contrary, I have the highest possible opinion of it provided it's kept in its place and not abused by being taken alone against dangerous game in thick cover. When it was first introduced it gained for itself an enviable reputation which it has worthily upheld. It took the big game hunting world by storm. Men soon got to know its amazing capabilities; but the trouble was that they did not discover its limitations equally as quickly—in fact, many of them refused to admit or even consider the possibility that it might have any limitations. However, with the introduction of Holland's .375 Magnum, men were compelled to realize that the .318, wonderful little weapon and all as it undoubtedly was, was nevertheless *not* the last word in rifles. At the same time, this in no way detracts from the excellence of the .318 provided it is remembered that it was never intended for use against dangerous game at close quarters. The makers themselves would be the last people in the world to recommend it for such work; in their catalogs and advertisements they only boost it for use against non-dangerous animals; their .425 is there for dangerous game. The makers do not wish to see their .318 used for dangerous animals because they know very well that if the habit is persisted in sooner or later someone will be disappointed if not disemboweled—as has happened to several men in the past; and when these so-called "accidents" occur, those who do not understand are apt to blame the rifle, in spite of the fact that the rifle is in no way to blame whatsoever.

Let us listen-in to two of them chatting and yarning at sundown over their whiskeys and sodas:

"That was damn bad luck about Brock, wasn't it?"

"Why, what happened?"

"What! Haven't you heard? Why, the poor devil was pulled to pieces by an elephant only a couple of days ago."

"Good God! That's the first I've heard of it. Poor old Charlie. What a hell of a pity. One of the decentest fellas you could wish to meet. But how did it happen?"

"God knows. You know how difficult it is to get hold of the real facts in a case of this description; you know yourself how, when tackling a herd of elephant in a dense, matted tangle of bush it's pretty well a case of every man for himself, since you can't see what's happening other than in your immediate vicinity; and I gather that his boys, other than his gun-bearer, were all too busy looking after their own skins to be able to see much—can't say I blame them much either!—when the stampede started. But so far as I can gather from his gun-bearer, Charlie shot one of the herd and the remainder came crashing thru the bush straight for him. He could see nothing until one brute in a welter of flying bamboo appeared right on top of him. He blazed off a shot, but it didn't appear to have any effect; and the elephant, a large cow which had apparently charged the sound of the shot whilst the others were merely stampeding, got him down and proceeded to tear him in pieces. The gun-bearer, who had been knocked down

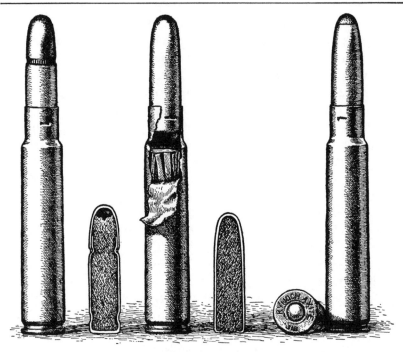

.318 RIMLESS NITRO EXPRESS.

Powder 54 grs. Smokeless; Bullet 180-gr. Metal-covered; Pressure 19 tons; M.V. 2,700; M.E. 2,920.

Powder 47 grs. Smokeless; Bullet 250-gr. Metal-covered; Pressure 19½ tons; M.V. 2,400; M.E. 3,200.

This shell was introduced somewhere around 1910, I think, by Westley Richards, or it may have been the previous year. It's a development of the 7.9mm Mauser cartridge, and a splendidly satisfactory general purpose weapon provided it's not abused by being taken alone against dangerous game at close quarters. It fulfils all the necessary requirements for general African use, and is probably the most popular and most widely used of all British medium bores. This is almost certainly because it does not require the long magnum action, which means that it can be built appreciably lighter and more cheaply than can various of its competitors.

The 250-gr. bullet, both as solid and soft-nose, has always been renowned for its great depth of penetration. The Westley Richards round-capped bullet in this weight is also most satisfactory. I cannot recollect any strange or particularly noteworthy shots when using this cartridge—it was just one of those fine, reliable, easy-shooting guns that always did its duty and never let one down. Owing to its ease of handling and light recoil, it's an extremely accurate weapon with as flat a trajectory as you could possibly want in Africa. I should very much like to have a Westley Richards double rifle handling this shell and regulated for the 250-gr. bullet.

The "L.T." pointed-capped bullet, both as 180-gr. as well as 250-gr., is in-when the cow came thru the bush, managed to get to his feet, pick up Charlie's second rifle, and put a bullet from it into the beast. She then cleared off and fell dead a little way farther on."

"Good God! Well I'm damn sorry to hear that about old Charlie. But you know, he's been asking for it for a hell of a long time."

"How do you mean, 'asking for it'?"

"He was using his .318, I suppose?"

"Of course. I don't think he ever used anything else. He had a second rifle—a .450, I think it was—but I don't think he ever used it; stuck to his .318 and concentrated on and specialized in brain shots. A bit of an artist, he was, on brain shots."

"That's all very well; but as I often tried to point out to him, if an elephant is practically on top of you a brain shot is an impossibility for any rifle under the sun. What the hell's the good of having a second rifle if you never use it? I don't know whether you're interested or not in such matters, but I am—tho I don't pretend to know much about it—and you know, it seems to me that the .318 has gone off a lot recently."

"Gone off?"

"Yes. It had a positively terrific reputation at one time: you could hardly meet a man who wasn't wildly enthusiastic about it—you could hardly get the blighters to speak about anything else but the .318. But you know, a hell of a lot of fellas seem to

---

tended for the lighter varieties of soft-skinned game. On them it behaves as it was intended to but it is ridiculous for men to expect the same pattern to perform equally satisfactorily on much heavier animals.

The round copper-capped bullet shown here has most excellent penetration. The envelope is steel, which greatly helps it from breaking up too soon but the cap being of copper it commences to flatten much sooner and so permits of expansion taking place. This type of bullet in this weight makes a perfect combination for general African use, and should be chosen in preference to the hollow "L-T" pointed-capped bullet which is only intended for the lighter animals.

The solid bullet shown is jacketed with cupro-nickel and has the usual thickness of metal at the nose. Nowadays, all British bullets in this class are given a "Nobeloy" ("Lubaloy" in America) non-fouling envelope, but I don't think there has been any alteration in the thickness of metal at the nose. The penetration of these bullets is quite remarkable, always provided they don't become rivetted at the nose or bent. But who can assure that? The amount of reinforcement given nickel-jacketed bullets is not sufficient to guarantee them keeping their shape under all conditions when used against the heaviest of all game.

The .318 can certainly be recommended for African hunting.

be getting themselves knocked about recently thru using the .318. There was Willis, chewed up by a lion last month—he used a .318; young Wright was killed by an elephant not long ago— he was using a .318; and that fella with the double-barreled name who was so badly mauled by an elephant—he was a great believer in the .318; and now here's poor old Charlie Brock gone and gotten himself killed—another .318 merchant. See what I mean? That's why I say that the .318 seems to have gone off a lot."

Can't you hear them? Isn't it exactly how they talk? But the .318 has not "gone off." It's ballistics have not been altered since it was introduced. It is merely that its devotees will not realize that it does not hit a sufficiently heavy blow to make it a safe weapon to take against dangerous game at close quarters. It will kill—but it will not always kill sufficiently quickly. So long as the animals are in the open, permitting you to choose your shot, all will be well; but in thick cover you can seldom pick your shot, and if a beast comes, various obstructions may prevent you getting off a shot until the animal is almost on you. It is then that you need a heavy bullet.

I have used the .318 extensively. For some years I used a Westley Richards .318 and swore by it; but I always had a heavier weapon for close quarter work because I realized the .318's limitations. Always provided that there is a more powerful weapon at hand for use in thick cover, you could not wish for a better or more satisfactory general purpose medium bore than Westley Richards' .318; it is a delightful little weapon to use, whilst its trajectory is as flat as you are ever likely to want in Africa. The weight-to-diameter ratio—or sectional density, if you prefer that term—of its 250-gr. bullet is probably better than that of any other bullet on the market with the possible exception of the 300-gr. bullet thrown by Jeffery's .333. The combination of long thin parallel bullet of good weight and reasonable velocity makes for very accurate shooting and great depth of penetration; whilst there is little or no tendency for the bullet to turn over or glance on passing thru grass, twigs or similar obstacles or on entering an animal's body.

Its many users are all enthusiastic about it—the only one man I ever encountered who had anything to say about it in the shape of a grumble was an idiot who had bought himself a special light model that had been sighted in for the 180-gr. bullet. Naturally, he did not get very accurate results when using the 250-gr. slug, and didn't realize that there was any need to bother with different sights or a different aim. When using the 180-gr. bullet he was disappointed in its penetration after all he had heard and read about the .318's ability in this direction! Well, what could you expect? But he was the only man I ever met who had used the .318 without being entirely satisfied. I did quite a lot of shooting with it myself, and certainly have no complaints.

Its pressure is high, but, judging by results, not unduly so. The only case I can recollect of anyone having any trouble that might be ascribed to pressure, was Bell. I seem to remember he tried out the .318 when hunting somewhere in the southern Sudan, and experienced a separation on one occasion: the base of the cartridge coming away and leaving the body of the shell sticking in the chamber. Whereupon he naturally discarded his .318. But I don't remember the date when that happened—possibly it was before the British cartridge manufacturers amalgamated. At any rate, it can safely be assumed that such are not frequent or the .318 would never have gained its enviable reputation. I certainly had no trouble when using it myself, and some of my shooting was done in excessively hot districts.

Was I thinking of having Westley Richards build me a new heavy double such as their .476 and wanted a medium bore magazine to go with it, I would almost certainly have him build me a .318; nor do I see the slightest reason for supposing that I would ever live to regret it.

The following rifles do not really come within the medium bore group; but some of them at least were so widely used once upon a time that I will bring them in here:

.315 (8mm) Austrian Mannlicher. This is a flanged shell corresponding to the 7.9mm Mauser. I've seen a few of them in use, but not many. The B.S.A. people used to make a magazine rifle to handle it because of its low chamber pressure. Except that it had a lower pressure than the 7.9mm, the ballistics of both were identical; and everything said about the Mauser cartridge would apply equally here. But men generally preferred the rimless shells for magazine rifles as it was found that they were less inclined to jam.

.311 (7.9MM OR 8MM) MAUSER: Powder 40½ grs. Smokeless; Bullet 227-grs. Metal-covered; Pressure 15½ tons; M.V. 2,025; M.E. 2,060.

Powder ? grs. Smokeless; Bullet 244-grs. Metal-covered; Pressure 16½ tons; M.V. 2,030; M.E. 2,240.

Some call this a .311″, others a .315″—but the true bore diameter is .312″ with a bullet diameter of .323″.

This, the German caliber corresponding to the British .303, is a very much better weapon. There used to be many men who swore by it for general use and were never happy if they didn't possess one. It's heavier bullet possessed very much better penetration than the .303 and made it a much better killer. There really isn't a great deal to say about it. Anything the .303 could do, the 7.9mm could do better; and it could do things the .303 couldn't do. It's not what we reckon a big game rifle out here; but is a quite satisfactory general purpose weapon for use in conjunction with a more powerful one.

I can find no record of the British manufacturers loading the 244-gr. slug; but I'm practically certain the Germans did, to make their Mauser the equal of the .315 (8mm) Austrian Mannlicher. And I'm also pretty sure that it was this loading that gave the little 7.9mm its great attraction for so many hunters. There is no question that this longer, heavier bullet would have appreciably deeper penetration than the 227-gr.—altho this latter was very satisfactory. Nevertheless, without exception all those with whom I ever discussed this cartridge declared that the German ammunition was infinitely better than the British; and the answer, of course, is to be found in the 244-gr. bullet with which they loaded it, altho they had originally loaded the 227-gr. The Germans would have marked their bullet weight in grammes on the ammunition packets, and few men out here could have converted grammes to grains off-hand, so that they probably didn't realize that it was a heavier slug—altho it was so much longer, they might well have done so.

Right up to the present day it has always been a popular light rifle for general use, in conjunction with a more powerful weapon.

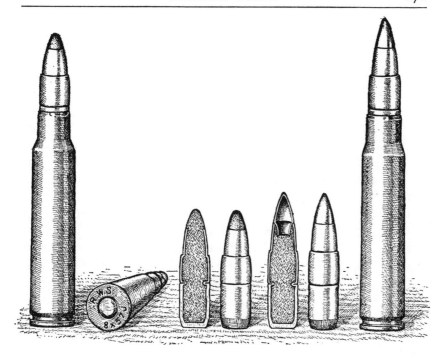

THE 8MM MAUSER

The British manufacturers call this the 7.9mm or 8mm Mauser, and both they and users of it who prefer the British calibration invariably refer to it as the .311 in order to differentiate between it and the 8mm Mannlicher-Schonauer, which is called the .315. It was the official cartridge of the late German Army, when loaded with a 154 grain solid pointed bullet.

The bullets shown are the "H" jacket bullets with their strong base which the Germans brought out somewhere in the '30s, if I remember rightly. The general design of these slugs is excellent. I never heard of the envelope busting up. But the only ones I ever saw in use had the pointed copper tube. Like *all* these hollow-nose slugs, they tended to break to pieces on impact or shortly after. The envelope would hold together, but the lead core would frequently have entirely disappeared. This meant that far too much weight had been lost. I many times advised users of these bullets in various calibers to keep on asking the Germans to make them plain soft nose bullets with the same strong jacket. Such slugs I guessed would be among the very best expanding bullets to be found anywhere. Judging by the illustration it would seem that the Germans did eventually turn out plain soft pointed slugs similar in every way to those I had been recommending for so long. These bullets should be very satisfactory. I have a hunch that Peters "Belted" and Remington's "Core-Lokt" bullets are very similar; but I have not as yet had a chance of using them. However, it would certainly seem that at least some of the American manufacturers are alive to the necessity for really good expanding bullets. More power to them!

Barnes was a great believer in it; Ryan used it extensively; Major Maydon has used it for some 30 years in preference to anything else; my old friend Mussa Issa was never without one in all his 40 years of hunting. I never possessed one myself, but used Mussa's quite considerably when he was trying something of mine. I found it a most excellent little weapon and a good killer; but cannot find anything noteworthy to say about it, altho I killed most varieties of game with it, including two or three elephant. It's an infinitely more satisfactory cartridge than the British .303.

.303 BRITISH. The following remarks only apply to the old "Mark VI" load, with its 215-gr. bullet. It was, of course, widely used thruout South Africa after the Boer war since quantities of surplus army rifles and ammunition were thrown on the market. Also, being the British army action the rifles have even been very much cheaper than Mausers. It's not a very powerful cartridge, and its penetration is nothing like so good as that of the corresponding Mauser calibers. However, it's perfectly capable of keeping your pot filled, and can be built very light for a weapon of that caliber—which has always been a very strong point with the average Britisher.

The first rifle I bought after I got to Africa and started off on my elephant hunting was a B.S.A. sporter chambered for this .303 cartridge. I purchased it in Bulawayo, Southern Rhodesia, along with a stock of 100 cartridges. They had Mausers there also, but neither I nor the salesman seemed to know much about rifles so I found myself fitted out with the .303 as a starter.

A lot of game has been killed with this cartridge; but a lot has been wounded and lost. Anyway, it's prohibited now thruout the greater part of Africa north of the Zambezi.

.300 MAGNUM (SUPER-THIRTY) FLANGED: Powder 55 grs. Smokeless; Bullet 150-gr. Metal-covered; Pressure 17½ tons; M.V. 2,875; M.E. 2,755.

Powder 50 grs. Smokeless; Bullet 180-gr. Metal-covered; Pressure 17½ tons; M.V. 2,575; M.E. 2,653.

Powder 46 grs. Smokeless; Bullet 220-gr. Metal-covered; Pressure 17½ tons; M.V. 2,250; M.E. 2,475.

.300 MAGNUM (SUPER-THIRTY)

BELTED RIMLESS: Powder 58 grs. Smokeless; Bullet 150-gr.
Metal-covered; Pressure 18½ tons; M.V.
3,000; M.E. 3,000.
Powder 55 grs. Smokeless; Bullet 180-gr.
Metal-covered; Pressure 18½ tons; M.V.
2,700; M.E. 2,915.
Powder 49 grs. Smokeless; Bullet 220-gr.
Metal-covered; Pressure 18½ tons; M.V.
2,350; M.E. 2,700.

Thruout British territory this rifle is almost invariably known
as either the 375/.300, or better still by the designers' own designation, "Super-Thirty." .300 Magnum is a far better and more
accurate description than 375/.300.

When this cartridge was first introduced it was Holland's
boast that it was the only rifle actually giving 3,100 f.s. velocity
with the 150-gr. bullet. However, not long afterwards they reduced the velocity to a round 3,000 f.s., contending that there
was no real difference in the killing effect between 3,000 and
3,100 f.s. but that there was an appreciable reduction in pressure
with the lower velocity. Accordingly, with the standard British
loading of:

150-gr.	3,000 f.s.
180 "	2,700 "
220 "	2,350 "

chamber pressure of all loads 18.5 tons, it will be seen that in
this guise the .300 Magnum is just a considerably stepped-up
.30–06. And it is apparent from the designers' own designation
that this was precisely what they had in mind when they were
designing it. Further, owing to its bigger, stronger, belted case,
it can always keep ahead of the .30–06 even when the latter has
been loaded to its ultimate maximum.

The longest shooting that takes place in British territory is,
I suppose, in the Himalayas in India. For the wild sheep and
goats of those high hills, the ovis ammon, burrhel, shapoo, mark-
hor, ibex, thar, and such, the 150-gr. bullet from the .300 Magnum
is generally preferred to all others. Even there, 300 to 350 yards is
considered the maximum range. Up to there the 150-gr. bullet
has a flatter trajectory and a higher striking velocity than either

the 180 or 220-gr. bullets. At the 300 yards the British loading gives the three bullets the following striking velocities:-

150-gr.	2,270 f.s.
180 "	2,100 "
220 "	1,870 "

In Africa, since the shooting is chiefly of heavier animals and usually at shorter ranges, the 180 and 220-gr. bullets are generally preferred. Holland's bullets for this rifle are very much better and more suitable than those usually supplied by British firms for high velocity rifles. The 150-gr. is a semi-pointed soft-nose; the 180-gr. a not-too-bluntly shaped round-nose with just a pin-head of lead showing—infinitely better than the copper-pointed some makers like; and the 220-gr. a plain round-nose soft-nose.

I have used all three of these bullets with the British loading and found that they all behaved most satisfactorily on the approximate size of animal for which they were intended. Everything the .30–06 will do is done better by the .300 Magnum—as is only to be expected. What is usually claimed to be the outstanding point about this rifle is its paralyzing effect when used on suitable animals—one-shot kills being customary. The 180-gr. bullet as supplied by Holland is the only bullet of less than 220 grains I can remember using that gave me even reasonably satisfactory results on anything but the smallest animals.

It is not, and was never intended as, a big game rifle—as we consider "big game" in Africa; but for killing the lighter varieties of soft-skinned game. I have, however, been intensely interested in recent articles in the *AMERICAN RIFLEMAN* describing the behavior of this rifle with the stepped-up American loading. The 180-gr. seems to be coming in for the most attention, which is quite understandable in view of the long ranges at which so much American shooting seems to take place nowadays; its greater momentum would undoubtedly help it to retain better its initial velocity when out in the vicinity of 400 or 500 yards. I see that the 220-gr. bullet is normally loaded at 2,500 f.s., only it's not 220 but 225-gr. This must make it a very much better killer than the regular British loading I used. Whilst the 180-gr. bullet has been boosted to around 3,100 f.s. I also gather that a slightly "wild-catted" version of the .300 Magnum has lifted the velocity of the 180-gr. bullet to 3,500 f.s. with energy better than 4,000 ft-lbs. If the bullets stand up to it, this must be an incredibly deadly load.

Quite apart from any question of chamber pressure, when velocities get up into these high figures the whole success of the rifle depends upon the bullet. If your bullet breaks up too soon its power will be dissipated and you will be disappointed.

I have never had any experience of velocities running upwards of 3,000 f.s. and 3,000 f.s. gives you as flat a trajectory as you could possibly require at all ranges up to 250–300 yards. Even when hunting the rare desert antelope of the drier parts of the Sudan and surrounding territories, and in the Kalahari and the desert country south of Mossamedes in Angola, you do not need to consider longer shots than that. Some types of American hunting are different, however, and doubtless these super-high speed weapons will prove of inestimable value there.

With American loading, and always presuming that the powders used are not too sensitive to high temperatures, then this .300 Magnum with its three weights of bullets and one of the new reinforced-jacket bullets, such as the Peters "Belted" or the Remington "Core-Lokt" in 220 or 225-gr. should be a most excellent weapon for all soft-skinned African game.

.30–06 U. S. A. This cartridge has always had a fair degree of popularity amongst those who only shoot soft-skinned game. Whether or not full-patch round-nose 220-gr. bullets are available for it I cannot say; but I have never seen them. The vast majority of regular hunters want their medium or small bore to be able to kill thick skinned animals occasionally, a weapon solely for soft-skinned game being looked upon as a mere luxury. The .30–06 is perfectly capable of killing anything in Africa provided suitable bullets are used, and is certainly a very much better killer than the British .303. Mind you, I am only referring to the old ballistics for the .30–06. According to the British ammunition manufacturers' ballistic tables they do not load this cartridge to the modern American stepped-up velocities. The British loading runs:

150-gr. bullet 2,700 f.s.
180 " " 2,500 "
220 " " 2,200 "

chamber pressure for all loads being 20 tons to the square inch. Now 20 tons is generally considered the maximum figure that should be used in very hot countries. To what extent has the modern American stepped-up loading boosted the pressure? I'm afraid I can't answer. That they must have been boosted is a practical certainty. Modern powders have undoubtedly helped; but it's difficult to believe that the pressures can still remain at their original figure.

That a considerable quantity of soft-skinned game, both heavy and light, is killed every year in Africa with the .30–06, and presumably with the old loading, is a fact. Many men are perfectly satisfied with it; but they are generally those who shoot only the smaller varieties.

Reports of the .30–06's killing power amongst Africa's lions every now and then find their way into American sporting magazines. Sometimes these accounts are misleading and liable to cause disappointments thru being entirely divorced from their context. I am thinking of an article I read not so very long ago in a famous American magazine in which the author was wondering if there was really any need for these modern super-high velocities. He pointed out that considerable quantities of American game of all descriptions were killed perfectly satisfactorily with the old .30–06 "War Horse" in days gone by, and how considerable quantities of similar game were still being killed with the same cartridge. He mentioned how a certain American sportsman had taken his .30–06 to Africa with him and subsequently wrote a book in which he described how on one occasion he cross-piled a "bunch" of half a dozen lions or so on top of each other with the same old weapon. He then went on to say that it had become quite customary with a certain type of American hunter of the present day to speak disparagingly of the .30–06 as incapable of killing an "over-grown cow" like a moose altho it apparently had no difficulty in blotting out African lions.

Now that's all very well; but as I am constantly repeating, the mere ability to kill is, by itself, not sufficient. Casual hunters adopt certain expressions they hear us using concerning rifles, and give them a quite different meaning as they use them. For instance, when we speak of a rifle being a fine "lion-stopper," we do not just mean that it is capable of killing half a dozen lions with half a dozen quick consecutive shots—any modern rifle almost is capable of doing that if the lions are obliging. What we mean is that the particular rifle in question is capable of *always stopping, crumpling*, a lion at the charge—a very different thing. When contemplating the rifle you always intend to carry around with you, you must not lose sight of the fact that in good game country you are liable to put up a lion, and usually several of them, at any moment. If there are females amongst them and you open fire, you can expect to be charged—you may not be, but you must allow for it because it's quite usual.

Further, it must not be forgotten that the wealthy visitor is almost sure to be accompanied by at least one thoroly experienced professional whose business it is to see that his wealthy patron does not get hurt. He will certainly be armed with a powerful rifle with which to back up the visitor's small bore. Accordingly, for a person to speak of shooting lions with a small bore without any reference to the heavier weapon that's at hand, can be highly misleading.

If you intend to bring a .30–06 along, first make sure that the pressures are not unduly high and that the powder used is of a type that will not be affected to too great an extent by changes in temperature. Of the three bullets I consider the 220-gr. is by far the most effective for all general African use. This is a very good weight for all the heavier varieties of soft-skinned game. It sets up well and remains in the animal's body. Yet, curiously enough, it was the 180-gr. bullet that seems to have given the .30–06 its name as a game gun out here. Most of the men with whom I have ever discussed it seemed to use the 180-gr. bronze-pointed bullet only. I do not like any of these bronze- or copper-pointed bullets, and reckon they would have been vastly more satisfied had they been using the 220-gr. slug. I know that one or two took my advice and were very pleased about it.

I have never owned a .30–06 because I have always wanted each and all of my rifles to be capable of killing elephant and I was never able to find any round-nose solids of that caliber; but I shot a fairly representative variety of African game with it, including a lion, and so got an idea of its capabilities. If the new American loadings will stand up to the temperatures, then, given the 225-gr. Peters "Belted" or Remington "Core-Lokt" bullets at velocities ranging between 2,400 and 2,500 f.s., I reckon the .30–06 should prove as good a general purpose gun for Africa as anybody could wish. And there is no reason under the sun why really hard-nose full-patch slugs could not be made for it.

(NOTE: I had just closed this section when my copy of the *RIFLEMAN* for May arrived, having been considerably delayed en route. And it arrived most opportunely because it contains a most interesting and, for me, most apt article by Edwards Brown, Jr. discussing the Ball and Armor-Piercing loads for the American service ammunition, used in the last war. Amongst other things it is stated that the average pressures of these loads ran 40,000 to 42,000 pounds per square inch for Ball and 48,000 pounds for A.P. "The pressure of 48,000 pounds per square inch," says the writer, "is not excessive and the maximum individual pressure allowed is 54,000 pounds per square inch. Some .30–06 sporting cartridges are loaded with pressures close to 54,000 pounds per square inch."

If we reduce that to British tons to agree with our other readings it will work out at a trifle over 24 tons to the square inch. We would certainly look upon that as very high indeed out here; and it's to be remembered that when the .280 Halger with its 180-gr. bullet showing a pressure of 24.5 tons was tested in Britain it was found that the action was appreciably strained. Obviously the American actions must be very strong and fully capable of withstanding the service pressures, because some of these rifles must have been used in some of the hottest parts of the world during the recent war. However, not having had any personal experience of such high pressures under tropical hunting conditions I am not in a position to discuss them.)

.275 OR .276 (7MM) MAUSER. This is an even more popular and very much more widely-used weapon than the .256 (6.5mm) amongst small bore enthusiasts. I much prefer it myself, and my little Rigby gave me the greatest possible pleasure and satisfaction. But it was usually as a small bore rifle that I used it, and not as a medium bore. I do not believe in these small calibers for the bigger animals. They were widely used when they first came in and men were beginning to realize the greatly enhanced killing power of the metal-jacketed bullet as compared with the old lead slugs. Also, the game were still comparatively unsophisticated and spent more of their time out in the open so that the hunter could pick his shot to a much greater extent than he can today. The little 7mm rifle is every bit as good a killer as the 6.5mm, and it has adequate penetration to enable it to find the vitals of any animal.

This was Bell's favorite weapon and it was with it that he killed practically all his 1,011 elephant. However, it is rarely used nowadays by regular hunters, other, of course, than as a genuine small bore for the smaller animals. The principal objection to these small calibers is that the expanding bullets cannot always be relied upon to penetrate sufficiently on the heavier kinds

7MM MAUSER CARTRIDGE.
Loaded with the 140-grain copper pointed bullet and nitro cellulose powder.

I have ever found these copper-pointed bullets the most unsatisfactory of all patterns on the market. If they hit a bone at fairly close ranges they almost invariably disintegrate whereas, if they slip in between two ribs they more often than not snick clean thru like solids. But this little weapon loaded with 140-gr. semi-pointed soft-nose slugs is my favorite of all small bores for killing the little buck we shoot for the pot. It is a grand little gun for that purpose.

Loaded with the 173-gr. round-nose bullet with which it was originally brought out it is a very effective weapon in the hands of a steady and experienced hunter. Bell, the greatest exponent of the small bore, killed 1,011 elephant, practically all of which he shot with his Rigby-Mauser of this caliber. He specialized in brain-shots and brought it to a fine art. There is no question that a 173-gr. in the brain will kill just as effectively as will a 750-gr. bullet—it's merely a question of putting it there.

of game, even of the non-dangerous beasts, and therefore solids must be used. But if the little slug is not perfectly placed, little damage is done and the animal may get away. Also, the light bullets are all too easily deflected by tough grass and similar obstacles.

This rifle, firing its 140-gr. H.V. bullet, is widely used in British East Africa for all the general run of non-dangerous game. I cannot condemn this practice too strongly. It results in an immense number of wounded animals getting away to die miserably or, even worse, to be pulled down and literally eaten alive by hyenas or other varmints that would be unable to kill them if unwounded.

.256(6.5MM) MANNLICHER RIMMED.

Powder 36 grs. Smokeless; Bullet 160-gr. Metal-covered; Pressure 17.5 tons; M.V. 2,300; M.E. 1,880.

This is one of the few cartridges I never used. Ballistically it is identical with the 6.5mm Mannlicher-Schoenauer, except for its lower chamber-pressure. Take note of the full-patch bullet shown in section—the jacket is of steel and is well reinforced at the nose. It is this feature that gave these little rifles their excellent penetration. In every way that is a really well-designed bullet, as the turn-in of the envelope at the base shows.

.256 (6.5MM) MANNLICHER-SCHOENAUER. This is the smallest caliber with which you could possibly expect to have satisfactory results in general African hunting. Its 160-gr. bullet has probably a better diameter-to-weight ratio than any other bullet on the market. It is very accurate and has excellent penetration, both when used as a solid and soft-nose. What must surely be the world's record bag with any rifle, much less with a small bore, is held by the little 6.5mm Mannlicher-Schoenauer in the hands of Banks, recently retired from the Elephant Control staff in

Uganda—three elephant to the one shot! He shot one which fell against two others, and all three of them tumbled over a precipice.

Blaney Percival, for many years Game Warden of Kenya, did most of his shooting with a 6.5mm. It has always been popular with those who like small bores. Naturally, other than on head or neck shots, you could not expect the little rifle to drop animals in their tracks other than the very smallest species. It will kill anything; but as with all the other small calibers, if the bullet is not vitally placed there is little or no external bleeding, which frequently means a lost trophy.

Let me quote from Banks, the greatest of all the exponents of the small bore. A lioness galloped across his front. He was carrying a 6.5mm Mannlicher-Schoenauer loaded with solids.

"I let drive at her," he writes, "and she carried on as though untouched. I thought that I had missed her clean, until I found her some way further on, stone dead. Search as I would, nowhere could I find either entrance or exit bullet hole, and it was not until she was skinned that I found the tiny wound channel through the kidneys."

But it has one very bad point, and that is its capacity for jamming at the worst possible moment. Time and again have I read, or heard some fella lamenting, how his 6.5mm Mannlicher-Schoenauer let him down—usually by having the fired shell stick in the chamber.

Percival relates how his misbehaved on two occasions when he was tackling lions. On one occasion he practically stubbed his toes on seven or eight lions in fairly long grass. They cleared off, and when the last one was about 30 yards away Percival took a shot at him. The others immediately spun around and stood growling, one moving slowly towards him. Percival found that the fired shell had remained in the chamber when the bolt had opened; so did the wisest thing he could have done—dropped down into the grass out of sight of the lions, and dug at the empty shell with the point of his hunting knife—the continual growling of the lions doing nothing to steady him. He finally managed to remove the stuck cartridge, reloaded, and gradually got himself into a kneeling position. There was one lion still watching the spot from over a fallen tree, so that there was only his head showing. Percival let drive at him, but admits that he clean missed

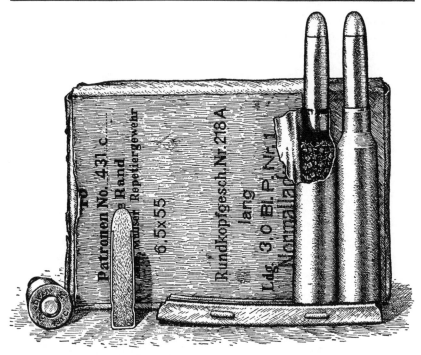

.256 (6.5MM) MANNLICHER-SCHOENAUER.

Powder 36 grs. Smokeless; Bullet 160-gr. Metal-covered; Pressure 17.5 tons; M.V. 2,300 f.s.; M.E. 1,882 ft-lbs.

This cartridge has always had a very considerable following amongst those who like small bores. Its long thin bullet of good weight for its caliber gave it excellent penetration and it's this, and this only, that has enabled it to add every kind of animal in Africa, I suppose, to its bag.

It's obviously absurd to even think of it as a big game rifle altho it's quite capable of killing anything. Its popularity arose in the early days of the transition from black powder to smokeless when hunters were intoxicated by the deep penetration of metal-jacketed bullets, and forgot that a big game rifle needed stopping power as well as the mere ability to kill. The lightness and handiness of these little short-barreled Mannlicher-Schoenauers appealed greatly, whilst many men found that the reloading process was easier and smoother with the revolving magazine than with the box pattern. However, it has long been discarded by regular hunters tho a few men still use it for the pot.

As I have said elsewhere, I never cared much for any of these small bores—other than for the very small buck for which they are reasonably suitable—because of the very small entrance hole to the wound and consequent poor blood spoor. Most men who used them to any extent were compelled to use solid bullets for everything, and this meant that unless the bullet was very accurately placed a long tiresome follow-up was inevitable with, perhaps, nothing to show for it in the end. This seemed to me too much like needless waste of time and energy.

him owing to the scare he had received and the anxious manner in which he had been rooting at the spent shell making him a trifle shaky.

On another occasion he wounded a lion which he had been driving out of some reeds. The lion charged and Percival's rifle again jammed. His gun-bearer then lost his head and ran, and the lion, as almost invariably happens in a case of that description, brushed past within a couple of feet of Percival, who had remained like a rock, and made after the fleeing boy. She, it proved to be a lioness, caught up with the boy and clawed him down, but fortunately died on top of him without doing any very great damage. But it was a matter of seconds—five more and she would have killed him.

Of course, I fully realize that all Mannlicher-Schoenauers of this caliber cannot be so unreliable, or the rifle would never have gained the popularity that it undoubtedly possesses. Nevertheless, I have heard and read of so many cases of it jamming, that I would never recommend it for dangerous game, quite apart from its caliber. I do not know of any bullet of less than 160 grains that can be used for general African hunting; and personally I do not consider that anything less than about 220 grains is likely to prove generally satisfactory.

The vogue for these little rifles did not last very long. Bell and Stigand were the two best-known hunters to use them; but Stigand was badly hurt by both elephant and rhino. He had a double .450 with which to back up his little 6.5mm, but was not using it on either of the occasions when he so badly needed it.

The bullets illustrated here show the exposed lead nose to come well around the shoulders of the bullet. I guess this pattern must have been preferred for European game to the British soft-nose-split type, because I saw some similar German shells shortly before the recent war exactly like those shown here. Personally, I prefer these to the soft-nose-split. I found that they do not break up so readily.

The soft-nose-split is excellent when it's a case of using a fairly heavy bullet against a soft-skinned animal—such as a 480-gr. slug for lion or tiger—and you want to help it all you can to ensure complete expansion before it has driven its way right thru the beast, but where all these lighter bullets are concerned for African use, I always found the plain soft-nose, with a greater or lesser amount of lead showing, depending on the weight of bullet and the weight of animal, by far the most satisfactory. The 6.5mm had an enormous vogue thruout Europe in days gone by, but I think that latterly it had been pretty well superseded by some of the higher velocity Magnums.

Percival, already referred to, Lyell and Powell-Cotton were others who liked either the 6.5mm or the 7mm. Powell-Cotton, however, had his scope-sighted and only used it as such a weapon should be used.

I have never been able to understand the, I can only call it, mania, some men used to have to want to use the smallest possible calibers for everything. Keith puts it so succinctly in his *"Big Game Rifles and Cartridges"* that I cannot refrain from quoting him: "Many hunters today," he writes, "are apparently small-bore crazy, seemingly wanting to kill as large game as lives with as light and small a bore of rifle as possible, throwing the lightest bullet obtainable; even to hunting big game with the .22 Hornet. Such men need their heads examined. Certainly it is not sportsmanship they display."

And that about sums up my opinion also.

An intensely interesting series of articles ran thru three or four issues of the *AMERICAN RIFLEMAN* around the beginning of 1947 on the *Development of the Sporting Rifle*. The writer of the series, S. R. Truesdell, sets out to make a survey of the rifles used by most of the better-known sportsmen and hunters who wrote books about their hunting adventures from the early '30s of the last century up to 1925. Just why he should have stopped at that date is a little difficult to understand, particularly since he brings in Commander David Blunt who only started his serious hunting career in that year, and whose excellent book *Elephant* was not published until 1933.

Such a survey, altho as I have said, is intensely interesting if you know anything about the subject yourself, can nevertheless be somewhat misleading in the case of an inexperienced man and tend to give him a wrong impression. The writer of those articles was solely concerned with the calibers used, and made no attempt to differentiate between black powder weapons and the more modern nitro-firing rifles of the same calibers. Possibly he didn't realize or know exactly which type was under discussion by the writer of some book he was studying, and who hadn't bothered to distinguish his rifle himself. This was an all-too-common fault of those early writers. The .577s and .500s are the calibers that are so often mixed up in this way. Most of the .500s written about by Indian and Asiatic hunters were black powder Expresses;

the .577s could have been either, tho most of them were also black
powder.   In Africa, altho the early .577s were B.P.s, thereafter
they were almost exclusively nitro.   No black powder weapon
can be compared with its more modern nitro-firing equivalent, and
they should not be lumped together merely by caliber.

Then another point that should always be brought out and
emphasized when big game hunting in both Africa and India, and
farther East, is being discussed generally, is the very different
conditions under which most of the corresponding species are
hunted and shot, and how much easier the Indian and Asiatic
beasts are to shoot as compared with their African contemporaries
—notably elephant.   The Asiatic elephant is easy to kill as compared with his much bigger African cousin.   In the days when
there was almost unlimited elephant hunting in Ceylon, for instance, those men who claimed the biggest bags—one claimed
1,200 elephant and another 1,500—shot those elephant with
ordinary breech-loading shot guns of 12 and 16 gauge with the
barrels cut down to 24 inches for the sake of general handiness.
They used ordinary spherical lead balls.   They would never have
made such enormous bags in Africa with such weapons.

The late Sir Samuel Baker is almost invariably mentioned in
connection with the 4-bore, and the .577 Express, and himself
claimed to have introduced the big gun into Ceylon but it is
generally overlooked that when he went to Africa to concentrate
on elephant he had Holland build him a battery of four double 10-
bores for the sake of their greater fire-power—a point worth
bearing in mind—and it was with those rifles he shot most of his
elephant.   He never shot an elephant with a nitro-firing weapon.

But the principal point that I must criticize—in the friendliest
possible manner—in the summing-up remarks of the writer of
these articles is in his tendency to run-down various of the most
widely-used calibers that only really began to be known around
the time when he closed his survey.   It's true he qualifies his
statement slightly by admitting this possibility, but there is no
getting away from his final remarks "But more probably there
was some inherent quality in the older calibers, such as the
Mannlicher, the Springfield, Lee-Metford, or the 7 and 7.9 Mausers
. . . and even in some instances the .250 Savage which none of the
newer cartridges could improve upon," etc.   He then goes on to

mention certain sportsmen who continued to use those calibers even after the more modern stepped-up magnums appeared. Well, it's quite understandable that a man might prefer to continue using a certain caliber that had given him good service for many years when used as a general purpose weapon with something heavier at hand to back it up when tackling dangerous game but it must not be forgotten that the vast majority of hunters never dream of writing about their experiences—they either don't feel qualified to do so, or else can't be bothered.

For instance, Truesdell states that "some rifles which have been highly touted, such as the Newton rifles, the .280 Ross, the .318 Westley Richards, the .333 Jeffery, the .350 Rigby, the .425, the Gibbs .505 and the .600 Jeffery, are conspicuous by their low popularity in the hunting fields." Mr. Truesdell would never have made such a statement if he had ever wandered around those "hunting fields" with his eyes open. The .318 is easily the most widely-used of the British medium bores and has an immense following; the .333 is also quite common; Rigby's .350 was the most popular medium bore up to the introduction of the .318 which was cheaper, and is still widely used, altho it has in large measure been superseded by Rigby's .350 Magnums. The .425 was another very popular big game weapon amongst those who preferred the magazine to the double and until the introduction of Rigby's .416. The two most powerful magazine rifles, the .500 and .505, were, unfortunately for themselves, introduced at a time when the price of ivory was rapidly dropping to next-to-nothing and there was no incentive to the ivory-hunter to buy new weapons —in fact ivory-hunting almost became a thing of the past except amongst a very few of us hardened old-timers who didn't care a damn about money provided only that we could make enough to cover expenses and keep our spare ammunition bags filled—whilst the .366 (9.3mm) is scarcely mentioned at all and yet it has ever been by far the most widely-used medium bore thruout Africa.

The "inherent quality" possessed by those older calibers, notably the .256 (6.5mm), .275 (7mm), .315 (7.9mm) and .303 British, was the inestimable advantage they had in that the elephant were still more or less unaccustomed to gun-fire and spent the greater part of their time in the open so that the hunter could pick his shot.

CHAPTER VI

The Small Bores

THERE ARE A GREAT NUMBER OF CALIBERS IN THE MAGNUM SMALL bore group. I have only listed a representative selection of them in the ballistic tables, because there is really nothing to choose between most of them from the point of view of killing power and flatness of trajectory. They are only in existence because competition was so keen and gunsmiths were eternally trying to bring out something new. There is really not the slightest need for so many calibers.

I am afraid that in the killing of these small buck and the use of suitable rifles for the job, I must plead guilty to a blasé attitude totally out of place in a hunter. For many years I just could not bring myself to look upon this as anything but an aggravating necessity—even the hunting and shooting of the larger antelopes was a "nuisance" and really beneath a hunter of elephant and buffalo! Hence my only arming myself for a long time with nothing smaller than .450. However, I eventually learnt sense, and came to realize that this could—all of it—be an intensely interesting and enjoyable sport and sideline to the hunting of the big fellows. But it was the using of suitable weapons that taught me. Nowadays I thoroly enjoy every hunt, be the animals hunted large or small. But all those wasted years might have provided me with a wealth of information concerning these small bores.

To some extent, perhaps, an excuse might be found for me—at any rate amongst the more leniently-minded—in the fact that by far the most of my hunting has taken place in Portuguese territory, and the Portuguese regulations limit a man to three rifles, a shotgun, and a handgun. As an ivory-hunter I *MUST* have at least two rifles suitable for elephant under all conditions, so that if one happens to meet with an accident I can still continue satisfactorily with the other; and since genuine elephant-rifles are not suitable for soft-skinned game, I generally added a medium bore to complete my battery. So you'll see, this left me no opportunity for experimenting with small bores. The only times when I did get that chance were when I replaced one of the large bores with a large medium and used it for meat for my men, and then got myself some exquisite little rifle for my own pot. But such luxury was only possible after a particularly good run after the elephant, and when for a change I took to hunting in more open scrub and bush. But when the call came to again return to the dense, matted tangles of thorn and heavy forest, the little rifle had to go and another heavy weapon replace it.

The 140 and 150-gr. bullets, provided of suitable pattern—and, by all accounts, the 100-gr. slugs also—are so intensely satisfactory for the shooting of all the little critters we collect for our own pots, that there really isn't anything to say about them. It's only when rifles and bullets misbehave that discussions start. At the ranges at which these rifles are generally used, the semi-pointed soft-nose slug at velocities ranging between 2,600 and 2,800 f.s. is just about ideal. Clean, one-shot kills are a practical certainty. I don't know much about weights, but would reckon that the little buck I have in mind would probably run from 100 to maybe 250-lbs.; Grant's and Thompson's gazelles, impala, oribi, bushbuck, reedbuck and similar little fellows. Klipspringer, duiker and, of course, the tiny dik-dik, little bigger than a good-sized hare, are all smaller.

I have had no personal experience of bullets lighter than 140 grains—other than an occasional shot at some little buck with a miniature rifle; but I have discussed the lighter bullets with a great many men who use them and swear by them for the pot. None of these men had ever tried them on wild hog; but they told me that they killed like lightning on all the smaller varieties of thin-skinned game such as impala, Grant's and Thompson's gazelles, and similar little beasts that simply swarm in most parts of the big game hunting grounds and are loosely called "buck." It is they the hunter usually shoots for his own pot.

These men had principally used rifles in the .240-bore group, and one of them a .250 Savage. He did not seem quite so satisfied as the others, and I gathered he would have preferred a heavier bullet than the 87-gr. slug he had been using. The others declared that they had never had anything but the most satisfactory results with their 100-gr. bullets thrown at roughly 2,950–3,000 f.s. Two men had used the .260, which throws a 110-gr. bullet at 3,100 f.s. They were entirely satisfied. I only came across one man who had used the .270 Winchester, 130-gr. bullet at 3,100 f.s. He was very pleased with it; but he shot in a cool district in the East African Highlands. I know that the .270 is quite widely used in various parts of Africa, principally the South; so it would certainly seem as tho the American powders were less affected by the heat than the British powders. Of course, some of the men who use the .270 must undoubtedly use British ammunition; because I know that the British firms load it, and they would hardly do so if it was never used. However, I consider its chamber pressure, 21 tons in Britain, too high for the tropics.

These 100-gr. bullets are widely used for wild hog in Austria and Spain—at least they were before the recent war—so there seems no reason why they shouldn't prove equally satisfactory for African hog.

Of the other calibers, the .256 (6.5mm) with 135-gr. bullet is one that I have never come across; but the .275 (7MM). RIGBY is, I think, easily the most widely used. It throws a 140-gr. bullet at 2,750 f.s. The semi-pointed soft-nose is infinitely preferable to the copper-pointed. I did not like the latter at all. If it failed to hit any bone larger than a rib it usually snicked thru like a solid without setting up at all; whereas if it hit a shoulder it usually blew to pieces. But the semi-pointed soft-nose is a peach. In my experience it always behaves as it should behave. Naturally, I refer only to the animals for which it was designed and not to beasts running up to 1,000-lbs. or more in weight. It is more than madness to expect satisfactory results when using such light slugs and high velocities on animals of that size. But when used as it was intended that it should be used, it will give you the greatest pleasure and satisfaction. One-shot kills are certain—instantaneous death following whenever you squeeze your trigger.

.275 N $\underline{\circ}$ 2 RIGBY. This is the flanged counterpart of the rimless .275 or 7mm, for use in double rifles. It fires a similar 140-gr. semi-pointed soft-nose bullet at 2,675 f.s. and is, I think, my favorite of all the small bores. Naturally, except that it is a double and the other a magazine, it's identical with the H.V. 7mm. It's a little difficult to see just what more men think they are going to gain by boosting the velocities of these little weapons. In countries where shots have to be taken at upwards of 400 yards, well and good; it's quite understandable. But as far as African hunting is concerned, I cannot see the slightest necessity for it. No animal could possibly be killed deader than my little .275 killed 'em; whilst it was a delightful little weapon to shoot.

The advantage of these H.V. loads over the old L.V. ones is that the more suitable weight of bullet sets up and stops in the little animals where the 173-gr. slugs with their lower speeds would not always do so; but by far the greater asset is the peculiar property of "shock" imparted by the high-speed bullet when it hits an animal of suitable weight. I have already discussed it in connection with the medium bores when used on the heavier animals for which they are more suitable; but it applies here also, and possibly even to a greater extent. Because if the old L.V. bullet is used the little buck will seldom be killed instantly, and the small entrance hole to the wound will leave but a very slender blood trail; but with these H.V. bullets he drops as tho struck by lightning.

.275 MAGNUM HOLLAND. This was brought out by Holland a couple of years or so after the introduction of the .280 Ross. It threw a 160-gr. slug at 2,675 f.s. It was the first of Holland's belted rimless cartridges, and was obtainable in flanged form also for use in double rifles at a slightly lower velocity of 2,575 f.s. It was widely used for some years after appearing on the market, but I have not seen one in use now for a very long time. Since Hollands have made no reference to it in their catalog now for many years, it would seem that they have abandoned it and only build it to order, concentrating on their .240 "Apex" and .300 Magnum.

I only fired two or three shots from the .275 Magnum. It appeared to be quite satisfactory.

.280 ROSS AND OTHERS. It was the Ross rifle that proved to be forerunner of the entire range of high velocity rifles. It was originally introduced with a hollow-point 140-gr. slug at the then unheard of speed of 2,900 f.s. Men were flabbergasted at its instantaneous killing power, and there was a rush to buy a Ross rifle.

Most firms built rifles to take one or other of the two shells that were brought out, flanged and rimless; and two other weights of bullet appeared—160 and 180-grain at 2,700 and 2,525 f.s. respectively; whilst Jeffery came to light with a special load in a rimless shell throwing a 140-gr. slug at 3,000 f.s.

But the inevitable disappointments crept in when men foolishly started using such light ultra high-speed projectiles against heavy and dangerous animals. Lions that the 140-gr. hollow point slug failed to stop killed a few men—George Grey, brother of a well-known British statesman, being the first of them, his five bullets blowing to atoms on a charging lion without having the slightest effect on him; "Fitz" Schindler was another; and there were several more.

Colonel Stockley relates an incident that occurred when a tiger attacked his dog one day on the path right in front of him. Stockley had also taken to the .280 when it first came out and was carrying his this day. He let drive at the tiger at 23 yards range, hitting him in the chest, and a second time at 5 yards, hitting him about 3½ inches back of the shoulder blade. The bullets smashed into minute fragments and the tiger, altho knocked down by the second shot, continued his rush and was found dead about 100 yards away in thick cover. It was particularly noticeable that the penetration was much less in the case of the bullet fired at the closer range. The first had managed to get past the breast bone and tore the big blood vessels, but the second had merely made a bad surface wound altho it had not had to encounter a heavy bone.

Then the straight-pull Ross action was responsible for a few fatalities and hideous injuries, thru sometimes blowing back in the firer's face, that it gave the death knell to this caliber; men coming to think that the evil reputation applied to anything .280.

.280 HALGER. This rifle secured a good deal of limelight when it first appeared. Its ballistics ran:

100-gr.	22 tons	3,800 f.s.
143 "	25.5 "	3,450 "
180 "	24.5 "	3,000 "

When it was tested in Britain with the 180-gr. bullet it was shown that the action was appreciably strained and it was considered extremely doubtful if the weapon would pass proof. An enthusiast tried it out in South Africa with the 100-gr. bullet. His

report was that the weight and unhandiness of the rifle—it weighed
10½ lbs.—together with the blast and recoil, stiffness in extraction
and slowness in reloading from the magazine, quite outweighed
the advantage of higher velocity and flatter trajectory in view of
the normal ranges at which it was used, and at which experience
had shown that velocities around 3,000 f.s. were ample.

Burrard mentions a friend of his trying one for deer-stalking in
Scotland, and his report was almost word for word the same as that
which came from South Africa.   These velocities were secured
simply by loading an immense powder charge behind the bullet and
firing it in the normal way—the inevitable result being a too-high
chamber pressure and an unduly heavy weapon for its caliber.

.300 MAGNUM HOLLAND & HOLLAND.   This and the Rigby
.275 N $\stackrel{\circ}{=}$ 2 are my favorites amongst the small bores.   Firing its
150-gr. slug the .300 Magnum is unbelievably deadly.   I can't remember ever having to give a beast a second of them—they're sure
dynamite.

The longest shot I can call to mind that I've ever fired in Africa
was with this rifle—239 long strides.   I had just shot a haartebeaste for my men on a bare open plain on which the grass had all
been burnt off, and the only other animal in sight was an impala
ram.   I had shot the haartebeaste with the 220-gr. slug at about 125
paces; and then seeing the little impala away off beyond him stop
grazing to look around and see what was happening, I slipped another shell, loaded with the 150-gr. bullet, up the spout, took a
sight slightly above the centre of his shoulder and squeezed.   He
might have been struck by a bolt from heaven.   Well, in the name
of all reason, what is to be gained by boosting the velocity higher
when its regular speed makes it behave like that?   And when with
its regular velocity enables it to be built so light and handy and
leaves it so pleasant to shoot?   That the stepped-up American
loading of these various calibers would make them any better is a
moot point *at the ranges at which these animals are shot*.   Anyway,
it would seem that the bullet manufacturers still have a long way to
go to keep pace with the hand loaders.

.30–06 U. S. A.   I have never used this rifle with its 150-gr. bullet, but can see no reason why it should not be very satisfactory;
nor have I come across anybody else who had used it.   But the
180-gr. bronze-point bullet is widely used.   This is the only pat-

tern I have seen in this weight, and I have several times stated that I do not like any of these copper or bronze-points. In my experience they are the most unreliable and unsatisfactory pattern of bullet on the market: sometimes refusing to set-up at all, and sometimes blowing to pieces on impact. The 180-gr. bullet supplied by Holland for their .300 Magnum would be excellent here, particularly with the American loading.

From the above it will be seen that I did not get good results when using the .30–06 as a small bore; but the fault was entirely with the bullets, not with the rifle. Had other types of bullet been obtainable I am quite sure I would have been pleased. The only 150-gr. slugs I ever saw for the .30–06 in Africa, were the solid pointed military type which, of course, would have been quite useless for game shooting; tho some men were carrying quite a few of them. Just what they wanted them for, I cannot answer.

.318. Its 180-gr. bullet brings this rifle within the small bore group. It throws it at 2,700 f.s. It's only obtainable in the Westley Richards patent pointed "L.T." capped pattern. But this type of bullet in this weight behaves extremely well on the size of animal for which it was intended. I shot quite a few small beasts with this bullet when I had a .318 and found it worked very well indeed. This bullet greatly increases the .318's general utility; because the regular 250-gr. slug is much too heavy for the small buck we shoot for our own pots. But altho I prefer the 140 and 150-gr. bullets, I must say that in its L-T pattern the 180-gr. is a sure killer. Whether this weight would meet with enough resistance to cause it to set-up properly in other patterns I cannot say, because the 180-gr. bullets in various calibers are generally used on somewhat heavier animals than those I have in mind. I don't remember any outstanding shots when using this rifle: it just did what was required of it without fuss.

MINIATURE RIFLES. The only miniatures with which I have had any personal experience are the .295 (or .300, the cartridges are the same), .255, .22 H.-P., and .22 Rim-Fire. Prior to the non-fouling .22 R.-F. ammunition appearing, I used to reckon the .295 the best of the lot; tho the .255 ran it close. I have heard fine reports of the .22 Hornet, but have not as yet had an opportunity of trying it.

The .22 Savage had a considerable vogue in South Africa when

it first came in. The only bullet available, at least in British loading, was a 70-gr. soft-nose pointed, with an immensely long point.
All was very well if it didn't hit a bone, but if it did it tended to
break up too quickly. Bell, that great exponent of the small bore,
speaks of shooting buffalo with it—naturally, picking his shots;
but he must have managed to get some other pattern of bullet. It
was a tremendously popular little weapon with farmers and others
for the pot. Some idea of its popularity may be gained when I
mention that John Rigby has for years been building best grade
double rifles to handle it. Some years since, a Walter Winans beat
the previous world's record with a Rigby double .22 high-power at
the running deer with a score of 38 out of 40. With a double rifle
two shots must be taken at each run, and there are four runs.
Under these conditions Winans scored 7 bulls with his first 7 shots.
Given suitable bullets there is no question of its excellence for
pottering.

I have read of the .22 Savage being used on at least one occasion
by a parson to shoot a man-eating tiger, and am glad that it was
he and not I! Still, he killed the tiger. However, I'm most certainly not recommending any such weapon for that kind of shooting; any more than for stopping a charging rhino as I gather a
certain well-known sportsman once did in East Africa—but he
very nearly didn't! (There is a case on record of a man killing a
rhino with a long .38 revolver—the word "revolver" was used,
but I cannot help thinking it must have been an automatic, because metal-jacketed bullets for revolvers were not obtainable in
those days. And we all know from reading the "blood-and-
thunder" variety of "whodunits" that a "revolver" in one chapter
becomes an "automatic" in the next, and possibly an "automatic-
revolver" in a later one!—he was taking photos of a rhino and
wanting to get a little movement and life into his pictures, he fired
a shot from his hand gun to stir up the rhino. He never intended
to hit the animal, but his bullet took the rhino in the neck and
dropped him stone dead! The only possible explanation would
seem to be that the bullet slipped in between two of the vertebrae
when the rhino was looking the other way and then when he
turned his head again sharply on feeling the bullet and hearing the
shot, he dislocated his own neck on account of the bullet being in
one of the joints.)

Altho I have had no personal experience of the .220 Swift, it might be of interest to mention that Bell got hold of one of the first of them to reach Britain, had Rigby mount a Zeiss scope sight on it, and used it deer-stalking in Scotland. He related his experiences with it in Britain's *GAME & GUN* not very long before the recent war. He said it killed the Scottish deer like lightning, and was supremely accurate. He killed one stag at better than 300 yards, the bullet taking the animal in the brisket. Bell thought he had clean missed because the stag remained motionless, and he couldn't figure it out as he had felt quite certain of the shot. He prepared to fire again, but it wasn't necessary: the stag suddenly keeled over, stiff-legged like a child's toy, stone dead. The little 48-gr. slug had mushroomed ideally and altho it had only penetrated about 2 or 2½ inches into the brisket, it had nevertheless totally paralyzed the stag's entire nervous system. Bell sent the bullet along to *GAME & GUN* to be photographed and it was used to illustrate his account. He had killed a considerable number of deer at the time he described this incident, and stated that the .220 Swift was the finest and deadliest weapon he had ever used on such animals, and far surpassed his beloved .275 Rigby-Mauser. And if Bell reckons a small bore is worth its oats, that's good enough for me.

The modern .22 Long Rifle Rim-Fire is really an astounding little weapon. Given a good scope sight and a steady shot it's almost unbelievable the variety of animals you can shoot with it. There was a fella in Tanganyika who habitually used it on all kinds of buck up to and including zebra. It's a simply splendid weapon for the elephant-hunter with which to collect something fresh for his own pot and give himself a change from jerked meat, or biltong. To a very great extent he can feed his men with it also. The beauty of it is that it makes no noise at all, and so doesn't put game on the alert as a more powerful weapon would. I would happily undertake to walk thru from Cape Town to Cairo armed with nothing but a scope-sighted .22 Rim-Fire and a powerful hand gun, and I am quite confident I would not go hungry.

I have never seen any of the numerous American high-speed ultra-small bores, such as the .218 and .219 and other wildcats and varmint guns, so cannot speak of them. For my own use, I believe in the scope-sighted .22 Long Rifle Rim-Fire.

BALLISTICS OF LARGE-BORE RIFLES

Rifle.	Weight of Bullet in grains.	Pressure in tons per square inch.	Velocity in ft. per sec.				Energy in ft.-lb.				Knock-Out Blow. Values.	Approximate Weight of Rifle in pounds.	
			Muzzle.	100 yd.	200 yd.	300 yd.	Muzzle.	100 yd.	200 yd.	300 yd.		D.B.	S.B.
.600............	900	14.0	1,950	1,690	1,450	1,250	7,610	5,720	4,210	3,130	150.4	14–17	12–13
.577............	750	14.0	2,050	1,730	1,450	1,210	7,020	5,000	3,510	2,440	126.7	11½–14	11
.505 Gibbs......	525	15.0	2,300	2,020	1,790	1,550	6,180	4,760	3,740	2,810	86.25	—	10½–11
.500 Rimless.....	535	16(?)	2,400	—	—	—	6,800	—	—	—	90.3	—	10¼
.500 3..........	570	15.5	2,115	1,880	1,650	1,440	5,730	4,490	3,450	2,640	86.5	10–12	9–10
.476............	520	16.0	2,100	1,890	1,680	1,490	5,100	4,130	3,260	2,570	74.2	11	9½
.475 No. 2.......	480	15.5	2,200	1,960	1,730	1,510	5,170	4,100	3,200	2,440	71.7	11–12	10½
.475 No. 2 Jeffery.	500	?	2,000	1,818	—	—	4,450	3,670	—	—	67.8	11–12	10½
.475............	480	15.0	2,175	1,930	1,700	1,490	5,030	3,970	3,090	2,360	70.8	11–12	10½
.470............	500	14.0	2,125	1,910	1,700	1,500	5,030	4,060	3,210	2,500	71.3	10½–11½	9–10
.465............	480	14.0	2,125	1,920	1,720	1,530	4,820	3,940	3,150	2,500	67.7	10¼–10¾	9–10
.450 No. 2.......	480	13.0	2,175	1,900	—	—	5,050	3,700	—	—	67.1	10½–11½	9–10
.500/.450........	480	15.5	2,175	1,990	—	—	5,050	4,220	—	—	67.1	10¼–11½	9–10
.450............	480	17.0	2,150	1,960	—	—	4,930	4,100	—	—	66.3	11–11½	9–10

BALLISTICS OF LARGE MEDIUM BORE RIFLES

Rifle.	Weight of Bullet in grains.	Pressure in tons per square inch.	Velocity in ft. per sec.				Energy in ft.-lb.				Knock-Out Blow. Values.	Approximate Weight of Rifle in pounds.	
			Muzzle.	100 yd.	200 yd.	300 yd.	Muzzle.	100 yd.	200 yd.	300 yd.		D.B.	S.B.
.440 (11.2 mm.)	332	15.0	2,450	2,170	1,650	1,430	4,430	3,480	2,010	1,510	51.1	—	8½
.425	410	18.5	2,350	2,110	1,910	1,710	5,010	4,100	3,330	2,660	58.5	10-11	9
.423 (10.75 mm.)	347	14.0	2,200	1,950	1,710	1,500	3,750	2,940	2,260	1,740	46.1	—	7½
.416	410	17.0	2,350	2,150	1,960	1,780	5,010	4,220	3,500	2,900	57.25	—	9¼
.405	300	17.0	2,200	1,940	1,690	1,470	3,240	2,510	1,910	1,450	38.2	—	8
.404	300	16.0	2,600	2,360	2,130	1,900	4,500	3,720	3,030	2,400	45.0	—	8¼-9
.404	400	16.0	2,125	1,930	1,750	1,580	4,020	3,310	2,730	2,200	49.0	—	8¼-9
.400 Jeffery	400	16.0	2,125	1,940	1,760	1,590	4,010	3,350	2,760	2,250	48.6	9-10	8½-9
.400 3-inch case	400	16.5	2,150	1,960	1,780	1,610	4,110	3,410	2,820	2,300	49.1	10-10	8½-9

BALLISTICS OF MAGNUM MEDIUM BORE RIFLES

Rifle.	Weight of Bullet in grains.	Pressure in tons per square inch.	Velocity in ft. per sec.				Energy in ft.-lb.				Knock-Out Blow. Values.	Approximate Weight of Rifle in pounds.	
			Muzzle.	100 yd.	200 yd.	300 yd.	Muzzle.	100 yd.	200 yd.	300 yd.		D.B.	S.B.
·375 Magnum	235	17.0	2,800	2,510	2,220	1,950	4,100	3,300	2,580	1,990	—	9½	8½
·375 "	270	18.0	2,650	2,430	2,210	2,000	4,220	3,550	2,930	2,400	—	9½	8½
·375 "	300	18.0	2,500	2,300	2,110	1,920	4,160	3,530	2,960	2,460	40.1	9½	8½
·369 Purdey	270	17.0	2,620	2,400	2,190	1,970	4,110	3,460	2,880	2,330	—	10	—
·350 Magnum	225	17.5	2,600	2,360	2,120	1,880	3,380	2,790	2,250	1,770	29.25	9¼	8¼
·333	250	18.0	2,500	2,300	2,120	1,930	3,470	2,940	2,500	2,070	—	9–9	8–8
·330 B.S.A.	165	18.0	3,000	2,700	2,410	2,130	3,300	2,680	2,140	1,670	—	—	8¾
·318	180	19.0	2,700	2,440	2,190	1,930	2,920	2,390	1,920	1,490	—	9¼	7¼–8
·318	250	19.5	2,400	2,210	2,030	1,850	3,200	2,720	2,290	1,910	27.25	9¼	7¼–8
·311 (7.9 mm.)	154	18.0	2,800	2,550	2,290	2,040	2,700	2,240	1,810	1,430	—	—	7–7
·303 Sporting	150	18.5	2,700	2,480	2,230	2,000	2,430	2,050	1,660	1,340	—	9	7–8
·300 Magnum (H & H)	150	18.5	3,000	2,750	2,510	2,270	3,000	2,520	2,100	1,720	—	9	7½–8
·300 Magnum (H & H)	180	18.5	2,700	2,500	2,300	2,100	2,920	2,500	2,110	1,780	—	9	7½–8
·300 Springfield ('06)	150	20.0	2,700	2,460	2,220	1,980	2,440	2,020	1,640	1,310	—	—	7½–8
·300 Springfield ('06)	180	20.0	2,500	2,300	2,100	1,930	2,500	2,120	1,770	1,490	—	—	7½–8

BALLISTICS OF MEDIUM-BORE RIFLES

Rifle.	Weight of Bullet in grains.	Pressure in tons per square inch.	Velocity in ft. per sec.				Energy in ft.-lb.				Knock-Out Blow. Values.	Approximate Weight of Rifle in pounds.	
			Muzzle.	100 yd.	200 yd.	300 yd.	Muzzle.	100 yd.	200 yd.	300 yd.		D.B.	S.B.
.375........	270	14.5	2,000	1,790	1,600	1,420	2,400	1,920	1,540	1,220	28.9	9–9½	8–8½
.400/.375........	270	—	2,175	1,930	—	—	2,840	2,235	—	—	31.5	9–9½	8–8½
.375 (9.5 mm. Mann-Schon.)........	270	17.0	2,250	2,040	1,830	1,630	3,030	2,500	2,010	1,590	32.5	—	7½–8½
.366 (9.3 mm. Mauser)........	285	16.5	2,175	1,960	1,760	1,570	3,000	2,440	1,960	1,570	32.8	—	7½
.360 No. 2........	320	14.7	2,200	2,110	1,830	1,660	3,450	3,170	2,390	1,970	36.2	9–10	8–9
.360 Westley Richards........	314	15.5	1,900	1,720	1,550	1,390	2,520	2,060	1,680	1,350	30.7	9	8
.400/.360........	300	15.5	1,950	1,760	1,580	1,410	2,540	2,070	1,670	1,330	30.1	9	8
.355 (9 mm. Mauser)........	245	17.0	2,150	1,920	1,700	1,500	2,520	2,000	1,580	1,230	26.7	—	7–7½
.355 (9 mm. Mann-Schon.)........	245	17.0	2,100	1,870	1,660	1,460	2,400	1,900	1,500	1,160	26.1	—	7–7½
.400/.350........	310	16.0	2,150	1,970	1,790	1,630	3,190	2,680	2,210	1,820	33.3	9	8
.350 Winchester........	250	17.0	2,200	1,970	1,760	1,550	2,690	2,160	1,720	1,340	—	—	7½–8
.333........	300	18.5	2,200	2,030	1,860	1,700	3,240	2,750	2,310	1,930	31.4	9¼	8–8½
.318........	250	19.5	2,400	2,210	2,030	1,850	3,200	2,720	2,290	1,910	27.25	9¼	7¼–8
.315 (8 mm. Mann-Schon.)........	200	14.0	2,200	1,970	1,750	1,540	2,160	1,730	1,360	1,060	—	—	6½–7½
.315 (8 mm. Mannlicher)........	244	14.0	2,025	1,840	1,670	1,500	2,230	1,840	1,520	1,220	22.4	—	7–7½
.315 (8-mm. Lebel)........	198	14.0	2,300	2,100	1,910	1,730	2,330	1,940	1,610	1,320	—	—	7–8
.303 Mark VI........	215	16.5	2,060	1,870	1,680	1,510	2,030	1,680	1,360	1,050	19.2	9	7–8
.303 Sporting........	192	17.0	2,200	1,980	1,770	1,570	2,060	1,670	1,340	1,050	—	9	7–8
.303 Mark VII........	174	18.5	2,450	2,250	2,060	1,850	2,320	1,960	1,640	1,320	—	9	7–8
.303 Savage........	180	17.0	1,975	1,750	1,550	1,350	1,560	1,230	860	730	—	—	7
.300 Magnum (H & H)........	220	18.5	2,350	2,170	2,000	1,830	2,700	2,300	1,960	1,640	22.15	9	7½–8
.300 Springfield ('06)........	220	20.0	2,200	2,020	1,850	1,690	2,370	2,000	1,680	1,400	20.7	—	7½–8
.311 (7.9-mm. Mauser)........	227	15.5	2,025	1,830	1,640	1,460	2,060	1,590	1,360	1,040	20.4	—	7–7½
.311 (7.9-mm. Mauser)........	244	16.5	2,030	1,850	1,670	1,500	2,240	1,860	1,510	1,210	22.0	—	7–7½

BALLISTICS OF MAGNUM SMALL-BORE RIFLES

Rifle.	Weight of Bullet in grains.	Pressure in tons per square inch.	Velocity in ft. per sec.				Energy in ft.-lb.				Approximate Weight of Rifle in pounds.	
			Muzzle.	100 yd.	200 yd.	300 yd.	Muzzle.	100 yd.	200 yd.	300 yd.	D.B.	S.B.
.280 Halger	100	22.5	3,800	3,480	3,160	2,840	3,210	2,690	2,220	1,790	—	10½
.280	143	25.5	3,450	3,270	3,100	2,920	3,780	3,390	3,050	2,800	—	10½
.280 ,,	180	24.5	3,000	2,860	2,720	2,580	3,600	3,270	2,960	2,670	—	10½
.280 Jeffery	140	18.5	3,000	2,820	2,630	2,450	2,800	2,480	2,160	1,870	—	8½
.280	140	18.0	2,900	2,720	2,540	2,360	2,610	2,400	2,010	1,760	9½-10½	7½-9
.280	160	18.0	2,700	2,520	2,340	2,170	2,590	2,250	1,950	1,670	9½-10½	7½-9
.280	180	18.0	2,525	2,350	2,200	2,040	2,560	2,210	1,940	1,670	9½-10½	7½-9
.280	160	18.0	2,700	2,550	2,380	2,230	2,590	2,310	2,010	1,780	9½-10½	8-8½
.275 Magnum	140	19.0	2,750	2,580	2,400	2,230	2,360	2,070	1,800	1,550	—	7¼
.275 (7-mm. Rigby)	140	17.0	2,650	2,500	2,330	2,160	2,220	1,950	1,690	1,450	8½	7½
.275 Rigby	130	21.0	3,100	2,890	2,680	2,470	2,770	2,410	2,080	1,760	—	7
.270 Winchester	130	18.0	3,100	2,880	2,640	2,420	2,350	2,030	1,710	1,440	—	7½-8½
.260 B.S.A.	145	19.5	2,600	2,440	2,280	2,120	2,180	1,920	1,670	1,450	—	7-7½
.256 Magnum Gibbs	135	21.5	2,800	2,620	2,450	2,270	2,350	2,060	1,800	1,530	—	7-8
.256 (6.5-mm. Krag) / .256 (6.5-mm. Mann. and Mann.-Schon.)	135	17.5	2,600	2,430	2,250	2,080	2,030	1,770	1,520	1,300	—	7-8
.250 Savage	87	19.0	3,000	2,710	2,420	2,150	1,720	1,410	1,130	890	—	7¼-7½
.246 Purdey	100	18.0	2,950	2,750	2,550	2,350	1,940	1,680	1,450	1,230	9	—
.242 Vickers	100	19.5	3,000	2,810	2,610	2,410	2,000	1,760	1,520	1,310	—	7
.240 Holland	100	17.0	2,950	2,770	2,580	2,400	1,940	1,710	1,480	1,280	8	6¾-7

BALLISTICS OF SMALL-BORE RIFLES

Rifle.	Weight of Bullet in grains.	Pressure in tons per square inch.	Velocity in ft. per sec.				Energy in ft.-lb.				Knock-Out Blow.	Approximate Weight of Rifle in pounds.
			Muzzle.	100 yd.	200 yd.	300 yd.	Muzzle.	100 yd.	200 yd.	300 yd.	Values.	S.B.
.275 (7 mm.)	173	17.5	2,300	2,100	1,880	1,680	2,040	1,700	1,360	1,040	15.6	7
.256 (6.5 mm.)	160	17.5	2,300	2,160	2,020	1,890	1,880	1,660	1,450	1,270	13.4	7-8

Rifle	Powder drams	Bullet grs.	Pressure tons	M.V. 24″ barrels	M.E.	Weight D.B. rifle
4-bore.............	12	1,882	7.0	1,330	7,400	20–24
8-bore.............	10	1,250	6.0	1,500	6,290	16–18
10-bore.............	8	875	7.0	1,550	4,660	13–15
12-bore.............	7	750	6.0	1,550	4,000	11–12

These charges are those that were considered most suitable for general purposes. But sometimes much heavier charges were used —up to 1 oz. in a 4-bore and 14 drams in an 8-bore. These were the charges generally preferred in Africa.

AN HISTORICAL 4-BORE CARTRIDGE CASE

This is an accurate, full-scale drawing of one of the actual cartridge cases once owned by the great Sir Samuel Baker; now the possession of Dr. George R. Hays, of Richmond, Indiana.

This brass case has seen much usage in its day, having been reloaded with heavy charges of black powder on countless occasions. Note how the primer pocket has been forced inward from the repeated loadings and heavy hammer blows. This failing was a common fault of these early brass cases and accounted for many of the misfires which all of these old-time big-game hunters tell of in their writings.

Bullet	Diameter	Bullet	Diameter
.600	.620″	.350 Magnum	.357″
.577	.585″	400/.350	.357″
.505	.505″	.35 Winchester	.357″
.500	.510″	.333	.339″
.500 Rimless	.511″	.330	.338″
.476	.510″	.318	.327″
.475 N≗2 and .475	.476″	.315 (8mm Mann. and Mann.-Schoen.)	.322″
.470	.483″	.311 (7.9mm)	.322″
.465	.476″	.303 British	.311″
.450	.458″	.303 Savage	.311″
.440 (11.2mm)	.465″	.300 Magnum and '06	.308″
.425	.435″	.280 Halger	.287″
.423 (10.75mm)	.423″	.280 Ross	.287″
.416	.416″	.275 (7mm)	.282″
.405	.410″	(including the Magnums, both Holland's and Rigby's)	
.404	.411″	.270	.280″
.400	.410″	.260	.268″
.375 and 9.5mm (including 400/.375 and .375 Rimless)	.375″	.256 (6.5mm)	.262″
.375 Magnum	.375″	.250	.255″
.369	.375″	.246	.252″
.366 (9.3mm)	.368″	.242	.248″
.360 N≗2	.367″	.240	.242″
400/.360 and .360	.367″	.22 Savage	.224″
.355 (9mm) (both Mauser and Mannlicher-Schoenauer)	.357″		

CHAPTER VII

An All-Around Rifle

Auctor: Is there such a thing?

Lector: Faith! you weren't long getting that in, were you? Don't you realize that this is the most debated question thruout the big game hunting world and ballistic circles everywhere?

Auctor: Sure, I do. But I want to know if you are one of those who maintain there is no such thing; or if you reckon there is indeed such a rifle and intend to tell us what it is right now, or keep us waiting until the last page, like the writers of the whodunits.

Lector: Well, your question is easily enough answered if by "all-around" rifle you mean a weapon that will prove ideal for long range 'chuck-shooting and at the same time prove equally satisfactory for elephant in dense bush, and the answer is an emphatic raspberry! No weapon ever devised by man could possibly be so flexible. But if you are prepared to be a mite more reasonable in your requirements, I reckon it might be possible to satisfy you.

Wait till I tell you about a fella I know, a London stockbroker, who is mighty keen on big game hunting but is a very busy man whose time is strictly limited. Not only did he not want to be bothered with a whole lot of different rifles with their inevitable packets of different shells and different bullets and different cleaning implements; but on account of his only being able to get away for comparatively short periods, he's gotta use a plane for getting around. He can't afford a big plane in which he could carry a lot of baggage, nor can he afford to charter one. So he scratched his head and put in a lot of deep thinking, and the result is that he had Holland build him up one of their special light double .375 Magnums which only weigh 8¾ lbs. with 25″ barrels, which is only

4-ozs. heavier than their magazine rifle and 4-ozs. lighter than similar magazine weapons built by most other firms. With this he has a little Zeiss 2½-power hunting scope sight that can be attached or removed without difficulty.

His first trip took him to Uganda and the Sudan. He only had about a week or ten days in each territory, but he bagged elephant and buffalo in Uganda, and lion and various lesser game in the Sudan. He returned mighty pleased with himself and his choice of weapons. The next time he could get away, he took the fastest ship he could find across the Atlantic (the regular air-service wasn't in existence before the war) and then a plane across the American continent. He shot the big Alaskan grizzly and brown bears, and declared the double .375 Magnum was just the right medicine for them. Caribou and moose were added to the bag, and the longest shot he had he estimated at between 300 and 350 yards at some sort of sheep—Dall, possibly—and said he found the 235-gr. bullet beautifully satisfactory. He had rather wondered how a double rifle would perform at that range, and admits that he was none too sure of it at the time; but after the shot he was even more pleased than before at his choice of weapons. His third trip took him into the jungles of the Central Provinces in India. Here he shot tiger, panther, bear and bison. His next trip found him in the Himalayas where he bagged bear, ovis ammon, ibex, I think, and thar. He then came out again to Africa and had more fine sport with the same rifle, obtaining a fine lot of heads and skins.

Now that fella had sense; he knew what he wanted and went after it. He didn't try to strain his rifle by asking it to kill chucks for him at 400 yards range when in the States; nor did he waste time and money travelling to America to shoot crows with the weapon he wanted to use in Africa against elephant and buffalo. His choice of a rifle is just about ideal. In fact there is no other weapon in existence with which such a wide variety of animals can be shot with an equal degree of certainty and satisfaction. Practically every caliber on the market from .256 (6.5mm) to .423 (10.75mm) has been called an all-around rifle at some time or another in ballistic sessions; but in every instance some serious short-coming can be brought up that wipes it off the list. There is no other rifle in existence of which so much can be said as it can of the .375 Magnum.

Auctor: But surely you can't mean that a double barreled weapon is preferable to a magazine? Have you forgotten that doubles can only handle the load and bullet for which they were regulated? An all-around rifle must be able to shoot more than the one bullet-weight.

Lector: Sure. But for some types of hunting the double is not merely preferable to any other pattern but, in my opinion—and that opinion is borne out by many other experienced hunters—it is definitely essential if the best results are to be obtained. And altho you are quite right when you say that double rifles will only handle the load for which they were regulated, the one outstanding exception is the double .375 Magnum. This weapon and its three different loads was definitely designed as an all-around rifle for the man who didn't want to be bothered with a whole battery of rifles. It reflects the greatest possible credit upon the designers that these different loads can be fired with equal accuracy from the one weapon, and also that all three of them should be so intensely satisfactory on the wide varieties of game all over the world for which they are so supremely suitable. In the case of a single barreled weapon it is merely necessary to alter the sights or the aim and any number of different loads can be used, but matters are very different where doubles are concerned.

Should anybody feel like raising a sceptical eyebrow in connection with my statement that a double .375 Magnum will group accurately with all three of its different loads, I might mention that a Holland double .375 Magnum fitted with ordinary open sights was sent around to the British *FIELD* for testing and report. Both barrels were fired consecutively, all three loads being used, three or four shots with each load. The composite group at 100 yards measured 2½ inches deep by 2 inches wide. The unbeliever can write either to the *FIELD* or to Holland & Holland who will be pleased to send him a copy of that report with a full-size reproduction of the target.

That sort of shooting is good enough for me. It might also be remembered that I have used two of these rifles and fired all three loads in both of them. I fired all three loads in each of the magazine models I had also, and never noticed the slightest difference in aim being required at the ranges for which they were intended to be used. One of the magazines threw its 235-gr. slug a mite higher than the other two, but the difference was negligible, possibly 1 to 1½ inches at 100 yards, certainly not enough to cause a miss. But the only difference in the doubles was what you would expect and want—the 270-gr. bullet grouping centrally in the bull at 100 yards, with the 300-gr. about 1-inch below it and the 235-gr. about 1-inch above. There was no divergence in the grouping of the two barrels with either weapon.

Now I've given you the experience of one man who wanted a weapon which he could use satisfactorily all over the world where big game were to be found; but the vast majority of sportsmen can not get around to the extent that that fella could, and anyhow I'm only immediately concerned with Africa here. Since magazine rifles are so widely used in Africa, for all types of hunting, there can be no question that in the hands of a thoroly experienced hunter who has used that pattern of weapon all his life, the magazine must be declared safe even if not necessarily quite so satisfactory for certain types of work. Daly, for instance, has probably had as much all-around experience of African hunting as any man, and much prefers the magazine action for all purposes. But then he has rarely used any other type of weapon and is imbued with the notion that if a man has a double rifle in his hands he is compelled to fire both barrels every time he presses the trigger. However, if you have a preference for the magazine, you can get the .375 Magnum in that guise also.

The only other weapon that could possibly compare with the .375 Magnum for all-around utility in Africa is the .400, with the .404 as its magazine counterpart. The .400 held the palm for many years as *the* all-around rifle until such time as the .375 Magnum appeared. The .404 has the advantage over the .400 that its H.V. 300-gr. load is altogether more suitable for long range shooting at light soft-skinned animals than the regular 400-gr. bullet. But, as I mentioned earlier, it is only obtainable as a copper-pointed affair and therefore is not too good for African use. There is only the one load for the .400; but it's a peach of a load for all heavy and dangerous African game, and with the soft-nose and split bullets very satisfactory on all but the smallest of African soft-skinned animals. As we have already seen, its trajectory is as flat as you are ever likely to want in this country. Nowadays the rifle is built to weigh 9½ lbs., which is the regular weight of the double .375

Magnum, and I have not the slightest doubt that the double .400 *could* be built still lighter to special order.

Personally, I think it a mistake to have these weapons built too light. If an irreproachably balanced weapon at 9½ lbs. is built to weigh but 8¾ lbs., I fail to see how it can be quite so well balanced at the lighter weight. Because the greater part of the reduction of weight *must* come from between the hands, from the breech ends of the barrels, which is just where you most want it. I'm not suggesting for a moment that any one of the best firms would turn out an ill-balanced rifle; but it's just that the lighter weapon could hardly be as well-balanced as the heavier. And after all, who could complain that a perfectly balanced and perfectly proportioned double rifle at 9½ lbs. is too heavy?

For African use the decision between these two rifles must really depend on the type of hunting in which you expect or intend to usually indulge. If you reckon that you would rather spend most of your time hunting non-dangerous game in open and fairly open country in reasonably cool parts, such as the East African highlands, with an occasional crack at the big fellows from time to time, then the .375 Magnum would certainly seem to be indicated, because its variety of bullets and loads will prove more generally suitable for the much wider varieties of animals you will be hunting.

But if you have a hankering for thrills and the excitements of tackling animals that can hit back, and prefer to do your hunting in thicker bush where the shots are nearly always at close ranges, and where a shot may be called for at any moment, but will also want to do a fair amount of shooting at "ordinary" game, then I would certainly recommend the .400. There is no getting away from the fact that its heavier bullet hits a heavier punch than does the bullet from the .375 Magnum, in spite of the latter's much higher velocity. At any rate I am quite sure it does on a head shot that fails to find the brain. In the case of a frontal chest shot, I'm not so sure. That the bullet weight is better for close range work is indisputable; but there is that peculiar shocking-power of the .375 Magnum at close quarters on chest shots that I illustrated when describing the big buffalo bull I brought down when he charged from close by. I have killed other buffalo on similar chest shots when they were merely standing looking at me, and on almost every occasion they collapsed instantly. The only charging buffalo I killed with the .400 I shot in the brain, except for one; in his case I placed the 400-gr. bullet just inside the point of the shoulder at a range of maybe 10 paces. It was a somewhat slanting shot, because he was not charging me, but one of my men. He fell to the shot and scrabbled a bit on the ground as I maneuvered into position to give him another. However, by the time I was ready it was apparent that he had had enough.

I have killed another bull with a very similar shot from the .375 Magnum, placing the bullet just inside the point of the shoulder as he charged me. He was coming with a bit of a swerve instead of straight. The result was almost exactly the same as in the case of the .400. The shot brought the bull to his knees and his nose and he rolled over and died as he tried to get to his feet. The shot had not pole-axed him with quite the same certainty as the other bull that got the bullet centrally in his chest. But altho there seems to be little difference in the stopping power of these two rifles on chest shots, there is no doubt about it where head shots are concerned. Here there is no paralyzing of the animal's entire nervous system. It's the weight of bullet that counts if for any reason a brain shot is impossible.

I have knocked elephant down with the .375 Magnum on head shots that failed to find the brain, but they were up again sooner than those I brought down on similar shots with the .400. On head shots at any animal a heavy bullet will always inflict a more stunning blow than a lighter bullet, irrespective of any questions of velocity. You will see this if you turn to the ballistic tables and compare the punch of the .470 and .416 bore rifles whose energy is approximately the same on account of the latter's higher velocity; but there is an appreciable difference in bullet weight. The .470 has a heavier bullet and hits a heavier punch. You will see the same thing if you compare the .375 Magnum and .400. The difference in the actual punch of the bullet on head shots is considerable; velocity has nothing to do with it, it's a question of bullet weight. And so it's for this reason that I must always recommend the .400 in preference to the .375 Magnum if the sportsman reckons to do most of his hunting in the thicker bush.

Auctor: That's all right as far as it goes; but you'll forgive me if I mention that it does not go far enough. You've given us your

ELEPHANT HUNTER'S CAMP

This is Fletcher Jamieson's dry-season camp. As you can see, he just has the fly of his tent pitched under a shady tree—and that's adequate. There's no earthly need to lug around a full tent in the dry season, which lasts in Central Africa for about seven months. A fly is necessary, however, because during the middle of the season there is usually a day or two when it drizzles in a most provoking way day and night. If you haven't a fly your bedding and provisions and everything else get soaked. You need one for yourself and another for your men—then everybody's happy; tho most men don't bother about one for their followers. However, I reckon it's a good investment.

It will be noticed that there is no thorn fence or *zariba* around this camp. Actually, it's really totally unnecessary unless you're in a very bad man-eater's area. The ordinary hunting lion won't worry you. He may stroll up to take a look at you but once his curiosity's satisfied he will wander away again. Don't bother your head about him.

It is rather touching to see how, in a man-eater's area, your coons, without saying a word to you and apparently by mutual consent amongst themselves, will light fires all around where you are sleeping and sleep in pairs around those fires. The idea being that if the lion attacks he will grab one of them and not the lordly white man. They are all blessed with the happy philosophy that it will be one of the others that will be the victim—and the chances are, naturally, in favor of it being one of the others. The chances are still more in favor of it not being the white man but there is no guarantee in these matters. White men have been taken from the centre of their camps, altho sleeping in closed tents.

It's best not to worry about such matters. As I look at it, if your bell rings you go—whether it's lion, elephant, snake, or a stroke of lightning and if it does not, then you won't go. And that's all there is to it. In support of that, take the case of Jamieson's death, which occurred since I wrote this book: he had just returned from a trip after elephant during which he killed six good bulls in three weeks, and as he told me in a letter written immediately before his death, experienced no less than four misfires out of seven shots at elephant. Yet it wasn't an elephant that put paid to his account, as you might have expected; he was accidentally electrocuted when working down his own well after returning home! So what?

DISSECTED ELEPHANT'S SKULL

Well, there it is. Mebbe that will show you why such a tremendous dunt is required to stun an elephant. The cellular bone mass that comprises his skull absorbs the shock of the bullet and dissipates it before it can reach the brain. Right in the foreground you can see the roots of the tusks. You will notice that they are very close together and come up *between* the eyes, reaching well above them. Many artists who draw pictures purporting to be African elephant show the tusks apparently coming straight out of the mouth. Actually, the tusks are not really teeth at all altho they come out thru the gum well up under the upper lip—just where in days gone by they used to puncture you for sinusitis. When taking the frontal brain shot, you've gotta be mighty careful or you will split a tusk and thereby ruin its value. The bullet must slip in between the roots of the tusks—the target is about 4″ x 3″ on a big bull, assuming you have the angle right.

You will appreciate that it's a big job dissecting an elephant's skull and searching for bullets to see what's happened to them, and is quite out of the question if you are poaching. An elephant brought down with a frontal brain shot, as this one almost certainly was, nearly always collapses in an upright position—all four "knees" giving way simultaneously. If he's charging, of course, that does not always hold—the weight distribution may cause him to topple over on his side. But if you have brought him down with a head shot examine him carefully to make sure he's dead—if you see a thick dark gush of blood coming from his mouth then you can be practically certain that your bullet has found the brain, and that he'll stay dead. If you don't see that thick gush, give him another—it's better to be sure than sorry. You needn't waste one of your costly large bore shells—a solid from your medium bore will do fine. But it's poor economy to save a shell and lose an elephant. Yet it's happened many a time.

I was reading not long ago where a fella dropped a rhino and being short of full-patch slugs for his .450 told his men to finish off the rhino with their spears. He actually photographed them doing so but the rhino got up and cleared off, and this fella had to give him another three shots from his .450 before he finally managed to kill him. So what did he save? Selous had a very similar experience, but lost his rhino entirely. If you are in any doubt, give him another then and there whilst he's a motionless target and you are right alongside him.

This picture will also give you some sort of idea why the question of angles is so important when elephant shooting. There is an immense amount of bone to be traversed by the bullet before it reaches the brain cavity, which is situated in the centre of the skull and just above an imaginary line drawn from the outer corner of the eye to the ear-hole. When taking the side shot you should aim immediately in front of the ear-hole and just above that imaginary line—assuming that you are at right angles. For the frontal shot you take an another imaginary line, between the eyes this time, and aim slightly above it—always provided the elephant hasn't gotten his head unduly raised. If the animal is standing on much the same level as you are, then this spot is okeh for ranges between, say, 12 and 20 paces. If you are in a very steady position, you could doubtless take the shot from a somewhat greater distance—I have killed elephant with the frontal brain shot at ranges running up to about 40 paces but I was comfortably wedged against a convenient tree, and rock-steady.

DRAWING WATER

That weird-looking vegetable growth in the centre of the photo is a baobab tree, originally known as the "Cream-o'-Tartar" tree. Some of them attain to a tremendous girth. The trunk is usually hollow and in many cases acts as a tank or reservoir to hold rain water. This is well-known to hunters who frequent the dry-bush zones. If the hunter is new to that sort of country and does not know himself, his coons will darn soon tell him if they happen to get thirsty. The elephant also know it, and I have seen many times where some old tusker had reared up on his hind feet, his fore feet resting high up against the trunk of the tree, as he reached in to the top of the hollow to try and get a drink. Naturally, he can only reach a certain distance down under such conditions, whereas his hunter can get at the precious water long after the elephant has to look else-where. The water keeps well in these natural tanks—if you don't mind a few dead bees and things. And if you are hunting in a dry-bush zone you will not bother your head about any such trifles as a drowned bee.

It's these natural tanks that save many an old and big tusker from visiting a waterhole "outside" for weeks and even months on end. The hunter who does not know visits those waterholes daily to look for spoor, and not finding any quits the district in disgust. "Aw, to hell with this! There ain't no big stuff around here. Let's go." And away with him; leaving the big tuskers in peace. . . . And don't those big fellas know it! But the man who knows treks out into the heart of these dry zones, which the elephant have come to look upon as sanctu-aries, and relies upon the baobabs for his water if it ain't too late in the season. Naturally, they all dry out eventually—you couldn't expect them to carry water right up to the next rains. (The dry season in Central Africa extends for about seven months.)

In some districts the natives use the hollow baobabs as cemeteries—just drop-ping their dead down into the hollow. Consequently, you don't look for water in a baobab close to any native kraal when in one of those districts!

Few men have ever seen a really young baobab, including many coons who have lived all their lives amongst them. However, they don't just "arrive" all fully-grown tho I have seen precious few *really* young ones myself. The young ones, a foot or two in height, are miniature replicas of the older ones, but not quite so wrinkled. They are like little old dwarfs.

Many a hunter has put a bullet into a baobab under the impression that he was shooting at an elephant: Cotton Oswell speaks of doing so somewhere. This, of course, is because the color is almost exactly the same as that of an elephant that has had the mud washed off him by rain. Nevertheless, the man who actually gets as far as firing would have been taking a mighty chancey shot at an elephant had it been one. I've been momentarily deceived myself, but refrained from firing because I couldn't see a "vital" spot into which to drive my bullet. But the mistake is undoubtedly easy to make.

REMAINS OF A DEAD ELEPHANT

The old and very popular belief that there is an elephant cemetery, a "place where the elephant go to die," somewhere in the heart of Central Africa has long been exploded. The notion being that the lucky hunter who stumbled across it would be set for life on account of the millions of tons of ivory that must be there for the picking up. The small point that ivory is an organic substance and therefore decays, like anything else, being conveniently forgotten. It was also put about by the early hunters that nobody had ever seen a dead elephant other than one that had died of wounds. Well, that is quite easily explained—scavengers, hyenas, jackals, vultures and ants will make short work of even an elephant carcass—then the jungle quickly grows up and hides his bones.

Nevertheless, I do not think that normally an old elephant just dies "anywhere." My notion is that as he feels old age getting the better of him he gets right away from any likelihood of encountering Man. Some favored place where there is good water and mud for his baths to keep the biting flies off, there will also be good feeding close by. A single aged critter, be he elephant or man, does not require a hell of a lot of food. There the old fellow will drowse thru the days in the shade, wandering down to the water in the cool of the evenings. He is very wise in his old age, and will probably not become bogged in the mud when bathing but will mebbe just lie down for a sleep one day and fail to wake up again. The inevitable scavengers will do the rest.

The elephant in the photo died of wounds. I have myself picked up quite a number of tusks in that manner—elephant wounded and lost by some other hunter. Normally, if you come on a dead elephant you take it for granted that he has been wounded some time before, if only because you cannot turn him over to examine the other side! But it would be quite possible for a big snake to kill an elephant— there are parts of the body where the skin is comparatively thin—for instance, between the toes, between the legs and back of the ears. And we know that arrow poison will kill elephant just as easily as it will kill lesser game.

Then elephant are occasionally killed by lightning. I once found five dead elephant all in a line. They had been standing under a tree and probably holding on to each other for moral support. The tree had been struck by lightning and the leading elephant had doubtless been leaning against it. The current had travelled right along the five of them. On another occasion I came across two others that had undoubtedly been killed by lightning also. They were unmarked, so far as I could see—there was no other hunter in the district. Accordingly, it is difficult to find any other explanation of them being found dead together like that if lightning is excluded.

ELEPHANT BULL

This is a comparatively small tusker, and was probably a persistent raider of native gardens. From what you can see of the bush it's what I would describe as nice easy bush. And nice easy bush it is as compared with some of the dense matted tangles of thorn in which so much of my hunting has taken place. In this type of bush you can close your elephant without much difficulty. It's only necessary to constantly test the wind. There is plenty of cover for you, and you can keep it between you and your quarry until you are in the position you want, so that there is no chance of him spotting some movement that might put him on the alert.

When you drop an elephant with any sort of shot, and are not in any immediate hurry to depart, watch for that upper hind-leg to stiffen until the foot is raised off the ground. It will tremble as it does so, and you know then for a certainty that your elephant has handed in his checks. But until that hind leg tells its story, your elephant may still have life left in him. Your coons will invariably touch his eyeball with a spear or long cane or bamboo and see if he reacts but that's not too certain, expecially if he has been brought down with a head shot. If you are in doubt, then when he is lying on his side like that you can easily drive a bullet from your medium bore straight in thru the top of his head, centrally. If he wasn't quite dead, there will be a convulsive jerk and that hind leg will tell you that all is now well.

RHINO

This is an exceptionally long horn carried by this fella who has been posed for his picture to be taken. It is 27 inches long. These scrub rhino very rarely grow horns anything like as long as this one. The forest rhino in Kenya are famous for their long horns. The longest known was cut into a walking stick and presented by a Masai chief to a Britisher. In that guise it was 44 inches in length, and was said to have been at least a coupla inches longer before being cut. Amongst those forest dwellers horns running around 40–42 inches are not really uncommon but the rhino of the plains and bush do not grow those long thin tapering horns. Around this neck o' the woods anything running over 20–21 inches is considered very long. The cow usually grows horns longer and thinner than the bull. The longest I have ever shot around here went 22½ inches and belonged to a cow but I traded a 24 inch horn from an old native hunter who had shot the original owner with his muzzle-loader. It was also a cow. A better price is paid by European buyers for horns running over 22 inches.

Rhino horn, not being horn at all, is lighter than you might think. A good average pair of horns from the bush rhino would turn the scales at around 7–7½ lbs. but somewhere around 5 lbs. is more usual. There is always a better price paid for rhino horn than for elephant ivory but the trouble is that you do not get the heavy horns like you do the heavy tusks.

ELAND BULL

I invariably feel a twinge of regret whenever I kill one of these grand beasts. They're so quiet and harmless that it seems wanton slaughter to shoot them. Selous reckoned that they were more suitable for some old English park than for the African veldt. If you get one down and he is still living, when you go to cut his throat he will just turn his head away and wait for you—for all the world as tho he was saying, "well, get to it, brother; hope your knife's sharp." Where another animal will throw his head around—watch out for the horns!—an eland won't. Yet I know of two cases where a wounded eland showed fight. Percival mentions one, and says that he was very nearly caught because it was so totally unexpected. But such cases are entirely exceptional. I have never myself had anything of the sort happen, and I've shot many eland.

A big old bull like this is lazy. When he gets to a goodly spot with plenty feeding and water close by he remains there until he is so fat that even an agile white man can run him down on foot, and, of course, he'd be money from home for any coon of the hunting tribes. The eland's pace is the trot. They quickly tire at the gallop, but can keep up a long swinging trot for miles without tiring. They are incredibly agile. They think absolutely nothing of jumping a 5-foot fence, in spite of their bulk. They are very easily tamed, and it seems extraordinary to me that such half-hearted attempts have been made to domesticate them. Their weight and strength and ability to feed themselves almost anywhere—they browse as well as graze, like goats, and are always in good condition—would seem to make them ideally suited for African farms.

Their flesh is of the very best, and also their fat. Until you've tasted the hump of a good bull you don't know what the African veldt has in store for you!

This big fella was brought down by a Holland double 500/.450—a perfectly satisfactory weapon for the job but the eland, being an antelope, is more lightly-boned than the buffalo, and a less powerful cartridge will prove equally effective. But the eland can "take it," and it's a real mistake to try and shoot them with some small-bore squirt throwing very light slugs—besides being grossly un-sportsmanlike.

It seems strange that lions haven't wiped out these animals long ago—they occasionally kill a young one, but I can't remember ever finding the remains of a grown one that had been killed by Leo. I take it that it's their alertness that saves them, and that long tireless trot.

HIPPO

Hippo are very numerous thruout Central African waters—even in quite small pools and streams. A big bull probably weighs around 2½ tons. They cause a lot of damage amongst the natives' food crops, even tho those crops may be miles away from the pools frequented by the hippo. They wander considerable distances during the night, as they have no enemies except man. I've seen them utterly ignore lion when ashore on moonlight nights (a lion would certainly have his work cut out to kill a hippo!).

There is but little sport attached to the hunting of hippo with a rifle, unless you are drifting around in some crazy little dugout trying to entice some rogue into charging you and so get a shot at him. I have heard of men speaking of hippo coming open-mouthed for the canoe on the surface; but in my experience they have always charged under water and then tried to jump up under the canoe and upset it. If they succeed they then turn on the canoe, or on any unfortunate that has happened to fall into the water close to him, and get busy with their teeth. And a hippo's bite is a fearsome thing. With a single crunch they will take a piece bigger than this typewriter out of the bows of an iron-wood canoe into which you couldn't drive a nail.

The most sporting method of hunting hippo that I have ever come across is to harpoon them. I have never seen this method practiced other than on the lower reaches of the Zambezi. The native hunters lash two or three of their oldest and lightest canoes together, both for added stability and because one or more of them are almost certain to be wrecked before the hunt is over. The harpoon is not thrown, but driven in with both hands when the hippo is sleeping. They can be certain of being charged at least once, tho they tell me that it is unusual for a hippo to charge more than the once. However, they occasionally get hitched on to a tartar which will charge then again and again. When the hippo charges, the harpooner and his paddlers slip over the stern of the canoes and swim rapidly and silently away from the danger zone. Then when the hippo has vented his wrath on the canoes, they swim back and clamber aboard again. They are accompanied by several small swift canoes which act as rescue craft in the event of the hunter's canoes being hopelessly wrecked, and also serve to keep crocs away—sometimes. I have accompanied several of these hunts, riding in one of the small outriders' canoes, and it has been a never-ending source of regret that I had no small movie camera with me. I am quite sure this sport has never been photographed. For sheer thrills and sport it beats the old-time whaling. Those coons deserve every hippo they kill—and they seldom fail to kill.

I have twice had hippo upset my canoe, which cost me a fine battery of expensive rifles each time. Accordingly, I have no particular love for the critters.

BUFFALO BULL

This is a fine bull with a grand pair of horns. He was brought down by a Holland double 500/.450. If you were ever lucky enough to get a buffalo looking at you like that, with his head more or less on a level with you, you would just slip your bullet in between his eyes but a buffalo carries his head low and if you whistle to him to make him look up at you, he will stick his nose out straight in front of him so that his face is horizontal. If you then place your bullet immediately under the boss of the horns—which looks, and is, so tempting, he will drop to the shot and be "out" for anything up to 10 minutes or so—but *he will not be dead*. Such a shot will almost certainly pass above the brain and make its exit thru the back of the head. You will joyfully examine your fine trophy, put your rifle up against him or against a neighboring tree, and sit yourself down for a smoke and a rest. And the next thing is that your "trophy" is doing his damnedest to make a trophy of you! It has happened time and again with buffalo, just as it has with lion.

I was very nearly caught like that once in my early days, and have never forgotten. I had dropped a good bull with a bullet under the boss of the horns and was quite sure that he was dead. I turned my back on him and looked for another to shoot but there was a yell of warning from one of my followers, and I looked around in time to see my bull on his feet and shaking his head to clear it. He was just in the act of charging one of my men when I dropped him for the second time. I then had my gun-bearer hamstring him. From that day to this, I have my gun-bearer trained to hamstring immediately any bull dropped with a head shot—just two quick slashes with his razor-snarp hunting knife—a present from me. I can then turn my back on him with the pleasing certainty that he is definitely anchored. And I would advise you to do the same.

A heavy bullet is essential for the best results in the type of scrub and bush beloved by the buffalo—there are so many little twigs and branches there to deflect a light slug. The African buffalo can take an almost unbelievable amount of punishment and still survive. I have cut great lumps of iron, from half to three-quarters of an inch in diameter, out of buffalo that were in fine condition and fat. One old bull had a lump of iron bar about three-quarters of an inch in diameter and about an inch and a quarter in length *right in the centre of his liver;* another, shot at the same time, had had a similar lump of iron bar, about half an inch in diameter and fully an inch long, driven clean thru his guts from one side of his belly to the other. Each and every puncture of the intestines, and each coil was punctured twice, had healed perfectly. These missiles, of course, had been fired by some coon armed with some old gas-pipe muzzle-loader. At least I call them "gas-pipe," but actually those old Tower muskets must have had pretty good metal used in the barrels. The coons make their own powder—coarse stuff it is, belching immense volumes of smoke—and load it by the handful! But one rarely hears of one of these old guns bursting.

CROCS

All Central African rivers are infested with these brutes. There are two varieties—the blunt-nosed carnivorous man-eating brute shown here, and the other with a long narrow snout that lives on fish—known as the *gharial* in India —and which is not known to attack man, tho human remains have been found in them, it being generally assumed that they have been acting as scavengers and have gotten hold of some corpse.

But there is no doubt about the blunt-nosed one. I have shot hundreds of them in the Zambezi and without exception I have found human relics in their bellies—either actual bones and partially decomposed flesh, or else beads and bracelets and anklets such as are worn by the coons. Their annual toll of human lives must run into thousands—probably tens of thousands. The coons themselves, particularly the women, are in large measure to blame. An instance from my own experience will explain what I mean. I was sent for to shoot a bad man-eater that had taken no less than four women during the past four days. The bank right there was very steep and the water below it deep. They had cut steps in the face of the bank to enable them to get down to draw water. Having filled their pots and jars, the women, one at a time, then stood up to their ankles on the lowest step and commenced to wash themselves. The croc was waiting his chance and grabbed. There was a great hullaballu and nobody else drew water that day. But the next day another woman was taken in exactly the same way and another the day following. The deaths of their sisters in no way deterred the others from behaving in an identical manner the day following. And it wasn't until four of them had been grabbed that they thought of calling me. It was the easiest shot in the world; I just called a bunch of women along to the place and had them talk and laugh as loudly as they could whilst I watched. Sure enough, in a very few minutes there was the croc right alongside the lowest step waiting for the next fool woman to come down. It was a simple matter to put a bullet down thru the top of his head.

The African looks upon all visitations such as the arrival of a man-eater, be it lion or croc, as witchcraft—somebody has transmogrified themselves into the lion or croc for the purpose of getting their own back on somebody who has done them a bad turn. They themselves, not having done anyone a bad turn, will be okeh—the man-eater won't worry them. And so they take no precautions whatsoever.

Some of these man-eaters grow to an enormous size—well over 20 feet. (I've heard of them in some of the Congo rivers running up to close on 30 feet.) If one of those big ones gets hold of you, you haven't a hope. Their weight is incredible, and they know how to use it. That, combined with the tremendous power of their tail—their motive force—is what enables them to drag even buffalo, and occasionally rhino, under water.

The croc does *not* bite off a limb like a shark would—he just holds and drowns his victim. If you read of some native fisherman having his arm taken off by a croc, it was not bitten off; almost certainly it was a fairly small croc—otherwise the man would have been swept off his feet—and when the fella's pals came to his assistance and grabbed hold of him and pulled, the bone of the arm was broken and the arm pulled off in the tug-of-war that ensued. I have been instrumental in rescuing two persons from crocs—one a white man and the other a native woman—and in neither case was the limb bitten off—the croc just pulled and tugged whilst I bashed him over the head.

The object in the centre of the photo is the Zambezi variety of dugout canoe. As its name implies, it is burned and scooped out of a solid log. Some of them are shaped much like a banana, but serve their purpose.

SABLE BULL

The animal in the photo is just a fair average representative specimen. Sometimes those grand scimitar-shaped horns sweep back much further over his withers. When young the bulls are red with a white belly like the cows but with maturity they become black where they were previously red, tho still retaining the white markings on the face and the white belly. They're magnificent animals and very good eating. Their hide is preferred by the Boers of South Africa for rawhide reims (ropes and thongs) to that of any other species except, mebbe, buffalo.

They only favor certain types of country, and you won't get them anywhere else. The light open forest and scrub they like, slightly undulating, makes for fairly easy stalking. Any good modern medium bore will prove satisfactory. But be careful! Sable antelope have killed many excitable and inexperienced hunters who have closed in too rapidly and too carelessly to finish off some wounded beast. They make a scythe-like sideways sweep with those curved horns that's very deadly. I saw a native woman that encountered a wounded sable bull and got one of those horns driven right thru her chest. I have myself had a wounded sable bull make a savage and most determined charge as I closed in to finish him off, but I was ready for it, altho it certainly didn't look as tho he was capable of making a charge. I repeat, *be careful* of these bulls when wounded!

LEOPARD

You seldom get a shot at one of these critters by day. They're always on the alert, and their markings blend so perfectly into their background that they are almost impossible to see until they move and then their movements are so quick, and their choice of resting place so well-chosen, that they are gone even as you spot them.

An ounce and a quarter of buckshot is *the* medicine to carry around when following up a wounded leopard. Their charge is incredibly quick, and the slugs give you a larger margin of permissible error than a single bullet.

You occasionally hear men claim that their dogs have killed a leopard lone-handed. Well, in view of my own experience of leopard and my knowledge of the ease with which they can and do kill dogs of all sizes—a dog is the leopard's favorite tidbit—I can only take those claims with a very considerable pinch of salt. I have never come across a genuinely authentic case of any dog having killed a leopard all by himself.

A leopard by day and the same beast by night are two totally different critters. A leopard's boldness when dark falls is astonishing—particularly in view of his shyness by day. They think nothing of coming right into your house or tent and removing your pet dog from under your bed. There is an authentic story told by Blaney Percival of a trader down on the East African coast who kept a leopard as a pet until he was full-grown. He was well-fed and perfectly tame, and the trader used to allow him to wander around at will during the day but he was always most careful to chain him up at night. One night he awoke to find a leopard licking his hand which was hanging down the side of the bed. Thinking that his pet had somehow managed to slip his chain, and knowing that he might be a different proposition by night, the trader got out of bed apparently quite casually and picked up a heavy sjambok—rhino-hide whip—and lashed hell out of that leopard, beating him unmercifully. The leopard beat it out of the back door into the compound. The trader threw down his whip and went out to chain him up again. But when he got outside he found that his own pet was still chained there! When he fully realized that he had been thrashing a wild leopard he got such a scare that it took half a bottle of whiskey to steady his nerves and permit him to get to sleep again. He disposed of his pet after that. There is not the slightest doubt that the suddenness and fierceness of the attack disconcerted the leopard. Had the man shown the slightest sign of fear he would almost certainly have been clawed down.

Leopards are found everywhere. They must be far more numerous than lions tho they don't go around in "prides." They are only in pairs during the mating season and even then it is more customary to find them hunting alone.

DUIKER

These little fellas live solitary lives altho there may be many of them in the district. It is rare to see them even in pairs, and that only in the breeding season. You can wander around by day and only see a very occasional one, and get the impression that there are very few about but clamp a flashlight on the barrels of your shot gun and take a stroll around by night, and you will pick up their big glowing eyes in the rays of the torch all over the place. There must be considerable numbers of them in most parts of Central Africa but their habit of lying-up in a tuft of grass by day, and lying very close, banking on the fact that you can't see them till they move, makes it seem as tho they were scarce.

Shooting them at night with a flashlight and a shot gun is no sport at all— just slaughter—but it's a convenient way of getting a bit of fresh meat if your pot's absolutely empty, and only permissible under such circumstances. I've had good sport shooting them with a bow and arrows by day but the aid of a well-trained shooting dog is almost essential. (Incidentally, it was an American bow I used, one of several brought out to East Africa by a party of American sportsmen who went after lion with those most deadly weapons if properly handled.) Steinbok, or stembuck, is another little critter, even smaller than the duiker, that gives excellent sport to the shot gun by day if you have a good dog to tell you where they are. They also lie-up in a tuft of grass, and lie even closer than the duiker—there are times when you have almost to kick them to get them on the move and then they go like a red streak, jinking like hogs. An ounce and a quarter of buckshot from a 12-bore is just the medicine for them then.

Most hunters are very fond of duiker venison, and it's certainly tasty but, of course, they carry no fat at all, and I can't say I've ever been particularly interested in meat that carries no fat. The little fella in the photo looks like an old man to me, judging by the length of his horns. If you were hunting for the pot by day, so that you could see the horns, you would pass that fella by and look for another with spikes not more than mebbe a couple of inches long. He would be much better eating than this one—which would be tough as an old pair of boots.

HYENA

Useful as scavengers but otherwise a sheer unmitigated nuisance. Their numbers must be literally legion. They are everywhere but you very rarely see one in daylight—they are essentially nocturnal. I reckon they come next to the magazine rifle as potential game exterminators. The number of newly-born game animals they must destroy is incalculable. They're the most daring critters at night—human habitations hold no terrors for them. On the contrary, they come around regularly to see what they can scrounge. Anything at all that smells of meat or fat is welcome—I have had one of them clear off with my fry-pan one night and crumple it like it was cardboard within about 20 yards of camp. They have the most powerful jaw muscles and teeth—will crunch bones that even a lion will leave alone. They don't crunch bones like a dog—several times—there is just the one loud crunch, that's all. You can always tell if it's a dog or a hyena you hear.

You often hear of the "laughing" hyena but you mustn't imagine their laugh is an expression of joy. It's a soulless, maniacal, high-pitched, chattering, "laugh," and is only heard when there are a bunch of the brutes sitting around waiting for some lion to finish with his kill and they fear he won't leave enough for them. It sends a shudder of horror thru even the most hardened—you can easily imagine just such horrible soulless laughter issuing from some ghastly torture chamber of the bad old days as some poor wretch is driven insane.

It's quite impossible to find a good word to say for the hyena. His mournful howl is heard nightly, even in the towns anywhere close to the game districts. His bite is a terrible thing. Living as he does on carrion, it goes without saying that his teeth are poisonous and a white man would probably succumb if he didn't receive medical attention very shortly after it, but thanks to his phenomenal vitality, the African can get over it. It's unusual for the hyena to attack humans except in those parts of Eastern Africa where the tribes, such as the Kikuyu in Kenya, do not bury their dead, but just leave them out for the hyenas to "bury." Up there the brutes are very bold, and it is not so very uncommon to see some unfortunate coon with a foot or half his face missing owing to the bite of a hyena when he was sleeping. Just the one bite and the piece is gone. They not infrequently take an infant from beside its mother during the night.

RHINO

This is just a fair average specimen of the common "black" rhino. In the light timber in which he was shot he was comparatively easy money. So long as the wind was right, it was merely a case of strolling up within range and shooting. But altho the timber is open, it is surprising how often you will find some infernal stick or branch in the line of fire when you come to aim. It is also quite remarkable how often rhino collapse in an upright position like the one in the photo. Occasionally, of course, they are posed like that to make a better picture but as often as not it's not necessary to pose them—they've done it for you.

There's nothing very remarkable about the rhino shown here. These scrub dwellers don't usually grow very long horns. By the way, a rhino's horns aren't "horn" at all—they are actually hair "cemented" together by some substance. They aren't attached to the bone of the face, but only to the hide—you slice them off with a sharp knife. They are greatly prized by Asiatics—especially the Chinese —for their aphrodisiacal properties; it was this that led to the virtual extermination of the Indian and Sumatran rhino. At the present time there is a "black market" value of some $300.00 U. S. an *ounce* for the horn of the Asiatic rhino. The African member of the family is less highly valued but there is always a good market for rhino horn.

The horn polishes up beautifully and is used for the handles of fancy walking canes and also for some specially-finished guns and rifles—fore-arm caps, grip caps and butt-plates. The hide polishes up equally well, and if properly prepared looks like an enormous slab of amber. It makes splendid and most beautiful card and occasional tables. It is also the best of all hides for the making of sjamboks or whips. It does not absorb moisture out of the atmosphere nearly so readily as hippo hide will nor does it crack so easily (tho if hippo hide is well oiled it is also very excellent). Both these hides make very fancy walking canes —usually with a light steel rod thru the centre to keep them stiff.

REMAINS OF A LION'S KILL

A common sight thruout Africa. Curiously enough, the presence of lions in a district does not worry the game in the slightest. They know perfectly well that once the lions have made a kill they will not interfere with them again for a coupla days or so, and possibly not then. The lions go roaring around—tho naturally not when actually hunting—the lion ain't such a fool as to advertise his presence then—but they roar when starting out for their evening's prowl down to the water and when returning, and they roar after a feed or sometimes to call a mate or a pal to share a feed; yet the game does not forsake a district in spite of all that roaring.

The lion normally kills every three days. He *may* get a coupla feeds off a kill, if the local coons don't find it and if the hyenas don't finish it whilst he is away for a drink but it would seem as tho a lion only needs one really good feed in about three days. He will have a snack now and then between feeds—a very favorite dainty in the lion menu is porcupine. In some districts known to me in which porcupines are very numerous the lions have a great time—there are circles of porcupine quills scattered all over the place. I guess the lions there must feel as I felt when out in Australian waters and I could get all the oysters I could eat for the mere knocking of them off the rocks!

About the only point worth mentioning in this photo is the remarkable number of ribs and small bones lying around—plus the fact that these are the remains of a young elephant which, according to Fletcher Jamieson, was killed by lions. It would seem to indicate that no hyenas turned up after the lions had abandoned the remains. Usually all such bones are gone, and there is little but the skull and vertebra, and possibly a thigh bone or two, left.

TWO BUFFALO COWS

These cows were shot by Jamieson there with a right and left from his Holland double 500/.450. And he could not have used a more suitable weapon for the job. They were obviously two well-placed shots or the two cows would not have fallen together like that—one at least would have run some way before dropping. That's a dry season photo with the grass more or less burnt off, and it's apparent that there is little cover to conceal the hunter. But with buffalo that does not matter. They, having few enemies, are not usually on the alert, and it is by no means difficult to approach within easy killing range. You don't get cows wandering around on their own, so there must have been a herd there. The bigger the herd the easier they are to approach. Their own curiosity is frequently their undoing. Particularly does this apply when there are a number of cows and heifers in the herd. They *must* see what it's all about, and push and jostle one another in an effort to get to the front until you find the whole darned crowd coming towards you. When that happens let them come. If you attempt to advance they will stop, so just let them come on until they are nicely within range.

Those two cows must have been brought down with neck or shoulder shots to have dropped in their tracks like that.

BUTCHERING A HIPPO

This crowd of men, women and children are impatiently awaiting the moment when they will be given the all-clear. That is, after the hunter's men have taken all they want—possibly the hide for whips and thongs, and of course, the fat and any meat they may want themselves. Then the fun will start! The locals will make a concerted rush, brandishing knives and slashers and bits of sharpened hoop-iron and anything else that will cut, and make for the carcass to get as much as they can. They slash and jab and cut, not only the carcass but themselves and one another. But nobody cares—what does an extra drop of blood matter when there's so much around? And anyway they often don't know they've been cut by someone else—they're much too excited thinking of the gorge they'll be having presently. I've seen a fella get about three inches of sharpened hoop-iron into his backside and, far from being upset, he just yelled to the fool who had stuck him to pull the damned thing out! There were yells of delight from the audience, but the incident was completely forgotten in two minutes, even by the victim himself. There were far more important matters to be considered than a punctured bottom!

The meat of a young hippo is quite good but that of a mature beast is too strong for my liking. Hippo meat is the most fattening meat I know or have ever eaten—the only food I know comparable with it for fattening you is—of all things!—locusts; young locusts in the hopper stage.

Hippo, owing to their amphibious habits, are generally shot in the head, when they submerge without a ripple if you have found the brain but it is not, perhaps, generally known that if wounded in the body a hippo will invariably make for the shore or a convenient sandbank, where, of course, he is easily finished off. But this is well-known to the various hunting tribes who wound them with bows and arrows—usually poisoned—or with spears. They then surround them when they come ashore and finish them off with spears.

ORIBI

Generally speaking these little critters are less numerous than the duiker altho in some districts they are quite common. Like the duiker they are pretty solitary. They are larger than the duiker, and their horns grow appreciably longer but otherwise they are really much the same. Having said that, there isn't a great deal more one can say.

Most men declare that the duiker is the best and tastiest of all these small buck whilst others will tell you that there is no soup on earth to compare with oribi soup. Personally, I honestly don't believe that one of them could tell which beast they were eating! The difference between the meat of any two small buck is not like the difference there is between, say, a duck and a chicken. As with anything else, much depends on the cooking. The meat of these little critters is pretty dry, and if you want the best out of it, you should shove strips of fat bacon thru it and cook it with them there. This makes all the difference, and you will have a most enjoyable and tasty feed.

On account of the type of country they frequent, these buck are almost always shot at fairly close range—the great majority are knocked over with shot guns. You don't often get a chance at them by day except in the very early morning and late evening, and then mostly only during the end of the dry season when the grass is all burnt off. A magnum small bore throwing a bullet of somewhere between 100 and 150 grains is the ideal medicine for them then. But if you want them for the pot, pass up a shot at an elderly one! They become incredibly tough with age. You can get a pretty fair idea of their age by the length of their spikes.

ELEPHANT RAIDER

This is a young bull that persistently raided the food crops. Efforts to discourage him—such as firing over his head—having proved abortive, there was no alternative but to kill him. Actually it's of little use doing anything else, because it has been seen that if you merely scare the elephant away from the crops they are marauding, without killing any of them, they just stroll along to another cultivated patch 10 or 20 miles away and continue their interrupted feed there. But the killing of one or more has a decidedly deterrent effect.

The background here gives you some idea of the matted tangles of thorn to which I have repeatedly referred. There are many stretches infinitely worse than the one shown here but this will show how infernally difficult it can be to get a clear shot even at an elephant once he gets in there. This fellow was killed just on the edge of the thorn. The chief and the bevy of beauties have trooped out from the village to see him and help cut him up.

And that brings up a point of real interest—the truly extraordinary way in which coons will arrive from nowhere after you've dropped an elephant. You bring him down miles from anywhere and have scarcely done examining him when you glance up and there is a naked black figure, spear in hand, gliding silently thru the forest or bush towards you. There are others behind him and when you look around, sure enough, there are others coming from over there, and all making straight for you. Every hunter of elephant has experienced this. They are with you much sooner than the vultures, much sooner, and it does not usually take long for the first of *them* to appear.

And another thing is the rapidity with which news of the kill gets back to the nearest kraals and villages. Time and again I have met the shoals of men, women and kids hurrying out for the free feed, tho I was only on my way back to camp after killing. And oh boy! do they have a time when they get out there! Yelling and shouting, laughing and singing, hacking and slashing and sawing at the great chunks of meat; fires lit all around the place with huge jagged strips of flesh thicker than your arm drying on rough frames over them, and all around them enormous lumps and slabs of the choicest morsels fancied by anyone impaled on sticks and stuck in the ground to toast against the flames. "Nigger Heaven!" Well, if it does not have amongst other things unlimited feeds of free meat it will be a sore disappointment for Jim Fish.

The quantities of meat consumed in these orgies is unbelievable—they eat it literally by the pound. The immense slabs toasting against the flames are merely *hors d'oeuvre*, an appetizer, in spite of the fact that they will be eating them all day. The real feed comes after sundown when the day's work is finished. Vast pots have been crammed with meat and guts and have been stewing all day; as the sun drops other immense pots are put on to boil for the inevitable porridge-cake, the African's staple. It does not matter how much he has eaten, if he does not get his porridge-cake he does not reckon he's fed. (I call it "porridge-cake" for lack of a better name or description—it's just meal poured into boiling water and stirred until it's thick enough to allow you to pick up a handful, roll it into a ball, and dip it in whatever there may be as relish—fish, meat or vegetable, and then cram it into your mouth.) They'll eat till they can scarcely stand, and this will go on for a day or two until the carcass is entirely butchered. They then ease up a mite and concentrate on drying some meat to take home. There's no waste.

DIVING FOR FAT

Not many elephant carry any fat worth mentioning but you occasionally come across a lone bull that will give you a coupla 4-gallon kerosene cans of excellent cooking fat when rendered down. The elephant likes such a wide variety in his diet, and does not mind a 50-mile stroll thru the night to get a change of feeding, that all this trekking around does not give him a chance to build up much fat. But an old lone bull that has found a spot that suits him, does not do so much traipsin around. Rhino at certain seasons carry good fat, and hippo practically always but the best of all is the eland bull, and the buffalo. Their marrow bones—and those of giraffe—if you've ever tasted them will make your mouth water whenever you think back!

The hero in the photo who's head-first into the carcass—or are there two of them?—will soon disappear entirely from sight. They'll wallow around inside, rooting out the choicest morsels, and then emerge covered in blood and gore, laughing and yelling and whooping for joy. They love this game. It matters not a hoot that there is no water within miles in which they can wash they're thoroly enjoying themselves. Those are the elephant's intestines they're lying on in the foreground—they're like pink automobile inner tubes.

They delight in playing practical jokes with these elephant carcasses, particularly when there is one somewhat bloated thru having lain in the sun for a coupla days or so. They entice some of their pals within range and then jab a spear into the blown-out belly. Naturally, there's an immense out-rush of stinking gas and muck and the unfortunate victim probably gets the lot in his face! But he does not care—he'll get some of his own pals the same way one of these days.

I might add that not a scrap of these elephant carcases is ever wasted—except, of course, when you shoot one amongst the Muhammadan tribes—they don't eat elephant. However, there are generally other pagan tribes not so far away, and they will soon get the word that you are shooting and will arrive to collar the free meat. The meat of an elephant will last a coupla families for the best part of a year but the African is very generous and will share with all his relatives and his wives' relatives—he'll never hear the end of it if he does not! But it takes African teeth to chew African elephant.

WATERBUCK BULL

These are amongst the commonest game in Central Africa. Wherever you find any considerable amount of water, there will you surely find waterbuck. If you are in a strange district and see waterbuck, you can bet on finding water close by. They are never found far from water. They are tough critters and can take a lot of punishment if the first shot is badly placed.

The meat is coarse and tough and very strongly-flavored unless it's a young one you've shot. They are quite eatable but I would advise you not to attempt a feed off a mature animal of this species. There is another very objectionable feature characteristic of these beasts and not found with any others and that is that what little fat they have congeals very quickly and very firmly. It may be hot enough on your plate and apparently okeh to eat, but as soon as you get the meat into your mouth the fat congeals on the roof of your mouth and sticks there. It's extremely unpleasant and takes a lot of removing. Personally, I wouldn't attempt to eat waterbuck meat if I could possibly get anything else— even a scraggy native fowl.

But if he can't be recommended for the table, the waterbuck can certainly be recommended as a sporting target. I suppose most beginners in Central Africa start their hunting career on waterbuck and lesser kudu. These two critters might almost be described as ubiquitous.

The one in the photo was shot with a Holland double 500/.450. This was a needlessly powerful weapon for the job. Any good medium bore throwing a bullet of not less than 220-gr. would have been far more suitable. Bullets ranging between 220 and 320-gr. are ideal for all such animals. But I do not recommend a bullet of less than 220-gr. The waterbuck, as I have already said, is a tough critter and covered with long coarse hair. Light bullets tend to break up much too quickly on these beasts. Normally the range works out at between 75 and 175 yards—the latter being a long shot. Unless they've been shot-up considerably they're not difficult to approach.

ELEPHANT COW AND CALF, A FOREST TRAGEDY

This old girl was a very persistent raider of food crops and had to be killed in spite of her young calf. It is an unfortunate fact that when an old cow takes over the leadership of a small troop consisting of other cows and immature bulls and leads them on marauding expeditions, they become incredibly bold and dangerous, chasing and killing the owners of the crops whenever they try to drive the elephant away. Long years of immunity from gunfire teach them to have an utter contempt for Man, because the licensee may not shoot cows. This was just such an old bitch. When she was dropped, she fell on her calf and crushed the life out of the little fellow. This is not an unique incident. Blunt relates an occasion when he had to kill a cow with a small calf, and when she fell the calf put his trunk into his mother's mouth, and she in her final death spasm grabbed the little fellow's trunk between her teeth and smothered him.

Cow elephant are more liable to attack the hunter than are bulls—doubtless the maternal instinct coming to the fore in defense of the calves. Where the bull swings his ears out at right-angles to his head when charging, the cow usually puts hers back, which gives her an extraordinarily vicious appearance. Her charge is just as deadly as that of a bull, and it will sometimes happen that others cows in the herd will charge with her. However, if you shoot her that will generally be sufficient to discourage the others, unless they are very close.

When shooting on license, with cows prohibited, it is really extraordinary how easily a cow can be killed! Sometimes, in very dense bush, it is extremely difficult to say with any degree of certainty whether that big brute in front of you is a bull or a big cow. Normally the tusks would decide the question but mebbe you can only get a glimpse of them—possibly there is a bull there as well, and it's *his* tusks you see—but if you take a chance and shoot, you may well find that you have clean killed a cow, where had it been a bull you would probably only have knocked him out for a few moments and could have let him go had he proved worthless. (A bullet thru the head that fails to find the brain will do no serious damage—it will doubtless give him a headache for a day or two, but he will soon get over it—judging by the numbers of fired bullets I have had brought to me at different times that were extracted from elephant—head as well as body shots.)

Cow ivory is usually short and thin, but of closer grain than bull ivory. It fetches a slightly higher price as its closer grain makes it more suitable for billiard balls. I have only once come across tuskless cows, and then, curiously enough, there were two of them standing together. Tuskless bulls are not so uncommon and are very dangerous—if only because if they get you down they tear you in pieces with their trunk where a tusker will more often than not try to use his tusks, and you *may* be lucky.

INYALA RAM

These are very rare, and the one here shown looks to me like a very good specimen. They live in very dense bush generally around the edge of heavy forest. You will seldom see them in the open other than immediately after daybreak. They are not unlike kudu in appearance, but much smaller and redder in color; whilst the rams have a very considerable mane.

I had never even heard of inyala when I shot my first, and reckoned I had dropped some local variety of lesser kudu. Had I only known it, there was an American fella offering three or four hundred dollars for a complete inyala skin and skeleton at that time! I have found them in one or two places where they were not previously known to exist. At one time they were quite numerous in Northern Zululand but the biltong hunters (market hunters) got to know of it and almost wiped them out. They make very fine biltong, or jerked meat—the South African Dutch are very fond of biltong.

Naturally, being so scarce, they are a greatly prized trophy but take a deal of patient hunting. Because of their rarity they are protected in most parts of Africa now but there are still one or two places where you may shoot them—if you can. . . .

ELEPHANT'S HEART AND TUSK NERVES

Whoever said that the vital spots on an elephant are small would do well to take a look at this photo. There is nothing very minute about that heart—it's only small in comparison with his bulk. But it must be remembered that the bottom of the heart is by no means so vital as the upper region. Selous mentions putting three small bore bullets thru an elephant's heart before he succeeded in killing him. I've seen a Westley Richards capped-bullet from a .577 blow a hole 5-inches in diameter thru an elephant's heart. He didn't require more than the one! As you can see, the heart is practically the same size as the coon's torso.

The tusk nerves, similar to the nerves in your own teeth, vary enormously in certain districts, and even in the same district. Some tusks are hollow for the greater part of their length—very disappointing to the ivory-hunter—whilst others have but little hollow. These latter are mostly very short, very thick, and comparatively straight. Their weight is far greater than you would think. They are much prized by the hunter.

Normally these nerves are taken out and buried close by the elephant's carcass —just why nobody seems to know. I have never known them eaten—and there isn't much in the meat line these Central African coons won't eat! But there it is.

The heart makes quite edible steaks, and I've enjoyed many a good feed of them. Yet the trunk, provided it's properly cooked, is by far the best part of an elephant. But the cooking is a lengthy business—you dig a hole, light a fire in it, and finally remove the ashes. Then put the chunk of trunk in the hole, with its hide on; put a bit of iron or something over the top and light your ordinary cooking fire on that. Cook your meals there for the next two or three days, and then remove the lump of trunk from the hole. Let it cool and you will find that the hide will slip off without any trouble and you will have what resembles a chunk of the most delicious brawn you ever tasted. Naturally, this method of cooking can only be practiced in your base camp but it's well worth while when time is no object. If improperly cooked the trunk is like chewing old automobile tires—only an African could manage it.

opinion on your two pet calibers; but there are others. What of the
.318? Aren't those .318 lovers gonna put up a squeal! I remember
reading in the *AMERICAN RIFLEMAN* some years ago that the
palm for all-around utility was held in Kenya at that time by the
.318. The fella went on to say that as the .318 had been specially
designed for a game killer and had a larger shell it was doubtful if
they could ever equal it with the .30-06. Well, I don't suppose
they could equal it with the '06; but what have you got to say
about the .318 as an all-around gun? There are plenty fellas who
would prefer it to either of your choices.

Lector: Sure. But they're fellas who have done practically all
their hunting in open country. I cannot conceive of any man who
has had real experience of bush work choosing a .318. I dealt
pretty thoroly with the .318 when discussing the medium bores.
It's a grand little weapon in its place; but its place is not in thick
cover. That the *RIFLEMAN'S* correspondent spoke as he did
concerning Kenya and the .318 is quite understandable. You must
remember that by far the greater part of all hunting in Kenya takes
place on the open Athi plains and in the Rift valley. There is
plenty thick cover in Kenya, particularly when you get down to
the coastal belt, but nearly all parties of hunters and sportsmen
head for the plains where game is plentiful and easily found. On
those open plains a .318 is undoubtedly one of the best and most
satisfactory weapons you could use; but that is putting considerable limitation on your all-around rifle, because some of the best
hunting is to be found in the bushveldt where greater stopping
power is called for than the .318 can provide.

It must never be lost sight of that you can drive a bullet from a
low powered rifle right thru a charging animal's heart without
stopping him. You can drill him thru and thru but he will still
come on and kill you before dropping dead himself. It has happened time and again. Elephant, buffalo, lion; they have all killed
their man before dropping dead themselves. Is it going to be of
much satisfaction to you to know that you have killed a charging
lion with a low powered rifle if he has first succeeded in killing you?
I very much doubt it. As I said before, if any of these animals are
encountered in the open the .318 will do very well and will probably prove just as deadly as a .577; but it's a very different thing in
close cover.

No rifle showing less that 40 K-O values can really be considered safe for use in thick cover, at any rate if elephant are on your list. If you are not hunting elephant and have had a reasonable amount of experience, then it might be permissible to use a slightly less powerful weapon. But if you do, my advice is stick to a heavy bullet. Don't look to velocity where close-quarter work is concerned. Use a rifle throwing a bullet of around 300 grains, such as the .366 (9.3mm), .360 N $\stackrel{\circ}{=}$ 2, 400/.350, or .333. Yet why go for a gun like one of those nowadays, when the .375 Magnum is there? The .375 Magnum is undoubtedly going to be *the* weapon in the future, because I understand that Winchester is concentrating on it and the .300 Magnum. Accordingly, its shells will be stocked thruout the continent like those of the 9.3mm were in days gone by.

The only other weapon that could conceivably be regarded as an all-around rifle is the 10.75mm (.423). There are quite a few men who swear by it; there are others like myself who swear at it. An all-around rifle must be a safe weapon to take against dangerous game as well as giving satisfaction when used against a wide variety of non-dangerous animals. Well, I can't consider a rifle that is unable to drive a full patch slug thru a buffalo's shoulder as safe. The 10.75mm is sufficiently powerful to stop a charge under most circumstances; but how can I recommend a rifle for the beginner that will cause him to be charged on many occasions where a better weapon would have put a charge out of the question altogether when first fired? I have already pointed out that a buffalo with a broken shoulder is a horribly dangerous proposition in long grass or thick bush; yet a 10.75mm will smash the shoulder without killing. So that, unless finished off at once, that buff will clear off with a broken shoulder. It can quite easily happen in the long grass beloved by the buffalo that some little time must elapse before the fellow brought down with the shoulder shot can be given another slug to finish him.

Then the 10.75mm fails thru lack of penetration when soft-nose slugs are used against some of the heavier kinds of soft-skinned game, including lion. It's staunchest supporters all admit this lack of penetration. There was one fella shooting buffalo in Assam who mentioned bringing down a very big bull with a shot on the shoulder from a 10.75mm. He said the bull was down for about five seconds, then got up and cleared off. This fella and a companion followed-up the buffalo on an elephant. The companion was armed with a double .470; yet they had to put five more shots, from both rifles, into that buff before they succeeded in killing him. They probably wouldn't have been telling the yarn at all had they been obliged to follow the bull on foot as they would have had to do in Africa.

I knew another man who dropped a buffalo with a shot in the neck from one of these 10.75s, thought he had killed him, handed his rifle to his gun-bearer, and was strolling quite casually towards his buff when the beast scrambled to his feet and came. If that fella hadn't been passing close to a convenient and easily-climbable tree, he could never have escaped. As it was, he just managed to pull himself up out of reach of the buffalo as the infuriated beast reached the foot of the tree. The buffalo then switched his attention to the gun-bearer; but that lad wasn't waiting to be caught. He dropped the rifle and swarmed up another tree. The bull savaged the rifle a few times, which didn't do it any good; and then cleared off, apparently little the worse for his adventure. They never saw him again. A safe rifle, that?

It was in just such a manner that many a man in the days of black powder and lead bullets was killed by buffalo. And it was this that gained for the buffalo his reputation for savage vitality and ruthless power. A buffalo can be killed quite easily with modern rifles if you don't lose your head or allow them to scare you; and they would never have gained such a reputation had men been more suitably armed in days gone by. It's extremely doubtful if a charging buffalo could have been stopped with certainty in the black powder days with anything less powerful than an 8-bore, or a very heavily-loaded 10-bore. But today you can stop him with certainty with a .375 Magnum—a medium bore rifle.

Auctor: But your own K-O values show the 10.75 to hit a somewhat heavier punch than the .375 Magnum.

Lector: I know. But only for bare head shots. In that discussion that ran thru *GAME & GUN* some years ago there was a good deal of talk about these two rifles, and more than one lover of the 10.75 tried to compare it with the .375 Magnum; others asked questions as to how it showed up in comparison. Let me show you some of the talk that went on in the correspondent columns. Here is an extract from a letter of mine at the time:

". . . Col. Alexander had told us how he pole-axed a buffalo in Assam with the bluff-nosed solid 300-gr. bullet from his double .375 Magnum at under 50 yards range. In reply to a question of mine, he stated that the bullet had taken it thru the shoulder blade. He then went on to describe how he shot another buffalo at 150 yds. range, hitting it behind the shoulder with a similar bullet fired from the same rifle. It was not even knocked down much less pole-axed. 'Jungli Bains' then wrote to describe how he had shot a buffalo at 180 yds. range with a 10.75mm (.423) Mauser and the buffalo was knocked down for a count of five, then got up and staggered off. On the strength of this he claims that his rifle hits a heavier blow than does Col. Alexander's—at any rate at ranges upwards of 150 yds.

"Unfortunately, 'Jungli Bains' omits to tell us where he hit his buffalo. But, assuming that it was neither in the head nor in the neck, then I contend that it must have been either in the shoulder blade or spine. From my own experience I have not the least hesitation in declaring that no rifle on the market, particularly when loaded with solids, is capable of knocking down an animal weighing upwards of a ton at ranges in excess of 150 yds. if the bullet fails to strike any bone larger than a rib. Accordingly, it is obviously unfair to compare the result of his shot with Col. Alexander's, since the latter definitely stated that his took the buffalo behind the shoulder.

"Now, quite apart from the theoretical aspect of the question—from the point of view of the ballistics of the two rifles—I can assure both Col. Alexander and 'Jungli Bains' that had Col. Alexander hit his second buffalo on the shoulder-blade, he would have killed it instantly. I speak from my own experience. I have shot a number of buffalo in the same way, but the most recent—only yesterday morning—was quite the most outstanding.

"I shot a very fine bull out of a large herd at a range of 177 very long strides, well stretched out so that they could not have been less than 36 inches in length, with the bluff-nosed solid 300-gr. bullet from my Holland .375 Magnum. The bullet took the bull on the shoulder-blade and he dropped instantly. All he was capable of doing was to lift his head just a few inches from the ground and then let it fall again. He was totally paralyzed, and was dead within certainly not more than a minute. Had there been even a tiny tuft of grass between me and him I should never have noticed that slight movement of his head, and would have written that I had pole-axed him stone dead at a range of 177 yards—and written it in all honesty and truthfulness. At the same time I shot three other members of the herd at various ranges between 150 and 170 yards. All three of them were hit behind the shoulder (two of them with the same bullet); all three ran for some distance before falling; all three loosed the same mournful bellow as they died— but the big bull never made a sound or a movement beyond that slight lifting of his horns. For all practical purposes of sport he could be said to have been killed outright.

"Which, I think, effectively answers 'Jungli Bains'' question concerning the relative power of the .375 Magnum and .423(10.-75mm)-bore rifles."

That letter was written some years ago; but subsequent experience has done nothing to make me alter the opinion contained in it. The 10.75mm has sufficient power to enable it to stop a charge, as my K-O values show; but its lack of penetration makes it a dangerous weapon other, perhaps, than when in the hands of an experienced man who knows the rifle and knows of this very serious fault. In my humble opinion the rifle in no way deserves the amount of space I have felt compelled to devote to it; but I have not grudged it, because this weapon has so many devotees who loudly recommend it that I dread the thought that, if I failed to emphasize its bad points, I might indirectly be to blame if some beginner allows himself to be persuaded to invest in one. I repeat, I consider it an insidiously and inherently dangerous weapon.

I hardly think it is necessary to consider the .416 and .425 bore rifles. Surely nobody would be thinking of using 5,000 ft.-lbs. of energy other than on dangerous game. They are both magnificent killers, and are eminently safe weapons to take against the big fellas; but unless your hunting was almost exclusively of them, you would hardly be wanting so much power. The only other rifle that might possibly be considered is Rigby's .350 Magnum, with the .350 N≗2 as its double barreled brother. These are certainly splendid arms and are most satisfactory over a wide range of animals, almost as wide as the .375 Magnum. The bullet is too light for elephant in thick cover; but I almost think that we may put elephant in a category by themselves. As an ivory-hunter, it is only natural that my thoughts should run constantly on elephant when discussing rifles, and I have to keep reminding my-self that there are thousands of sportsmen and hunters who have not the slightest intention of ever going after those big grey ghosts of the forest, but who are keen to hunt lesser beasts. Personally I would have no hesitation in using the .350 N$\underline{o}$2 for all other animals; but I would like to see the beginner throwing a slightly heavier bullet at rhino in thick bush or when following-up a wounded lion. These two rifles—their ballistics are identical—have much greater stopping power than their ballistics and bullet weight would seem to indicate, and this is undoubtedly due to the speed and depth of penetration of the bullet. I had excellent results when using these rifles, but never used them alone because I was concentrating on elephant and wanted heavier bullets as I was hunting in very thick bush.

If elephant are not on your list, and you have a decent shot gun in your battery, as you are almost certain to have, or better still a "Paradox," with which to back up your rifle if you are un-lucky enough to wound a lion, then, assuming that you are a steady shot and take the greatest care to place your bullets where they will do the most good, you can use any of the better medium bores for general all-around African hunting. However, I'm afraid it's asking rather a lot of the totally inexperienced beginner to come up to the above specification! So, if you don't want to be bothered with a large battery of rifles, my advice is to use either a double .400 or a double .375 Magnum.

CHAPTER VIII

Sights, Sighting and Trajectories

IT's AN EXTRAORDINARY THING TO ME HOW CARELESS THE AVERAGE man is over this question of sights. The majority don't seem to give a thought to it at all, and are quite satisfied to accept the rifle "off the peg" with whatever sights happen to be on it. The gunsmith who built the weapon couldn't possibly know for what particular purpose it was eventually going to be used, and therefore could do no more than fit a compromise in the way of sights.

I must admit that the greater number of British gunsmiths seem to have not the remotest idea of the sighting requirements of a big ga ue rifle, if one may judge by the sighting combinations they normally fit on their stock rifles. A lot of the trouble is undoubtedly due to the fact that the few men who have written on this matter have been mostly those who have done by far the greater part of their hunting in very open country, and fill most of their space and give the bulk of their advice in connection with sights suitable for that type of shooting. I can hardly bring to mind a single man who has written a book about African hunting who has even mentioned the sights on his rifle; if he has it was probably only to bemoan the fact that the ivory bead had dropped off his foresight without anybody noticing until he wanted to use the rifle. There are, however, just two or three of the best gunsmiths who really do seem to know what is needed; but they are very definitely the exceptions.

Just as there are different rifles for different types of hunting, so also are there different combinations of sights which should be fitted to these weapons to give the user the greatest possible advantages. Of what earthly good is it having a superbly suitable weapon for certain purposes if you completely nullify its suitability by having it fitted with totally unsuitable sights?

One of the greatest mistakes that gunsmiths make is in mounting the backsight too close to the breech on double rifles and single loaders. There is not the same likelihood in the case of magazines because of the long bolt action; but on doubles this is a point of the greatest importance. When I say too close to the breech, what I mean is, of course, too close to the shooter's eye. There was an experienced hunter in Tanganyika who found that he habitually got about 40% high shots with his double .470. He heard or read somewhere about this possibility of the backsight being too close to the breech, had his shifted some 3½ inches towards the muzzles, and found that those high shots were a thing of the past. I had myself noticed long years ago that I could pick up the sights on most magazine rifles quicker and much more clearly than I could on my doubles—which seemed strange; but when I learnt about the correct position of the sight and measured mine, I found that they were all from 3 to 4 inches too close to the breech. There are some gunsmiths who illustrate in their catalogs and keep on display in their showrooms beautiful best grade double rifles with the backsights mounted immediately in front of the chambers, or even in one case I know of, right over the chambers! And the rib so short that there was no possibility of shifting the sight farther forward. It's only fair to state, however, that there are just a few firms who are very particular to mount their backsights well away from the shooter's eye.

It's a very simple matter to find out the distance that best suits you—just make an imitation backsight out of anything at all (but don't let it be white or it will catch your eye too easily), and slip this on the rib of your shot gun. Then slide it towards the muzzles until you can see it reasonably clearly when aiming at some object. Measure the distance from there to the heel of the butt, and then when ordering or buying a new or secondhand rifle you can always have the sight mounted the same distance from the breech.

You may be told that the longer the sightbase, or sight radius—the distance between the two sights—the more accurate the rifle. That is perfectly true in theory; but theory and practice don't always coincide. It's what happens in actual practice that matters to the hunter, and it actually happens that you can shoot with a much greater degree of accuracy when you can see your sights clearly than you can with a much longer sightbase in which the backsight is merely an indistinguishable blur.

I found that 24½ inches was the distance that best suited me, but had all my backsights mounted 26 inches from the heel of the butt to allow for age creeping on. Because as is well-known now, a man's eye's powers of accommodation—their ability to rapidly alter their focus from near to distant objects—fails with age, and I didn't want to be bothered having to have my backsights altered at intervals, since there are no gunsmiths around this neck o' the woods. Altho on paper my rifles may not be so technically accurate as they were, I know that I can shoot much more accurately with them than ever previously—and that's all that matters to me.

The usual sights consist of a foresight and an open barrel backsight.

FORESIGHTS. The customary pattern is the bead, and this is certainly the best type for use in conjunction with the open sight. For African use I am certain that the beads usually fitted are much too small. A very fine bead may be necessary if you are shooting very small animals at long range in open country wherein the light is good; but the general run of animals shot in Africa justify a larger bead which can be picked up much more quickly if a quick shot is called for. You have only to tell your gunsmith what you want and he will fit it. For the big rifle I like an extra large bead because it can be picked up instantaneously in heavy forest wherein the light is frequently bad. Since this weapon is only used at close quarters against large animals there can be no objection. In the case of smaller animals too large a bead might blot out too much of your target; but that does not apply to your big gun. Have each and all of your rifles sighted with particular reference to the work for which they will mostly be used.

Some men like the face of the bead to be rounded; but personally I much prefer it to be flat and inclined slightly at an angle to catch any light that's going. Whether or not there is really any practical disadvantage in the rounded bead I cannot say, tho the theorists will put forward objections. I have used both patterns successfully. The flat-topped blade foresight is not too good with open sights, other possibly than in very open country. It should be used in conjunction with a plain flat-topped backsight, not with a V or U. For quick shots at close quarters there would be a grave risk of taking too much of it and shooting high.

Ivory-tipped foresights are delightful to use so long as the ivory tip stays put; but it shrinks in the heat and drops out all too often, besides being liable to be knocked off. White metal or platina can be fused onto metal and cannot be lost. Most beads are fitted with platina, which is very satisfactory. My own preference is for gold-faced beads; but the gold should be dull and not highly-polished. Enamel-faced beads I also found excellent; but don't get cheap ones. The price of a foresight is a very small matter when compared with the total cost of the rifle, so get the best.

OPEN BARREL BACKSIGHTS. I have only seen two patterns of these in Africa, the V and the U. The British makers always fit the former; but the Germans seemed to prefer the U. I don't like it. It necessitates a small bead foresight, and in my experience tended greatly to blur. But the open V should be broad and shallow. Here again gunsmiths have a habit of fitting a deep narrow V in conjunction with a tiny little foresight, even on powerful double rifles. Such a combination is all wrong. It's quite impossible to pick-up the almost microscopically small bead as it nestles away down at the bottom of the deep cleft of the V if a quick shot is called for, or if you are trying to aim at some big black animal such as a buffalo as he stands in the deep black shadow in heavy forest; whilst the shoulders of the V blot out the entire countryside. Have the backsight wide, so that the shoulders come well out over the barrels on each side, and the V cut just deep enough to accommodate the bead of the foresight—so that the top of the bead is level with the shoulders of the backsight. Have all sharp corners and points smoothed off, so that the V becomes more of a smoothly-rounded depression than a definite notch. This, after much experimenting, I have found by far the best shape and pattern, both for quick shots at close quarters and for longer shots.

The backsights should slope slightly towards the muzzles on all your big game weapons. If you are told that this will cause it to dazzle you in more open country, that will be quite true if the sun happens to be in a certain position behind you; but not otherwise. In heavy forest the light is often poor on account of the branches of the trees meeting overhead, and you will find a sight sloping towards the muzzles a very real help. It will not by any means *always* dazzle you when used in the open, and I consider it advisable to have the weapon sighted in the best and most suitable way for the most difficult work it will have to perform, and wherein matters can very easily become a question of life or a sticky death. The shots you'll take with this weapon in more open country will usually be much easier. The vertical backsight that so many men advocate can also dazzle you if the sun is in the right position; but my principal objection to it is that it can, and sometimes will, merge completely into its background when you are aiming at a dark-colored animal standing in deep shadow. I found this a real handicap on more than one occasion when hunting buffalo, as I found that it was necessary to lower the foresight until it disappeared and then raise it again to make sure that I was taking the bead, the whole bead, and nothing but the bead. That sort of thing is much too slow when the buff may have been wounded.

Do not be persuaded to have a collection of those fascinating little leaf sights in addition to the standard backsight that almost all gunsmiths love to fit. They are only a temptation and will inevitably end in a high miss. Don't I know it? Don't we all know it? Yet I have known men to buy rifles because they were ostensibly sighted for some fantastic range like 600 yards or even 1,200! The fixed standard and then four or five of these little leaves each marked for an additional 100 yards. Westley Richards must have had a psychologist on the staff of his export department once upon a time! I remember seeing two fellas in Rhodesia looking at his .425-bore magazine rifle in a store. It was fitted with a 28″ barrel and in addition to the fixed standard sight for 100 yds. had four leaves each for another 100, and then a tangent marked up to 1,200 yards. Said one fella to the other: "Man! but that must be a powerful weapon. Think of shooting a buffalo two-thirds of a mile away! I must get one of those rifles." And he did, and so did his companion. I often wondered afterwards how many buffalo they shot at 1,200 yards; how many they even saw at half that distance!

Have but the one backsight, have it regulated to give you a 2 or 2½-inch bullet rise at 100 yards, study the trajectory curve of your rifle and in the event of a somewhat longer shot than usual being called for, just aim a mite higher on the animal's shoulder to allow for the drop of the bullet at that range. If you do this, there will be no fear of you missing high thru having over-estimated the range.

At first glance it may seem a horribly theoretical business to study the trajectory curve of a rifle, but actually it only means remembering one, or at the most, two figures, the amount by which your bullet drops at 250 yards, and possibly 300. And that last can be happily forgotten because you will seldom if ever shoot at 300 yards in Africa—altho you may think that you are!—and in any case the drop will be almost exactly double the drop at 250; so there should be no difficulty in remembering it if you have memorized the drop at that range. I'll come back to this again when we get to trajectories.

APERTURE OR PEEP BACKSIGHTS. Men out here (and in many other places) have a notion that these are only suitable for target work. But the peep-sight is by far the best and quickest of all iron backsights for use in open country. Use the largest possible aperture and have the sight mounted as close to the eye as you safely can. On magazine rifles I like it mounted on the tail end of the bolt, but this can not always be done with safety to one's shooting eye.

But it must be remembered that when a peep-sight is being used the open backsight must be folded down or removed entirely from the rifle. If not, you lose all the advantages of the peep-sight. And *don't think about using it*. Don't *try* to centre the foresight in it; your eye will do that of its own accord. Just look thru it—not *at* it; place your foresight on the spot you want to hit; and squeeze. Nothing could be simpler or quicker.

As fitted on double rifles, they have to be mounted on the grip and frequently prevent a comfortable grip of the rifle. But Holland have a pattern of their own which is let into the strap of the action and folds down quite flush with the grip. But on doubles they would be very liable to become entangled in things, or festooned with grass or trailing creepers, so I do not recommend that they be carried ready for instant use. However, if you use a double for your medium or small bore, or in the case of an all-around rifle, you can carry the weapon with the open barrel sight raised and the peep folded down, and then if you are offered a shot at long range, you will have plenty of time to fold down the open sight and raise the peep; thereby giving yourself all the advantages of a sightbase almost double that given by the open sight and of a perfectly clear view of your target, which you cannot get with the open sight. This is a real help if the animal is partially concealed in bush or grass.

The open backsight should be fitted with a small strong bolt to definitely hold it up when you are hunting around, and prevent any possibility of it being accidentally pushed down. It should also have a strong spring to keep it down when not wanted. But these are small details and any good gunsmith will fix you up.

Those who haven't used the peep-sight may think that I make too much song and dance about it, and that it's really not worth the trouble of having it mounted on doubles, particularly if it can't be carried ready for instant use. Let me assure you it is well worth it. I have vivid recollections of a day when I was very badly off for meat for my men. The wind had been blowing about from all points of the compass, and no matter what I tried I just could not get a shot. It was infernally hot, but we had absolutely nothing to eat in camp and I simply had to get something. Finally, when it was getting along towards sundown, I got my chance. It was no easy shot, and had to be taken quickly lest the treacherous wind would again scare the animal, as it had done so often during the day. I was offered a shot at a lesser kudu bull at almost exactly 200 yards. He was almost entirely concealed from view behind bush and small trees. I had no scope sight. I was so tired, I simply couldn't see him at all over the open sights—there wasn't much of him visible, but what little there was disappeared entirely when I tried to aim. Then I remembered my peep-sight. I flipped down the open sight, raised the peep, and dropped that kudu with complete certainty.

The peep-sight's only real disadvantage is said to be that it cannot be used in a bad light; yet I have on more than one occasion killed animals with the aid of the peep-sight when it was so dark that I couldn't use the open sights at all. But then I always insist on extra large apertures on all my peep-sights, and have them mounted close to the eye—as close, that is, as one safely can.

When I speak of a peep sight being fitted as close to the shooter's eye as safety permits, you will please bear in mind that I am solely concerned with African shooting. I am fully aware that in America shooters are constantly being warned of the dangers of getting the peepsight driven back into their eye when the rifle recoils—especially when shooting "up the side of the mountain." I'm certainly not gonna disagree with that but then in Africa you practically never get such shots—whilst you may literally spend a "lifetime" in the African bush without ever firing a shot from the prone position. In all the years of my hunting career, and out of all the thousands of rounds of ammo I've fired at game, I can only remember *two* shots fired from the prone position and both of those were exceptional cases; so exceptional that I will take time out right here to tell about them.

The first was a monstrous man-eating croc that had been playing havoc with the local injuns for a long, long time, and took a coon I knew only the previous night. I was determined to get him. I stalked him across a big sandbank at midday, pushing ahead a little heap of sand in front of me as cover. It took me about an hour to get into position for a certain shot and oh boy! was I roasted by that white-hot sand—to say nothing of the sun! But I got the brute.

The other was when I was canoeing down the river and stopped overnight on a large stretch of sand that ran out from the bank. Being the dry season, we were all just lying on rugs or mats on the clean white sand. There was a good moon. Since I knew that lions were apt to come gamboling along these sandbanks, playing around like kittens, my Manton double .470 shared my sleeping rug with me, loaded with soft-nose-splits. Something woke me during the night and my hand dropped to the rifle grip as I looked up without lifting my head. But it wasn't lions. It was a troop of waterbuck that were coming along for a drink. I must have heard their hooves crunching the sand. As we needed camp meat, I slid forward the muzzles of the rifle, rested them on my pillow, and let drive. But, I repeat, those are the *only* two shots I can remember firing from the prone position—and nobody would have tried using a peep sight at night.

I believe in handling and shooting a rifle exactly as I handle and use my shot gun. I like to stand up straight to my shot and as fully 96% of my shots are fired like that—with the remainder from the kneeling position—I have my rifles built with plenty downpitch and a fairly high comb so that I can keep my head well up and use both eyes, even if I'm steadying the rifle against the side of a tree. If you shoot like that you can have a peepsight mounted on the tang with perfect safety irrespective of the power of the rifle. I have *never* had the butt of a rifle leave my shoulder when firing. Even the time that old double .600 gave me a double-discharge which knocked me down, I distinctly remember that the butt remained on my shoulder until the up-throw of the barrels took the entire weapon backwards over my head as I fell into my gun-bearer and the bush. The butt did not slide off my shoulder and whizz back to knock my companion's head off. I could have been using a tang peep sight on that occasion and still have the use of my shooting eye.

But I fully appreciate that if you are doing much belly flopping and then "stock-crawling," a peep sight too close to the eye might well be dangerous. But that does not apply to African hunting conditions. I had Holland build me to order one of their .375 Magnums solely to try out their then-new peep sight mounting, which I think must be located similar to the Howe-Whelen bolt-sleeve mounting, which I've heard about but never seen. I found this mounting most excellent, and used it extensively. It was with this rifle that I killed the 411 buffalo and more than 100 elephant, besides some lions and a considerable quantity of lesser game. There was a folding open barrel backsight as well but I never used it. I did all my shooting with the peep sight, which was about 2 inches closer to the eye than the original mounting directly on the end of the cocking piece.

Personally, I wouldn't hesitate to have a peep sight mounted on the tail end of the bolt on *any* magazine rifle, including the .500 and .505. I used such a sight on my Rigby .416 Mauser with the greatest satisfaction, and killed many elephant and lion with it when they were encountered in the open. It was solely because of its aperture sight that I used the .416 because it's unwise to try using a peep sight on a heavy double other than in the open, as it might interfere with quick reloading and become festooned with grass, trailing vines, creepers, or something of the sort in thick cover. So far as I know, Holland are the only folks who fit the peep sight on the tang of double rifles so that it drops into a recess in the long strap they fit and there is therefore no fear of it, when folded down, interferring with your manipulation of the safety catch. And by no means all my rifles were Hollands, nor were they all built to order for me.

But if there is any likelihood of you "stock-crawling" or if you are in the habit of shoving your head very far forward when aiming, or if you have foolishly bought yourself a badly-fitting weapon, then let nothing I've said persuade you to have a bolt-head sight fitted on your rifle if it's a magazine, or a tang sight if it's a double or single-loader.

TELESCOPE SIGHTS. The sole object of mounting a scope sight on a rifle is to give greater precision in aiming. There is NO other object. They are not the "lazy man's tool," as I have sometimes heard them described; the idea presumably being that they save the fella the trouble of getting closer. I have killed many elephant at ranges between 30 and 60 yards with the aid of scope sights that I'm quite sure I would not have succeeded in killing with any other type of sight. I had tried both open and aperture sights and was quite unable to get an aim. I had to slip my bullet thru a tangle of branches and leaves, and the foresights prevented me seeing what I was doing. There have been other times when the big bull was standing on the far side of a bunch of cows and immature animals, and it was impossible to get into a better position because I would have given my wind to other members of the herd. It meant skidding my bullet across the back or neck of some beast so as to get it into the big fellow. The slightest mistake would spoil things. Open or aperture sights weren't good enough. For a tricky shot of that nature where the fraction of an inch out will ruin all, the scope is ideal.

Then there is the man whose sight is failing. I had a good friend in a German hunter of great experience who was so short-sighted that he always carried a pair of 6X Zeiss prismatics around his neck when hunting, even in scrub and bush. His tracker pointed: "M" used his glass to see whatever there was to be seen and then took over his scope-sighted rifle and got into action. If he didn't kill most of his elephant with it, he certainly killed a large proportion of them that way. His two double rifles were fitted with the most gigantic bead foresights I have ever seen—he couldn't see anything smaller. If there were no such things as scope sights, he would have been compelled to quit elephant hunting many years before.

The various disadvantages that their detractors put forward against scope sights may have held good in days gone by but they certainly can't uphold them today.   Naturally, I'm not concerned with cheap scopes cheaply mounted.   In the past the Austrians used to supply a scope on their Mannlicher-Schoenauer for a mere $25 extra.   Needless to say they sold a lot of them—there are always those who will buy anything that seems cheap—but it goes without saying that they were little better than useless.   But best grade modern scopes are a very different proposition.   Provided you have them properly mounted they will stand up to about anything.

The scope sights that have always given me the greatest satisfaction were the Lyman "Alaskan," the Hensoldt "Dialytan," the Zeiss "Zeivier," another small Zeiss that only weighed 7 or 8-ozs., on big game rifles, and a Weaver on miniatures.   There are doubtless others, but those are the best of those I have used.

Many British gunsmiths used to be averse to fitting scopes on the larger calibers—upwards of .400; but now I think they will all do so.   Experience has shown that, *provided they are properly mounted*, best grade scopes will stand up to nearly anything.   They have been fitted on double .465s and .470s for tiger shooting at night.   I well remember how astonished some of these firms were when I asked them to fit scope sights on some of my larger weapons; however, word got around and the next thing was that they were getting similar orders from some of the Indian princes.

I have never yet had an opportunity of trying out the Leupold scope; but I have been hearing such good reports about it that I shall be using one by the time this book appears in print.

I was greatly intrigued by a remark of Keith's in his *"Big Game·Rifles & Cartridges."*   He states that a scope sight is not too good when shooting towards a low-hanging sun, and that under such conditions you should remove the scope and use your iron sights.   Now this is directly contrary to my experience.   I have always reckoned that when the sun was low on the horizon in front of me, a scope sight was incomparably the best of all sights with which to take the shot.

I remember on one occasion I had to shoot-up a number of hippo that had been making a nuisance of themselves.   It was my job to teach them a lesson, and to do that effectively I needed to kill three or four of them. I paddled across a small lake to a cluster of rocks in the centre of it on which the hippo were sunning themselves. I knew they would slip into the water on the far side of the rocks when they saw me coming but I guessed I could take up a good position amongst the boulders from which to get busy. The hippo did as I expected, but they would not get out of the rays of the setting sun which were blazing right off the water into my eyes. I tried open, and then aperture, sights, but it was quite useless. I could not get any sort of aim at all. So I took over my scope-sighted rifle and killed four of them without the slightest difficulty.

I have also heard it said that a scope-sighted rifle would be entirely unsuitable for use against lions—that the scope would be a liability. That may be so if you have foolishly allowed your gunsmith to mount the thing away up in the air so that you can't rest your cheek against the comb of the rifle when aiming but I certainly don't agree otherwise. Naturally, you wouldn't attempt to follow-up a wounded lion with a scope-sighted rifle but if you have encountered a bunch of lions in open country and open fire with a scope-sighted rifle on which the scope is mounted in the correct low position, and you find yourself being charged by one of the females after killing a male or two, I personally reckon you will stop that charge with greater ease and certainty than ever you would with any other pattern of sights. The reason for this is, that with the scope the aiming post is in constant focus with your target. You have nothing to bother about except holding that post on the right spot and squeezing your trigger whenever you feel like it. With iron sights you have to switch your eye rapidly backward and forward between backsight, foresight, and the lion to make sure that all three are in line. You experience a curious impersonal sensation when watching a charging lion thru a scope sight that helps to keep you from becoming flurried but which isn't easy to describe. You find the same sort of thing when taking a running shot; you just swing with the beast, keeping the aiming post well forward on his shoulder, and squeeze the trigger whenever you feel like it. It's as easy as following thru your binoculars the fortunes of your favorite in a steeplechase.

But it's absolutely essential that you have your scope mounted as low down as possible. You will not be wanting to use the open sights when the scope is on the rifle—why should you? This used to be made a big point with the British and Continental firms before the war but the sole reason behind it all was that they didn't want to go to the trouble of bending the bolt lever of magazine rifles so that they would clear the eye-piece of the scope. Until all scopes are built with an eye-relief of about 6 inches, permitting them to be mounted with the eye-piece on the receiver of the rifle, immediately in front of the bolt lever, then the bolt levers will have to be bent back so as not to foul the scope. There is no reason whatever why all bolts could not be manufactured this way; there already is a pattern in which this has been done. I refer to the Enfield '14.

On double rifles the matter is simpler but it would be a great advantage if the scopes had sufficient eye-relief to enable them to be mounted with the eye-piece flush with the breech ends of the barrels.

Auctor: Your mention of scope sights for running shots being easier than with open or aperture sights is directly contrary to what I have always heard and understood. I seem to have always heard that scope sights were slow for such work.

Lector: As I have already stated, I belong to that school which never attempts to press trigger until it can clearly see its way to make a kill. In my early days I several times attempted what appeared to be very easy shots at running animals, with both open and aperture sights—I don't of course mean open and aperture sights used together at the same time—but the results were invariably the same; I hit the animals too far back.

Pick up any book on African big game hunting and read on until the author describes how he took a running shot at a lion or other beast, and how the lion "acknowledged the bullet with a grunt of rage" but carried on, and how on subsequent examination it was found that "my first shot had taken him too far back." It is always the same, and the explanation is to be found in the fact that, with ordinary iron sights a man will give a final glance at the sights the instant before he squeezes the trigger just to make absolutely sure that they are as he wants them, and this momentarily takes his eye off his target. This will inevitably cause a momentary check in the swing of the rifle which will cause the bullet to hit the animal too far back. I know that there are men who try to intercept an animal by aiming at a given point ahead of him and then firing the instant they think he is close enough but you will never kill by such a method other than by a fluke.

The only method of shooting a moving target with any degree of certainty whatsoever is to swing with the target and fire without checking the movement of the muzzles until after the trigger has been pressed. The slightest check in the swing of the muzzles will mean a miss behind in the case of a bird, and a hit too far back in the case of an animal. The greatest exponents of the shot gun will tell you that checking the swing is one of the greatest difficulties they have to overcome and that they frequently miss a bird in spite of all their practice thru this very fault, so what hope has the big game shot in Africa who gets no practice at all, as you might say, since running shots are not frequent?

For years, after those early disappointments, I never attempted to shoot a running beast other, perhaps, than an elephant stampeding directly across my front at very close range. But after I took to using low-powered, low-mounted scope sights I found that it was almost as easy to hit a running animal as it was a standing one. Because with a scope sight there is no taking your eye off your target for a last glance at the sights, since the aiming post of the graticule is superimposed on the part of the animal you want to hit and in constant focus with it.

On one occasion I bagged four buffalo with a scope-sighted .375 Magnum; the first, a big bull, standing, and the remainder as the herd stampeded across my front. With open or even aperture sights I should not have attempted it; I should have been satisfied with the first, and then followed-up the herd and bagged another, after which I should have done the same thing again and continued until I had gotten my four. It might have taken me half a day to kill them all, whereas, with the scope sight I bagged all four in about half a minute.

Auctor: Don't you think you might say something about reticules or graticules or whatever they call the things? Which patterns do you prefer and why?

Lector: Glad you're there to jog my elbow from time to time. There is so much to say if genuinely helpful advice is to be given, that omissions are all too easily made in a book of this description. I ought not to have overlooked the question of which of all the many different aiming devices one sees in scope sights are the best.

Since one of the principal advantages of a hunting scope over a target scope is the much larger field of view given you by the former, why go and clutter it up with a lot of fat black pillars and side bars? A favorite type of graticule consisted of a fairly thick vertical post with a sharp pencil point and a couple of horizontal side bars, just as thick, extending over fully a third of the field on each side. What was the object in them? Another type had the vertical pillar with the sharp point and a medium-fine horizontal cross wire. That was better, but I do not like that sharp point for general African use. It is not always easy to get it into definite focus and it has an infuriating habit of disappearing altogether when you are aiming at some big dark-colored animal standing in deep, black shadow. The plain cross wires were, I think, better, but by no means ideal. Personally, I much prefer a flat-topped vertical post designed to coincide with the bottom of a 4″ bull at 100 yards. Whether or not there is a medium-fine cross wire along with it seems immaterial, to me at all events; I can shoot just as well with it as without. I find this pattern by far the best for general African use, either by day or night; in fact it makes by far the best night sight there is, always provided the scope is properly mounted.

And speaking of night sights brings us to the question of power. For African hunting you do not need a powerful sight; on the contrary, a low-powered scope gives you a much larger field of view and better light-gathering qualities. For night work a low power is essential. From 2 to 3 magnifications will be found not only ample, but by far the most generally satisfactory. In fact I might have said from 2 to 2½. The animals are of good size and the ranges close; your scope is merely to enable you to take a clear and surer aim, not to magnify your target.

I have frequently heard it said that the sportsman who hands his rifle to an African coon to carry for him won't long enjoy the benefits of a scope sight. Well, that certainly hasn't been my experience. I have found that the African, not having been accustomed to many possessions, is far more careful of anything I hand him to look after than I would be myself. It's true he'll turn things upside down always in preference to having them the right way up (the Indian, incidentally, is just the same), which makes it inadvisable to carry liquids around unless the containers are exceptionally well corked, and will invariably look at a picture paper upsidedown but I cannot remember ever having to reprimand any man of mine for dropping or knocking down a rifle of mine. Whenever my rifle has been sent clattering to the ground, I have been the guilty party by standing the rifle against a tree, sitting down with my back to the tree, reaching around to get the makins or something out of my hip pocket, and have my elbow send the rifle flying. Besides, scopes can be mounted and removed from the rifle so easily nowadays without the need for tools, that there is no real need for it to be always carried on the rifle if you are scared of the boy dropping it. It can be carried in its holster. Apart from my own experience—and I have never yet had a scope injured— there was that German friend of mine who never removed the scope from his rifle, nor did he ever have it injured.

A scope sight is not essential for African hunting; you can get along very well without it. But if you have ever tried a properly mounted low-powered hunting scope, you will not be satisfied without one. You may only want it now and then; but when those occasions arise, you will be mighty glad you had it.

TRAJECTORIES. As I have already stated, the trajectory tables which I give at the end of this chapter are taken with the author's kind and generous permission from *Notes on Sporting Rifles*. It will be noticed that the rifles are all sighted so that they will group approximately in the centre of a 4″ bull at 100 yards, and that is all that you need bother about. When ordering a rifle, tell your gunsmith to take the "6 o'clock" aim on a 4″ bull at 100 yards and have the rifle group not lower than centrally in the bull—then test it yourself and make sure that he has done so. The only exceptions are the .577 and .600 bores, which ought to group along the bottom edge of the bull or better, perhaps, centrally in a 2″ or 3″ bull at 50 yards. Since such weapons would only be used at close quarters that is ample for them. But for the others, if you have them sighted in this manner, you will not have to bother your head about estimating ranges.

Of course, if you do all your hunting in very open country at ranges which generally lie beyond 300 yards, then you will naturally give yourself a greater bullet rise at 100 yards, so as to get the benefit of the flattest possible trajectory *at the ranges at which you mostly shoot.* But that does not apply to Africa. If you give yourself a bullet rise of 3 or 4 inches at 100 yards in Africa and then try to take a shot at a lion's head when he puts it up out of the grass 90 or 100 yards away, you will probably clean miss him. The idea is to have the rifle so sighted as to give you as flat a trajectory as possible over the ranges at which you generally fire, whilst keeping the bullet so low that there will be no risk of you missing animals at closer ranges. And experience has shown that a bullet rise of 2″ to 2½″ is just about right. Since 300 yards is generally considered the ultimate maximum at which you would attempt to shoot an animal in Africa, and very, very seldom as far as that, all we need consider is the first 300 yards of the bullet's flight. And the accompanying diagram showing the trajectory curve of the bullet from a .240 "Apex" rifle which has been properly sighted to give the owner the greatest possible benefit from the flatness of the trajectory, will clearly show what I mean:

Muzzle	*100 yds.*	*200 yds.*	*250 yds.*	*300 yds.*
	2.0	0.0		
Line of Aim ———————————————————————————————
0.75		0.0	3.0	7.8

Note:—Measurements above and below the line of sight are given in inches.

It will be noted that the bullet starts off below the line of aim. That is because the sights are mounted some three-quarters of an inch above the axis of the bore; the bullet then cuts the line of aim and rises 2 inches above it at 100 yards. That is the highest point of its curve. It then begins to drop and again cuts the line of aim at 200 yards. Thereafter it continues below the sight line until at 250 yards it is 3 inches below. But what does that matter? The man behind the rifle has nothing to think about over those 250 yards except holding steady and squeezing the trigger. A 3-inch bullet drop is nothing; from the muzzle right up to there the rifle has been shooting well within a 3-in. circle, which is very much closer than 99 men out of 100 could hold under practical hunting conditions. That is therefore the only figure he need remember; in fact, if you come to think of it, he needn't even bother to remember that; he should now have a mental picture of what is happening to his bullet; accordingly, he need only remember to aim a trifle higher on the animal's shoulder. Once you know the bullet curve of your rifle, this aiming higher is perfectly simple. But *you must know it,* and not merely guess at it.

Therefore the proper sighting for this rifle is for 200 yards and for 200 yards only. If it is sighted for 100 yards and then given a number of additional leaves for various ranges, this splendidly flat trajectory is really being wasted, because its real object is to cut out the bug-bear of trying to estimate the range. Everybody is inclined to over-estimate the distance; have you ever heard of a man saying that he under-estimated the range and had his bullet kick up the dust between him and the animal? Not in Africa, anyway. On the other hand, what is easier than thinking the animal is farther away than he really is, flick up another leaf, and have the bullet whizz over his back?

To take another example:

The H & H .375 Magnum, firing the 270-gr. bullet, shows the following trajectory curve:

	Muzzle	100 yds.	175 yds.	200 yds.	250 yds.	300 yds.
		2.0	0.0			
Line of Aim						
	0.75		0.0	1.5	6.0	13.0

Note—Measurements above and below the line of aim are given in inches.

Here again the only figures you need to bother about are 6 inches and 13, well, call it a foot—a difference of 1 inch at 300 yards is not worth considering and makes it easier to remember. But once you *know* your bullet-drop and are not merely guessing at it, you will find that you do not think in terms of inches at all—you just hold a wee bit higher on the shoulder than you normally would.

All modern rifles in the same group have, for all practical purposes, similar trajectory curves; as I have already stated, a difference of an inch at 250 or 300 yards is not worth considering when it comes to actual hunting—the animals do not measure off exactly the distance they stand from you. For instance, to take the .240 whose curve we have just followed, all rifles in this group—.240; .242; .246; .250; .260; .270; .275; .280—will all have identical trajectory curves. And then, if you are inclined to imagine that this business is altogether too complicated as there are far too many curves to remember, just ask yourself: how many rifles have you and in how many groups do they fit? Most men have only two rifles—a large bore and a medium. The large bore will not be used beyond the range for which it will comfortably stand sighting, so that you have nothing whatever to remember with it; so that just leaves you with the medium bore, and you have only to remember its drop at 250 yards if it is one of the Magnums. If it is one of the older rifles, you can remember its drop at 200 and again at 250; and remember that the drop at 250 is just about double that at 200. Surely that isn't very difficult. If you add a small bore to your battery, since it will probably be a Magnum, you need only bother about its drop at 300; the drop at 250 is too slight to need actual remembering. In a word, if the animal looks very far away, just aim a mite higher than you normally would and let it go at that because the beast almost certainly isn't as far away as you think he is.

In connection with these trajectory tables, the following are Burrard's own words:

"The trajectories given are those obtained with ordinary sporting rifles fitted with 24″ barrels in the case of those weapons which are usually made in magazine form, and 26″ barrels in the case of doubles. In actual practice the charge of powder used in a double is slightly less than that used in a similar magazine-actioned rifle so as to allow a slightly larger margin for excess pressure. The result of this is that the M.V. from a double is not quite so great as that given by a single rifle, and the resulting trajectories will be found to be approximately the same if the double is fitted with slightly longer barrels.

"Allowance has been made in every case for the actual line of sight being above the centre of the bore. . . .

"The plus sign denotes the rise of the bullet above and the minus sign the drop of the bullet below the line of sight at the particular ranges given.

"For purposes of practical convenience the intermediate distances for rifles which should be sighted for 150 and 175 yards have in both cases been given as 100 yards. This will enable the sighting of all rifles to be carried out at this convenient range. As a matter of fact the culminating points of the trajectories actually occur at

80 and 90 yards respectively, but the figures given for 100 yards may be taken as being sufficiently near, for all practical purposes, to the actual greatest rise of the bullet above the line of sight in each case.''

It should be borne in mind that if a rifle is sighted for 150 yards, or any other distance for that matter, that merely indicates the second intersection of the bullet with the line of aim. Its trajectory is not flat merely for the distance indicated, but for some distance beyond that point until it has dropped, say, 3 inches below. The distance beyond will vary according to the bullet's capacity for overcoming air-resistance, and that will depend upon its weight, shape and diameter. Speaking generally, you can allow yourself from 25 to 30 yards or thereabouts beyond the distance for which you have the rifle sighted.

RIFLE WHICH SHOULD BE SIGHTED FOR 250 YARDS

Rifle	Bullet	Ranges in Yards				
		100	150	200	250	300
.280 Halger............	100	+1.8	+2.5	+1.5	±0	−2.8

RIFLES WHICH SHOULD BE SIGHTED FOR 200 YARDS

Rifle	Bullet	Ranges in Yards			
		100	200	250	300
.375 Magnum.........	235	+2.4	±0	−4.0	−10.5
.300 Magnum.........	150	+2.0	±0	−3.0	−8.0
.300 Magnum.........	180	+2.4	±0	−4.0	−9.7
.280.................	140	+2.0	±0	−3.0	−8.0
.280.................	160	+2.2	±0	−4.0	−9.7
.275 Magnum.........	160	+2.2	±0	−4.0	−9.7
.275 Rigby............	140	+2.5	±0	−3.7	−9.25
.260.................	110	+1.9	±0	−2.9	−7.5
.256 Magnum.........	135	+2.5	±0	−4.5	−10.0
.250 Savage..........	87	+2.2	±0	−3.5	−9.2
.240.................	100	+2.0	±0	−3.0	−7.8

RIFLES WHICH SHOULD BE SIGHTED FOR 175 YARDS

Rifle	Bullet	Ranges in Yards				
		100	175	200	250	300
.404	300	+2.3	±0	−1.8	−7.1	−15.0
.375 Magnum	270	+2.0	±0	−1.5	−6.0	−13.0
.375 Magnum	300	+2.4	±0	−1.9	−7.4	−15.4
.350 Magnum	225	+2.2	±0	−1.7	−6.9	−14.4
.333	250	+2.3	±0	−1.7	−6.9	−14.7
.318	180	+2.0	±0	−1.6	−6.4	−13.6
.256	156	+2.5	±0	−2.1	−8.0	−16.6

RIFLES WHICH SHOULD BE SIGHTED FOR 150 YARDS

Rifle	Bullet	Ranges in Yards				
		100	150	200	250	300
.505	525	+2.0	±0	−4.9	−13.0	−25.4
.500	570	+2.2	±0	−5.2	−14.0	−27.0
.476	520	+2.2	±0	−5.2	−13.5	−26.0
.475 N ≗ 2	480	+2.2	±0	−5.0	−13.0	−24.6
.475	480	+2.2	±0	−5.1	−13.1	−25.3
.470	500	+2.2	±0	−5.0	−13.0	−24.5
.465	480	+2.2	±0	−5.0	−13.0	−24.5
.425	410	+1.7	±0	−4.2	−10.8	−20.6
.423 (10.75mm)	347	+2.2	±0	−5.1	−13.2	−25.5
.416	410	+1.7	±0	−4.0	−10.5	−19.7
.405 Winch'ter	300	+2.2	±0	−5.3	−14.0	−27.0
.400 Jeffery	400	+2.1	±0	−4.9	−12.6	−23.9
.366 (9.3mm)	285	+2.0	±0	−5.0	−12.0	−22.5
.360 N ≗ 2	320	+2.1	±0	−4.4	−11.8	−21.8
.350 (400/350)	310	+2.1	±0	−4.9	−12.6	−24.0
.318	250	+1.7	±0	−4.0	−10.4	−19.6
.300 Magnum	220	+1.7	±0	−3.8	−10.1	−19.2
.275 (7mm)	173	+1.9	±0	−4.5	−11.2	−21.3

TRAJECTORIES OF MINIATURE RIFLES

Rifle	Ranges in Yards			
	25	50	100	150
.22 Long Rifle (R.F.)	+1.4	±0	−8.25	−27.0

CHAPTER IX

Marksmanship in the Bush

You do not need to be a crack shot to be a successful African big game hunter. Steadiness and patience are of far greater importance than actual marksmanship. Naturally, you've gotta know how to shoot, how to aim and how to squeeze your trigger instead of yanking at it, but you don't have to get discouraged and postpone your proposed African expedition just because you can't put them all in the black at 600 yards on your home range. I've never done any target shooting in my life, other than zeroing a batch of service rifles at 25 yards but I always manage to keep the pot boiling and, given a decent rifle, seldom need more than the one cartridge to do it. I'd probably look the veriest tyro on the range but there's many a fine target shooter who's quite useless in the Bush. Big game shooting is an utterly different sport from target shooting—as different as baseball from cricket. And just as you use entirely different tools in those two games, so do you require entirely different tools for the two different types of shooting—different weapons and different sights—whilst the methods employed are also quite different.

There's a certain type of imaginative man who likes to give the impression that he knows a hell of a lot more about hunting than he actually does, and who almost invariably starts his book with a foreword or preface in which he disparages every other writer on the subject with the idea of conveying the impression that the reader is at last going to get the real inside dope on the business from a genuine hunter, someone who really knows. That done, he then goes ahead, giving his imagination full play, and spins any kind of goddam yarn he fancies, feeling pretty sure it will be swallowed. Almost invariably, sooner or later, you will

236

come to where this hero has dropped some animal stone dead in its tracks with a clean brain shot at some incredible range like 750 yards. You will meet others who will try to tell you the same thing. Well, we all know that the most extraordinary flukes will occasionally come off—particularly where the vagaries of stray bullets are concerned—but the point is, what the hell was the fella doing shooting at an animal 750 yards away? If he was the hunter he would like to have you believe he was, how come he couldn't get any closer than that?

Then there is the question of judging ranges. African hunting takes place under such a wide variety of totally different conditions —from the wide open plains thru different types of scrub and bush to light forest and then into heavy forest with or without dense undergrowth—that I defy any man to be able to estimate correctly the distance away that an animal may be standing under each and all of these conditions. A man who does most of his shooting on the open plains may in course of time become fairly proficient in judging distances in the districts with which he is familiar, but that same fella would be quite lost if taken to light timber country, and vice-versâ. Open country generally makes an animal look much farther away than he really is, especially in the early morning, but it can be extremely difficult when there is nothing to give you a comparison. For instance, you can see the line of an animal's back as he passes thru some kind of scrub growth where the plains are slightly undulating; it might be a rhino passing thru fairly high stuff, or it might be a lion slouching along thru quite short stuff. The line of the back of these two animals is almost identical; they each carry the head low; they each have high withers and hips and a hollow back. But altho the difference in size is considerable, it can be very difficult to say just which it is when there is nothing around to give you an idea of the height of the stuff thru which the animal is walking. There are certain types of timber which seem to magnify an animal, either giving the impression that it's a much larger beast than you at first thought, or else that he's very much closer than he really is. There are other types of bush which seem to act like telescopes looked thru from the wrong end—and they are by far the commonest.

But the fact to be remembered is, that provided you have your rifles sighted-in in the manner I suggest in the chapter dealing with that subject, you do not need to worry about range—no matter what you may think the distance is, it's a hundred to one that it's well under 200 yards. I have repeatedly stated thruout this book that the average range at which animals are shot in Africa—in any part of Africa—will average between 75 and 175 yards, with just an occasional, very occasional, shot at 200. Let those boastful individuals shout all they like about killing at 650 and 750 yards; you think in terms of actual facts—and the actual facts are that the range practically never exceeds 200 or at the very most 250 yards.

The only parts of Africa I know where a slightly longer shot might have to be taken is when hunting that somewhat rare desert antelope—its name eludes me for the moment—which is found to the south-east of Malakal in the Sudan. It's a white beast with long, straight horns not unlike a small oryx. From the nature of its habitat it's not too easy to approach, but to compensate for that, it's not hunted to any extent. A 250-yd. shot *might* be called for here. Then there's the giant eland, also found in the Sudan. It's also very rare and, I think, strictly protected. It's generally found in somewhat undulating country inclined to be stony, with open scattered timber and not too much undergrowth. The big fellow is very shy and generally on the alert. It's very difficult country in which to make a close approach: the small stones, more or less concealed in the short grass, are all loose and persist in rolling whenever a foot is placed on the ground. I seem to remember Selous, describing his assignment to collect specimens of these eland for the British Museum, saying it was the toughest he had ever undertaken. A scope-sighted Magnum would undoubtedly be a great help to you here. However, I do not think you are likely to get permission to shoot one of these animals.

The only other place I can think of at the moment where you may be called upon to fire at upwards of 200 yards, is if you are trying for one of the scarce variety of gemsbok that are found in the desert country to the south of Mossamedes in Angola, Portuguese West Africa. Even there, however, it is extremely improbable that it will be necessary to shoot beyond 250 yards. And the same applies to that weird, semi-amphibious beast, the sittatunga. The swamps of Lake Bangueolo are *the* place for them, but owing to their habit of living in the sudd, your only chance of getting a shot is to try and catch them on the firmer ground around the edge of the swamp at first crack of dawn. The going is so difficult for you, that a close approach is practically impossible if they are any distance away when you first spot them. Under these conditions a longish shot may be necessary but 250 or thereabouts should be far enough. Here again you will find a scope-sighted Magnum a real help—the light can be very tricky at earliest dawn, and there is usually considerable mist rising from the swamps at that hour. You will find it very deceptive, and will appreciate a low-powered scope.

So you see, even for these, the most difficult of African shots on the most difficult of African game to approach, as far as my experience carries me the statement I made a little while ago—that the range practically never exceeds 200 yards, or at the very most 250—still holds good.

I am by no means alone in stating this so emphatically. Let me quote from Major H. C. Maydon, a very keen and observant amateur who has been hunting whenever he could get the opportunity for the last 30 or more years, and who amongst various other books edited the *Big Game Shooting in Africa* volume in the Lonsdale Library. Speaking of range etc., he writes:

"Choose a carbine or short rifle since it is easier to carry in thick bush and you will not need long shots. Try to get a rifle with a flat trajectory up to 200 yards and tear off all other sighting leaves. They only put you off or get pushed up by accident at the wrong moment, or persuade you that you can kill further than you ought. The best range is the nearest possible, with 200 yards as your limit. Never farther than 200 yards? Well, almost never. When you must break that golden rule, take a full sight and pin your faith in Nimrod. He'll play up if you are playing fair. . . . Shoot as much ordinary game as you can with the magazine rifle until you have learnt something of stalking, of judging distances, of native guides, of fatal shots, and, above all, of your own self-confidence. Then, and only then, collect your heavy rifle and go for the heavy game."

Now there is genuine advice from a real hunter who honestly wants to assist those with less experience than he has had, and who is not concerned with any boastful claims anent his own prowess or skill. Compare that with the claim made by another writer whose book is in front of me right now and in which he states that on one occasion, thanks to knowing the trajectory curve of his rifle, he was able to kill a stampeding elephant at upwards of 600 yards with a brain shot, by aiming some three feet above his head and three feet in front of him! True, he mentions that such shots could not always be brought off to order, but the impression given is, nevertheless, that such shots are by no means unusual for a man of his skill and experience. It does not occur to him to tell us anything about trajectories. You will frequently see game at considerably more than 200 yards range but why open fire right away? If you are anything of a hunter you will be able to get very much closer. If you can't be bothered doing so, then the veldt is no place for you. You are here to hunt—if long range target shooting appeals to you more than hunting, then surely the rifle range will suit you better than the African veldt.

Mirage, that bug-bear of the target shot, will not worry you under ordinary hunting conditions out here. In hot dry open country, such as you will find in the North-West Frontier province of Kenya, for instance, the mirage is considerable, and you will see a herd of zebra or other game apparently standing up to their hocks in a shimmering lake of water; but it would seem as tho the mirage acted both ways and prevented the animals getting a clear view of you as you approach, because under such conditions you will have little difficulty in getting within your 250 yards altho there is no cover at all, and you will then find that the lake has either disappeared entirely or else is now beyond your quarry. Doubtless, if you were to try a shot from the prone position, you would be bothered by mirage still, as well as being well grilled by the scorching hot ground but if you shoot from either the squatting position or take a standing shot, as I always do, steadying your rifle on your gun-bearer's shoulder, you will have no difficulty in killing clean. In all similar districts, where the temperatures run around 120 or more in the shade—if you can find a bit of shade!—you will find the same thing; but generally speaking mirage would only begin to worry you beyond the ranges at which you should shoot.

Many men, shooting in the East African highlands, complain that their rifles shoot from a foot to eighteen inches high, particularly in the early morning when most shooting takes place. They blame it on the rarefied atmosphere. Now the Highlands of East Africa vary between 4,000 and 9,000 feet above sea level, and altho the difference in atmospheric pressure will be quite apparent to those unaccustomed to such altitudes, they could not possibly affect the velocity of a bullet to the extent of throwing it three feet high, as I once heard a man state. He said that the lowering of atmospheric pressure spelt a corresponding increase in velocity. As a matter of fact a lowering of atmospheric pressure actually means a slight *decrease* in velocity, since the bullet meets with somewhat less resistance during its passage up the bore and therefore gets ahead of the expanding powder gasses, as it were, which causes a slight reduction in barrel pressure and therefore a reduction in muzzle velocity. But this is entirely theoretical; in actual practice the change in velocity is so slight at the altitudes at which shooting takes place, that it can be ignored. Admittedly, after the bullet has left the muzzle it then meets with less resistance, and consequently retains better its initial velocity. Accordingly, the only effect a high altitude can have is to slightly flatten the trajectory, and even there the difference will be hardly noticeable —certainly not at African altitudes.

In the Himalayas in India it is quite usual for sportsmen to hunt at altitudes ranging between 14,000 and 18,000 feet above sea level. Burrard mentions doing so with a pal of his who was using a .375 and a .303; Burrard was using a .280 and a .400. They were most careful to observe all shots so as to check theory by actual practice over this question of altitude. Burrard states that neither of them noticed any change in sighting being necessary, and reckoned that his .280 gave him a slightly flatter trajectory at ranges between 300 and 350 yards. Now such altitudes are very much higher than any found in Africa, at least as far as the hunter is concerned, and therefore the rarity of the atmosphere cannot be the answer to those men's trouble who find their rifles apparently shooting high in East Africa.

Personally, I have little doubt that refraction of light is to blame. In the early mornings and late evenings there must be layers of air lying at different heights above the ground all at different temperatures, because it cools quickly and considerably in the Highlands in Africa when the sun drops, and begins to heat up again pretty rapidly next morning after the sun is up. An animal seen under such conditions will have its position distorted until it appears to be standing a foot or more higher than it actually is—just as a fish seen in water will probably not be within a foot of where you stab a spear in unless you are looking practically straight down on him.

Speaking generally, and this is borne out by every other hunter with whom I have ever discussed such matters, it can safely be stated that one always over-estimates the range in Africa. In my early days, before I knew anything about trajectories, I used to be fascinated by those little leaf sights, each marked for an additional 100 yards or meters, with which almost all British and Continental rifles are fitted in addition to the fixed standard backsight. I used to carefully estimate the range and then flip up one of these little leaves, aim most carefully, and then—have my bullet skim over the animal's back. Again and again it happened, but for long it didn't occur to me that the fault was mine—that I was over-estimating the range.

Sometimes, if the animals haven't been shot at much, and a wild shot is fired, they will just stand there looking around and wondering what on earth is happening. I remember on one occasion, when I was very new to the game, I was trying to kill some wretched little beast for the pot. He and a companion were standing in an almost dry water course with a high perpendicular bank immediately behind them. I judged the range at slightly under 300 yards, put up the 300-yd. leaf—I was using a brand-new .303 sporter, "Mark VI" ammo—aimed a bit low and let drive. My bullet hit the bank feet above the little buck and knocked some dirt and small stones down. The little beast looked round at the bank and then looked round towards me, but otherwise didn't move. Realizing that I had overestimated the range, I put down the 300-yd. leaf and flipped up the one for 200 yards. Again I fired, and again the bullet smacked into the bank above the little buck. He decided it was no place for him and with his companion headed for more peaceful pastures. On another occasion I was given either four or five shots at a reed-buck and missed them all in exactly the same way. I can think of yet another similar occasion with a wart hog. Misled by the ground mist in the very early morning which enormously magnified the animal, I at first thought it was a buffalo. I crept up closer, however, and then saw it was only a hog. But I again overestimated the range and clean missed him with my first shot. That was the last time I ever used leaf sights or any other kind of adjustable sight. And what misses I have had since then are at any rate not due to overestimating the range.

Nevertheless, one's eyes can play one strange tricks at times. There are two occasions that come immediately to mind. I was hunting for meat for my men and spotted a kudu bull with his harêm. I had no difficulty in getting within about 80 yards of him. I was using a 9mm Mauser by Churchill. I saw the bull standing broadside on to me, and not having learnt the shoulder shot at that time, I placed my bullet close up behind his left shoulder. The cows cleared off and the bull took a wild gallop around in a circle that would probably have taken him some fifty yards or so had 'he been running straight. He then collapsed. I was quite confident of the shot and just waited for him to fall. However, I was always anxious to see if my bullet had indeed taken the animal where I had intended it to, because I was mighty keen to become a good game shot, so I went along to examine him. He was lying on his right side, which was unusual, as animals generally fall on the wounded side when shot with "ordinary" rifles—not so with the Magnums—and I was astonished to see no bullet hole behind his shoulder. I told my men to turn him over, and there sure enough was the bullet hole behind his right shoulder. His *right* shoulder, mark you; yet I could have sworn I placed the bullet behind his left shoulder. How can you account for that? "Optical illusion" jumps immediately to the lips; but that's altogether too easy. I could readily believe that my eyes had been deceived so that I imagined the bull to be looking towards my left when in point of actual fact he was looking towards my right; but I cannot believe that my rifle was also deceived. Because in that case my bullet should have taken him thru the flank just in front of the right hip, surely? The answer? I haven't the remotest idea.

The second occasion was very similar and took place some two or three years later. I was again hunting for meat for my men, and this time it was sable antelope I spotted. I took the shot at about 90 or 100 paces. I had by now learnt the shoulder shot and the bull dropped in his tracks with, as I supposed, my bullet thru his left shoulder.   But it wasn't thru his left shoulder—it was thru his right shoulder.   My rifle that time was a Farquharson-actioned falling-block single-loader by Greener built to handle Rigby's 400/.350 shell.

My eyes?   I've never had any trouble with them; it's only within the last few years that I've taken to wearing glasses for reading.   Hooch?   No; I'd learnt my lesson by that time.   So what? To this day I can't answer.   There have only been those two times in all the years I've been hunting but they are as vividly before me today as they were when they happened.

There's one word of advice I might slip in here: Always take plenty shells with you when you go hunting.   There is nothing more infuriating than to have a wounded animal in front of you and not a single shell left with which to finish him off.   It happened to me once, and I've taken darned good care that it never happened again.   I went out with a Martini-Henry carbine (577/.450) to shoot something for my own pot.   This is, of course, a single-shot weapon, and a killer at close ranges.   I spotted a klipspringer—a small antelope—up on the side of a rocky kopje. I fired for his shoulder, but the smoke prevented me seeing clearly what had happened altho pretty sure of my shot.   However, I saw a klipspringer leaping in its characteristic way from rock to rock, and naturally imagined that it was my little beast because I could see that he was wounded.   I scrambled up the side of the kopje and then realized that my bullet had gone thru the animal at which I had fired and then into a companion.   I didn't know there were two of them there.   My little fella was stone dead but there was now the wounded one which must be put out of its misery, and I had not bothered to bring any extra shells along. It was a horrible business, because the light was failing and it was impossible to go back to camp, get some cartridges, and return again before dark.   My boy found the wretched little beast dead a couple of hundred yards away next morning.   Maybe it was as well I didn't attempt to follow that evening, or it might have gone much farther.   But it taught me never again to go out without plenty shells.

I knew a fella who lost a mighty elephant bull in the same way. He didn't go out with only one cartridge but he only had what were in the magazine of his rifle, and he was one of those idiots who believed in "filling him full of lead." He took a head shot which went a trifle too high, and then emptied his magazine into the elephant as he cleared off. One shot wounded him slightly in the lungs, and another in the hindquarters. The remainder were apparently misses. The bull was pretty sick both from the head shot which had passed close to the brain, and also from the lung shot. He ran about half a mile, and then pulled up. The hunter followed in the hope that he might find him dead but had to return to camp as he had no more ammunition with him and the light was failing. He knew his men could never run there and back before dark; accordingly, there was nothing to do but quit. He went out next day but the bull had moved off during the night and he failed to find him. He quit the district a day or so following and when out hunting myself a day later, I came on this magnificent tusker, looking fairly sick but still very much alive, and killed him without any difficulty.

It's better to bring back a belt or bag of shells unfired than to run short—you can always use them later—and anyway you won't be carrying them yourself.

In East Africa I suppose more shots are fired from the squatting position than from any other. Personally, I do not like that squatting position—maybe it's an acquired taste. In bush, scrub and forest, of course, it's out of the question. Fully 96% of my shots are fired from the standing off-hand position and by that I do not mean any of those weird positions and attitudes adopted by small-bore marksmen in competition shooting. You hold your rifle in the most natural and comfortable position, not only with the shot in view, but also in such a manner that you can reload with ease, speed and the least possible amount of movement and noise on your part, and so that you have complete control over your weapon at all times. In a word, you handle it as you would handle your pet shot gun. When hunting game you can forget pretty well your target-shooting lore—at least as far as African shooting is concerned. Your trigger-squeeze is about the only thing that remains the same. Forget all about your rifle—you know it's a good'un; you know your shells are okeh; right, forget about 'em; above all, *forget all you've ever heard about muzzle-blast and recoil.* Concentrate on placing your bullet where it will do the most good and you won't even notice the recoil or report.

By "squatting" position, I mean sitting down on the ground, both feet flat, knees drawn up, and elbows resting on the knees. It's very popular on the open Kenya plains where the grass is seldom more than a foot high, if that. But as I say, I very much prefer to drop on one knee, *with my backside well down on that heel*, and steady my barrels against the outside of my gun-bearer's thigh, he bracing his leg firmly against the ground. You get a beautifully steady shot like that.

And don't, I beg of you, *DON'T*, do as this guy did I'm going to tell you about. He was very nervous of buffalo, but very keen to shoot one. His own account of how he went about it is an excellent illustration of how it should *not* be done; but also an equally excellent illustration, I'm afraid, of how it is done all too often. He finally got his chance when he struck fresh spoor coming out of a dense patch of bush known to be a refuge for buffalo. Here is how he describes it:

". . . .Everything went in my favour. When within approximately one hundred and fifty yards, I singled out the largest animal, took a standing aim just behind the left shoulder and away sped the bullet on which my cherished hopes rested. Instantly the herd, which proved to be seven bulls, came thundering down along the track they had previously made—instinctively, I presume, taking the shortest cut back to the safety of their beloved Jassie.

"It seemed that I was in imminent danger of being trampled into oblivion. This, however, did not at the time cause me the least anxiety—*I simply rammed clip after clip of cartridges into the magazine and fired into the herd.* When within fifteen or twenty yards they swerved slightly and thundered past, heads down in a cloud of dust. I caught sight of a spurt of blood from the shoulder of one, evidently the one first fired at. . . .

"Now wild with excitement I tore after the vanishing herd, shouting and cursing at Mondoropuma for not lending a hand.

"This gentleman was safely up a tree. . . . He implored me not to go any farther, but all fear of buffalo had left me, and I plunged on as hard as I could go. A child could have followed the splashes of blood left by the herd; *goodness only knows how many I had wounded* in my desperate endeavour to bring one down.

". . . .A short time was spent following up fresh blood spoor left by the other buffalo I had wounded, but these were abandoned at the edge of the Jassie where they had taken refuge. Why no trouble was experienced from following *at least four or five of these wounded animals* I cannot attempt to explain. Perhaps some other unfortunate hunter reaped the benefit." (The italics are mine.)

Well there it is. And he is so proud of it that he has written it all in a book so as to tell the world. If I had ever behaved in such an outrageously unsportsmanlike manner, far from telling the world about it, I should hide it away in the depths of my evil past and sincerely hope that the world would never get to hear about it.

Did he do a single thing right? He was scared and yet used a totally unsuitable rifle—a .303 magazine (215-gr. bullet, M.V. 2,060, M.E. 2,030, K-O value 19.2); he opened fire from the comparatively long range of 150 yards; he planked himself on the track made by the troop when they emerged from their sanctuary and along which his common-sense, if he had any, ought to have told him they would very likely return; in a frantic mixture of panic and anxiety to get at least one, he blazed off wildly into the brown of the herd—unaimed shots. He admits wounding "at least" four or five apart from the one he killed—the first one at which he fired. If he was anything of a rifleman he ought to have known exactly where his bullet had taken the bull, and therefore, since he had been hunting for some years, he ought to have known that the beast was mortally wounded and therefore his without any more shots having to be fired. He then admits tearing after the wounded animals as hard as he could go, in spite of his tracker's warnings— (I certainly don't blame that hero for seeking the safety of a tree, since he had been with this man some considerable time and must have had his own opinion of him as a hunter!).

Now I have seen and heard of this sort of thing again and again, not only with buffalo but also with elephant and rhino and on countless occasions have heard men describing exactly similar occurrences. They don't seem to realize that such accounts of their ineffableness are merely nauseating to the real, genuine hunter. But men who could behave like that are beyond shame and would readily find specious excuses for themselves.

I headed this chapter *Marksmanship in the Bush* but really there's precious little to say on that aspect of African shooting—

as I find now that I've come to discuss it. Marksmanship, as such, is really of secondary importance in view of the size of the animals shot and the comparatively short ranges at which they are shot. The great thing is to pick your spot and put your bullet there— not just anywhere at all into the "brown" of the beast.

You can fill these African beasts with lead and still lose them if your first shot was badly placed. I can give you an example of what one of them can stand: I was shaking and rotten with malaria once upon a time, and my men had absolutely nothing left to eat—I simply had to go out and try to get them something. Now malaria plays the devil and all with your vision whilst the fever is on you. I first of all mistook two or three wart hogs for as many lions and then clean missed a sable bull antelope at barely 60 yards. I reeled along and presently came across a roan antelope bull at about 90 paces. I had two rifles with me—a 9mm and a 10.75mm. I used the 9mm and hit but didn't know where. We followed the roan and I got another shot shortly afterwards. And then another, and another. And still the wretched animal wouldn't fall. I was pretty nearly blind by now, but simply had to get that meat. I exchanged the 9 for the 10.75 but it didn't seem to be much better. However, after several more shots, we found the unfortunate roan's stomach and the greater part of his intestines lying on the veldt, so I perked up a bit; I guessed he couldn't get much further without that lot. Still, it took another two or three shots from my shaky and nearly blind state to finish him. Now that's not a nice story, and I don't like telling it but the malaria was directly to blame and the absolute necessity for getting my men something to eat. Altogether, I fired 13 shots into that wretched roan before killing him—simply because the first was badly placed.

The South African Dutchman, the "backveldter," is taught to shoot the hard way. His father hands him a rifle, probably an 8mm relic of the Boer war, almost as soon as he is big enough to carry it, and two shells. He is told that he is to go out and bring back some meat; the second cartridge is to enable him to finish off a beast if he is unlucky enough to only wound with his first shot. If he fires his rifle and fails to bring home the bacon, he will get the daylights walloped out of him with the rifle's own steel cleaning rod. And that's not merely a threat—it's one of the few promises the youngster can be perfectly certain his father will keep! If he kills clean with his first shot, he can do what he likes with the other—no questions are asked concerning it. Numerous backveldters have told me that this is how they all learn to shoot. It makes them good meat-getters from the very beginning; and if they were permitted to use only single-loaders all would be well. The trouble is that they all use Mausers and are never satisfied until they've had a shot at everything in sight with hair on it.

With reference to placing your bullet in the right spot, not merely for humanitarian reasons for the sake of killing the animal with the least possible infliction of pain and suffering, as well as to save yourself needless tramping, it also ensures that you do at least know at what you are firing. At first glance that may sound like the wanderings of delirium, but I can assure you it is nothing of the sort; more than one gay hunting party has ended tragically thru one member of it shooting and killing a companion by accident. A party of four guns was beating thru a patch of grass and low bush into which a lion had been seen to make his way. They couldn't keep in sight of one another, and one excitable sportsman, seeing a movement in the bush on his half-right front, let drive and shot his own brother dead. Another similar case was that of a party driving wild hogs in the same way, and one of them not waiting to see what it was that moved, blew off a pal's face with a soft-nose bullet from his 9.3mm Mauser. Yet another, which comes nearer home, was that of a professional guide and hunter taking a very keen but excitable visitor around. They were hunting in a patch of thick bush known to contain rhino. The guide was in front. Suddenly the visitor thought he saw something, swung up his rifle and blazed off—shattering his guide's right elbow with a .470-caliber slug. And there were many, many, more.

There is one type of shooting that appears to beat hunters in all parts of the world and that is when they are shooting steeply downhill. They either don't give a thought to it at all—until after they've missed!—or else they give too darned much thought to it in the light of all they've heard and read about the difficulties of such a shot, and all the different theories that have been forwarded from time to time concerning it. Such shots are few and far between in African hunting; but they occur occasionally.

My own explanation is the awkward and strained position you are compelled to adopt to get your eye in line with your sights.

The almost inevitable result being that you take too much fore-sight and so shoot high. Try aiming at a mark on the carpet a few feet in front of you, and then aim at a picture on the wall. You will find the latter much easier, simply because your sights come up and level themselves up in line with your eye; whereas, when aiming downwards you have to force your head and neck for-ward and downward to bring your eye to the line of the sights. Don't bother your head with questions of gravity and bullet-drop at various angles, or any other theoretical explanations. Just re-member that you are firing from an infernally uncomfortable posi-tion and that if you aren't careful your bullet will pass over the animal's back—and make the necessary allowances. That is, when shooting downhill aim low, and the steeper the angle the lower you must aim.

Auctor: When you gave us Major Maydon's advice to beginners, you may remember he said something about taking a full sight if you are shooting beyond 200 yards. I know there are many men who vary the amount of foresight they take for different ranges, and you frequently hear the expression, "I took a very fine sight," or "I took a full sight," or something of the sort; and there are some gunsmiths who actually recommend this method of aiming in their catalogs. What is your reaction to that?

Lector: I'm afraid that was an unfortunate choice of wording on Maydon's part tho I agree that there are a great many men who say they aim in that manner. The whole object of a bead foresight is to enable and help you to always take the same amount of foresight when aiming—the bead, the whole bead, and nothing but the bead. Those who advocate altering the amount of foresight for different ranges forget that by doing so they are violating one of the first principles of aiming. Bring a little common sense to bear, son. Since judging distances accurately was one of the greatest diffi-culties the big game hunter had to overcome prior to the intro-duction of the high velocity rifle, and since the slightest variation in the amount of foresight can throw your bullet hopelessly out, how in the name of all reason can you expect to be able to estimate the correct amount to take for any given range? Besides, you will have two guesses to make instead of only one—you will have first to guess the range, no easy matter and then guess the amount of foresight to take for that guessed range! Well? Don't you think you'll have a better chance of putting your bullet where you want it if you follow my advice? If you have your rifle sighted as I suggest you have nothing to guess at all—you just take a normal aim for all ordinary shots, and if the animal seems to be standing much farther away than usual, why, you merely hold a mite higher on his shoulder, that's all. There is no guessing called for.

And anyway, always bear in mind that the old-timer's maxim holds as good today as ever it did in the days of black powder, especially where dangerous game is concerned: "Git as close as y' can, laddie; an' then *git ten yards closer.*" Get as close as ever you possibly can, and then make dead certain of your shot. The shoulder shot is by far the best for all animals, particularly dangerous game, (and incidentally the biggest target). Do not think in terms of behind the shoulder—the vital spots lie *between* the shoulders. Slam your bullet thru the bone and the animal will drop instantly—I am, of course, assuming that you are suitably armed— with spinal concussion and will die of rapid internal hemorrhage owing to the bullet and particles of broken bone tearing their way in thru the main arteries situated at the top of the heart. He will not get to his feet again.

Now practically without exception all beginners are imbued with the idea of "behind the shoulder." This is undoubtedly because the old-timers invariably spoke and wrote of aiming in that manner. But then, when you get back to the days of muzzle-loaders and black powder breech-loaders with their lead balls, this was the only place where there was reasonable certainty of the ball penetrating sufficiently to kill. A spherical lead ball on the shoulder might break the bone but would certainly fail to get thru it, unless you were using an enormously powerful and unwieldy weapon on small animals. The black powder Express breech-loaders were not much better in this respect. Accordingly, right up to the end of the last century, when John Rigby pioneered the modern nitro-express back in '98 by introducing the .450 cordite, men were still speaking in terms of "behind the shoulder." (The old buffalo-hunters of the '60s in the States invariably went for the lungs or the "armpit.")

But with modern rifles and ammunition things are different. The metal-jacketed bullet will have no difficulty in getting thru the bone of the shoulder-blade provided you are using a suitable weight of bullet for the animals you are shooting. There is no need to mash up both shoulders. A solid will probably drill a neat little hole thru both, with or without stunning but a soft-nose will set-up on the first shoulder, inflicting a terrific punch which *will* stun, and will then tear thru those vital arteries and usually stop against the opposite shoulder, with or without breaking it. The animal will rarely regain consciousness before death overtakes him; if he does, he certainly will not get to his feet. In other words, the animal is yours the instant you squeeze your trigger, and you know it—there is no doubt.

When hunters realized the penetrative power of the metal-jacketed bullet they at once took to this shoulder shot so as to be certain of definitely anchoring their beast. Because where dangerous game are concerned it is not the original stalk and shot, but the following of a wounded beast that is so dangerous. A brain or neck shot will, of course, drop an animal in his tracks but an animal moves his head and neck much more than his shoulder, and these targets are very much smaller. The shoulder is the largest, steadiest and most vulnerable of all targets and just as instantaneous, for all practical purposes, as either head or neck.

An animal shot thru the heart or lungs can run from 60 to 140 yards or more at full speed before collapsing. If heavy rain comes on to wash the blood off the grass or bush, you may fail to find him in thick cover. I have picked up several elephant that had been shot thru the lungs by other hunters and gotten away thru this very cause. (An elephant shot thru the lungs can go half a mile before halting.) Then cow elephant often come to the assistance of a wounded bull and help him away. I myself lost a good bull in this manner once. I'd knocked him down in an impossible tangle of bush. I'd had to slip my bullet thru a little gap about 4 inches in diameter and then into his shoulder. But he must have moved his hindquarters the instant before I fired, without my being able to see, so that my bullet did not take him at right angles thru the shoulder but must have raked him diagonally. He fell, and I felt certain that he was mine. I tried to see if there was anything else worth shooting, but failed to see another bull. My followers, whom I had left squatting under a tree, saw the whole performance. They told me that three big cows had come and, one on either side and one behind, had literally boosted the bull onto his feet and in that formation had wheeled around and gone. I followed them from early in the morning until near sundown, but they never even stopped for a breather. Except for one small smear of blood on a fallen tree over which they had shoved him, there was no blood spoor at all; the cows pressing against him on both sides either stopped all external bleeding or else collected the blood on themselves. I never found him.

Further, in Africa it may be taken that the solitary animal is the exception. If a powerful rifle is used for a lung shot on soft-skinned game, the bullet will all too frequently go clean thru and maybe wound another beast standing beyond the one at which you have fired. Then there is the man who is badly off for meat for his men. If he takes a heart or lung shot, the animal will clear off at speed; he may not be too certain of his shot and in his anxiety to get the meat for his men may be tempted to take another one or two shots at other members of the herd. Only to find eventually that there was no need for them as the first animal had been mortally wounded. So that he has killed two or three animals unnecessarily, where one would have sufficed.

Deer-hunters in the States and deer-stalkers in Scotland and other places who are shooting solely for sport and pleasure and whose bag may be limited to a single beast a year, men who look upon venison as a treat and who like to share it with their especial friends who may not be able to collect their own, would not even dream of blasting a hole thru a deer's shoulder—it would spoil too much meat. In Africa, however, things are very different; you will have no especial cronies to whom you would like to send a shoulder or haunch of venison—they wouldn't thank you for it anyway by the time it reached them! No matter how small the beast is, you are not going to eat it all yourself; your cook-boy will see to it that all the choicest cuts are reserved for you; he and your gun-bearers and personal staff will eat the remainder if it is a small animal, your porters will get their share if it is one of the larger beasts.

You need not worry about meat being wasted out here just because there's a bullet-hole thru it and it is somewhat blooded. Your coons will eat every scrap, every morsel of it. They are not particular as to niceties in butchering. I have seen them collect the remains of a big buffalo bull that had been killed by a lion some thirty-six hours previously in a very hot district. It was literally green and whistling to high heaven. They hacked it in pieces with yells of delight and carried it back to camp in triumph. There they cut it in lumps and crammed it into the pots. After stewing it for an hour or two they struck into it—this was real meat! meat that could smell as strong as this smelled must be really find food and would be sure to make them strong! Not a scrap was wasted—tho a whiteman would almost certainly have died of ptomaine poisoning.

No; you needn't worry about meat being "wasted" or "spoilt" in Africa just because it has a bullet-hole thru it.

Auctor: You've several times mentioned that the average range at which game is shot in Africa works out between 75 and 175 yards. I take it that this means the general run of African hunting. But what about the big fellows, as you call them? I gather they're shot at very much closer ranges than that. Why not be a little more specific. You have frequently used the expression "at close quarters" and "at point blank range" and so on. Well, just what is implied by those expressions?

Lector: Okeh; tho I have a notion I told you before when discussing the various rifles.

Anything over 40 yards is a long shot at elephant and much the same applies to rhino in thick cover. I should think the average range at which my elephant are shot would probably work out at somewhere between 12 and 20 paces—sometimes very much closer. Rhino, in the same way, at from 15 paces to perhaps 8 or 10 feet. Buffalo are generally shot at from 20 to perhaps 120 yards, tho when it's a case of being charged unexpectedly by some beast wounded by somebody else, the range can be reckoned in feet—sometimes not many! I have not been charged by an animal wounded by myself for many years—I take far too much care in the placing of my shot. And in my figuring this has paid me handsomely. Instead of spending maybe days following-up a wounded elephant, I can devote that time to hunting others.

There's a word of advice I might slip in here. Every experienced hunter knows it but the beginner all too easily forgets. It's this: *Never move your feet from the spot upon which you were standing when you fired without first reloading your rifle.* It matters not if it's only a guinea fowl or a wild goose, reload before attempting to approach to examine your kill. Animals can "come to life again" in the most extraordinary way, and if you make a habit of always reloading before closing in even with non-dangerous game, there will be no fear of you forgetting when you knock down your first or your twenty-first lion.

Col. Patterson of "*Man-eaters of Tsavo*" fame relates how on one occasion he shot a lion which dropped instantly to the shot and lay still. Patterson's followers ran up and clustered around the lion, which was apparently stone dead. He himself came up, propped his rifle against a tree, and was just closing in to have a look at his kill, when the lion suddenly scrambled to his feet and chased one of the men up a tree. Blaney Percival also tells how he dropped a lion seemingly stone dead and rode up for a closer look, only to have the lion "come to life" again without any warning. He had to ride hard until a safe distance away before pulling up and finishing off the lion. Since his only weapon was his .256 (6.5mm) he didn't dare attempt any heroics when close.

In the case of such animals you can literally walk straight into the "jaws of death" if you have foolishly approached without your rifle being ready for instant action. In the case of non-dangerous beasts you may lose your trophy or your meat, for which you've hunted so hard, if you forget this precaution or allow yourself to become careless.

It happened to me once and I've never since forgotten. I'd had a very hard and difficult morning's hunt for meat, and at last got a shot at a big roan antelope bull. I fired from about 125 paces and the bull dropped instantly, rolled over on to his back, and lay there with all four feet in the air like you'll sometimes see a friendly dog do, inviting you to rub his tummy. I'd never seen an antelope behave like that before, but he sure didn't look like clearing off, so, having something pressing on my mind, I propped my rifle against a tree and allowed my gun-bearer to go ahead and attend to the throat-cutting. Presently I heard a shout and looked round to see what was the matter. And there I saw my gun-bearer on his back with *his* feet in the air this time, and the roan getting nicely into his stride at full gallop! Before I could grab the rifle, he was gone.

It appeared that my gun-bearer found that his knife was too blunt and was stooping to pick up a stone on which to sharpen it when the roan came-to, scrambled to his feet, knocking my hero heels over head as he did so, and departed at speed. (I think this business of blunt knives has been responsible for more of my gray hairs than anything else in Africa! The African simply will *NOT* think of sharpening a knife until he actually wants to cut something with it. It took me literally years to train my men to sharpen their knives *before* we left camp, and not wait to look around for a stone out in the veldt when they wanted to cut some beast's throat.)

I killed that same roan two or three days later. He was apparently little the worse for his adventure. I forget what rifle I was using that time but the caliber makes no difference on these occasions—I don't doubt but that a pistol bullet would have exactly the same effect. What happens is that the bullet hits one of the projections on the under side of the spine, which brings the animal down with spinal concussion—in other words, knocks him out for a few moments but does little actual harm. This roan I was lucky enough to kill a couple of days after dropping him in that manner, didn't appear to have suffered any ill-effects. I don't doubt he had a stiff and somewhat sore back but he was grazing away quite contentedly when I again sighted him, and I had no means of knowing that it was the same animal until he was dead and I had a chance to examine him more closely. It was a powerful rifle—a .475 or, .475 N $\stackrel{\circ}{=}$ 2—and the bullet snicked clean thru.

The question is so frequently being asked: "Which is the most dangerous game?" that perhaps it would not be out of place to try and answer it here.

As I see it, the answer is each one in his own particular field. But really it is a most difficult question to answer; so much has to be taken into consideration—whether or not the animal is being hunted; whether he is alone or accompanied by others of his species; the conditions under which he is being hunted; and whether or not he has been wounded, either recently by yourself or in the past by somebody else. Each and all of these points must be considered before an answer can be given to the original question. I have not said anything about your arms. It is understood that if you have taken the trouble to read as far as this you will at least know what *NOT* to arm yourself with.

No hard and fast law can be laid down about any wild animal;

they will occasionally do the weirdest things, in utter and complete contra-distinction to all the recognized habits of their respective species. There are credible reports of a hippo that developed a taste for dogs and fowls, and of another with a partiality for goats, whilst I have also heard of a man-eating elephant and of an eland, usually the quietest and most inoffensive of animals, treeing a hunter. However, speaking generally, it may be fairly safely stated that a rhino is the only animal in Africa which is at all likely to attack unprovoked. (Exception must be made for buffalo suffering from rinderpest, or which have recently had and recovered from it. I have it on excellent authority that such buffalo are apt to attack without any other provocation than the mere presence of man in the vicinity. I have only heard these reports from Kenya.)

Bearing in mind the phenomenal power of the modern nitro-express rifle, the absence of smoke, and metal-covered bullets, I fail to see how elephant can possibly be considered the most dangerous game to hunt as so many men maintain. In the days of black powder and lead bullets maybe he was—but that is an entirely different matter. The only real danger when tackling a large herd of elephant is the possibility of the herd, or a portion of it, stampeding directly towards the hunter. In heavy forest and in dense bush the danger then is more apparent than real, because there is almost always a large tree or a particularly dense clump of bush which even stampeding elephant cannot stamp flat, behind which you can shelter while the terror-stricken animals crash past on both sides of you. But in an ocean of 10- or 12-foot "elephant" grass there is no such friendly shelter—save possibly, if you are lucky, an anthill—and since you will not be able to see them until they loom up in the grass within a few feet of you, in these circumstances elephant-hunting must be considered as one of the most dangerous pastimes, but not, I think, otherwise.

There is always danger when hunting in, or passing thru, thick bush or scrub in which rhino are likely to be encountered, as you are liable to be attacked at any moment from very close quarters. And a rhino can go thru stuff that even a stampeding elephant wouldn't face, like it was wet paper. But provided that you are suitably armed, *and carrying your own rifle*, you should be able to turn the brute at least, even if you fail to knock down or kill him.

Buffalo are frequently described as the most dangerous beasts to hunt in Africa—and, for that matter in Asia—but to my mind very much the same applies to them as to elephant. The only difference is in stopping a charge. A charging elephant (not to be confused with an elephant stampeding towards you—a much more difficult proposition) can usually be at least turned by slamming a heavy bullet into his face, even tho the bullet may be badly placed. And once a charging elephant is stopped or turned it seems to knock all the fight out of him for the time being—his one and only idea being, apparently, to get away. Which is not to say that he won't charge again if you follow-up. But in my experience, and in that of every other hunter with whom I have ever discussed them, there is only one thing that will stop a charging buffalo and that is death—either yours or his. I do not think that buffalo are any more dangerous than elephant, except that they are, of course, smaller targets and can travel on three legs which an elephant cannot.

Auctor: You know you've done a whole lot a talking about buffalo thruout this book. Folks may be wondering why you have so much more to say about them than about other game.

Lector: I have done so because next to elephant I prefer to hunt buffalo more than any other game. He's a magnificent fellow, and a grand fighting foe when wounded. Also, I have a hunch that visiting sportsmen will be shooting far more buffalo in the future than they did in the past. Except for Kenya, where the rinderpest nearly exterminated the buffalo towards the end of the last century, these animals have been increasing to such an extent in all Eastern Africa, and do so much damage to the natives' food crops and cotton gardens, besides being the worst spreaders of the dreaded tsetse fly, that they are classed as varmints almost everywhere and can be shot without restriction for the price of a gun permit.

Since a lion is such a very much smaller target than any of the above three animals, and can merge so perfectly into his background, he is, obviously, very much more difficult to hit when charging—at any rate in scrub or reeds or similar cover. A wounded lion that has managed to get into a clump of grass or thicket of bush is an extremely dangerous proposition to follow-up —far more so, to my way of thinking, than any of the larger species.

Personally, I consider that a leopard is, potentially, the most dangerous beast in all Africa—but only when wounded, and then only if the hunter is armed with a rifle. He is so very much smaller than a lion and so incredibly quick, that he makes a very tricky target when charging.

If, however, you are armed with either a 12-bore Magnum "Paradox" or a 2¾″ or 3″ smooth 12-bore, loaded in either case with slugs, then he immediately becomes a very much simpler proposition, since the margin of permissible error is greatly increased over that permissible when a single bullet is used.

On reviewing the question, I rather think that, speaking generally, I should be inclined to put lion at the top of the list, tho, as I have already stated, the whole thing depends upon the circumstances in which the animal is encountered.

Auctor: I realize, of course, that you write as a professional hunter, and since your work is principally amongst dangerous game. . . .

Lector: I seldom shoot anything nowadays other than elephant, rhino, buffalo and man-eating lions—except for an occasional beast for the pot.

Auctor: Exactly. And so, as I say, it is I suppose only natural that your thoughts should tend to dwell almost exclusively on the big fellows. But on reading over what you have written don't you think that you have, perhaps, rather overdone it?

Lector: "Overdone it!" In what way?

Auctor: Well, what I mean is, you must remember that few if any of those who will read this are even thinking of becoming professional hunters. If they do come out here to Africa on a big game hunting expedition they will not be concentrating exclusively on dangerous game in thick cover. Yet your advice thruout has been almost entirely in connection with rifles suitable for dangerous game at close quarters. I have little doubt that every visiting hunter from the States will be wanting a smack at the big chaps but most of their hunting will be for trophies of non-dangerous animals. Now do you get what I mean?

Lector: Sure; sure; I get you all right. But don't you see, the way I look at it is this: Any of those fellas who are thinking of taking a run out this way have certainly done plenty hunting in Canada, Alaska and the States before they took the notion to roam farther afield. They don't *need* to be told how to shoot non-dangerous game and they won't even need to be told how to hunt it when they get here, it's so darned easy after the hunting they have been doing and to which they are accustomed. You have to hunt your game in America; and you have to hunt your dangerous game in Africa; but where non-dangerous animals are concerned your American hunter will tell you it's easy—and he's right.

Accordingly, I have concentrated principally on the more dangerous side of African hunting since fewer mistakes are permissible there than when hunting animals that can't hit back. It will doubtless have been noticed that such difficulties as I experienced, or such unpleasant incidents as came my way, in the past were due almost entirely to unsuitable weapons and inexperience. Confidence is half or more than half the battle: confidence in yourself and confidence in your rifles and ammunition; and you cannot have confidence in yourself—or at least it won't be of any use to you—if you cannot place complete confidence in your rifles and their shells; if you never know when the darned things are gonna jam or misfire or otherwise let you down—inevitably in a tight corner.

The American hunter will find the shooting of African non-dangerous game easy. It is easy: game is plentiful, incredibly plentiful in some areas; the animals, generally speaking, are large; the ranges close. There are certain species that are rare in some districts, and take a lot of hunting but if you know where to go, you can get them in other parts of the continent without the slightest difficulty. The visiting sportsman, naturally, can't be expected to know all this but there is no reason for him to be dependent solely upon the hunter and guide he employs in one territory—that fella may know nothing about the neighboring territories.

Most visitors have but a limited time at their disposal in which they must collect their trophies. One of the most coveted of all trophies is that of the greater kudu. These animals are very scarce in British East Africa, where most visitors go, and you may spend weeks of your precious time in very hard and difficult hunting before you get your kudu head—you may not get him at all. But the greater kudu is by no means so scarce in other parts of East Africa. You could collect yourself a fairly representative selection of heads in British territory and then, with maybe only a week or ten days left, you could take a plane down to Portuguese territory—having previously been in communication with somebody in those parts, or who knows them, and who will meet you with everything ready, take you out to where the kudu are to be found, and let you bag your fine head in plenty time to catch your ship which will have come down the coast from British East with the rest of your kit on board.

Most visitors think in terms of one territory only. In days gone by that was almost imperative but today you can get planes to take you wherever you want to go, and so can visit several territories if you wish to and sample the different types of hunting, and collect trophies in one that you couldn't in another. It's only necessary to get in touch with someone in the different territories you intend to visit well beforehand so that all arrangements can be made, and no waste of time ensue when you arrive.

Most of the guides are only familiar with their own territory; tho a few of them may also know the neighboring one. For instance, it's extremely improbable that a Kenya professional would be of much service to you in, say, Southern Rhodesia or Portuguese East or West Africa. But you could use the Kenya men whilst you were up there, and then use a man from Rhodesia for his territory and the neighboring Portuguese areas. Moving around in this way you could have a much better showing when you get back home than you could if you confined all your activities to but one territory.

CHAPTER X

Bullet Design and Construction

SOLID, OR FULL-PATCH, BULLETS. THIS IS A MATTER OF THE VERY utmost importance, yet it's a never-ending source of amazement to me how utterly indifferent the vast majority of men are about the design of the bullets they use. It does not appear to occur to them that they could do anything about it if the bullets didn't behave themselves too well. They appear to be quite satisfied with whatever the makers care to supply and never think that the makers are not themselves hunters and will rarely alter their bullet design unless they receive complaints from the men who actually use them.

The ordinary nickel-jacketed solid or full-patch bullet has not been altered since metal-jacketed bullets first came in with the smokeless powders. The only change that has taken place is that they are now given a Nobeloy cupro-zinc non-fouling jacket instead of the old cupro-nickel one, which gave rise to "nickeling" or metallic-fouling in the bore, particularly with the smaller calibers. I do not think, however, that the non-fouling envelopes are supplied for calibers ranging up from .375 (9.5mm).

Now these full-patch nickel-covered bullets are reasonably satisfactory, and the result is that men just go on using them without ever thinking of complaining when they misbehave themselves. In my opinion a solid, or full-patch, bullet should be sufficiently strong to obviate any possibility of it being distorted, much less broken open, no matter how heavy or massive a bone it happens to strike, or no matter how close the range may be. After all, bone is but bone; it's not homogeneous armor-plate; and it should not be difficult to design a full-patch bullet of any caliber that could be slammed into the mighty hips or spine of an elephant at point-blank range without running the risk of having the bullet distorted, riveted on the nose, or even broken open.

The only nickel-jacketed solids I have ever known not to be distorted to a greater or lesser extent were those thrown by the .577 and .600-bores. But then it must be remembered that I by no means recovered all the bullets I fired into elephant. It is quite possible that the 750 and 900-gr. bullets thrown by these two big guns would also sometimes be found distorted and I should not be the least bit surprised if other hunters could produce bullets of these two calibers that had failed to retain their shape.

In gunsmiths' catalogs you will frequently see a photo of "fired bullet extracted from clay." It looks very nice. There is no mark on it other than the rifling grooves, and it looks exactly like its unfired brother which is also illustrated. But such photos are quite meaningless to the practical hunter. There is no sort of comparison between clay and bone. The bullet might just as well have been fired into a tub of water or lump of butter for all the information it gives him concerning its capacity for standing up against massive bones.

If a solid bullet becomes distorted it will be very liable to lose its direction after entering the animal at which it was fired, and thereby fail to reach a vital spot altho perfectly placed. In fact, unless the vital spot aimed at is pretty large, if the bullet becomes distorted you will be very lucky if it gets there. This, besides being disappointing in that you will have to give the beast a second shot, can even mean a lost trophy. And it can be definitely dangerous in that you may have a difficult follow-up without knowing just how hard hit your quarry may be.

It happened to me once with the 480-gr. bullet thrown from a .450. I picked up the spoor of a troop of elephant early in the morning, followed them thru very difficult country, and eventually caught up with them as they were making their way along a deep kloof to get down to the river for a drink. I scrambled up on one wall of the kloof and got above them, but was just too late to put my bullet down thru the top of the big bull's head. But as I was shooting almost directly downwards, I endeavored to place my bullet on his spine immediately abaft the withers. However, my rough and hurried scramble had put me a mite out of breath, with the result that my bullet was not too well placed. The bull staggered to the shot but did not actually fall. He reeled around a rocky projection, which prevented me giving him a second bullet but I didn't worry as I felt certain that the bullet must have driven down thru lungs and heart.

After the remainder of the herd had stampeded, I made my way down into the kloof expecting to find my bull dead a short distance away. But there was no dead elephant to cheer me. There was a fairly good blood spoor, however, and I continued along it in high hopes. But my hopes waned somewhat as hour followed hour and he led me into the most ghastly tangles of thorn-bush. His spoor showed that he was pretty hard hit, and that he had frequently halted but the wind was wrong and it was quite impossible to make detours to get it right. It was quite one of the most difficult hunts I had ever had, and I am quite sure that the only reason I wasn't charged several times when closing in to where he had halted was that the bush was so dense he would have been unable to see me and a wounded elephant, like any other animal that means to be nasty, likes to give himself the advantage of a small clear or fairly clear space for his charge. It was late in the evening before I finally managed to kill him. I found that my bullet, the first one, had smashed one of the lateral projections of the spine, which had not merely deflected it slightly but had bent it appreciably lengthways. The result had been that instead of driving straight down thru lungs and heart to kill, it had taken a curved course downwards passing thru the outer edge of the left lung but missing the heart, alongside of which it passed, to lodge under the hide at the forward edge of the left armpit. Had that bullet not been bent it would probably have killed within 50 yards. I had been on the elephant's left side when firing, so that the bullet should not have been on the same side.

There was another occasion when I had a very similar experience when using a 9.5mm Mannlicher-Schoenauer on buffalo. I fired for his spine when he was lying down facing away from me. But instead of flopping out, as he should have done, to my disgust he scrambled to his feet and lurched into the grass before I had time to give him a second shot—I was not accustomed to this action, or, indeed, to any magazine action at that time. I had a very nasty job in front of me now, and was proportionally glad that I had a heavier rifle to take over for it—as well as I remember, a double .475 N⁰2. Except that, as is always the case under such circumstances, it was a somewhat nerve-racking business, there is nothing remarkable to relate in the subsequent follow-up. I eventually killed the bull and found that the 270-gr. solid from the 9.5mm had been badly distorted and bent against the spine, but had failed to smash it. One of the vertebrae had been cracked and its lateral projection broken; the bullet had then made rather a mess of the bull's liver and stopped in it. The bull had been very lame and obviously had difficulty in managing his left hind leg but in long grass he was still a very dangerous proposition. Now I felt pretty sure that had that bullet not been bent it would have had a very much better chance of breaking the spine, instead of slithering off it, as it were, and merely smashing the projection.

It's true that I can't remember ever having the actual nose of these nickel-jacketed solids break open but that's not sufficient. I've had the nose of most of them deeply cut and grooved at times, and not infrequently considerably riveted whilst the lengthways bending, with or without other distortion, is quite common. Further, it is not particularly unusual to have the envelope of the bent bullets split right along one side from the base almost to the shoulder. In other words, these nickel-covered full-patch slugs are merely hard-nose bullets; the reinforcement of the jacket is only sufficient to prevent the nose from breaking open. Well, that's not enough.

I said earlier that it ought not to be difficult to design a full-patch bullet that would really stand up to its work, and always retain its original shape. This is proved by the fact that John Rigby supplies such bullets for all his special calibers: .416, .350 N⁰2 (Magnum), .350 Mauser-Magnum, and original .350 (400/.350). These bullets are *steel*-covered and have a really useful thickness of metal not only at the nose but well down past the shoulders. Then the end of the envelope is truly turned into the base of the bullet and the lead core well swaged over that turn-in.

Well, in my experience, and this is borne out by every other hunter with whom I have ever discussed such matters, these solids of Rigby's are the *only* perfect full-patch bullets in existence. They do NOT become distorted, rivet, or break-up. I have never seen the nose of one of these bullets even marked much less damaged, no matter how massive a bone it encountered nor how close the range.

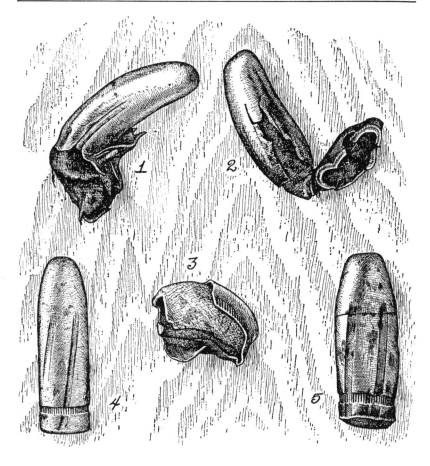

BULLETS TAKEN FROM ELEPHANT.

Take a look at these 535 grain, solid, nickel-jacketed bullets which were fired from a .500 Mauser rifle by the late Fletcher Jamieson. This drawing shows clearly the distortion that can happen to the ordinary full-jacketed bullet when fired into really heavy and solid fleshed animals.

Bullet No. 1 was a heart shot from behind the shoulder, thru the heart, and then pulled up against the opposite leg bone, having turned over sideways enroute.

Bullet No. 2 was a similar shot to No. 1.

Bullet No. 3 was a lung shot from the point of the big shoulder joint, raking thru the lungs towards the off-side hind leg.

Bullet No. 4 was a lung shot that hit no bones; its shape leaves nothing to be desired.

Bullet No. 5 was a side brain shot. The bones of the skull not being as hard as those of the shoulder would account for its not breaking up. Nevertheless, there is considerable distortion—just compare it with No. 4.

In the days when I was using Rigby's original .350 in my falling-block single-loader, I didn't know the solids were steel-covered—I didn't even know at the time that medium bores were available as doubles; I thought that only large bores were built like that—and at the time I couldn't explain just why my .350 seemed to be so much better than corresponding calibers. Now, of course, the answer is clear; it was undoubtedly due to the splendid steel-covered bullets and the absolute certainty of their maintaining their course after entering.

I've broken buffalo necks and backs with the 225-gr. steel-covered solids thrown by Rigby's .350 Magnums without the bullets being in any way distorted, and at times the ranges were very close but I have had the 300-gr. Nobeloy-jacketed bullet thrown by Holland's .375 Magnum badly riveted on similar shots. I admit the envelope wasn't ruptured but that's beside the point. Exactly the same applies to the .416. I've shattered elephant necks, spines and hips with these bullets, but have never seen the nose more than faintly marked—it was not cut or grooved as nickel-jacketed bullets would all have been on similar shots, assuming nothing worse, even much heavier bullets. I class these steel-covered bullets of Rigby's as tops, and cannot for the life of me see why *all* full-patch bullets are not made in the same way.

I do not know if John Rigby himself had any African big game hunting experience, tho his rifles and cartridges would certainly seem to indicate that he had plenty, but if he hadn't, then he was wise enough to get hold of a really keen and observant hunter of wide experience and listen to his views on just what was wanted for African hunting. Then, having picked his brains clean, he turned-to and designed the perfect weapons on which his reputation has been built, *and the perfect bullets for use in them.* He has only slipped-up once and that is that he does not supply any special steel-covered solids for the .470 which he has adopted to replace

---

Jamieson's brother informs me that in his experience the bullet from this .500 Mauser always travelled far enough to do all the damage that was necessary to put the elephant out. They sometimes went right thru the elephant and he stated that he has never known one actually to disintegrate.

Well; that may be, but I certainly would not be satisfied. The amount of distortion in bullet No. 5 is permissible, but the manner in which the other three (Nos. 1, 2 and 3) have broken up is all wrong, and might easily mean a wounded and lost elephant that should have been killed clean.

the .450—for that matter, he didn't supply any special bullets for the .450 either, but then at the time it was introduced it wasn't yet realized that something better than the nickel-covered slug was desirable. But I certainly reckon that he would do well to give us bullets for the .470 similar in every way to those he supplies for his .416. And not only with regard to the envelope, but also in connection with the shape.

The perfect full-patch bullet should be slightly less blunt than the printed letter U. But the sides should be almost exactly parallel right up to the shoulders—Rigby's .416 and .350s are as nearly perfect as possible but the solid thrown by the .470 has a long taper towards the nose. I don't like it. You will find it illustrated somewhere in this book; just compare it with corresponding bullets of other calibers. Doubtless its ballistic coefficient is better than theirs but when ranges run under 120 yards or so, we don't need to worry about any such technicalities as coefficients of shape. What we want is a bullet that can be relied upon to hold a straight course after smashing its way thru heavy bones.

It has been clearly shown that the pointed solid is totally unreliable for game shooting, as there is no telling what the bullet is going to do if it happens to hit a bone at anything short of an exact right angle. (I saw a fella shot during one of the wars I was in with a pointed military bullet on the point of the hip as he was lying down. Instead of breaking the bone and driving into his innards, it changed direction and traveled straight down along his leg to make its exit at the ankle. It broke no bones at all. That fella was mighty lucky that a pointed bullet had been used.) When these high velocity rifles first came out all makers supplied pointed solids—Rigby for his .350 Magnums, and Holland for the 270-gr. bullet thrown by their .375 Magnum, and so on, but they quickly discarded these in favor of the round nose when it was found how utterly unreliable they were.

All the best bullets are parallel-sided and then given a not-too-bluntly-shaped round nose, then why does the .470 still continue to have that long taper towards its nose? Possibly its penetration is a little deeper than that of its contemporaries but what of it? Since they have adequate depth of penetration to kill, what is to be gained by increasing that depth at the expense of less certain maintenance of direction after entry? I may be wrong about this but my experience was that the solid bullet thrown by the .470 was not quite so sure as that thrown by the .465, for example. I repeat, this may merely be an illusion because I didn't like the shape of the solid .470 bullet, and was looking for faults when using it. But I had to give three big bull elephant a second shot after bringing them down with frontal head shots which I couldn't help feeling ought not to have been necessary. Admittedly, I killed a number of elephant with similar frontal brain shots when using the .470, and the one bullet was sufficient; but I could have sworn that my bullets were perfectly placed on the three occasions mentioned. Unfortunately, circumstances prevented me tracing the course of those three shots, so that I cannot say with any real degree of certainty if it was indeed the shape of the bullets that was to blame. (The dissecting of an elephant's head is a big job— take a look at the photo of one that my friend Jamieson cut open.) But when we know that the parallel-sided round-nose bullet is entirely satisfactory, surely it's unwise to experiment with degrees of taper approaching that absolutely unreliable sharp point—and which we *know* is so useless. The .470 was introduced by Grant & Lang during that scurry amongst the British gunsmiths to bring out an acceptable substitute for the .450 when all weapons of that caliber were banned in India and the Sudan, and it was not realized as fully as it is today that solid bullets *must* have a rounded nose, and the less taper the better.

The only reason I can think of why there has been no alteration in the shape of the .470 bullet is that the British are so little rifle-minded and so little interested in such details, that they just don't bother to squeal and continue to accept whatever they are given. Except by just a mere handful of us old-timers, there is really very little hunting of the big animals nowadays. In India it is only the occasional man-killing elephant that has been proscribed as a "rogue" by government that may be shot tho in Burma there are rather better opportunities. But anyway, the Asiatic elephant is a very much easier animal to kill than his big African cousin, whilst in Africa, you are limited to two or at the most three elephant a year in British territory, and comparatively few men of the present generation out here have the slightest ambition to go elephant-hunting—it's too much like hard work; they like to do their hunting within reasonable distance of where they have parked their car

—walking does not appeal to them at all. Of those few of us who still prefer to tramp the elephant trail to any other way of life, it's just possible that the various .450s or .465 is more generally used than the .470 or possibly, as in the case of Jamieson, the .500 or .505 Mausers are preferred. As far as the hunters employed by the governments of Uganda and Tanganyika are concerned, nowadays these men do comparatively little hunting themselves—their duties are the supervison of the well-trained and well-armed native hunters who do practically all the work. The result is that there are not enough keen regular hunters to put up a sufficiently loud squeal about the shape of the .470-caliber solid. If we don't care for the shape of the bullet, we just discard the rifle and replace it with another corresponding caliber the bullets for which coincide with our notion of what a solid bullet should look like.

I know that when I have my new battery of doubles built I shall insist that the makers of the ammunition be persuaded to give me solids similar in every way to those they supply for Rigby's calibers. It will doubtless cost me more, but I shall not quibble about that provided the bullets are identical with Rigby's. I reckon they are well worth the difference. If it's Rigby I decide on to build the rifles, he will have to guarantee that *all* the solids are of the same pattern irrespective of the caliber. For some reason the other makers have been very dilatory over this question of full-patch bullets; they ought to have forgotten their petty jealousies and followed Rigby's lead.

EXPANDING BULLETS. *Auctor:* I wish you would give us your views on expanding bullets. Out of the umpteen varieties obtainable, which do you consider the best? I have often noticed in the correspondence columns of sporting journals that a man lauds to the skies one type of bullet which he has found satisfactory, and then only perhaps a week later, somebody else is equally emphatic in condemning that very same bullet fired from an identical rifle. What is the earnest seeker after knowledge to do in the case of such contradictory reports?

Lector: From the very fact that there are so many different patterns available, it is surely obvious that there is no such thing as an ideal expanding bullet. If there was then it, and it only, would be manufactured, since there would be no demand for anything else. The nearest approach to the ideal was the solid soft lead bullet thrown by the old black powder weapons but with the much higher velocities of the present day it cannot be used.

It is almost invariably the case that when a man condemns any particular type of expanding bullet he does so in general terms and without any reference whatsoever to either the weight of the bullet or the weight of animal against which it was used. If an expanding bullet is intended for use against some of the heavier varieties of game, it will be designed for penetration combined with expansion. Naturally then, such a bullet would be little if any better than a solid when used against one of the lighter animals, since it would not encounter sufficient resistance to cause it to set-up before it had passed clean thru the little animal's body. In exactly the same way, if a bullet is designed for the rapid expansion necessary for one of the lighter varieties of soft-skinned game, it will blow to pieces on striking a bone on one of the heavier varieties. A sense of proportion must be maintained and a suitable weight of bullet chosen for the weight of animal most likely to be shot.

And then, don't forget velocity. Velocity is the controlling factor in the rapidity or otherwise of expansion. A bullet which might expand perfectly on a given animal at a range of 100 yards, might pass thru like a solid if it hit the same animal in the same place at a range of 300 yards. Further, if a bullet has been designed to expand correctly at ranges between 200 and 300 yards, it would probably blow to pieces if it hit a similar animal at 50 yards.

Accordingly, in view of all these factors which have to be taken into consideration, it is clearly impossible to design an expanding bullet which will behave satisfactorily on all types of game at all ranges. It is up to the hunter who intends to shoot a wide variety of species over widely differing country to supply himself with a variety of different weights and types of bullet if he is to obtain satisfaction. If he does not intend to shoot quite so widely, and does not want to be bothered with an assortment of bullets, then he must choose the best type of bullet for the type of shooting in which he principally indulges, and do the best he can with it for other kinds of game and other types of country. In other words, he must compromise. But he must remember that a compromise is only a compromise, and that no compromise can ever be one hundred per cent satisfactory to all the parties concerned.

With regard to the different patterns of expanding bullets—here again common sense must be brought to bear and a thought given to the weight of animal it is most desired to shoot, and the range at which he will usually be encountered. To a very great extent this question of bullet weight and type is mixed up with the choice of calibers, because a certain type of bullet might act perfectly if of a certain weight where it would prove useless if appreciably lighter —and vice versa. But if only one rifle is to be used for all types of shooting, well—three different weights of bullet are obtainable for the .375 Magnum, because the designers realized the necessity for such in view of the widely differing weights of animals that might be shot, as also did they realize that it was necessary that all these different weights should be of different patterns—some being of a type that will expand more readily than others.

Nevertheless, irrespective of the type of bullet, by far the most important consideration is its weight, because even a fairly light bullet of a type that does not expand too readily might be better on occasions than an appreciably heavier bullet of a type that expands very easily. For instance, I should very much rather face a lion with the 270-gr. semi-pointed soft-nose bullet thrown by the .375 Magnum, than with the 300-gr. copper-pointed bullet thrown by the .404, because the latter pattern is designed for rapid expansion on fairly light animals at long range, and would probably disintegrate almost on impact on a frontal chest shot at a lion.

The principal object of expanding bullets is not merely to cause greater internal laceration, but rather to cause the bullet to remain in the animal's body and thereby expend its entire energy on the animal instead of whipping clean thru and wasting its energy on a tree, anthill, rock or the ground, or whatever else eventually stops it. This is a point which is by no means always realized. I have frequently had men tell me that their rifles obviously had more power than mine because theirs were capable of driving an expanding bullet right thru an animal, whereas my bullets almost invariably remained in the animal's body. As a matter of actual fact their rifles had considerably less power than mine, and even that was being wasted. This was proved by the fact that my animals were either dropped stone-dead where they stood or else did not travel more than at the very most one-fifth to one-quarter of the distance that their beasts ran after receiving the bullet.

I wonder if anybody has ever attempted to compute just what

proportion of a bullet's energy is expended on an animal, and what proportion is wasted, when it passes clean thru. It would, of course, depend on a number of things—whether or not it was of the expanding variety and, if so, of what pattern; the extent to which it set up; its weight and the weight of the animal; the range at which the shot was taken; whether or not a bone was struck; and, of course, its striking-velocity at the moment of impact. I should imagine that the account of a series of experiments on this point would make fascinating reading.

In India the old B.P. .577 Express is generally preferred for tiger to any of the Nitro-Expresses in the .470-bore group, since it is claimed that its heavier lead bullet, in spite of its low velocity, inflicts more of a knock-down blow than does the metal-jacketed bullet from one of the latter rifles. The theoretical mathematical muzzle energy of a .465 or .470 is roughly 1,000 ft.-lbs. greater than that of the B.P. .577; but even if the bullet from one of the former rifles does go right thru on a broadside shot behind the shoulder which fails to strike any bone larger than a rib, where the lead bullet from the .577 would not, who can say that it has not expended just as much energy on the animal as the latter? It probably would not knock down the tiger but then neither would the .577 B.P.

In a letter to *GAME & GUN* a correspondent stated that so far as he knew no satisfactory metal-jacketed bullet had ever been invented, and that in his experience they invariably blew to pieces on impact if they happened to encounter a bone.

One is compelled to wonder with just which rifles this man has had any experience. If he had been using little featherweight expanding bullets with ultra-high striking-velocities then, naturally, an animal such as a tiger immediately becomes a pretty massive-boned animal, since he would only be shot at close ranges and these little bullets were never intended for such work. But if on the other hand he was using a bullet of reasonable weight, then that same tiger automatically becomes a comparatively lightly-boned animal and soft-nose metal-jacketed bullets will behave perfectly satisfactorily on him even if they do encounter a bone. It is merely ridiculous to say that *no* metal-jacketed expanding bullet will do other than disintegrate on an animal such as a lion or tiger. Does he wish us to believe that he has seen a 900-gr. soft-nose bullet thrown by a .600 blow to pieces on a tiger?

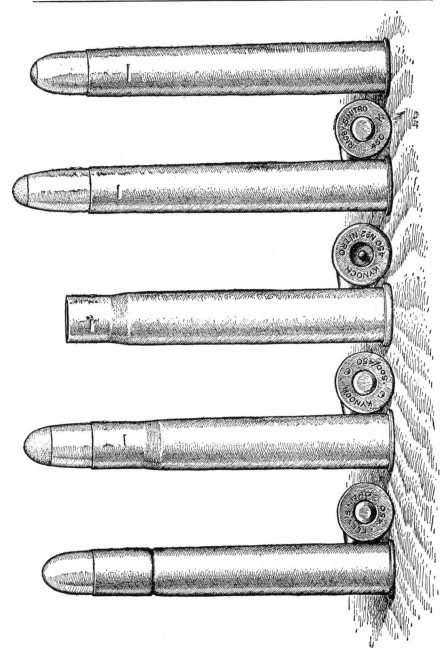

Probably this illustration should appear back in the chapter on The Big Bores, among the things I tell there about the .450 cartridges. However, it shows the different types of soft-point expanding bullets as turned out by the British ammunition makers, so we have decided to place it here among the talk on expanding bullets and then tell about both cartridges and the bullets they are loaded with.

Here you have the three old veterans, the .450 Nitro-Expresses. The two outer ones are the same, the one on the left having been made by Eley Bros. prior to the amalgamation of the British ammunition manufacturers. You will note that three different exposures of lead are shown. That of the 500/.450 is par ticularly interesting as being the only bullet I can remember seeing turned out by Kynoch with Eley's very considerable amount of lead showing. I guess it must be an old cartridge from which the illustration was taken, made immediately after the firms merged and before Kynoch had decided to abandon this pattern in favor of the soft-nose-split they came to prefer. However, I must say I consider this type of bullet better for lion and tiger than the more modern soft-nose-split. I can't think why Kynoch dropped it. In my experience it never lost weight as the split variety can and sometimes do.

The bullet shown second from the right is the kind Kynoch supply nowadays if you ask for plenty lead showing. It's my favorite for buffalo in these weights. You can bank on killing any buff with these bullets on any reasonable shot—I have never had one break-up or lose any of its original weight even after being slammed into one of these massive-boned critters at point-blank range. For frontal shots at lion it takes a lot of beating; but tends to drive thru without getting a chance of fully expanding on broadside shots. Altho the mighty chest muscles of a lion offer great resistance to a bullet; the same cannot be said of side shots. After all, a lion is comparatively lightly-boned, whilst he definitely comes within the soft-skinned category. On a side shot you need to use a bullet that sets up reasonably easily. The snag is that you never know when tackling lion just when you may have to face a charge, and therefore when you'll be wanting a bullet that *will not* blow-up. It is, therefore, imperative to use bullets that can be relied upon to hold together when out after lion.

The bullet shown away out on the right of the illustration is what you get when you ask for lead barely showing at the nose. It will kill elephant on side shots, and mostly will on frontal chest shots; but naturally can't be expected to do so on a frontal head shot. Accordingly, I always recommend a man to load up with hard nose slugs when elephant-hunting—you can then kill him from any suitable position. But these bullets are splendidly satisfactory for rhino. Possibly, if you were trying to shoot one up the backside you would do better with a hard-nose slug; but I don't think many rhino are shot thataway. You can also use this bullet for buffalo; but on a shot behind the shoulder that fails to strike any bone larger than a rib, will probably drive clean thru, only partially setting-up; it won't have encountered sufficient resistance before getting out the other side. It's very deadly on end-on shots.

If you want to see what the N $\stackrel{\circ}{=}$2 shell looks like inside, and in what way it differs from its companions, just turn to the illustration of a .475 N $\stackrel{\circ}{=}$2 shell shown in section on page 81. That shell was intended to take the place of the .450 N $\stackrel{\circ}{=}$2, and is of identical design. That massively-strong rim and head was specially designed for cordite, and the notion behind it all was essentially sound. Nevertheless, *all* these shells are made of such strong brass today, that you have nothing whatever to worry about with any of them.

Here is the way in which these British expanding bullets work out in actual practice:

(1) Westley Richards' round-capped..............slow expansion
(2) Soft-nose, lead barely showing at tip..........slow expansion
(3) Soft-nose, plenty of lead showing.............normal expansion
(4) Soft-nose-split...........................rapid expansion
(5) Copper-pointed...........................very rapid expansion
(6) Westley Richards' "L.T." pointed capped.....instantaneous expansion

For a number of years I would use nothing but 480- and 500-gr. full-patch bullets for buffalo. Then one time I ran out of solids and was compelled to carry on with plain soft-nose slugs (480-gr.)— plenty lead showing at the nose. I have continued using them ever since.

The disadvantage of solids is that, when tackling a large herd, there is grave risk of the bullet driving clean thru and maybe, in fact almost certainly, wounding perhaps several other members of the herd. With soft-nose 480- and 500-gr. metal-jacketed bullets this does not happen. The bullet mushrooms perfectly and invariably remains in the buffalo's body—on a clean shot behind the shoulder it will bulge the skin on the far side, yet, at the same time, I find that these plain soft-nose bullets will kill with certainty on both head and neck shots and are equally capable of smashing the spine and also of killing practically instantaneously on a shot thru the shoulder-blade—on this last the buffalo drops instantly in his tracks and is incapable of rising again; he dies within a minute or so of rapid internal hemorrhage owing to the bullet and, possibly, particles of broken bone driving thru and amongst the large main arteries situated at the top of the heart.

Accordingly, if these bullets behave so effectively on massive-boned animals weighing upwards of a ton, how can anyone possibly suggest that they would blow to pieces on striking even a rib on a soft-skinned animal, such as a lion or tiger, the very heaviest of which do not weigh more than 600 to 700 lbs. and generally appreciably less?

The foregoing remarks are not made on the strength of shooting perhaps half a dozen buffalo with expanding bullets. Towards the end of last year I used my .450 N$\stackrel{o}{=}$2 for which I had a number of soft-nose bullets (480-gr.)—plenty lead showing at the nose. In the four or five months during which I was amongst them, I shot and killed 92 buffalo, which was just a trifle under my usual annual bag during those few months when I make a point of concentrating on them. I have done the same for many years, and for a long time now have sworn by the 480- and 500-gr. soft-nose slug for buffalo.

As a matter of actual fact, the vast majority of men who use 480- and 500-gr. bullets for lion and tiger generally prefer to use the soft-nose-split variety so as to ensure the bullet setting-up sufficiently on animals which can only offer a very moderate degree of resistance to such comparatively massive projectiles.

Another correspondent mentioned in a letter that he had killed an African buffalo bull at roughly 100 yards range with the 270-gr. semi-pointed soft-nose bullet from a Holland .375 Magnum. In reply to a question of mine he stated that the bullet took the buffalo on the shoulder and killed him instantly. Now this shoulder shot undoubtedly brings the animal down with spinal concussion—stuns him. But, I contend, it will only kill if it is then capable of finding its way in thru the broken bone to lacerate the main arteries at the top of the heart. If it cannot do that, then the animal will eventually recover consciousness, get up, and clear off with a broken shoulder. But if the bullet has found its way in sufficiently, death takes place from rapid internal hemorrhage before the animal recovers consciousness. If a bullet disintegrates, therefore, it cannot kill on a shoulder shot. This is why men who use ultra-high velocity featherweight expanding bullets on fairly heavy animals fail to kill clean when placing their bullets in this spot.

For my own satisfaction I also shot a large buffalo bull with the semi-pointed soft-nose bullet from my Holland .375 Magnum at about 50 yards range, placing the bullet on the shoulder. The bull was killed instantly. I recovered this bullet and found that it had mushroomed perfectly and that the lead core had left the metal envelope about one inch behind. But I cannot see that this is a fault, as it is sometimes declared to be, because the primary object of the metal envelope is to enable the bullet to take the rifling at the high velocities of the present day and, to a lesser extent, to prevent the bullet setting-up too quickly. Accordingly, having done its duty as this one undoubtedly had, what does it matter if it then parts company with the lead core?

(Author's note:—The foregoing paragraphs were originally written a number of years ago and appeared as an article entitled

Expanding Bullets in a number of sporting journals. Since, with the exception of the first to publish it, all the others asked permission to re-publish it, it would appear that the observations and views expressed meet with general approval amongst those qualified to judge. Accordingly, I have reproduced it here almost word for word as it originally appeared.)

On reading Keith's most informative *Big Game Rifles and Cartridges* I was surprised to see his remarks in connection with expanding bullets, because I find myself in disagreement with them and it has been pleasantly surprising to find that so many of our ideas entirely coincide, even altho our stamping grounds are so far apart. On pages 27 and 28 he writes as follows:

"On broadside shots at the lungs of all species of our big game, I want to state here that I always want my bullets to penetrate completely through the animal with good expansion, leaving a good blood trail on both sides of the animal. I know this is contrary to most experienced riflemen. They claim that any bullet that goes completely through an animal and out the other side wastes most of its energy, and I have many times seen them state that they always wanted their bullets to stop in an animal. At the same time they will tell you that they want the bullet to always have adequate penetration for possible raking shots from the rear, and wish to penetrate with certainty through the rump, intestines and paunch on into the chest cavity. When I see such statements in print, I often wonder . . . how, with common horse sense, they can expect a bullet to go thru the thin walls of an animal's ribs and either blow up completely, or else stop under the skin on the off side, and still expect that same bullet when fired from the rear at the same animal to penetrate the heavy rump bones, guts and what not and on into the lungs. It is an impossible thing to expect. Any bullet that has sufficient penetration for such rear end raking shots as to ever reach the chest cavity, will always go completely through an animal broadside; whether he be shot through the lungs or the shoulders makes no difference, and if that bullet cannot penetrate completely through and out the animal on any broadside shot, then it has absolutely no chance whatever of ever getting forward into the boiler room when planted in his rump."

It is so long since I hunted on the American continent, and even then my hunting consisted principally of caribou, moose and bear, that I do not feel qualified to speak of American game, but I cannot help wondering if Keith has not overlooked the extraordinary resilience of an animal's hide.   Out here in Africa I have frequently had occasion to remark on the amazing variety of animals, shot at all ranges, that have fallen to the soft-nose 300-gr. bullet from my .375 Magnum on broadside shots and, with the exception only of the smallest, almost invariably have that bulge on the far side with the beautifully mushroomed bullet under it.   The elasticity of the hide would seem to be the only answer; and therefore I cannot agree that Keith's was a really fair comparison.

That an animal with two holes in him will leave a better blood spoor than if he only had one is indisputable but my experience out here is that if the bullet remains in the animal it kills sooner than if it has whipped right thru.   It is for that reason that I have decided to use the 300-gr. soft-nose in my .375 Magnum in future instead of the 270-gr.   If the latter on a broadside shot fails to hit any bone larger than a rib, it will set-up but more often than not pass thru, whereas the 300-gr. will always remain in the animal.

It must not be imagined for a moment that the foregoing remarks are in any way intended to be a criticism of Elmer Keith or his most instructive book; on the contrary, it is clearly to be seen that Keith is a genuine hunter who knows his stuff and is most keenly observant of everything that concerns his profession.   If I ever returned to the States for a roam thru the woods, I should make it my business to look up Keith and have a long, long yarn with him before hitting the trail.

When the Ross .280, the forerunner of all the present-day high velocity rifles, was first introduced, the bullets were all as sharply pointed as possible to give them the best ballistic coefficient and thereby help them to retain their velocity at the longer ranges. But it was found that the sharp pencil points of lead become badly distorted in the magazine box owing to their inertia, acting against the backward movement of the rifle under the shock of discharge, causing them to tap against the front of the magazine.   This distortion seriously interfered with their accuracy and frequently resulted in thin slivers of lead being torn off as the cartridge was driven by the bolt into the chamber, giving rise to leading at the breech end of the barrel.

The copper-pointed expanding bullet was then introduced.

This was merely an adaptation of the old copper-tubed lead bullet but instead of the tube being cut off bluntly, it was given a point for the sake of its ballistic coefficient. But it had the fault common to all hollow-nosed bullets—it matters not if the hollow is left open or plugged with wax, wood or a copper tube—they all break up too soon other than on the very lightest and smallest of animals shot at long range.

So the makers altered the sharp pointed to the modern semi-pointed soft-nose. These are a great improvement but in magazine rifles are still a long way from perfect. In powerful rifles they still become slightly distorted. If several shots are fired and the magazine then recharged, leaving one or two of the original shells to stew in their own juice whilst still more are fired over their heads, you will find that the exposed lead has been tapped back over the nose of the bullet until it is in a thin sliver all ready to be stripped off when that shell is chambered. Normally, the distortion is not sufficient to seriously interfere with the accuracy but personally, when using magazine rifles I used to make a point of not leaving any shells longer than was absolutely necessary in the bottom of the magazine; when recharging I would first remove those still in the magazine and put them on top. Further, if there was the slightest sign of distortion, I would take my knife or my thumb nail and pare off the lead until it was once more slick with the nose of the bullet. In double rifles you have nothing to worry about.

These semi-pointed soft-nose are amongst the very best of modern expanding bullets. The small percentage of lead exposed and their very good shape give them adequate penetration. They set-up well, but do not break up. It is worthy of note that John Rigby, who has ever concentrated on Africa, has entirely discarded the copper-pointed bullet for his .350 Magnum and .350 N $\stackrel{o}{=}$ 2 rifles, and for many years past has only supplied the semi-pointed soft-nose; the 270-gr. bullets thrown by Holland & Holland's .375 Magnum and Purdey's .369 are semi-pointed. The same applies to the smaller calibers. No copper-pointed bullets are available for Holland's .300 Magnum; Rigby's .275 calibers throw semi-pointed bullets.

The copper-pointed bullet is designed for instantaneous expansion. The soft-nose-split for rapid expansion. The various soft-nose, with a greater or lesser amount of lead showing, will vary their rate of expansion in accordance with the amount of lead exposed—the more lead showing the quicker the expansion.

Somewhere in the thirties, I think it was, the Germans brought out a "strong-based" bullet for use in their stepped-up 9.3mm Mauser. The base of the bullet and the walls of the jacket, for about half to two-thirds of the way up them, had about two or three times the normal thickness of metal. It was said to be very satisfactory but the only ones I saw were copper-pointed. If other patterns were available they would have been excellent. There were occasions when the lead entirely disappeared, yet the reinforced jacket continued to plough thru the animal. I saw a kongoni shot with one of these bullets as he was quartering away from the gun. The bullet took him in the flank and the strong jacket was found under the skin near the point of the shoulder; there was no sign of the lead core. That bullet would have been very much better had it been plain soft-nose instead of copper-pointed. But for some reason best known to themselves the Germans did not bring out this bullet for their 10.75mm, tho it would have been eagerly accepted by lovers of that caliber.

I would very much like to see some of these new American bullets in action—the Peters "Belted" and the Remington "Core-Lokt" in particular. By all accounts they are very satisfactory. The British manufacturers have been somewhat dilatory in this connection. The only special bullets are the Westley Richards patent capped. Provided the right pattern is used they are splendid.

Auctor: Ah, yes; I wanted to ask you what you thought of those. They had a tremendous vogue when they first came out and many men still swear by them; others, however, do not.

Lector: I am one of those who do. When they were first introduced they were obtainable for practically every caliber on the market at that time; subsequently, however, other calibers were introduced for which they were not obtainable. The reason why some men dislike them is that they have only used the "L.T." pointed hollow-capped pattern, generally in a light rifle, and naturally found that it lacked penetration when used against some of the heavier animals. They were never intended for such work but those men did not take the trouble to examine the two types and see for themselves the difference between them. They just satisfied themselves by condemning the W.R. capped bullet, altho they knew nothing whatever about the second pattern, which would have proved perfectly satisfactory on the occasions when the first type failed. If you examine the two patterns, the "L.T." hollow-pointed and the round-capped, you will see that they are entirely different and obviously intended for quite different purposes. See them in section and the difference is immediately apparent—the pointed cap is hollow and extends well into the nose of the bullet. This means that it *must* set-up to almost its full extent almost on impact irrespective of whether it hits a bone or not and so if a fairly light bullet of this pattern is used on a fairly heavy animal it will probably fail to penetrate sufficiently —but that is not the fault of the bullet; it is the fault of the man who used the wrong pattern. The round-capped bullet is quite different—it more closely resembles a soft-nose with an exceptional amount of lead showing at the nose; the cap is then placed over this exposed lead so as to protect it and prevent the bullet packing up too soon. It is splendidly effective on all the heavier varieties of game, having excellent penetration.

The .318 is undoubtedly the most widely used of all Westley Richards' calibers and the one for which one mostly sees these capped bullets but it is noteworthy that it is almost invariably the "L.T." pointed-capped bullet that is being used. I have seldom seen the round-capped in use; yet it is the round-capped that should be used for the greater part of African shooting with this caliber. With a bullet of 250 grains the rapid expansion of the "L.T." bullet makes it suitable for small light buck but its expansion is too rapid for the heavier species. It is also to be remarked that the round-capped pattern is the only one available for all the heavier calibers with which deep penetration is generally required—the .450s, the .500s and .577s. The only large bore for which the "L.T." pointed hollow-capped bullet is obtainable is Westley Richards' special .476, and it was obviously with tiger-shooting in view that he designed a hollow-capped slug for that caliber so as to ensure full expansion of the 520-gr. bullet on a soft-skinned beast.

An additional advantage claimed by the inventors is that these capped bullets will not jam in magazine rifles, as many men complain happens with the ordinary soft-nose bullets owing to the soft exposed lead tending to nick and catch on the entrance to the chamber. (I have never known this to happen with a good quality weapon, and suspect that faulty assembly is to blame. It is to be noted that all such complaints that I have heard have come from those who habitually used cheap Continental rifles— South Africa in particular. I have never experienced the slightest tendency of the bolt to jam on any of the good grade magazines I used, and there were occasions when the bolt was whipped back and slammed forward again several times almost as rapidly as it would have been with a self-loader.)

Provided that the more suitable of the two patterns is chosen, and which is the more suitable depends entirely on the weight of bullet and the weight of animal, then Westley Richards' capped bullets will be found to be splendidly effective on all animals for which expanding bullets are required. So much so, in fact, that if a choice is being made between two rifles of approximately the same power and you find it difficult to decide which one to buy, if Westley Richards' capped bullets are available for one and not for the other I should be inclined to let that be the deciding factor. They are the only pattern of expanding bullet you can get for the .425, and I have known the 410-gr. "L.T." bullet so set-up on kudu, sable, water-buck, eland and similar animals that it wouldn't go down an 8-bore. Yet I have never known one of these bullets to break-up. I've known of the round-capped pattern thrown by a .577 blow a hole between 4 and 5 inches in diameter thru an elephant's heart when fired from in front. A round-capped 300-gr. slug was available for the .375 Magnum but how come I never used it is just one of those things. If it's obtainable in future, I've every intention of trying it.

There is a contention frequently put forward, chiefly by men with Indian experience, and it crops up regularly whenever expanding bullets are being discussed. Since I came across it again only yesterday I feel compelled to refer to it; tho really it will not bear close examination. However, since it occurs so often, it would seem that a very considerable number of men must believe it. Here it is:

"So far as I know, no satisfactory soft-nose bullet has yet been invented; it usually consists of an exposed lead tip, enclosed in a nickel sheath. The results from these bullets are excellent so long as they do not encounter a bone but who can ensure this?

"Again and again I have known these bullets, on striking bone, to disintegrate into fragments, making a dreadful superficial wound, but failing to kill or disable.

"My belief is that this phenomenon is due to the velocity, and the lead core being in a semi-liquid state owing to the terrific heat set-up; it may be borne in mind that shots at dangerous game are usually at close quarters and there has been little time for cooling off."

There is a good deal more of it, but that is enough. You will note that there is no reference to bullet weight—the writer speaks generally—tho, since he mentions dangerous game and since the remainder of his letter concerns rifles suitable for tiger, it's but to be assumed that he has bullets of generous weight in mind.

However, the weight of bullet has nothing to do with it and is quite immaterial. But a little consideration will show that his contention cannot be upheld. Surely the greatest heat that any bullet has to withstand is the heat of the expanding powder gasses on its base when the cartridge is fired? If that is so, then surely the lead core of a solid or full-patch bullet is in greater likelihood of being in a melted or semi-liquid state than the lead core of a soft-nose slug, since the lead of the latter is protected by the closed base of the bullet where that of the solid is not? And since the suction at the rear of a flat-based bullet approaches that of a vacuum, surely there would be greater likelihood of the melted lead being sucked out of a full-patch bullet en route to the target, which would result in practically no penetration at all, if indeed the lead core of any type of bullet ever experienced sufficient heat to melt it?

And talking about muzzle-blast—I've been asked if I've ever noticed any effect from the "blast" of a high-power or extreme capacity and high pressure cartridge when the rifle is held close to an animal? Can this severe blast affect an animal to any extent? Can it tear its hide, or slice out flesh, or blow its jaws apart, at a range of a few inches or feet? And have I ever derived anything from "muzzle-blast" for disabling animals?

To all of this I must answer "No." I have never noticed anything that I could put down to the actual blast. And there was the case of Percival I referred to when he fired his .450 Nitro into a lion's chest with the muzzle actually touching the lion. Yet that lion wasn't killed or even disabled by that shot and the .450

Nitro is an extremely powerful cartridge. There were 70 grains of cordite there along with the 480-gr. soft-nose bullet. Percival makes no mention of anything peculiar having taken place and altho he was not a gunbug, Percival was an extremely observant fella. That shot, you'd think, *ought* to have blown a hole in the lion into which you could have put your head and I can't imagine that Percival would have overlooked it. Yet there's no mention of anything of the sort having happened. On the contrary the lion was busy with his teeth for some little while afterwards until Percival managed to blow out his brains. And so, if a .450 Nitro won't "blast" an animal out of existence even when the muzzle is touching him, I'm certainly not gonna rely upon muzzle-blast to stop my critters.

Auctor: I'd like your views on the practice of cutting the nose of full-patch bullets to make them expand. From all I can gather all you old-timers made quite a regular habit of it and I distinctly recollect one of you saying that the cut solid made a very much better expanding bullet for the "Mark VI" British .303 than any he could buy.

The Danger of the Cut Solid. *Lector:* There; does that tell you what I think of the practice? And you most assuredly can *not* class me with those who make a habit of mutilating their bullets—it's a thing I've never done, and a thing I've not the smallest intention of ever attempting. Ever since the earliest days of metal-jacketed bullets men have made a habit of cutting an X in the nose of solid or full-patch bullets, or of rubbing off the nose of the envelope on a file until the lead core is exposed and then scooping out some of the lead, for the purpose of converting them into expanding bullets. I think it was first practiced, and certainly most widely practiced, in South Africa after the Boer war, when vast quantities of surplus army ammunition were thrown on the market. Men going out for a lengthy hunting trip would buy a case or two of this at a purely nominal price, and then mutilate the nose of the bullets to make them expand. Those old "Mark VI" .303s had a really hard nose, having plenty metal there, and seemed to stand it pretty well. Nevertheless, it's a horribly dangerous practice and yet one sees it done on all sides.

These men do not seem to realize that when they cut or remove the metal from the nose of a "solid" or full-patch bullet, the envelope has become merely a tube. In the case of a soft-nose bullet the lead core is inserted at the nose, the base of the bullet being solid; it is therefore quite safe. But the lead filling of a solid is inserted at the base; accordingly, if you cut off the nose, there is nothing at either end of the lead filling—the envelope has been made into a tube around the lead, with nothing at either end.

A bullet must fit the barrel tightly if it's to shoot accurately. It must fit sufficiently tightly to seal the bore against the expanding powder gasses when the cartridge is fired. That it does so is shown by the grooves cut in it by the rifling. In other words, the bullet meets with considerable resistance during its passage along the bore. That resistance must be borne by the envelope. In the case of an ordinary bullet there is nothing to worry about, since one end of the envelope is closed; but if the bullet has been mutilated by having that closed end opened, there is grave danger of the lead core being blown out and leaving the metal envelope sticking in the bore.

Now just visualize what happens when the next shot is fired. Most rifles that one sees in Africa are dirty and rusty, and one has frequently heard men say, "Oh, that does not matter—the first shot will clear all that muck out." All that muck and rust increases the resistance the first bullet encounters. The shot is fired, the envelope sticks in the bore, and the lead core is blown out. The man thinks he has missed: "Never mind; it was all that muck in the barrel. It will be all right now." He slams another shell up from the magazine and lets drive again. The second bullet gets along fine until it meets up with the envelope left by the first. Its passage is instantly checked but the expanding powder gasses will not be checked. The result is that enormous pressure is immediately set up. No firearm could possibly withstand it; something has to give way. The barrel bursts, the stock is shattered, the action ripped open, and the bolt driven back into the shooter's face. That is what happens in theory and it's what *can*, and sometimes *does*, happen in practice.

You can get away with this cut solid business for years sometimes if you are lucky—most fools are allowed a little latitude—but there is no guarantee that the gods who look after fools will not sooner or later get tired of the job and leave you to stew in your own juice.

If you run out of expanding bullets, well, it's just too bad; you will have to do the best you can with solids. But use them as solids—let nothing induce you to mutilate them.

I have gone into this question of expanding bullets at considerable length, because it is a very much more important matter than many men seem to realize. The whole pleasure and even success of your expedition can be spoilt by unsuitable bullets. If dangerous game are on the *tapis* the use of unsuitable bullets could have serious results.

CHAPTER XI

The Revolver or Pistol as Auxiliary

FEW MEN IN AFRICA CARRY A REVOLVER OR PISTOL, EXCEPT FOR THOSE
who have developed the sport of hunting lions and leopards on
horseback with the aid of a pack of hounds. It was Paul Rainey
who introduced this method into East Africa by bringing over
from America a pair of well-trained cougar hounds. However,
this game is only played in British East Africa and the hand guns
are usually carried on the horse, or rather on the saddle, and not
on the rider. When hunting on foot a revolver is a thing you may
never need in a lifetime in the Bush—but if you do need it, you
are liable to need it darned badly.

I used to always carry a revolver in the days when most of my
shooting was done with single-loaders, and still do when after
lion. But otherwise nowadays I don't, because my hunting consists almost exclusively of elephant and buffalo. It's useful with
which to finish off a wounded non-dangerous beast if you are
running short of shells for your rifle—but be careful; some of these
antlered "non-dangerous" animals can kill with a single swing
of their horns altho otherwise crippled. Many a hunter has been
killed by sable antelope when approaching too lightheartedly to
finish them off. I had a wounded sable bull make a savage and
most determined charge on one occasion, and I only managed to
bring him down when within a matter of feet.

But don't weigh yourself down with a great .45 or .44 Special
and a belt of shells, which you won't be wanting, when hunting
on foot. They're all right if you're forking a horse all day, or to
wear in a cold climate where you'll have plenty clothing on but
out here we wear as little clothing as possible, and that loose-
fitting. A heavy gun on your belt becomes uncomfortable and a

nuisance, and will sooner or later set-up "prickly heat"—that most irritating rash caused by overworking of the sweat glands, and greatly aggravated by the pressure of a gun belt, as it collects the sweat and prevents it evaporating or running down. Besides, I'm not advising anybody to go hunting with a hand gun. A revolver or pistol should be looked upon solely as a stand-by for use in an emergency. Since, if it's wanted at all, the range will probably be a matter of inches, there is no real need for a heavy gun.

I used to recommend an automatic pistol of not less power than the long .38 Colt Auto because of the metal-covered bullets; in those days metal-jacketed slugs were not available for revolvers. But since World War II metal-covered bullets are obtainable for at least some sixguns, such as the .455 and .38, so if for any reason you prefer this type of weapon there is no reason why you shouldn't carry it. Experience has shown that the plain lead bullets fail badly in penetration on the mighty chest muscles of a lion.

Blaney Percival, who was a great believer in a long-barreled .45 Colt revolver, but who did all his hunting on horseback, relates how on one occasion he fired a great many shots from his revolver at a lion, first from motives of humanity and then in self-defence. He had been riding along slowly when suddenly a lion sprang up out of the grass very close and made threateningly towards him. Percival drew his revolver—he had no rifle with him—and fired a quick snap-shot which took the lion fairly in the eye. The animal reared up and crashed over backwards into the dry river-bed. He scrambled to his feet and moved slowly away, shaking his head. Percival, thinking he was badly wounded and nearly dead, emptied his gun into him. And then the fun started! The lion whipped around and came; Percival galloped for dear life, then, having out-distanced the lion, pulled up and reloaded and returned to finish off his beast. But Leo was by no means on his last legs. Percival's brother, hearing the shooting and knowing that Percival had no rifle with him, came out and killed the lion with a rifle. Altho the first shot from the revolver had taken the lion in the eye, Percival said that not one of the lead bullets had penetrated more than 2 inches into the great muscles of the chest and shoulders; some had slipped in quite easily between the ribs. As metal-covered bullets were not available for the revolver in those days, Percival took to the .45 Colt Automatic. But on the few occasions he speaks of when he was hunting on foot, there is no mention of his having a hand gun on his belt; yet he was far more likely to need it then than when mounted. Take note of those two occasions when he was shooting lions and experienced a jamb that I have already mentioned.

Self-consciousness is an ingrained trait in the average Britisher. In my humble opinion it's the acme of conceit to imagine that the rest of the world can find nothing more interesting to observe or discuss than you and your doings but there it is. The ordinary Britisher has a positive horror of appearing the least bit "different"; he *must* conform to his own conventions and ideas of the "fitness of things." And one of these is that it's "not done" for anyone to carry a revolver—folk might think that one was playing at being a cow-puncher! But they turn a condescending, supercilious and slightly-amused eye on Americans who carry them, and wonder if the poor mutts really think they are necessary, or is it just that they like to imagine they are back again in the days of their own wild and wooly West—"when men were men and women durned glad of it!"

Admittedly, it's totally unnecessary to weigh yourself down with a belt containing 40 or 50 shells as well as the revolver, but I personally reckon that a great many of those Britishers who get themselves mauled by lions might have saved themselves that mauling, with the possible loss of an arm or a leg, if not of life itself, had they been carrying a revolver or pistol in a sensible type of open-topped holster. The majority of them don't even carry a knife, tho that would be better than nothing, but it's not in the same street with a hand gun firing metal-covered bullets—even lead slugs would be better than nothing.

If you have failed to stop a charging lion and he has gotten you down and is now getting busy with his teeth, you can blow out his brains with your revolver from a range of two or three inches—which you will find infinitely more satisfactory than trying to gouge out his eyes with your thumbs or catch hold of his tongue with your hand, merely to have your hand crushed to pulp, as has happened to many a man in the past who was too shy to carry a hand gun on his belt in case somebody laughed at him or twitted him about it.

I personally know eight or ten men who have been mauled by lion, tiger or leopard, apart from those I have heard or read about, and in every case they are partially crippled. Some have lost arms or legs, and others might as well have had them amputated for they are of precious little use to them. Not one of those fools was carrying a revolver tho from their own description of their mauling it is apparent that they could each have saved themselves had they been doing so. Let me recapitulate two or three of these incidents—not hypothetical cases but actual adventures that took place—and let us see if my contention cannot be sustained that the men concerned could have saved themselves had they been carrying a hand gun.

Here is Blaney Percival's own account of the time he was brought down by a lion. There is no mention of a revolver on this occasion, which would seem to indicate that he only carried it when on horseback. He writes as follows:—

"It was a detestable place through which to follow a lion, though unwounded, but, having begun, we went on, and beat out every scrap of cover big enough to hide a rat. I had begun to think we must have passed over him somehow, when he suddenly got up close in front—a fine lion with a dark mane. I could not get in a shot until he was some distance away, and then only succeeded in hitting his foot. Though not seriously hurt, he turned into the bushes again, and when we reached the place where he entered, a man whom I had posted outside the cover to watch told us that the beast had gone into the grass below a small tree he pointed out. I walked towards the place, and when within 30 yards he charged straight out, growling horribly, mouth open, mane up. My bullet, as I afterwards discovered, caught him on one of his canine teeth, smashing it to atoms, but doing no other damage. It sufficed to turn him, and he went off towards the reeds, receiving a second bullet in about the right place. Thick cover was only about 20 paces distant and he succeeded in reaching it, but, as stone throwing and shouting failed to move him, I concluded he was done for, and, posting men round the place, sat down for half an hour, hoping he would die.

"As the event proved, he had a great deal more life in him than I supposed. Having rested, we took up the blood-spoor, and crept into the reeds, very carefully and slowly, I leading and two

Masai, Yondi and another man, with shield and spear close behind. We had gone only a few steps into the cover when I heard the rush of his charge through the reeds. Next moment his head broke out within 3 yards. I fired once, and again as he up reared over me. I have some confused recollection of going down under a heavy weight, and a general sense of scuffle. Rather shaken and dazed, I looked up to find Yondi across my knees, the lion on top of him, busy with his teeth. Hampered as I was by the combined weight of man and lion on my limbs, it was very difficult to get cartridges from my pocket. I had had the usual couple ready in my fingers when I fired, but dropped these when the lion knocked me over. I succeeded in extracting two more from the pocket, loaded, and, holding the rifle by the middle of the barrel, slid the butt over my shoulder, and put a bullet into the lion's ear at about 3 inches, killing him instantly. Then Yondi and I managed to struggle from under the brute. Our feelings—mine at least— were reflected in the haste with which we retreated from the neighbourhood of the lion, dead though we knew him to be.

"Yondi was cruelly mauled; he had a fearful bite in the thigh, and one foot was badly torn. I did what I could for his injuries. . . .

"To this hour I am not very clear what happened. As far as I could make out the muzzle of the rifle took the lion's chest, and thus threw me backward. The two Masai instantly sprang in, drove their spears home, and diverted his attention to themselves, when Yondi was caught and thrown across me.

"The man could not walk. . . . Yondi has never quite recovered from his injuries, and still limps from the effect of the wound in his thigh. As soon as he recovered he came back to me and has remained ever since, doing such light work as he can."

Now there cannot be the slightest doubt that Percival would have been killed or at least badly mauled if it hadn't been for the courage of his Masai spearmen. But the unfortunate Yondi might have escaped with a lesser mauling had Percival had his Colt with him that day. You can readily appreciate how much quicker he could have killed the lion with a revolver than was possible when he had to fumble for those spare shells in his pocket and reload the rifle. He had been using a Rigby double .450.

Then to take the case of Lieut.-Commander Coombe to whom I

have previously referred. In describing his adventure he has written as follows:—

"Again, early next morning, I stalked up to the kill. My belief was fully justified. They were all there, two old males lying on either side of the kill and the rest in one long line about twenty yards apart.

". . . At length, however, one sat up, leaning on his elbow. This was my chance, and I fired. The whole lot immediately sprang to their feet, and one of the lionesses, looking extremely nasty, came towards me.

"I shot her and the whole lot made off, including the second male lion, who, after he had gone fifty or sixty yards, stopped to look back. I think he was wondering why his mate did not follow him. I now took a very foolish risk. It is generally accepted by men who really know something about shooting that a shot should never be fired unless you are sure of your shot.

"This lion was a very difficult shot. He must have been 100 to 150 yards away and with his body looking away from me, though his head was turned in my direction. The size of his mane decided me and I fired. It was subsequently discovered that the bullet had gone through the fleshy part of the hind leg into his stomach.

"Off he went into some long grass a short distance away. I did not follow him immediately. I decided I would try to recover the lion I had fired at the evening before.

". . . I now decided to follow the lion I had wounded. There was not much blood, and what there was seemed to get less and less. I had been after him about half an hour, and considered that he must have escaped into the big bulrushes into the swamp, which was only a short distance away. I therefore said to my boys: "Oh, well, we won't get him now. We'd better return." It was at that precise moment, with a roar, that he charged from about twenty-five yards away. I was carrying my 7mm Mauser with which I had shot all my previous lions, and my native gun-bearer had my .450 double-barreled rifle, and another native my 12-bore shot gun.

"I fired with the 7mm and turned quickly to get the big rifle, but the boy had taken to his heels. I, therefore, turned to face the lion, but unfortunately not having time to reload, I was only able to thrust the rifle as hard as I could into his face.

"His first action was to chew my left knee and shin bone. I was absolutely defenceless, didn't even have a knife. My one thought was to keep him as long as possible below my body level. I tried to put my fingers into his eyes, but it was difficult, the skin was so loose. I thrust my right leg into his face, which he immediately got hold of. During all this I was yelling for my boys to come and shoot him. There didn't seem to be much hope. They had completely disappeared. I then thought if I got my hand into his mouth I could grasp his tongue. I did this and managed to hold the top of his tongue for a bit, but the saliva made it slippery and an elusive thing to hold on to, so my grip did not last long.

"It was at this moment that I heard the voice of my old farm boy, Chimoyra, behind me. There he was, the plucky fellow, with my heavy rifle pointing straight at me, or so it seemed, stalking up to shoot the lion.

"I managed to direct him to one side, and when within about five yards he fired. The shot went through the lion's shoulder and he fell over on to his side, luckily not on top of me. It was a most noble act on the part of the boy. He had never to my knowledge handled a gun before, but without the slightest hesitation as soon as he had seen my gun-bearer (a local native) decamping he had run after him, snatched the rifle from him, and come to my rescue. I was, of course, now in a pretty helpless state. Both my legs had been badly mauled and also my right hand. . . ."

Well, don't you agree that he would have come a damn sight better out of the encounter if he had had a six-gun on his belt?

Then to take the case of "X" (I won't mention his name because to the best of my knowledge and belief he has never published an account of his mauling, and he might not like to have me do so. However, I know him well and doubtless if he sees this will be able to recognize himself).

The tale concerns a Malayan tiger. The local "Injuns" came up in a great state one evening to tell X that a tiger had killed a coolie close by the village. X had no gun, but one of the villagers had an old Snider—the original British breech-loading Service rifle—an adaptation of the old muzzle-loading musket. You would have thought that X, having been born in India and having lived all his life up to then in the East, would have known better but he took the old Snider from the villager, who was only too keen to relinquish it, and set forth to do battle with the man-eater. He saw the brute on top of the body of the dead coolie about 50 yards away, and immediately let drive. The tiger dashed into a clump of reeds and X went after him. He had barely entered the reeds when the tiger sprang on him. One swipe of a paw removed X's right ear and a good deal of his face. The tiger then lay down beside him and commenced chewing one of his hands in what X described as a "contemplative manner," for all the world as tho he was sampling a whiteman for the first time and wanted to compare the flavor with that of the coolie he had just killed. X, naturally, was in no mood to judge time, but he reckoned that this went on for quite an appreciable while. Presently the tiger stopped chewing, tho he still held X's hand in his mouth. X followed the direction of his gaze and saw two or three of the local Injuns creeping up to see what had happened. The tiger made a rush, the Injuns departed at speed, and X decided it was as good an opportunity as he was likely to get. He also legged it like hell in the opposite direction, and got clear.

There are only two fingers left on that hand; all the rest were chewed off, and the sinews of the remainder of the hand and arm so badly torn that the whole thing is permanently crooked at right angles to the rest of the arm and no better than a hook.

I reckon X could have finished up with but the loss of his ear had he had a hand gun on his belt. I have been over that adventure with him several times, and his account of it never varies. He admits himself that a revolver would have saved him but "damn it, John, one doesn't carry a revolver; it's not done, old boy, it's not done."

Maybe not but I was mighty glad I was carrying one on two different occasions: once when a leopard sprang on me out of a tree without the slightest warning; and again when a wounded lioness came for me. She was one of a party of five. I had killed her companions with a Martini-Henry (a single-shot rifle) but only wounded her. When she charged I knocked her down but failed to kill her and she was on me before I had completed reloading. But the .455 Webley revolver settled both animals' hash. The leopard had made something of a mess of me—they will use all four feet as well as their teeth, where a lion or tiger will usually only use his paws to hold and then bite—but the lioness didn't even draw blood. The leopard was shot with the muzzle of the revolver actually touching his chest; the lioness had her brains blown out from a range of 2 or 3 inches just as her mouth closed on my knee.

Just as this book was about to go to press, I casually mentioned in a letter to my publisher that I had killed a lion a night or two before with my old .455 British Service Webley revolver and metal-jacketed slugs. He insists that I tell the yarn here. So here it is:

I and my good lad Ali were sleeping in the open, just the two of us. Somewhere in the night I woke up convinced that I had smelled a lion. We can hear lions roaring and singing to themselves almost nightly as they drift down to the river for a drink and then wander away again but they did not usually come around where we stayed. It was a stinking hot night, so we had no fire.

There was an old daisy, some kind of half-breed, who had a goat kraal about 50 yards away, and occasionally hyenas would come around trying to get at the goats. But I was certain it was no hyena I had smelled. My only weapon was my old Service revolver, a faithful friend ever since the end of World War I. It spends its life under my pillow. I got hold of this but didn't like to go wandering off leaving my companion fast asleep like that in the open—in case things went wrong. So I put my hand on his shoulder, and, like the well-trained lad he is, he was awake on the instant and not a sound out of him. I told him what was in the wind and suggested he slip into the grass hut until I got back. This was merely a shanty we used when it rained, and for cooking; it had no door. Ali just gave me one look, and then reached down and picked up the fine hunting knife I had given him, and which he keeps like a surgeon's amputating knife, drew it from its sheath, threw down the sheath, and nodded to me to get going. I knew it was useless to protest. We have been comrades in so many escapades over so many years that it was unthinkable for him to remain behind like a woman and let me go looking for a lion with nothing but a hand gun.

So off we went. I had no flashlight but the moon served my purpose. There was an old disused hog pen or sty or whatever you call the thing about 15 feet from the goat kraal and we sneaked up behind this and peeked around it. I was quite right. It was a lion. He was prowling around slowly, looking for a weak spot in the side of the kraal, or possibly hoping that the occupants would make a concerted rush from his smell and break it down— a favorite trick of cattle-killers. I reckoned it would be a good thing to slip inside the old hog pen, which was stoutly built of poles about 4 inches in diameter well-sunk in the ground. It had the remains of a thatched roof. I figured it would at least break the force of the lion's rush if things went wrong. I didn't fancy the notion of going lion-hunting with nothing but a revolver but I figured it would be better to get after him whilst he was occupied with thoughts of goat, than wait for him to come sneaking over our way. Ali and I are both Muhammadans and therefore are not in the habit of messing around with hog pens but under the circumstances did not hesitate to slip into this one. It was well dried-out anyway. The poles were about 2 or 3 inches apart.

I tried to see if I could aim but could not see my sights at all. I then tried to see if I could get anything approaching an aim by looking along the edge of the semi-octagonal barrel but that was no good either. So I decided to take the shot from the level of my hip next time Leo came around. Altho I had practiced shooting a rifle off both shoulders, I had done practically all my revolver shooting in the past with my right hand. But, thanks to World War II, there isn't quite so much of that hand now as there used to be, and I find that I can't manage a big gun like the Webley with it. So I was, perforce, compelled to use my left, which was not really such a handicap as it might seem, because I have always been ambidextrous.

In due course the lion appeared from my left, making just about as much noise as a puff of smoke. I waited until he just wasn't opposite, and then let him have it. I had hoped to take him thru the shoulder-blade about halfway between the centre and the withers, where the bone should be getting a mite thinner but as I afterwards discovered the bullet smacked into his spine at the top of the withers—say 3-4 inches or thereabouts higher than I had intended. He dropped instantly and lay flat on his side, his back towards me. I immediately gave him another in thru the top of his head. That one was better, and took him within mebbe an inch of where I had meant it to. On receipt of it he gave a convulsive jerk and kick of the upper hind leg proving conclusively that it was it that had killed him, and not the first one.

Whether or not the first would have proved fatal I'm not enough of a medico to say—one doesn't take chances—if wise—with lions that drop instantly to the first shot when placed as that one was. But there was no doubt about the second. I ran out to make sure but there was no need for any more. And I looked up to find Ali beside me, naked knife in hand.

Now don't get me wrong here. I'm *not* recommending anybody to go lion-hunting with nothing but a hand gun. I don't care what make, type, or caliber of weapon it is a hand gun in Africa should be looked upon simply as a stand-by, a reserve, and *not* as a weapon of offense. It can save your life in an emergency when used in self-defense, sure, but it can cost you your life if used foolishly.

A coupla nights later I killed a hyena in the same place. He'd gotten hold of a young goat by one hind leg thru a hole in the kraal and was trying to drag the little critter out. It was the goat yelling its head off that woke us. This time I didn't bother to get into the hog pen, but just crept around it and let drive for the varmint's shoulder. The metal-covered slug plowed thru and killed him.

If you are concentrating on lions I should advise you to carry a hand gun on your belt but be sure that the butt of your rifle won't clash against it when you are stalking. Something like a Smith & Wesson .38 Special with round-nose metal-covered bullets, or a .38 Colt automatic, should nicely answer all questions. A powerful pistol or revolver is a very comforting thing to have under your pillow at night. Many men rely upon a loaded shot gun at night but if a lion attacks and you are the object of the attack, you will not be able to get that shot gun into action. With a revolver you have at least a hope. Since the hand gun is merely a stand-by, and if you have to use it it will be from a range of mere inches, nevertheless a lion can do appalling damage in a matter of seconds—and a leopard is even worse—so it would be unwise to rely upon one of those delightful little .25 caliber waistcoat pocket fly-swatters.

CHAPTER XII

A Summing-up

Auctor: Now then, old-timer, you've covered a good deal of ground up to here. Don't you think it would be a good thing to have a general summing-up? It should help to clarify matters.

Lector: Okeh. Actually, the whole thing can be compressed into a very few paragraphs. My sole object in discussing the question so fully was to assist the reader. If a man knows the whys and wherefores, the reasons why this or that weapon is preferable to some other, he will be in a better position to make his choice. To merely recommend certain rifles and types of rifle, without telling him why, would not be particularly helpful. He must know the *reason* why. And it is my earnest hope that I have succeeded in doing so.

Speaking in broad, general terms, the question of a choice of rifles is really quite simple if only one will use a little common sense:

(a). Small bores and light bullets for the smaller varieties of soft-skinned non-dangerous game such as are usually shot at medium and long ranges—say between 150 and 250 yards;

(b). Medium bores throwing medium weight bullets for the heavier varieties of soft-skinned non-dangerous game such as are usually shot at medium ranges—say between 100 and 200 yards; and

(c). Large bores throwing heavy bullets for heavy and dangerous animals such as are shot at close quarters usually in thick cover.

This can be still further modified:

	Caliber	Bullet	Velocity
For (*a*)	.240–.318	100–180-gr.	2,650–3,000 f.s.
For (*b*)	.318–.375 Magnum	220–320-gr.	2,150–2,650 f.s.
For (*c*)	.400–.600	400–900-gr.	1,850–2,400 f.s.

Auctor: Well, that seems clear enough. And now your own personal choice for the different groups.

Lector: I would very much like to try out the little .240 but will confine myself to those weapons of which I can speak from actual personal experience:

	Doubles	*Magazines*
For (*a*)	.275 N $\stackrel{\circ}{=}$ 2	.300 Magnum
For (*b*)	.375 Magnum	.375 Magnum
For (*c*)	.400 and .465	.416 and .500

I should like to emphasize that I would be just as happy with a .400 as with a .465 for class (c), and have only mentioned the larger caliber to recommend it from amongst its numerous contemporaries should something more powerful than the .400 be desired.

CHAPTER XIII

Miscellaneous Odds and Ends

CLEANING RIFLES. It may seem trite to remark that a hunter's best friend is his rifle but occasions will occur when you will agree that it sure is. Obviously, therefore, it behooves him to look after it. All too many hunters in Africa are content to just hand the rifle to one of their servants to clean. That's no good; you must clean it yourself. What can the boy possibly know about the proper cleaning of nitro-firing rifles if corrosion is to be avoided? He will probably give it a pull thru and then just wipe it over with his hands which he has dipped in some oil that has dripped out of the sump of your car or truck. It's not his fault he does not know any better. Yet there are many men who appear quite satisfied with that method. Blaney Percival mentions an occasion when he was trying to take a shot at a lion, only to experience an apparent misfire, and on throwing open the breech found that, "the wretched boy who had cleaned the rifle had pushed all the cartridges into the magazine." You see, he hadn't even bothered to load his own rifle but had left it to his servant.

It's a never-ending source of amazement to me how a man of Percival's experience could have been so careless but he is by no means exceptional. I have known several hunters who never in their lives bought any sort of cleaning materials whatsoever for their rifles. I remember one who would have been mauled by a lion had I not shot the brute. I don't care about going out with another man unless I'm very sure of him but on this occasion there were three lions to be tackled which had been making a nuisance of themselves, and this fella asked me to come along to give him a hand as he didn't feel confident of his own ability to kill all three and he wanted them wiped out. So, much against my will, I went—and as it transpired, it was maybe a good thing that I did.

We found the lions in a little clear patch under some tall white-thorn trees, where no grass grows. There were three of them, a male and two females, and they had just enjoyed a full feed on a water-buck. They were lying around sunning themselves, disinclined for trouble or even movement. The lion and one of the lionesses were close together and separated by about two or three times her own length from the second lioness. So, since I was using a double .465, I nodded to my companion to take the lioness on her own whilst I dealt with the two closer ones. He was using cut solids in a 9.3mm Mauser. I killed my two with a quick right and left, and was surprised not to hear my companion's rifle synchronize with my first shot, as it should have done. Reloading rapidly, I was glad I had fitted my ejector springs, because I saw the second lioness coming open-mouthed for my companion who was struggling with his rifle. Since the brute had only been about 35 yards away, and since I'd had to reload, she was nearly home when I brought her down with a bullet thru the shoulder. I asked my very scared and white-faced companion what on earth had ! appened to him; and as soon as he was able to speak he started cussing his rifle. I finally discovered that he had "oiled" it with melted hippo fat the last time he used it, about a week previously! Hippo fat—which solidifies like lard! The striker wouldn't, couldn't, fall; the pull of the spring was only able to drag it slowly forward.

Men have a notion that the cleaning of nitro-firing rifles that have been shooting British ammunition is a hell of a job necessitating a whole bucket of boiling water. That's all bunk. Admittedly, the nigger in this particular wood-pile is the potassium chloride deposited in the bore after each shot. This has nothing to do with the powder, but is the result of firing the potassium chlorate contained in the cap composition in all British caps, or primers. The chloride is invisible and cannot be removed by any "ordinary" methods of cleaning and this is the cause of the "after rusting" so many men complain about. They "clean" their rifles, oil them, put them away, and then two or three days later find that they are badly rusted inside. Potassium chloride is not acid, as it is sometimes said to be. Chemically it is the same as sodium chloride, or common salt, and salt would act just the same if it was in the barrel of your rifle—see how readily gun-barrels rust in the neighborhood of the sea. Well, you all know how readily salt dissolves in water, or in the gravy on your plate but how it will not dissolve in oil. Accordingly, all you have to do is to take advantage of the chloride's natural affinity for water. Pour a cup of boiling water thru each barrel that has been fired—cold water will do just as well, but boiling water is easier to dry out because of evaporation. Use a funnel with a short spout or neck so that the chambers get their share of the water. Wipe out the water, which will remove most of the muck, and then rub a phospher-bronze wire brush well-dipped in a good alkaline gun oil thru the bore a few times. After that, wash out the bore with a stiff bristle brush dipped several times in similar oil, then rub a couple of clean flannel patches thru it. It should now be like a new pin. Finally, run a wool mop dipped in a good oil thru the bore just once so as to leave a film of oil as a rust preventer. That's all.

If you happen to be hunting in a very dry zone, where every drop of water is precious, you may reckon you can't spare a cup of water for each barrel; well, that'll be okeh too. There'll sure be some dregs of tea or coffee left in the pot, won't there? Just dip a couple of clean patches in that until they're well saturated; they'll do. If it comes to that, you can probably think of something else that's mostly water and quite capable of dissolving salt; well, if the worst comes to the worst, use that. Anyhow, in such dry districts, there will be but little moisture in the atmosphere, and therefore little likelihood of rusting setting-up in your rifles.

It might legitimately be asked: then why the hell don't the British use non-fouling caps and be done with it once and for all? And the answer is that they have tried all combinations to see if they couldn't produce a "non-fouling" cap equally as good and equally as certain as their present chlorate caps, but, altho they had no particular difficulty in making "non-fouling" caps, they found that they were neither so sensitive nor so hot as the chlorate caps; nor, and this is very important, did they suit so well the British powders. Everybody who professes to know anything about cartridges for either gun or rifle will know that the caps must match the powders if the best results are to be obtained. Also —and this is the *most* important point—they are not yet entirely stable over a period of years.

So the British very wisely, in my opinion, continue to use chlorate caps. And as I have mentioned elsewhere in this book, in all the years, and in all the thousands of rounds of British ammunition I have fired, I have only personally experienced one misfire, and never experienced a hangfire. And that solitary misfire was almost certainly the shell that dropped into the water. Well, since the water treatment of a barrel is so simple, I, personally, am quite willing to put up with it if by doing so I am assured of equally reliable results from my ammunition in the future.

Apart from the mere cleaning of the bores, the mechanism of the rifle should be examined, wiped and oiled. This is a simple matter with magazine rifles and really should not be difficult with doubles. But there is one point I should like to stress and that is the absolute necessity for testing the mechanism of all weapons before leaving camp. I have already hinted at it when mentioning that fella whose 9.3mm refused to fire and in an earlier section I mentioned a fairly close shave I had when unexpectedly attacked by a buffalo that had been wounded the previous day by some coon armed with an old gas-pipe muzzle-loader. But I didn't tell you how very much closer it might have been if I hadn't made it a practice to always test the working of my rifles before leaving camp. The rifle I was using that day had been put away for a few days' rest, and altho I had given it the usual thoro cleaning, I had apparently overlooked the fact that the last day it had been used had been exceptionally hot, and the sweat from my hand must have worked its way in under the safety slide—and there are few things that cause rust to form so quickly as human perspiration does—salt again? When I tried to move the slide I found that a terrific effort was necessary. Accordingly, I unloaded and, with a toothbrush dipped in oil, did what was necessary and put it right. Had it not been for that custom of mine, that buff would surely have got me. Elsewhere in this book you will find where another sportsman very nearly had himself and his wife and kids run down by a peevish rhino thru the very same thing. As I said before, it's no good leaving this sort of thing to your servants; you must see to it all yourself. Sure, it's very nice to have Jim Crow doing every darn thing for you, waiting on you hand and foot, and when you leave Africa you miss him but there are some things the hunter of dangerous game *must* see to himself—and those things are everything, *EVERYTHING*, connected with his rifles and ammunition.

SAFETIES. The safety slide on a double hammerless rifle that is to be taken against dangerous game should be non-automatic. Yet, with one or two notable exceptions, nearly all gunsmiths make them automatic unless specifically instructed not to.

The inexperienced man would probably never give a thought to such an apparently trivial point; and if he did, it would very likely be to the effect that the slide should be automatic as it usually is on shot guns. No greater mistake could be made. Nothing would be easier than for him to forget to shove forward the slide again after reloading if he found himself being attacked. It has happened again and again, and not merely with the new hands, but with thoroly experienced men. Let me give you an instance or two to help drive home my point:

Jimmy James, a cheery soul, was a man who had done a considerable amount of hunting on and off. He was hunting a notorious man-eater that had been causing consternation over a large area for a period of at least three years, and was known to have killed more than 200 natives. He had almost certainly been started off on his man-eating career thru being wounded by a sportsman who failed to finish him off, because he was a fine, dark-maned lion, and that is unusual in a man-eater. Several sportsmen had tried to get him but he was very cunning, and altho one or two of the hunters had had a shot at him, he was still going strong.

Jimmy arrived by truck in the centre of the man-eater's area, pitched camp, and in due course word was brought in of a kill not far away. Jimmy went out with his double .450 and a bunch of the local Injuns, in case he wanted them to drive the lion out of cover. Sure enough, the lion was much too wise by now to stick around in the open, and had dragged the body of the man into a thick clump of bush. But this bush was separated by about 60 yards from a continuous stretch of long grass. Jimmy reckoned his Injuns could drive the lion out of the bush, and that he would be bound to make for the long grass, so he planked himself down on the route he guessed the lion would take—but parked himself rather too close to it. Signalling to his men to start the beat, Jimmy knelt down behind a tuft of grass.

In due course the lion appeared. But he knew as much as Jimmy did about this sort of thing; he had been driven and shot at on several occasions and knew just what it all portended. He did not just come slouching across the open, as the hunter had hoped, but sneaked out, and, making himself as small as only a lion can when he does not want to be seen, he covered half the distance to the grass before Jimmy saw him. When he did, it was only a glimpse he caught. He fired, knocked the lion down, but the bullet was placed too far back. Had he not been almost directly in the lion's path, all might have been well but unfortunately he was. The lion got up, saw the hunter in front of him and nicely within charging range—about 25 yards—and came, roaring. The moment he fired, Jimmy broke the breech with the intention of reloading, as he expected he might be charged. But, seeing the lion coming, he realized he wouldn't have time to complete the business so he closed the breech and waited until the lion was almost on him before firing, as he now had but the one available shot. His men were eyewitnesses, and waited breathlessly for the shot—but it never came. . . .

Jimmy had forgotten to push forward the safety slide after opening the breech that time. Had he succeeded in reloading, he might have remembered but not having actually reloaded, he never gave it a thought until too late. Lumley Hall was another who was killed shortly before the recent war in such an almost identical manner that to relate his case would amount to repetition. I had frequently warned Jimmy of the danger of the automatic safety, and offered to convert it for him to non-automatic but he was a happy-go-lucky individual blessed with the philosophy that unpleasant things never happened to oneself, but always to the other guy. Poor Jimmy!

Then there was a pig-headed old fool I knew who was using a double .450 for elephant. It was also fitted with an automatic safety. I offered to convert it, because I knew that this fella had never used a double rifle before. But I was told to mind my own business; that if the makers of the rifle saw fit to make the safety automatic that was good enough for him. A few days afterwards he had a mighty narrow escape from an enraged elephant. He had wounded the beast, followed him, and then when the elephant charged, knocked him down. But instead of finishing him off at once with his left barrel, he attempted to reload. The elephant scrambled to his feet and came again. Old Nell tried to fire, but had forgotten to push forward the safety slide after breaking the breech. He turned to run and the elephant came after him. But the old fool couldn't run because he had ruined his feet in days gone by when in the British army by wearing boots two sizes too small for him because he reckoned they were "genteel." The elephant was so close that the spray from his trunk when he reached it out to grab the hunter wet the back of his shirt across his shoulders! And then, fortunately for himself, the hunter tripped and fell sideways off the elephant's path, just avoiding his feet. The bull either didn't see what happened, or was unable to pull up in time, anyway, he rushed past, and the man was able to scramble to his feet and dodge away down wind. But if that elephant had had two tusks instead of one, Nell would certainly have been impaled, but he happened to fall on the tuskless side.

And then just one more:

Commander David Blunt was tackling a large herd of elephant one day, he reckoned there were about 80 of them, in a patch of fairly thick bush with a good deal of long grass here and there. Having shot three or four, including the Master bull, he came on a solitary bull and killed him.

". . . next second," he writes, "a panic-stricken party of cows and calves came crashing through the bush on my left about six abreast and four deep. There was no avoiding them, so I threw up my rifle, but *found the safety catch on.* I had just time to blaze off a round, dropping one cow, but this did not stop them, so I fired my last cartridge and dropped another cow. This effectually stopped the stampede. . . . My gun-bearer and I 'froze,' the distance between us and the leading elephant being only eight paces." (The italics are mine.)

It is quite obvious that Blunt, having dropped the bull, broke the breech with the intention of reloading that barrel, which act put the safety "on," and was probably just closing the breech when the party of cows and calves came stampeding straight towards him. Being a magazine enthusiast he was naturally accustomed to forget all about the safety until he had finished firing so that when using a double on this occasion he can be excused for forgetting about it. Nevertheless it shows how infernally dangerous the automatic safety can be.

I have gone into this question in considerable detail and at some length, because I consider it a matter of the utmost importance. I could quote many more instances of similar occurrences that either resulted in unpleasantly close escapes or in actual fatalities, and that were due entirely to automatic safeties.

Auctor: Yes, I fully agree with all that. But tell me, what happens if one finds that the excellent secondhand weapon that one wants to buy is fitted with an automatic safety? Can it be converted to non-automatic? And if so, will it be expensive?

Lector: No decent gunsmith from whom you are buying a secondhand double rifle would charge you a cent for the job of converting the safety from automatic to non-automatic. It is only necessary to remove the little connecting-rod between the top lever and the slide of the safety—a matter of only a few minutes. If you already have a weapon with an automatic safety you can convert it yourself if you can use a turnscrew; failing that, then any gunsmith will do it for you for a dollar or so. Decide for yourself whether or not your life is worth that.

BARREL LENGTH. Experience has shown that there is no *best* barrel length for a big game rifle any more than there is for a shot gun. Doubtless, if you were shooting at some fantastic range like 1,000 yards you might find a 28″ or 30″ barrel more accurate than one of the 24 inchers but we are only concerned with sporting ranges, and it has been shown again and again that 24″ barrels will shoot as accurately as could ever be required in practical sport.

There are very real disadvantages in too long a barrel—that extra length spells extra weight in the butt to balance it; in other words, an increase in the over-all weight of the weapon, and most men like their sporters as light as possible, besides, a very long barrel can never give you quite so perfectly balanced a rifle as a barrel somewhat shorter. Then there is the general handiness of the finished weapon—a very important requirement in a sporting rifle. But one of the greatest disadvantages of too long a barrel, and one which one seldom sees mentioned, is the more exaggerated "flip." If the rifle was always fired in the same temperatures as those which existed when it was originally sighted, all would be well but the temperature varies enormously in the Tropics between midnight and midday. This means a variation in velocity and therefore a variation in the degree of flip and so in grouping. A short, stiff barrel is in every way preferable to a long, thin one for African use.

In the ordinary magazine rifle, there cannot be the slightest necessity for a barrel of more than 24 inches. The only two magazine rifles that are habitually built by British firms for stock with 26″ barrels are the .30-06 and the .318; apart from those, 24 inches is the customary length. In the case of a large bore magazine, which will normally be used in thick cover, I personally reckon that 22 inches would be better than the normal 24″.

In the case of double rifles, the question of barrel length is really a personal matter. These weapons are naturally much shorter and more compact than magazines, and are easier to balance perfectly owing to the greater concentration of weight between the hands that is possible with this pattern of weapon. But I think that the length of barrel should bear some relation to the length of stock, and it must certainly bear some relation to the manner in which you hold your rifle. For instance, a very tall man requiring a very long stock would naturally tend to favor longer barrels than a very short fella. The tall man would probably find 26″ or 27″ barrels balancing better than 24s; whilst in the same way the little fella would almost certainly find 24″ or 25″ barrels preferable to anything longer. My first doubles were fitted with 28″ barrels and I found them very satisfactory; I then came down to 26″ barrels and found them infinitely preferable; after that I started using 24″ and 25″ and swore by them. Nowadays I wouldn't dream of having a double or single built for me with longer barrels than 26 inches; the 27″ and 28″ barreled weapons actually seem clumsy and ungainly to me now. Further, altho on paper there is an undoubted falling off in velocity and therefore power when the barrel is shortened—in calibers ranging from .400 upwards it may be taken as roughly 25 f.s. for each inch reduction —these weapons have an ample reserve of power, and I can definitely state that I have never noticed the slightest falling off in killing power due to difference in barrel length, and in some of them I have used the same cartridges in three and even four different lengths of barrel.

After a vast deal of experimenting I have finally decided that 25″, 25½″ and 26″ barrels are the best and most suitable for me. The most irreproachably balanced rifles I have ever owned or handled have been fitted with 26″ barrels.

But if you have a fancy for short barrels get them by all means.

There are many others who swear by 24″ barrels. And after all, if a rifle fitted with 28″ barrels will kill an elephant at 50 yards, it will kill him just as dead if fitted with 24″ barrels. Balance and handiness are the prime requisites of a rifle for Africa.

CARRYING RIFLES. I suppose the great majority of men in Africa only take over their rifles when they actually sight the game. I used to do the same myself but it's a mistake. After being caught napping three or four times, I learned my lesson and ever afterwards have seen to it that I was never without a rifle in my hands, even when it appeared that I was least likely to want it. You can encounter game in the African Bush in the most unexpected manner in the most improbable places. I'll give you an instance or two, and will be surprised if other hunters cannot corroborate.

I was hunting one time in light open forest with little or no undergrowth and at a season when the grass was short. It seemed in the last degree improbable that one could stumble across elephant unexpectedly and without having ample time in which to take over the rifle from one's gun-bearer. I was trying out the .577 at the time, and as the only lighter weapons I possessed were a .470 and a .450 N$\stackrel{\circ}{=}$2, both of which weighed 11-lbs. exactly, I could see no earthly reason why I should lug one of them around myself. The .577 would do all I wanted it to, and since it weighed 13¼ lbs. I let my gun-bearer carry it always, only taking it over when actually closing my beast. On the day in question, we had been following a small troop of elephant with at least one good bull amongst them. Somewhere around midday my gun-bearer dropped out to answer a call of nature. Normally I would have taken the rifle from him rather than wait, and then let him catch up again to avoid needless delay but in view of the open nature of the forest, and the fact that the spoor led straight on as far as we could see, and visibility was extremely good, and that there were no clumps of bush that could possibly be concealing the elephant, and nothing moving anywhere in view, I didn't bother to do so this time.

So, since tracking was easy, I and the local guide, armed with a spear that was more of an ornament than anything else, strode along the spoor just about as fast as we could walk. We had covered about 100 or 150 yards when some slight movement behind a large anthill caught my eye. I found myself looking at a splendid tusker who was gazing straight at me with mild curiosity. He was barely 30 yards away. It was his ear swinging out that had caught my attention. He had been plastering himself with red clay so that he was exactly the same color as the anthill behind which he was standing, and the anthill being in a slight depression had seemed much smaller when viewed from 150 yards away—much too small to hide an elephant. I glanced around to see if by any chance my man was coming with the rifle, but he was squatting there in some sort of daydream of his own gazing in the opposite direction. I motioned the spearman back and whispered to him to slip along and get the rifle; I, remaining where I was, and hoping the bull would have patience. However, long before the rifle arrived—naturally, he couldn't just leg it like hell, grab the gun, and then come hareing back with it; no self-respecting elephant would stand that. The man had to move quietly and apparently casually away—but as I say, before he got back with the rifle, the elephant had satisfied his curiosity and decided he knew of a healthier spot. It wasn't until sundown of the next day that I caught up with him again and was able to add him to the bag. He was a much better bull than the herd bull, and so we dropped the other spoor and went after this fellow. Had I had a rifle in my hands I could have dropped him easily then and there and saved all that time.

On another occasion I had been hunting for meat for my men, but had only managed to get one fairly small beast. It would be very much better than nothing, but we still wanted more and wanted it today, because I wanted to get out again after the elephant next day. There was a strong wind blowing and we were walking directly downwind towards camp. Surely the last thing in the world you might expect under such conditions would be to bump game. Consequently, when my gun-bearer dropped out to remove a thorn from his foot, it didn't even occur to me to take the rifle from him. It was a .350 Rigby Magnum he was carrying, but had it been a field gun it would have held no interest for me right then, and the wind directly behind us. I might have been a couple of hundred yards from the rifle when I was flabbergasted to see a haartebeaste bull cantering slowly straight towards me across the *dambo* which started there. Whether lions had scared him, or whether some coon wandering around searching for wild honey or something had bumped him, I don't know; possibly the wind, on leaving the fairly open scrub thru which I had been coming and striking the open *dambo*, had eddied and carried the scent of man from the wrong direction, I dunno. But anyway, there he was coming along at a slow but steady canter. When he was about 80 yards away, he halted, swung around broadside on and looked back the way he had come. And I, crouching behind a small bush and praying that my gun-bearer would see what was happening and come sneaking up with the rifle before the haartebeaste got the wind again, this time from the right direction.

Well, I sure didn't deserve that meat, but maybe the god of hunters figured I'd learnt my lesson by this time and would not be such a fool again. Anyhow, he allowed my hero to make a really fine stalk with the rifle, shove it into my hands, and allowed me to drop the haartebeaste just as he caught the wind from our direction and his head was swinging around to look this way.

The hunter should always carry a light rifle himself. But see to it that it's no mere squib; there's no telling what questions you may be wanting to ask it. It must be something packing a reasonably heavy punch. I'm not recommending you to carry one of your heavier weapons, as they might tire you unduly but don't let yourself be caught out like I did without a gun of any sort. It happened to me about three or four times but that one with the haartebeaste was the last.

But if you decide against carrying the rifle yourself, then in my opinion there is only one way your gun-bearer should be trained to carry it, and that is, just a pace and a half in front of you so that you won't tread on his heels, and yet can reach out a hand and grab the rifle off his shoulder if it's wanted in a hurry. And he must carry it *muzzles foremost*.

I have frequently heard this method condemned. Men contending that it "strains" the rifle. How *can* it "strain" the rifle? The fella will carry the rifle in the easiest possible way, that is, with the point of balance immediately behind his shoulder so that the muzzles or butt as the case may be will press up slightly against his hand. Obviously, therefore, the amount of "strain" must be exactly the same irrespective of whether the rifle is butt foremost or muzzles foremost. The object in carrying it in this manner is that it is always pointing in the direction in which it is most likely to be required, and is immediately convenient for you.

To have it carried behind you, as some men recommend, is all wrong. You would have to turn around to get it, possibly only to find that your man had dropped out a short while before and hadn't yet caught up with you. Even when carrying my own rifle, as I always do nowadays, and my gun-bearer is carrying my second one, I insist on him carrying it immediately in front of me. He can please himself whether he carries it butt foremost or muzzles foremost, but it must be in front of me so that I don't have to turn around if I want to exchange with him.

SLINGS. Most men who carry their own rifles use a sling. I did so myself for ten or a dozen years but have not done so since. There is always something new to learn, and I have little use for the fella who reckons he knows it all, who can never admit that possibly he was wrong, or who cannot change an opinion once he has formed it. I have recommended slings and I rather think I have even described them as essential. Well, I no longer think so, and latterly have had my rifles built without sling fittings.

Still, if you fancy a sling there's no very good reason why you shouldn't use one. The following was the manner I always found best when hunting in thick cover and carrying the rifle by the sling: Carry the rifle with the sling over the right shoulder (assuming that you shoot from the right shoulder) and the rifle upsidedown, muzzles foremost. The muzzles are kept pointing up at an angle of about 45 to 50 degrees, so that there is no fear of blowing your tracker's head off, and steadied by the right hand on the barrels and the right forearm and elbow pressing against it— the sling should be adjusted to permit of this being done. If you want the rifle quickly it is only necessary to drop your right hand to the grip and turn the barrels uppermost, at the same time as the left hand comes across and grasps the barrels. The sling will slide off your shoulder and down past your elbow as you turn the rifle over but to make quite certain that there will be no hitch, it is advisable to have flat sling swivels instead of eyes. The rifle is pointing in the direction in which it is most likely to be required, and has been gotten ready for action with the least possible delay and—a very important point—with the least possible amount of movement on your part.

If you carry it as most men do, more or less vertically behind the shoulder with the sling to the front, then before it can be brought into action it must be swung around past your elbow. This, besides taking longer, means considerably more movement on your part; whilst there is always the possibility of the rifle knocking loudly against something or getting hung up on a trailing vine, creeper, or something of the sort.

Your heavier weapons should not be fitted with slings. They are apt to be a nuisance when exchanging rifles with your gunbearer.

Altho many men will tell you that they would never use a sling in thick cover because of the possibility of it becoming entangled in things, I must admit that in all the years I used a sling I never had it get hung up on anything.

RECOIL PADS. I strongly recommend these being fitted to all guns and rifles, other than miniatures, in the Tropics where practically all shooting takes place in shirt-sleeves. Altho you seldom feel recoil when firing at game, since your every sense is concentrated on placing your bullet where it will do the most good, a very severe recoil can have most unpleasant after-effects. If you are firing from an awkward position a rifle which normally appears to have no recoil at all can make itself felt on occasions, and a tenderness about the shoulder may very easily make you flinch next day and this can have but one result.

The British and Continental method of attaching recoil pads is to screw them right thru their vulcanite plates or mounts into the butt of the rifle. The heads of the screws are deeply countersunk, and rubber plugs are used to conceal them. I have never known one of these pads come adrift; in fact it would be practically impossible for them to do so. Unfortunately, however, they soon lose their pristine beauty. Standing heavy rifles down on stony ground to rest them against a tree or the carcass of some animal, soon causes little pieces of rubber to chip off around the edges, especially around the heel. Be the hunter and his gun-bearers ever so careful, this invariably happens sooner or later, and the pad develops a rat-gnawed appearance.

By far the finest pads I have ever seen are those supplied by Purdey. These are covered with soft leather which greatly improves their appearance and undoubtedly greatly lengthens their life. Because if they are not protected, the hot sun will perish them. This hardly concerns the visiting sportsman, because he is unlikely to be long enough in the Bush for it to matter but if you ever wanted to sell a gun it would make a big difference to the price you were offered if it had been fitted with one of these leather-covered Purdey pads.

RECOIL. Since it would appear that the recoil of powerful rifles is a serious bugbear for many men, it might be of interest to discuss it and give my views and experiences in connection with the more powerful weapons. For instance, here are questions that are sometimes asked: How does the recoil of heavy magazines like the .500 and .505 compare with that of corresponding doubles? Does the recoil from the heaviest magazines ever slow up the bolt functioning for following shots? Does the bolt ever "freeze" from recoil or pressure? What about the muzzle blast from short barrels on the heavier calibers? And, above all, what of the recoil of the .577 and .600 bores?

I will take these questions in turn presently and see what I can make of them; but first a few words in general. I sometimes wonder just how much of this recoil nuisance is fact and how much is due to an over-active imagination. I seem to recollect Hosea Sarber, writing in the *AMERICAN RIFLEMAN*, tell how he knew visiting sportsmen coming up to Alaska armed with .375 Magnums which they had been scared to sight-in because they had been hearing things about recoil—they didn't want to shoot their guns more than was absolutely necessary to kill their bears.

That some men are more sensitive to recoil than others, is indisputable. In the case of a shot gun a few shells may have no effect, but after two or three hundred have been fired in rapid succession the shooter may suffer from "gun-headache," the effects of recoil being cumulative. But that cannot apply to sporting rifles used for hunting, since so few shots are fired "at a sitting." Presumably, therefore, what worries these men is the fear of getting their shoulder hurt. Personally, I have always been punished more severely by the vicious jab of some medium and small bores than I ever have by large bores.

There are three factors that affect the extent to which recoil is felt even more than the question of caliber, and these are weight, balance and fit. No greater mistake can be made than to insist on your gunsmith building you a rifle appreciably lighter than the accepted weight for that caliber, if you are at all sensitive to recoil. Recoil is a direct consequence of the Laws of Motion—the force that drives the expanding powder gasses and projectile out of the muzzle is employed equally in driving the rifle back against your shoulder. Obviously, it can drive a light weapon back more viciously than it can an appreciably heavier weapon. Balance, as I have explained elsewhere, minimizes to an enormous extent the degree to which recoil is felt, because no effort is required to hold the rifle at your shoulder and therefore your own muscles act as the finest of all recoil pads. In the same way, if the stock is of the right length and bend it permits you to mount the rifle correctly for every shot so that the butt beds properly into your shoulder. If the butt is well into your shoulder the rifle can't kick you; it can only shove—a shove can't hurt.

Now to answer those questions: I have already mentioned how pleasant I found the .500-bore Jeffery-Mauser to shoot. I had expected considerable recoil, but I was most pleasantly surprised to find how little there was. There is not a great deal of difference in power between it and the double .500s: it gets its power by increased velocity to compensate for reduced bullet weight. Any man fit enough to tramp around the Bush hunting elephant could shoot it with ease—exactly the same remarks apply to Gibbs .505. Except that they are magazines, and therefore less handy and less perfectly balanced than doubles would be, there is really nothing to choose between them. I have never even heard of the recoil of these great magazines slowing up the bolt functioning for following shots, and certainly never noticed anything of that description myself when using them. I experienced no trouble whatsoever, much less did the bolt show any tendency to "freeze." The pressures are very reasonable in both these cartridges—15 tons in the .505, and about 16, I think, in the .500. I do not know what powder they used but since they are a comparatively new weapon, I should imagine it would be nitro-cellulose.

With regard to muzzle blast from short barrels: I have never used barrels shorter than 24″ on any large bore tho were I to get a .500 or .505 magazine I should insist on 22″ for the sake of general handiness. I have only once heard of anybody having shorter barrels than 24″ on a double—that fella had Jeffery build him a 22½″

barreled double .475 N $\stackrel{o}{=}$ 2 for buffalo-hunting. I considered it too
short but didn't get a chance to shoot it. As far as the other
weapons are concerned, I cannot remember ever experiencing anything unpleasant in the way of muzzle blast. That there is an
appreciable blast from the muzzles of a .577 or .600 is but to be
expected but I cannot say that it ever worried me in any way, and
I did a good deal of shooting with the .600 in particular, tho I also
had a .577 after parting with the .600.

Now where these two grand guns are concerned there is a hell
of a lot of bunk spoken, written and believed. The .600 is generally
reckoned to be something of a man-killer. Time and again have
I heard men blowing off about the .600, or read their out-pourings.
It's obvious that they have heard somebody else saying these
things and reckon it's up to them to say them too so that others
will think they have really used the big elephant gun. I have
never come across a man who had used one for any length of time
who had anything but praise for its killing power.

This myth of the punishing effect of shooting a real elephant
gun arose in the days of the old large bore black powder weapons—
4-, 6-, and 8-bores in particular. In the case of those old cannons
there was not so much exaggeration because of the immense charges
of black powder that were normally used—up to 16 drams in a 4-
bore. Black powder gives a considerably more severe recoil than
a corresponding charge of smokeless powder. Selous said that the
punishment he received from his old Dutch "Roers" affected his
nerves to such an extent that it seriously interfered with his
shooting for the rest of his life, and he heartily wished he had
never had anything to do with them. Neumann was another great
hunter who suffered from recoil. Speaking of a double 10-bore he
had built for him by Holland when his beloved .577 Express was
out of order, he said that the recoil was terrific and altho the rubber
recoil-pad prevented it from hurting his shoulder, he suffered badly
from gun-headache every day after using the thing; in addition it
knocked his fingers about cruelly. (It's always been a mystery to
me why he didn't have another .577 built instead of the 10-bore,
in view of his known dislike of large bores.)

My first .600, a cheap-grade weapon I bought secondhand in
my early days, weighed 18-lbs. The fella from whom I bought it
warned me that it had a nasty habit of occasionally double-

discharging—the discharge of one barrel jarring the other barrel off simultaneously. I thanked him for telling me, but didn't see what I could do about it. One day I sneaked up to within about 15 paces of an elephant bull and let rip. Sure enough, off went both barrels. I was sent flying into a thorn bush, the rifle leapt clean over the bush, but the elephant was blasted clean off his feet! He must have been, because normally he will fall on the wounded side, but this big fellow fell away from me. When I succeeded in scrambling out of the bush and getting to my feet, I rather feared I would find myself with a broken collar-bone at least, because I also had heard these tales about the .600-bore's man-killing propensities. But I found that my shoulder wasn't even hurt much less broken—and don't forget that was both barrels simultaneously.

Another popular belief is that those men who use these big elephant guns only do so as the lesser of two evils—when it's a case of either being mauled by an elephant or of having one's shoulder broken or dislocated by the rifle. That's all plain bunk. There are no unpleasant effects from shooting the .600 provided it's a high-grade weapon and fits you reasonably well. You bring it up, its balance and weight keep it rock-steady—more so than any other weapon—you squeeze the trigger. Sometimes there will be an orange-yellow haze—that's the muzzle flash; if the conditions permit you may see the bullet strike thru it, you will hear the "clup" as it does, you will feel a strong, steady shove against your shoulder, and then the muzzles will begin to rise. If anyone tries to tell you that it's mere waste of money having a double .600, and you might as well have a single, because the muzzle jump is so bad that you could never get a quick second shot if you wanted one, you just say "nuts!" That fella don't know what he's talking about. I cannot remember the muzzles of my 24″-barreled Jeffery double .600 ever rising more than from 5 to 6 inches. By the time I had slipped my finger to the second trigger, the sights were back in line again. I never felt any ill-effects either at the time of shooting or later. Altogether, I killed somewhere between 60 and 70 elephant with it besides a few rhino, some buffalo, and a lion—that lion was blasted into eternity as I have never seen a lion blasted before or since!

Some time ago a fella was sitting up for tiger one night in India.

He was armed with a Jeffery falling-block single .600. It weighed
13 lbs. He took a shot at the tiger and was nearly knocked out of
his perch in the tree by the recoil. He only wounded the tiger,
and next morning proceeded to follow him up. The tiger charged
from close quarters. The sportsman waited his opportunity, fired,
hit the tiger centrally between the eyes, killing him instantly. He
said he hardly noticed the recoil. Do you get it? The previous
night he had nothing to distract his attention and thought too
much of the recoil, with the result that it nearly knocked him out
of the tree but the following morning, knowing that he was
almost certain to be charged and that he had but the one available
shot with which to stop that charge when it came, he was entirely
concerned with placing the bullet where it would do the most
good—the result was that he didn't notice the recoil. Yet the
actual recoil must have been exactly the same on each occasion.

There is the answer to the recoil bug-bear—forget about it.
Given a well-balanced weapon that fits you, just concentrate on
putting your bullets where you want them and leave your rifle to
take care of its own recoil.

RELIABILITY OF DIFFERENT MAKES OF AMMUNITION. Prior to
World War I it was the recognized thing thruout Africa that if
you wanted to commit suicide decently your best plan was to use
the British-loaded ammunition in German Mausers! In those days
there were two or three firms loading ammunition, nothing was
standardized, neither the ballistics nor the cartridge dimensions;
cheap materials were used in an effort to undersell one another and
collar the market.

However, after that war these firms all amalgamated in Imperial Chemical Industries and the ammunition is now all under the
name Kynoch and manufactured under the one roof. All parts are
standardized as well as the ballistics. In all my experience I have
only had two of their cartridges misfire. I have never experienced
a hangfire or weak round. Of those two misfires, one was a .450
N$\stackrel{o}{=}$2 cartridge that dropped into a pool of water when I was
having a drink. It could not have been under water more than
maybe fifteen or twenty seconds, and that certainly should not have
been enough to hurt it. I kept it separate for a long time intending
to use it some day when it wouldn't matter much if it misfired
but it finally got mixed up with some others and I shot off the lot

at non-dangerous game. One of that lot misfired, and I naturally presume that it was that one.

The other was a belted-rimless .375 Magnum that had been lying around quite a bit. I gave it and some others to a fella who was going out after some meat and he afterwards told me that one of them had misfired and showed it to me. I was able to recognize it. But those are the only two in all the years I have been using Kynoch shells since just after the first world war.

By the way, it will be noticed in many of the cartridge illustrations in this book that the British load a fat jute wad between the bullet and the powder whenever cordite or Axite is being used. This wad is case-size, and the chump might be forgiven for asking how the heck they get that fat wad down past the neck of the shell, because its diameter is considerably greater than that of the bullet in many cases. And the answer is that the powder and wad are loaded before the shell is necked down, it then passes along to the necking machine for the final neck constriction before the bullet is inserted and crimped. It has been said that the object of this wad is to prevent the very hot gasses generated by cordite, and Axite—one of its derivatives—from melting the lead core of the bullets; tho it is to be noted that they also use it when loading soft-nose bullets, the base of which would be closed. Be that as it may, the primary object of the jute wad is to prevent the white-hot gasses of the burning cordite from causing devastating erosion as they tear past the bullet before the latter is properly seated in the rifling. This caused the British many a headache around the turn of the century when they were bringing out their original .303 Lee-Metford Service rifle. It was found that the barrels would not stand up to more than about 200 rounds before they were completely eroded away at the breech end. It was then that some bright spark thought of the jute wad, and it saved the day. Incidentally, it also has another function, and that is that it holds the powder down tight against the primer—there is no dead air-space in these shells—which must help considerably in matters of ignition, as the sticks of cordite have the most inflammable part, the ends, pressing against the primer.

Auctor: That's very interesting, and I'm glad to hear your explanation for the presence of that jute wad, because I see the British don't use it when loading nitro-cellulose and neither do the Germans with their flake powders. But tell me, how do your barrels stand up to cordite? You said that this jute wad saved the day in connection with the British Service .303; but there's a whale of a difference between its load of a mere 31 grains of cordite and the 100-gr. load you recommend for the .600. How do the barrels of these big guns make out when firing such heavy charges? Do they have a very short life?

Lector: If you clean your rifles as I suggest they should last any ordinary man a lifetime. I've fired more than 2,000 rounds thru one .375 Magnum and when I sold it the barrel was like a new pin inside. There was no visible indication of wear, much less of erosion; the grooves and lands of the rifling were as clear-cut and sharply defined as they were when the rifle was new. Some of my larger bores, in particular a .450 N $\stackrel{\circ}{=}$ 2, a .465, and a .470, had an immense amount of use. As almost invariably happens with double rifles, the right barrel gets a lot more use than the left, yet there was no sign of wear anywhere thruout those barrels after some hundreds of rounds. How many hundred I couldn't tell you off-hand but it must have been many hundreds.

Burrard describes experimenting in this direction with a .303 target rifle fitted with a best grade nickel-steel barrel by Jeffery. He was shooting at 600 yards, using the old "Mark VI" ammo—215-gr. bullet at 2,050 f.s. He said that after 3,000 rounds he began to get unaccountable shots at 600 yards but the rifle still shot okeh at 500. The barrel now took a .304″ gauge. Now that's more than double our sporting ranges, and it's gonna take the average sports-man a good deal more than the normal lifetime of occasional shooting to blaze off 3,000 rounds at game. I haven't the slightest doubt that any high grade rifle would fire 5,000 rounds at normal African ranges. How many non-professional hunters shoot any-thing like that quantity? It's rust that eats away their barrels; not honest wear and tear.

The only clean barrels that I have ever seen definitely worn out were those belonging to that old fool I mentioned before and he wore his out by stupid and utterly needless cleaning! Incessant cleaning. You can't clean something that's already clean but you can wear away the finest of steel by never-ending rubbing. And that's what he did. His barrels were spotless, shining but twice a day, whether he fired them or not, he would spend at least an

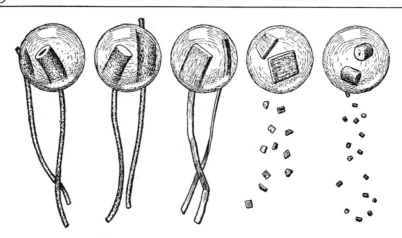

POWDERS USED IN BRITISH AMMUNITION

  1. Cordite M.D.T.   2. Cordite Mk. 1
  3. Axite   4. German Flake Nitrocellulose Powder
          5. American Tubular Grain Nitrocellulose Powder

The compositions of Cordite are—

	Cordite Mk.1	Cordite M.D.	Axite
Nitroglycerine	58	30	30
Nitrocellulose	37	65	63
Mineral jelly	5	5	5
Potassium nitrate	−	−	2

M.D. signifies modified, referring to the change in composition from Mk.1.

In sporting cartridges, Cordite Mk.1 is used in the form of strands ("strings") while Cordite M.D. is in the form of tubes and is then known as Cordite M.D.T. Chopped Cordite is merely Cordite Mk.1 cut up into small cylinders; it was formerly used in the British Government .455 Revolver cartridge.

Axite is still made in the form of flat strips. It is now only used in .333" Flanged and Rimless cartridges. It could be confused with L.E.C. (Light Express Cordite) which is also in flat strips. Axite has a darker colour and the strips are thicker than those of L.E.C.

L.E.C. is used in some of the Winchester cartridges, e.g. .401 Self-Loading and .32–40, and in most of the old black powder Expresses. For the latter purpose it has the advantage of being smokeless while giving pressures suitable for weapons not designed (or proved) for full power loads.

NITROCELLULOSE POWDERS

These are used in all the modern Express cartridges and in most rimless cartridges which are used in single barrel bolt-action rifles. The old medium velocity Expresses with flanged cases, which were originally loaded with Cordite, are still loaded with Cordite. The difficulty of changing the powder for these cartridges is that they are used in double-barreled rifles and that although there is generally no difficulty in obtaining the ballistics with N/C powder, the characteristics such as pressure/time and pressure/space rises are generally different from those with Cordite. This affects the point of impact of cartridges fired from the two hour rubbing them out, morning and evening. He quite literally rubbed them away—the rifling was barely perceptible.

I haven't had a great deal of experience with German powders. Having found the British ammunition just about one hundred per cent reliable, I was entirely satisfied. Besides, I do not think that the Germans regularly loaded the big shells I generally use, tho I have little doubt they would have done so had I asked them to. But I noticed that the man who started me off in a study of ballistics and similar matters, my friend the German hunter, himself used British built best grade doubles for close-quarter work, and used British ammunition in them. He used German shells in his custom-built scope-sighted magazine. Those facts impressed me very forcibly. Altho I had had a fair amount of experience by then, I knew nothing whatever about rifles and ammunition except what I had learned by actually using the various weapons. I distinctly remember that his was the first .465-bore rifle I had ever even heard of much less seen!

barrels. These double-barreled rifles were originally regulated with Cordite-loaded cartridges, which means that the right and left barrels give approximately the same point of impact at, generally, 100 yards and the change in the powder might upset this regulation and cause the bullets either to cross before reaching 100 yards or to diverge. To correct the rifle with the new powder would, therefore, often mean re-regulating it which is a troublesome and expensive job.

WADS

Before the advent of smokeless powder, wads were intended to lubricate and clean the bore. When nitroglycerine smokeless powder, with its small amount of residue, and metal-covered bullets, came into use, the wad became a means of protecting the base of the bullet from the very hot gasses and of forming a gas-tight seal as the bullet left the case, particularly in worn barrels. Thus a typical combination of one or more waxed felt wads between jute wads, as in many of the old black powder Express cartridges, became a single jute wad in the corresponding Nitro Expresses.

The jute wad may have some slight effect in improving ignition of the cordite by keeping it down against the flash holes, but this is not one of its main functions.

BULLET ENVELOPES

For many years it has been the practice both in England and on the Continent of Europe to use steel jackets for bullets with muzzle velocities more than about 2,500 f.s. Such steel envelopes were seldom, if ever, unprotected, they were generally covered with about a 5% coating of cupro-nickel or gilding-metal. The jackets of some bullets, however, were made of solid gilding-metal. Generally it is found that it makes very little difference to the ballistic results whether coated steel or gilding-metal envelopes are used.

But the German ammunition had a very good name always, tho, as I have said, it was only in connection with the shells for their Mausers. Those were the only type we saw out here, except when some sportsman had one of those three-barreled combination guns with a special 8mm barrel under the two smooth-bores. I am sure they would have loaded anything they were asked to load—for they were anything but bad business men; however, I never saw any large-bore shells of theirs except for the Jeffery .500-bore Mauser. Altho I cursed German ammunition once upon a time, it's only fair to add that stuff that let me down had been lying around for a very long time, and had not even been kept in packets.

I see a great deal of discussion nowadays in American journals concerning "head-space." I should imagine that there would be far greater possibilities of trouble of that sort arising when the shells are made by different firms than when they are all made in the same machines. That men with magazine rifles experience more misfires than we do with our doubles is a fact but then there are many more magazines in use than doubles.

I have never experienced any particular difficulty in extraction in any rifle but I have heard many men speak of it—magazines being the offenders. They told me that the method they employed to get the thing out was to wrench at the bolt lever with anything they could find to give leverage until something gave way!

I have not as yet had any experience with American shells but have heard from several sources that they're tops. This, however, only applied to expanding bullets; I have heard nothing about American full-patch bullets, and wonder sometimes if the American makers realize the absolute necessity for a really well-reinforced nose on all solid bullets intended for African use. This is absolutely imperative and I would draw their attention to the really excellent and most carefully drawn illustrations of British solids shown in this book and remind them that even amongst these the only truly perfect bullets are those supplied by John Rigby. With the exception of the .577 and .600, I have had solids distorted, and sometimes badly distorted, from all other rifles after being slammed into elephant—but not Rigby's.

SINGLE-TRIGGERS. This, of course, applies only to double rifles. The only double barrels that I have ever seen with single-trigger mechanism were Westley Richards' but I have little doubt that you could persuade other firms to give you single-triggers on their best grade weapons if you insisted on it. The advantages claimed for only having one trigger instead of two on a D.B. weapon are so well known now that I hardly think it is necessary to go into that here. Generally speaking, I would not recommend a beginner to use them because if you have one D.B. weapon so fitted, then you must have all your D.B.s, guns and rifles, similarly fitted. If you were only shooting non-dangerous game, then it wouldn't matter how many triggers you had but when you are close to dangerous beasts you do not want to be having to remember things that you might very easily forget.

You see, it would be absolutely essential that the mechanism should be of the selective variety, so that you could fire either barrel first, and you would have to remember to shift whatever mechanism there was after firing the right barrel before you could dare to open the breech for the purpose of reloading without firing the left, so that if you were suddenly attacked before you had gotten the shell into the chamber you could snap-to the breech and fire the left barrel. If you had forgotten to shift whatever type of slide or other control there was in the selective mechanism before opening the breech, then you would find yourself snapping the lock of the empty right barrel when endeavoring to stop the charge, because the opening of the breech re-sets the mechanism of the single-trigger device.

Besides, it is very, very seldom that you are called upon to fire so quickly that you couldn't take the shot with two triggers. Really powerful rifles jump to a greater or lesser extent on being fired, so that you could hardly expect to fire them as rapidly as an auto-loader. Nevertheless, in fairness to Westley Richards' selective single-trigger mechanism I must admit that on two or three occasions when tackling elephant in very thick stuff, and there were only two or three, *and I knew exactly where they were*, so that I didn't mind firing the left barrel without first reloading the right, I am pretty sure that I was enabled to get two where with an ordinary double-trigger rifle I would not have gotten more than one. It was occasionally the same with rhino and buffalo, when I would just get the merest fleeting glimpse of a vital spot as the animal passed across a small gap in the foliage on the heels of the first shot, or even as the first beast fell and exposed for an instant a companion. One step in that stuff, and your quarry disappears. However, taking everything into consideration, I decided that it was better in every way to stick to two triggers for dangerous game, and so discarded my .577.

It is frequently stated that a single-trigger mechanism, being complicated, must detract from the general reliability of the weapon. But I can't admit that argument. I grant that certain types of single-trigger are entirely unsuitable but there are others that would appear to be perfectly okeh. And since these mechanisms are fitted on shot guns that may be called upon to do more shooting in a season than the rifle will do in its entire life, and be expected to stand up to that hammering year after year—and do it satisfactorily—I utterly fail to see why they should be considered unreliable if fitted to a rifle. At any rate, Westley Richards have fitted many double rifles of all bores, from the .22 Hi-power to the .577, with their single-trigger mechanism with perfect satisfaction to the users.

The late Jimmy Sutherland, who was said to be the first of the professionals to have his bag of elephant run into four figures—altho he always had a gang of native hunters out too—used and swore by Westley Richards' single-trigger mechanism on his pair of double .577-bore Nitro-Express rifles. He would hardly have continued using them for so many years had they not been absolutely satisfactory. Sutherland's methods, however, were very different from mine and just because he found that single-triggers were fine, must not be taken as implying that they would be equally fine under different conditions. Sutherland hunted in, generally speaking, appreciably more open country than I do—or at least, call it less dense (I have hunted there, so I know)—and he always used a pair of rifles with his gun-bearer reloading for him when necessary. Well, as I have already explained, I do not hold with that method—at any rate not under present-day conditions; I advise a man to learn to rely upon himself, and himself only, and the rifle in his hands.

(Note: After finishing my talk dealing with my experiences when shooting the .600-bore, it was gradually driven in on me as a result of considerable deep, prolonged and careful thought that I have been laboring under a delusion for many long years but that little fact did not dawn on me until I had finished discussing the recoil of the .600. Since because of many arguments concerning the .600, I had taken particular note of the muzzle-jump, I was able to say that I had invariably found that the sights were back in line by the time I had slipped my finger from the front to the back trigger. Accordingly, it will be immediately obvious that I could not possibly have fired the left barrel any sooner had the weapon been fitted with single-trigger mechanism. For all practical purposes the muzzle-jump of the .577 can be described as the same as that of the .600, so it will be quite apparent that I was kidding myself when I imagined that I got off those second shots so much faster with the single-trigger than I could have done with two triggers, for the simple reason that the sights would not have been back in line any sooner. Yet it has taken me all these years to realize it!)

DOUBLE-PULL TRIGGERS. This refers to magazine rifles only. I cannot understand why gunsmiths almost invariably fit double-pull triggers on their magazine rifles unless specially ordered not to. I cannot see the object of a double-pull trigger. I am quite sure no double barrel rifle has ever been so fitted. And I am quite certain that it is a real mistake to have a magazine fitted with a double-pull trigger if you also have a double rifle in your battery. Because if you have been using your magazine rifle extensively and then change to your double, you will be very apt to fire your first shot before you intend to, thru automatically "taking up the slack," or tightening your finger to take up the first pull as you had to do on your magazine.

There was a fella I knew in Somaliland who had a very much closer affair with a lion than he had expected or wanted thru this very cause. It was his first lion. He got word that lions had broken into a kraal or zariba and killed some camels; so out he went, armed with a .318 magazine and a double .470. The lions, three of them, were lying under a small thorn tree beside an anthill with a good deal of longish grass around and then a clear space. This fella, being new to the game, didn't feel like sneaking up close and tackling three lions on his own so he got the local Injuns to advance in a semi-circular formation, beating drums and tin cans and yelling as hard as they could in the usual manner, and see if they couldn't drive the lions out into the clear space. They were also to fire the grass. But as usually happens when any of these coons try to think for themselves, one mutt fired the grass separately so that his fire raced ahead of the main blaze.

The result was that the lions broke separately in different directions. However, one big chap came straight towards the sportsman who was waiting for him with the .470. At the very edge of the grass, when barely 40 yards away, he halted and looked back. It was a gift of a shot but our hero tried to take up the slack of his trigger as he had been accustomed to on his magazine and, as he put it himself, "my rifle went off of its own accord." The lion took one look at him, and came. So that now, instead of an easy, certain kill on the edge of the grass, the fella had to kill his first lion during a charge and had but the one available cartridge with which to do it. He steadied and had the sense to wait until the lion was about 25 yards away before firing. But the beast came on for another twice his own length as tho untouched, and then suddenly pitched forward on his nose. The hunter loosed a yell of delight and was in the act of rushing forward to examine his trophy, when he found himself grabbed by the shoulder and there was his gun-bearer shoving the loaded .318 into his hands and taking the empty .470 from him. And just as well too because when he again looked around there was his lion once more on his feet—sick and dazed, surely, but alive and still dangerous. Another unhurried shot, and all was over.

Percival mentions an occasion when he was offered an easy shot at a bad man-killer—not a man-eater—and clean missed in just the same way thru trying to take up the first pull as he had to on his magazine.

Insist on single-pull triggers on all your magazines.

HAIR, OR SET-TRIGGERS. I do not recommend these for normal hunting. If you have allowed yourself to become accustomed to the hair trigger for deliberate shots, when you are offered a quick shot you will not have time in which to set the trigger and will inevitably find the normal firing trigger heavy. The result will be that you will be inclined to yank at it, and thereby pull off your target.

The only occasions in Africa when I like a hair trigger are when I am comfortably steadied against a convenient tree and have to dwell on my aim for a long, long time waiting for some beast to move maybe half a pace forward so as to expose a vital spot thru a tiny gap in the foliage. One must then be ready to fire on the instant; there is no time for deliberate squeezing of the normal firing trigger. The other occasion is very similar—dwelling on your aim in the same way when waiting for a shot at a shy hippo. In either case you will have but an instant if you are to put your bullet in the right spot. And even at that, a properly mounted scope sight usually spells the difference between success and failure.

But if you have double set-triggers fitted, you must insist that the normal firing trigger have a perfectly normal trigger pull of around 4 lbs. On almost all rifles I have ever handled fitted with hair triggers, the firing trigger had such an absurdly heavy pull that it was practically impossible to fire the rifle accurately without the hair trigger mechanism being in action. And I certainly do not recommend setting the hair trigger for running shots. It would seem that your pressure of the normal trigger helps to steady you and your rifle for such work.

Auctor: Look here, altho doubtless some of your readers will know as much as you do about double rifles, if not more, many of them will probably never have used such weapons. For their benefit, why not discuss the actual technique of reloading a double rifle after firing both barrels. It's understood, of course, that an ejector will sling out the fired shell or shells when the breech is opened but what's the procedure with a non-ejector? Do you drop the barrels and reload from the "topside", or do you elevate the muzzles and let the empty shells drop out? Will they drop out? Do you have much trouble with fired shells sticking in the chambers, and what happens if they do?

Lector: It would be a very clumsy and ungainly business, besides being slow, to elevate the muzzles of the rifle so that the fired shells would drop out; it would also occasion a considerable amount of contortioning and movement on your part. No, you press down the barrels and quietly remove the fired shell; if you are close to game you drop it down the front of your shirt or somewhere where it won't make a noise, and then slip another into its place, also quietly. If you were to just let them fall out, they would almost certainly clatter against the breech or butt. To the hunter, "silence is golden"; hence my recommending non-ejectors in close cover.

The first movement of the barrels as the breech is broken starts primary extraction. This is effected by the extractor "toe" or cam, which is a projection on the knuckle of the action. When the barrels revolve around the knuckle on the breech being opened, the extractor cam remains stationary, since it's part of the action, and consequently the extractor is pushed out to the rear of the barrels. Considerable leverage is derived from the weight of the barrels which thus helps the extraction of a tightly fitting cartridge. This primary extraction takes place irrespective of whether or not the weapon is fitted with ejectors. It is very strong and very certain. I have never known it fail.

On two occasions when, curiously enough, I was using the .450 N$\stackrel{\circ}{=}$2, which generates the lowest chamber pressure of any nitro-express rifle—a mere 13 tons—excessive heat must have been at work on the cordite. When I came to reload I found that the breech didn't want to open. I had to use quite considerable force to start the barrels moving. With a little jerk they did so, and thereafter there was no further difficulty. When I examined the fired shells, they themselves—they are massively strong—showed no indications of unduly high pressure but the caps did. It was clear that they had been driven back into the striker holes in the face of the standing breech. As soon as I had managed to force them clear, all was well.

For the actual shell itself to stick in double rifles must be very rare. I have never had it happen. The cartridges used give low pressures in the first instance, and the cases are very strong. In days gone by, when black powder cases were first loaded with cordite, it was quite common but today the makers use very strong brass in these shells.

Auctor: You mentioned something about shells for doubles being slightly underloaded so as to allow a slightly greater margin for excess pressure. To what extent are they underloaded?

Lector: Usually two to three grains, occasionally four grains. The result is that the double shows from 50 to 100 f.s. lower velocity than its magazine counterpart. I do not know of any case wherein the difference is more than that. And then to offset this, there is the fact that doubles are usually fitted with slightly longer barrels than magazines.

A case to which this does not apply is that of Rigby's .350 N$\stackrel{\circ}{=}$2. Its ballistics are equally as good, if not even a mite better

TROPICAL AMMUNITION PACKAGE

Showing how ammunition is packed and hermetically sealed in small lots for storage and use in the Tropics. Such cartridges are often specially loaded with what are termed "tropical charges."

TROPICAL CHARGES

With cordite, the temperature at which it is fired has an appreciable effect on the pressure and velocity obtained. When first introduced, it was found that rifles which shot correctly in England with full charge cordite cartridges gave trouble when used in tropical countries, partly due to the increased strain from the higher pressure and also from the difference in elevation caused by the increased velocity. To overcome this difficulty, full charge cartridges are used for sighting rifles in this country and reduced charge cartridges ("tropical charge") are supplied for use abroad. A temperature of 120°F is accepted as representing tropical conditions and the reduced charge of cordite is that which gives, in cartridges heated to this temperature, the same velocity as given by the full cordite charge fired at our normal temperature of about 65°F. The actual reduction in weight of charge is about 7½%. This temperature effect is not connected with the age of the ammunition.

With nitrocellulose powders pressures are scarcely affected by change in temperature alone, but velocities are affected about half as much as with cordite. If nitrocellulose loaded cartridges are not airtight and are stored under hot dry conditions, pressure and velocity may rise owing to loss of moisture from the powder. Conversely, under damp conditions, the powder may absorb some moisture with a consequent drop in ballistics.

Nitrocellulose powders for sporting rifle cartridges are made in Great Britain in the form of short tubes or thin square flakes.

than his .350 Mauser-Magnum; in addition it is usually fitted with 26″ barrels as against the 24″ barrel of the Mauser.

But in any case, the difference is too slight to be worth considering.

DOUBLE HAMMER RIFLES. *Auctor:* You mentioned a very interesting point about shooting a double hammer rifle, wherein you only cocked one barrel at a time. Is this customary? And if so, why?

Lector: In the days of the old large bore black powder weapons it certainly was customary—if you didn't you would inevitably get a double discharge each time you fired. It was necessary to keep one barrel at half cock until after you had fired the other. This was not such a disadvantage as it might appear, because the volume of smoke emitted by those old cannons precluded any possibility of getting in a quick second shot anyway. With good grade modern weapons, however, there is no such fear; you may safely cock both barrels when you reckon you may be wanting them. In the case to which you refer I was just wandering around looking for meat for my men. It would be extremely unwise to go wandering around that way with a double hammer rifle at full cock; a fall would almost inevitably jar it off. Accordingly, when I was offered a quick shot at close range, there wasn't time to cock both hammers—normally, there wouldn't have been any need to. I was carrying the rifle on my right shoulder, butt foremost. As the barrels came down and the butt came up, my thumb clamped down on the right hammer—just as your thumb clamps down on the hammer of a revolver when you are shooting single-action; you don't actually draw back the hammer, it's the barrel chopping down that leaves it back under your thumb. And so with the rifle.

I am very fond of the double hammer action because of the absolute silence in which it can be loaded and cocked. I know of more than one man, sitting up at night for man-eating tiger, who scared off his beast by the click of his safety as he prepared to shoot with a hammerless rifle. If you draw back the trigger at the same time as you draw back the hammer on a hammer rifle and then let the trigger go, you will have cocked without a sound of any sort. Then there is the delightful ease with which the breech opens; powerful double rifles are fitted with extra powerful main springs to obviate any possibility of a misfire; those springs have to be compressed as the breech of a hammerless action is opened and the locks cocked. There is nothing of that with the hammer rifle—you cock with your thumb, one lock at a time. I would happily finish the remainder of my career with nothing but best-grade double hammer rifles. Incidentally, such weapons can occasionally be picked up secondhand at very low prices—not because the hammer action is no good, but simply because fashion favors the hammer-less. If you get such a chance, provided the weapon is in good condition, you need not hesitate—it will satisfactorily answer any questions you are ever likely to ask it.

ORDERING AMMUNITION. Always give full details of what you want when ordering ammunition. For many of the most widely used calibers there are two or three different lengths of shell which are *not* interchangeable. Mention the length of case for which your rifle is chambered, the powder charge for which it is proofed, the weight of bullet for which it is sighted and regulated. All this information is stamped on the breech ends of the barrels along with the proof marks and in many cases it is also engraved on the outside of the left barrel. You cannot give too many details. For instance, there are two .577s apart from the black powder loads and the L.V. Axite load, a 3″ shell and a 2¾″; there are two .500s in both cordite and black powder, a 3″ shell and a 3¼″, to say nothing of the rimless .500; there are three .450s, a .450 N°2, a 500/.450, and the straight .450, as well as the black powder .450s; there are two 450/.400s, a 3″ shell and a 3¼″ in addition to the old B.P. loads and Purdey's special light .400; whilst there are six .375s including the flanged and rimless magnums; there are three .360s and three .350s.

You can imagine how infuriating it would be if you were away out in the "Blue" and found that the consignment of ammunition which has taken six or seven months to reach you does not fit your rifles when it at last arrives! I've known it happen on one never-to-be-forgotten occasion, and have heard of it happening several times.

USING RESTS. By the way, if you are steadying your double rifle against a tree, don't press the barrel against the tree. If you do, and fire the other barrel, because of its natural sideways swing it will tend to jump away from the tree, which will throw the bullet wide. In the same way, if you are firing the barrel that is pressing against the tree, it will be unable to swing out as it wants, and so that shot will also fail to reach the mark. You should put your hand against the tree and steady the rifle against it—just as you do when resting your rifle *on* something hard. Everybody knows by now that a rifle will throw high if it is rested on a rock or something but it does not always occur to men that doubles must be permitted to take their natural sideways swing. You don't notice this sideways swing when shooting, but it's there.

I remember my unfortunate gun-bearer's indignation one day long ago when I steadied my double .450 N $\stackrel{o}{=}$ 2 on his shoulder to shoot a buffalo. We were squatting on an anthill waiting for the herd to graze slowly towards us. I wanted a nice young heifer for the pots and so waited for them to close in, rather than advance towards them, as that would have caused all the younger members of the herd to take refuge in the centre and just left the bulls and older cows on the outside when they saw me coming. I had my hand on my man's left shoulder, the barrels of the rifle resting on the thumb of my hand. Having picked my beast, I let her have it, firing the right barrel. My gun-bearer clapped his hand to his ear and twisted around with exactly the same look on his face that I had seen in by-gone days on the face of a red Irish setter I peppered the first time I was out grouse-shooting in far away County Donegal. I had forgotten about the sideways swing of the double rifle, and on firing the right barrel it had swung sideways and clouted the boy on the ear. He thought I had clouted him with my fist, and wondered what the hell!

FIT OF A RIFLE. It pays on all sides to have your rifles fit you properly. In other words, you should have them built to your measurements, just like a suit of clothes. This will not cost you a cent extra; the only snag is that you will have to exercise your patience if you need anything exceptional in the way of length or bend. Be sure that the stock is well bent, or has plenty pitch-down, or whatever you like to call it. Practically all your shooting will be from standing or squatting position—prone shots need not be considered. I was compelled to discard a beautiful little double .450 B.P. Express of Holland's because it had apparently been built for some man who shot in a country where nearly all his shots were fired from the prone position. The stock was so straight that if a quick shot was called for, I invariably went high.

If your rifle fits you properly, not only can you swing it into action with a far greater degree of rapidity and certainly, but you will not feel recoil to anything like the same extent as you would with a badly fitting weapon. Personally, I have never had the recoil of a big game rifle worry me—always excepting the .425

magazine—but some men are more susceptible. Such men should make very sure that their rifles are of the correct length and bend, and that they are perfectly balanced. The rifle should really be balanced for you yourself if you are at all worried about this question of recoil. The actual recoil, of course, is precisely the same irrespective of any questions of balance and fit but the reason why the recoil appears so much less on an irreproachably balanced rifle is to be found in the fact that you can hold such a weapon at your shoulder without any effort at all and consequently the muscles are more or less soft and relaxed and so act as cushions and absorb the recoil; whereas, with an ill-balanced weapon your muscles are tensed and strained when holding it to your shoulder and therefore transmit every particle of the shock to your entire body.

The reason why I say that the rifle should be balanced for the individual himself is because different men have different ways of holding a rifle, and a weapon that suits me perfectly need not necessarily suit the next man equally as well. Actually I am lucky in that respect, as it would appear that my general measurements are normal, which permits me to use any reasonably-shaped weapon.

WEIGHTS OF DOUBLE-BARREL RIFLES. The groan that usually went up whenever double rifles were mentioned, that they were too darned heavy, no longer has a leg to stand on—unless, of course, you are foolish enough to buy a cheap weapon. Such "standard" guns are almost invariably much heavier than better grade weapons of the same caliber. The standard, or regular, weights at which double-barrel rifles have been built for many years were ascertained as a result of much experience, and were the weights found to be the best and most suitable for the greatest number of sportsmen. They permitted of perfect balance, were not too heavy for the average man to handle with ease, and they absorbed a very great deal of the recoil so as not to be unpleasant to shoot with. Because it must be remembered that where the larger calibers are concerned, the rifle must be up to a certain weight or else the recoil will be altogether excessive even tho only one or two shots are fired. In the case of a .577 or .600 an excessive recoil might prevent you getting in a quick second shot should it prove necessary.

However, by the use of newer steels gunsmiths are now enabled to build their double rifles down to practically the same weights as corresponding singles and magazines. For instance, the following table shows the comparative weights of doubles and singles, the singles being with or without magazines, in the regular weights and alongside I have shown the new light weights at doubles can be built to special order. The only exceptions, I think, are in the case of Holland's .465 which he normally builds at 10¼ pounds, and Purdey's .465 which he is now building at 10 pounds.

Rifle^c	Weight of S.B. lbs.	Normal weight D.B. lbs.	New weight D.B. lbs.	
.600.................	12–13	16–18	14½–15½	
.577.................	11	12¼–14	11½	
.505 Gibbs...........	10½	—	—	(magazine)
.500.................	10	11½–12	10½	
.470.................	9½–10	11–11½	10½	
.465.................	9½	10¾–11¼	10¼	
.425.................	8½–9	11	10½	
.423 (10.75mm).......	7½	—	—	(magazine)
.416.................	9¼	—	—	(magazine)
.400.................	9–9½	10–10½	9½	
.375 Magnum........	8½–9	9½	8¾	

(NOTE: Holland & Holland have just informed me that up to the end of '39, by using tungsten steel for their barrels, they were able to build their D.B. .465 down to 9-lbs. 6-ozs. to special order. Tungsten steel is no longer available; but they are trying out some new alloy which they hope will permit of equally good results. At present the regular weight of their .465 "Royal" is 10¼ lbs.)

LOADING MAGAZINE RIFLES. The vast majority of men in Africa fill their magazines and then slip an extra shell up the spout. And with the exception of John Rigby, who definitely states in his catalog that you should always load from the magazine platform, gunsmiths suggest this manner of loading, presumably with the idea of giving their rifles that seemingly greater fire power. Personally, I consider it an exceedingly dangerous habit, and have repeatedly said so both verbally and in print, and am going to do so again right here.

Auctor: Dangerous! Did you say dangerous?

Lector: I did and I mean it. Not only do you run the risk of breaking your extractor without knowing that you have broken it, which would result in your being unable to fire a quick second shot should you want it but there is also a very real risk of giving yourself a dangerous jam in a tight corner.

Look here, if you are in the habit of charging your magazine and then slipping that extra shell up the spout of a weapon fitted with a 4-shot magazine, you will inevitably come to think, subconsciously, in terms of four shots in reserve. Well, if you have fired three or four shots at a bunch of lions or elephant and then decide to reload, the temptation to slip that extra round up the spout will be almost irresistible. If you attempt to do so, you will have to use two hands and then if you suddenly find yourself being charged you will run a very grave risk of giving yourself a serious jam in your hurry to complete operations. On the other hand, if you realize that and refrain from shoving that extra shell in, then you will now have one shell less in reserve than the number upon which you have been accustomed to rely, and this might very easily mean that you will find yourself snapping an empty rifle in an attempt to stop a charging animal, because you will find it very easy to forget the number of shots you have fired if things are warming up.

But if you have always been accustomed to just charge the magazine and then close the bolt, you will subconsciously come to think in terms of the magazine's capacity only. You will be able to reload with one hand only, and will always have the same number of shells in reserve. In a tight corner, having fired the last cartridge in your rifle, you will automatically lower the butt from your shoulder and commence reloading. There will be no futile snapping of empty weapons in the face of some savage beast. Because, altho you may not be consciously counting your shots, nevertheless, subconsciously you are. I'm no magazine enthusiast, but I found that I always knew instantly when my rifle was empty; how much more so in the case of a man who always uses this pattern of rifle.

ORDERING RIFLES. Blunt reckons that if two rifles are taken out after elephant they should be of identical make, bore and action. Well, that would certainly prevent any possibility of trying to load the wrong shells into one of them but I think he goes a mite too far. I can't see that there's any particular harm in taking out two or more rifles of different bore, so long as the calibers are not too closely related.

But I certainly agree that there can be no greater mistake than to have two or more big game rifles of widely differing action. For instance, I have already mentioned how I gave up a double .577 because it was fitted with single-trigger mechanism, and was the only double-barreled weapon I possessed so fitted. In the same way, I consider it would be very inadvisable to have one double rifle fitted with the ordinary top lever and another with the under-snap lever; if you like the under-snap lever, then you must have all your double-barrel weapons similarly fitted. Also, if you have one non-ejector in your battery, then you should remove the ejector springs from all your other doubles.

The idea is to have all your weapons working in the same manner so that there is nothing to have to remember when using one of them that you don't have to think about with the others. This will make it possible for you to get into the way of handling, shooting, and reloading any and all of your rifles quite automatically and without conscious thought—just as you can handle the controls of your automobile.

If you are buying secondhand weapons, get anything altered that does not conform—preferably by the maker of the rifle.

Auctor: But is it really so essential?

Lector: It is, son. And not merely for the beginner, but also for the thoroly experienced man. That German hunter friend of mine was a hunter of very great experience, and had all the characteristic thoroness of his race, but he was very nearly run down by a troop of stampeding elephant one day thru forgetting which of his rifles he was using. He had two British built doubles which he had bought secondhand in London. He shot from the left shoulder. One of the rifles had the top lever working in the normal way, that is, out to the right, but the other had been built for some other southpaw and the lever worked out to the left as it should do for a man who shot from the left shoulder. My friend didn't take both weapons out with him when he was hunting, but used them month and month about, and he had just changed over this day. In the excitement of just dropping a cow that made a vicious attack on him, he forgot he was using his other rifle and was unable to open the breech to reload when the rest of the herd came his way. Since he had killed a bull immediately before being attacked by the cow, the rifle was empty.

BROKEN STOCKS. *Auctor:* Look here, you have several times hinted at the possibility of a hunter's rifles being injured thru meeting with an accident. Just what happens when you are away out in the Blue? Suppose, for instance, you were unlucky enough to break a stock. Can you patch these things up yourself, or does it mean that the rifle is out of action until you can send it to a gunsmith?

Lector: It is because of the possibility of a rifle being put out of action entirely that all professional elephant-hunters have at least two rifles, both of which are equally suitable for elephant. The ivory-hunter cannot afford to be left without a thoroly suitable weapon. A good rifle is not easily put out of action; the usual knocks and falls and tumbles inseparable from such a life do little real damage. However, if a stock is unlucky enough to be broken, unless you carry a lot of tools around with you and can use them, that weapon must be considered as off the pay-roll, at least until you come across a native carpenter or blacksmith—maybe one of those heroes who build the old gas-pipe muzzle-loaders in secret places in the Bush. Even if it's only a carpenter, and it's extraordinary how many of these fellows there are, in all probability he will be able to make a thoroly sound job of things.

The usual method is to cut a couple of brass or steel plates, shape them nicely, drill holes thru them and right thru the stock, and then rivet them together. I've known men use rifles for years after they had been repaired in that manner. If the stock is only cracked, even badly cracked, thru the "small," you can bind it tightly with raw hide straight from the animal and then put it in the sun to dry and shrink. That green hide binding will set like iron bands and last indefinitely. Incidentally, it will frequently give you a very much better grip than you had before. I repaired a rifle that way myself on one occasion and used it for three or four years afterwards without any further attention. It was a Holland rifle and had the usual long strap that Holland always fits, which reaches right back over the comb. Whether or not it helps much under ordinary circumstances I cannot say—most gunsmiths don't bother with it—but I was certainly glad it was there when I cracked the stock clean thru. It would probably have been completely broken if it hadn't been for that long strap, which must have helped considerably to reinforce the small of the butt.

Speaking of broken stocks reminds me of that great lion-hunter, "Yank" Allen. Allen is credited with having shot more lions lonehanded than any man in history. He was retained by a large cattle ranch in Southern Rhodesia for many years to shoot out the lions that played havoc with the stock and altho I cannot give the exact figures of his bag, I do know that he was credited with well over 200 on the books of the company. He used, unless memory fails, a double .577 B.P. Express. A tall, steady, unhurried Texan, he was a fine shot and in the event of a charge waited until the lion was practically on him before firing, and made dead sure of his shot.

Tackling three lions one day, he fired but only wounded. The wounded lion came for him and in taking one step back to give himself a comfortable position, Yank put his foot in a hole, or tripped over a tuft of short grass, or something, and lost his balance. Jabbing the butt of the rifle down in an effort to save himself from falling, his weight broke the stock off at the small. He just had time to grasp the heavy barrels by the muzzles, and swinging them as a lumberman would swing his long felling axe, bring them down with such force on the lion's head that the animal's skull was crushed like an eggshell.

In this case, of course, Yank had no alternative but to take the risk of the unfired barrel discharging but I would like to mention that it's a horribly dangerous thing to do, besides being stupid, to attempt to finish-off a wounded beast by bashing him over the head with the butt of your rifle. Yet there are men who do it in their excitement. I warned an Indian against it, once upon a time but apparently he took no notice, because I heard later that he had gone out one night to shoot a leopard that was trying to get his goats. He had one of the old type of 8mm Austrian Mannlichers— not the Mannlicher-Schoenauer. He had broken the stock once before in exactly the same way, and had it repaired by a native carpenter. With the aid of a shooting head lamp he crippled and mortally wounded the leopard, but instead of letting well-enough alone he had to swipe the leopard over the head with the butt of his rifle. And the result was that the rifle was jarred off—he hadn't put the safety "on"—and he received the 244-gr. soft-nose bullet upwards thru his own groin—which gave him eight or ten very unpleasant hours before he died.

The African is pretty good at makeshifts—since the world began he has had to make things for himself or else go without. Give him a bit of training in the use of tools, and he becomes remarkably ingenious but he is not in the same country block as the Indian "mis'ri." It's simply unbelievable what some of those Indian gunsmiths can do. I remember seeing a rifle that a peevish elephant had gotten hold of; the stock was smithereens; the under lever (it was a falling-block .500 Nitro) was badly twisted; whilst the barrel was bent thru an angle of more than 45° and twisted as well. I'd have chucked the thing away as useless for any purpose. But the fella who had it took it to an Indian (Sikh) gunsmith, and in four or five days it was returned to him to test. I was present when the owner tested it at a target. To my unspeakable amazement it was even more accurate than when new! The owner sent it back to the gunsmith—who had no elaborate factory or workshop—to be finished. When he finally received it it looked like a brand-new gun. I wouldn't have believed it possible. The cost? Equivalent to about $4.50 U. S.

The "bush gunsmiths" to whom I've referred do not actually build the muzzle-loaders from scratch. But whenever one of the old Tower muskets—Brown Bess?—bursts, which is remarkably rare or when some peevish elephant or buffalo has had a bit of fun with one of them, the bits and pieces are brought along to the "gunsmith." Others will have been brought in in the same way, and he pulls them all to pieces and then builds up one "new" weapon from the relics of mebbe several. He's quite capable of putting an entire new stock on them; and I've seen modern breech-loaders, double and magazine, that had been in a fire completely restocked by one of these fellas—and not at all a bad job he made of them, considering the materials and tools he had at his disposal. The cost? Mebbe a coupla goats or a can of black powder.

They make their own powder too but very much prefer to use the store-bought stuff. The latter is more certain and causes less smoke, besides being stronger. Their's is very coarse. These guns and powder *work*. I don't suggest they'd hold their own with a genuine Kentucky rifle as far as accuracy is concerned but then the African does not bother about accuracy—his notion is to get so close that he pretty-well scorches the critter's hide with the muzzle-blast. Accuracy does not count with him.

Then, sights. The wise man always carries a spare foresight identical with that on the barrel in the trap in the heel of the pistol-grip on each and all of his rifles—just in case. But if you have been exceptionally unlucky, you can easily whittle yourself another that will prove entirely satisfactory from a certain white-thorn tree that grows in most parts of Africa—and what outdoorsman is not an accomplished whittler? I have never had to fit a spare sight when out hunting, but just for fun have whittled myself sights of this description and found them most excellent—I refer to blade foresights for use with aperture backsights. I also had a couple of native ivory-carvers who fashioned me several ivory bead foresights with their own homemade, string-driven, lathe. They were most satisfactory—I used one of them for about three years.

And here's a small tip that may come in handy some day—maybe you'll tell me that old man Noah used it when he went dove shooting that time but it's just possible that the next fella may not have heard of it. It has nothing to do with rifles but every hunter carries a shot gun which he'll be wanting to use from time to time, and if you use one of those light English guns, like I do, you'll know that they are delightfully easy to carry, handle and shoot but, since you can't have everything, there's a snag attached to them, and that is that the very thin barrels with which they're fitted are very liable to become dented unless you're inordinately careful. Well, I slightly dented the right barrel of my little 12-bore one day, and since the nearest gunsmith was at least 1,200 miles away and there was no means of getting the gun to him, and anyway I wanted to use it, things didn't look so good. I am no gunsmith myself and in the Bush am not able to lug around a kit full of tools.

However, as I sat gazing at my gun and mentally kicking myself for my carelessness, it occurred to me that I had once heard or read somewhere, or possibly it just entered my head of its own accord, that water was practically uncompressible. So I got a cork, plugged the muzzle of the right barrel, filled it with water, and then with a chunk of soft wood, one end of which I had whittled into a handle of sorts, I gently tapped over and around the dent. It came up in the most gratifying way, and by the time I had finished and dried the water out of the bore, the most careful examination inside and out, from both ends of the barrel, failed to show the slightest indication of where the dent had been.

OBJECTION TO VERY LIGHT RIFLES. *Auctor:* In view of the positive mania there is, and always has been, in Africa for very light rifles, would you mind explaining why you dislike them. I fully appreciate the necessity for a powerful rifle when tackling the big fellows in the thick stuff but all hunting does not take place in thick cover. And since in more open country there is not the same risk of stubbing your toe on an animal before you see him, provided the bullet thrown is not so light that it will disintegrate on impact, why should not a light rifle prove perfectly satisfactory? It would be very much easier to carry than a heavier weapon.

Lector: Certainly, it would; and a walking stick would be even easier to carry and would be of greater help to you if you were tired. But a walking stick would not be of much use to you if you wanted to shoot anything, and I contend that a featherweight rifle will not be of much more service to you than a stick when you are dog-tired at the end of a long, hard day. Such a weapon absolutely refuses to keep still if you happen to be fatigued—and you are often fatigued in the African Bush. At 6 o'clock in the morning you may be able to place your shots beautifully accurately with the little rifle but just see what sort of a performance you will put up at 6 o'clock in the evening after tramping all day in the sweltering heat! Suppose it is getting along towards sundown and you are on your way back to camp when you are offered the chance of a lifetime; do what you will, that little light rifle will not settle down steadily in your hand; finally, with the muzzle of the rifle describing circles all over the animal, you in desperation yank at the trigger and hope for the best, and away goes your fine trophy. The small bullet means a small entrance hole to the wound— assuming that you have hit the animal at all—and this in turn means little or no blood spoor; the light is failing, you cannot follow far; eventually you are obliged to give up the chase and plod wearily on with yet another heart-breaking disappointment to round off a disappointing day. Had you used a heavier rifle it would have settled down much more steadily in your hand and therefore permitted of a more accurately-placed bullet in addition to which the larger bullet would have caused a more reliable blood spoor and done more damage even if it had failed to kill outright.

If you are hunting in more open country there is not the same necessity for you to carry the rifle yourself since you see the game sooner; there is little likelihood of you wanting to take a snap-shot. Personally, I like my rifles to weigh from 9½ to 10½ lbs., and would not care to use a rifle weighing less than 8½ lbs.

But this, of course, will depend on the physique of the man behind the rifle. It would be impossible and useless to attempt to lay down any definite figures as to the maximum or minimum weights of rifle that should be used. Nevertheless, I think that any man fit enough to go big game hunting is fully capable of carrying an 8 lb. rifle all day and once he has accustomed himself to that he will have no difficulty in managing an appreciably heavier weapon.

Single-barreled Single-loaders. *Auctor:* I don't know whether you have forgotten or not, but a long time ago you promised to say something about single-loaders.

Lector: I have not forgotten, and have quite a lot to say about them too. I have been saying it for years, verbally and on paper, in books, sporting magazines and newspapers. Because in my humble opinion magazine rifles ought to be banned from the realms of sport.

Auctor: Hell! But that's gonna cause a squeal! Can't you just hear all those fellas with their super-accurate bolt-actioned wild-cats beginning to moan!

Lector: They needn't. Altho you mentioned single-loaders, and I mentioned that magazine rifles should be barred, I guess we can modify that slightly. There could be no objection to bolt-actioned rifles having a magazine that would just hold a cartridge and a half—making a 2-shot weapon out of it. To explain what I mean by a cartridge and a half: If the magazine held two shells it would be impossible to prevent men from putting those two in and then a third up the spout but the magazine could be so designed that when the second shell was put in the magazine the bolt could get hold of it and carry it into the chamber, but it would not be possible to press it down and close the bolt over it. And so I speak of a magazine capacity of a cartridge and a half. There could be no real objection to this.

In most of the States there are regulations in the game laws prohibiting the use of repeating shot guns with a capacity of more than three shells, and I see no very good reason why there should not be regulations out here which would prevent the use of magazine rifles with a capacity of more than two, or at the very most three, cartridges.

Personally, however, I would much prefer the falling-block single-loader. With this type of weapon there is no rushing the shot in the hope of getting another; if you are given a second, there is again no rushing it, because it would be unreasonable to expect a third. The result is that each and every shot is fired as it should be, and a clean kill eventuates. That curious psychological factor which seems to arise when a man knows that he has three or four shots in immediate reserve would not appear. I can't think *why* a man shooting solely for sport and pleasure should *want* to make a big bag at a "sitting." Lions in particular seem to affect men this way. Why? The ordinary hunting lion does no harm—then why should men want to shoot them in large quantities irrespective of age or sex or anything else? The man-eater is an entirely different proposition—I hold no brief for him and if a bunch of lions take to cattle-killing they must be killed or discouraged. But this does not concern the ordinary sportsman—there are professional hunters who can be called upon to do this sort of work.

With a scope-sighted single-loader you should get your beast every time. It would teach you to take the greatest possible care with every shot you fire, and this would mean fewer wounded animals. And look at the vastly greater satisfaction your hunting would give you if you knew that you were a one-shot killer. Oh no! it's not hooey. Selous did practically all his hunting with falling-block single-loaders, and they weren't modern magnum scope-sighted ones either. For 30 years he used a falling-block .450 Metford B.P. Express by Gibbs; and then had a similar weapon built by Holland, I think, to handle the old Mark VI .303 cartridge and used it until it also was "worn out." After that he had Holland build him another single-loader for their old 400/.375 shell.

When I first started experimenting with magazines I used to only load two shells into them to avoid any possibility of being tempted into blazing off the contents of the magazine into the stampeding herd as I had seen so many men do. But by far the greater part of my shooting has been done with doubles and single-loaders. And my experience has been that if the gods are on your side that day, you'll get your several beasts just as surely with a single-loader as you will with any magazine—and remember I write as a professional who has all too often to shoot for quantity rather than for quality. I'm firmly convinced that if the governments concerned would prohibit the use of magazine rifles with a total capacity of more than at the most three cartridges—and preferably two—and insist that all rifles, other than heavy powerful weapons obviously intended for use against dangerous game at close quarters, be fitted with scope sights, it would be the greatest step forward towards genuine game preservation or conservation that has ever been taken at one stride. I am sure that it is no exaggeration to say that there must be literally tens of thousands of animals wounded thruout the big game hunting world every year thru the use of magazine rifles and open sights, and which would not have been so wounded had scope-sighted single-loaders been used.

VERTICAL STANDARD ON ALL AROUND RIFLE. *Auctor:* By the way, in your chapter on sighting you recommend that the standard backsight should be made sloping towards the muzzle as this makes it more suitable for use in the bad light found in heavy forest. But what about the all-around rifle? It will not always be used in heavy forest and a sight sloping towards the muzzles will undoubtedly dazzle you sometimes in open country and maybe lose you the trophy of a lifetime. What do you suggest?

Lector: A quickly detachable scope sight, of course.

Auctor: Yes; but supposing the fella simply couldn't rise to the price of a good scope.

Lector: Well, if the rifle was being built for me I should certainly have it sighted in the most suitable manner for use in thick cover if it was sometimes to be used in there, because it might very easily develop into a matter of life and death. There is not the same likelihood of such contingencies arising in the open, and if they do the animals must of necessity be close when the pattern of sight is of little moment provided it's practical. However, if the weapon is to be used considerably in the open country with open sights, I should imagine that a vertical barrel backsight would be the best compromise—it would not be likely to dazzle you in the open unless the sun was very close to the horizon behind you, whilst it's not too bad in heavy forest. Yes, undoubtedly your all-around rifle should be fitted with a vertical standard barrel sight if it's not to be fitted with a quickly-detachable scope sight for use in open country.

CASES. A good rifle deserves a good case. Bumping and jolting around in trucks over our apologies for roads will soon make a mess of your fine guns if you don't look after them. By far the best pattern is the dove-tailed oak case covered with leather and fitted with brass corners and, of course, straps and a lock. These cases are costly but they will outlast several of the ordinary canvas-covered wood boxes, which just can't take it. Besides you can usually pick up good used ones wherever you are buying your rifle. The all-leather leg-o'-mutton type is not too good. Everything you possess is subjected to a whole lot of rough, very rough, usage out here.

CAUTION. I would sound one word of warning where all double rifles are concerned, hammer or hammerless: *Never snap the locks of a double rifle if the chambers are empty.* If you do you run a grave risk of breaking your strikers. If there is nothing in the chambers the strikers may come too far thru the holes in the face of the standing breech, and may stick there. Then when you next open the breech the extractors may ride up against the points of the strikers and break them off without you realizing what has happened. You load, go out to shoot, and your rifle refuses to fire because the broken strikers are unable to reach the caps.

There is a certain type of moron who cannot pick up a gun without pulling the trigger. If there is the slightest likelihood of one of those creatures having fiddled with your rifle during your absence, examine it most carefully to see that the strikers are okeh. All the best makers supply a couple of spare strikers with the spare foresight in the trap in the heel of the pistol-grip for just such eventualities. Anybody who can use a turnscrew can fit a new one in a matter of minutes. The steel used in modern best grade rifles is so good that the possibility of a striker breaking in normal use must be a very remote possibility. I have never had it happen, and I have done a great deal of shooting with these rifles— far more than with any other type.

If you want to snap your locks, either to accustom yourself to the trigger-pulls or to practice reloading, use snap caps. These are merely nickel-plated steel cases like short cartridge cases, with a plug of hard rubber in place of the customary cap or primer. The strikers impinge on the rubber plug and return to their original place. With these in the chambers you can snap your triggers to your heart's content with the pleasing certainty that you cannot hurt your rifle.

Some men are scared that if they don't snap the locks to ease the springs when the rifle is not in action the springs will weaken. That may be so where coil springs are used, as in magazine rifles, but V springs are used in doubles and you may cheerfully forget them. I once bought at a government auction a hammerless double of by no means best grade that had been confiscated some 15 or 20 years previously from an elephant-poacher, put away in its case with the hammers cocked, and forgotten about. It functioned perfectly for me. If you would be happier with the springs eased, use snap caps or, if the weapon is to be put away in its case, then press the face of the standing breech against the table or something and let the strikers impinge on the wood but if you do this you may have difficulty in re-assembling the weapon later. Actually, it's quite unnecessary.

PISTOL GRIPS VS. STRAIGHT HAND STOCKS. The only rifles I have seen fitted with straight hand stocks were featherweight squibs specially built for some ladies. They were lovely little tools and delightfully easy to handle and shoot. I have never seen double rifles so fitted. Yet when using two triggers it would seem that the straight hand stock should be preferable to the pistol grip, thru allowing more play and freedom of movement to the firing hand. On a light shot gun I certainly prefer the straight hand grip irrespective of how many triggers the weapon may have. In the case of a powerful rifle, however, the recoil would probably prove a snag and might easily give rise to bruised fingers. In days gone by, many of the old black powder weapons were fitted with straight hand stocks with or without a twist of metal back of the trigger guard to form a grip of sorts. Owing to the excessive recoil of those old cannons many men used to complain of fingers injured. Neumann comes immediately to mind, who suffered so badly that he invariably wore gloves—and that in tropical Africa!

If I could find somebody else to pay for it, I should certainly like to try out a double-rifle fitted with a straight hand stock but I don't intend to experiment at my own expense!

Auctor: Here's a damfool question that has nothing to do with rifles, but which has piqued my curiosity: You have more than once made some mention of your men cutting off the animal's tail. You mention that they will sometimes do this before cutting the throat. How come? Is this just African cussedness, or do they have some superstition about cutting its tail off first? I can understand them cutting off an elephant's tail to prove ownership but *why* cut off the tails of all other animals?

Lector: Amongst the Muhammadan tribes the throat of an animal must be cut by a True Believer before death to make its flesh lawful food; but Islam is lenient in the case of an animal dropped stone dead by a well-placed bullet, provided the throat is cut immediately so that there is a slight flow of blood, the flesh may be eaten. The Muhammadans, therefore, invariably cut the throat first. But as far as pagan tribes are concerned, they seldom bother to cut the throat unless they have a calabash or something in which to catch the blood. Those that do cut the throat probably have some hazy notion that because they have seen the Muhammadans doing it it must be something good.

As far as cutting off the tail is concerned, apart from proof of ownership, the real reason is to satisfy those who have to go out to cut up the animal and bring in the meat that there really is an animal for them to cut up—particularly should the guide go astray and fail to find the dead beast.

And here is something that surely deserves mention—the African's sense of direction. In all the years of my hunting career I can only remember one coon failing to find an animal killed by me earlier in the day. Now after zig-zagging and twisting and turning for hours in heavy forest with plenty undergrowth and no landmarks, you eventually drop a beast, it's not too difficult after years of experience to be able to point directly towards camp, just as the African can—no looking up or around for landmarks or to see where the sun is—instantly, and with absolute certainty, his arm stretches out and he points directly towards your camp. Any real bushman or plainsman can develop this instinctive sense of direction in time—just as the born seaman can. The Grand Banks skippers come immediately to mind but it is a very different thing to then continue after the herd and drop maybe three or four more beasts in different parts of the forest, return to camp, collect your companions, and then lead them, straight as the bee flies, to where those dead animals are lying. There is no question of following up the morning's spoor—it would take far too long, and anyway the African does not need to. Straight thru the forest he goes, as tho he had a map of it in his black head, talking and laughing and looking for nothing but the easiest way thru the thicker patches, he will guide his party so direct towards that carcass that if it was dark they would all stumble over it. I am not exaggerating.

I have known Africans to go astray when returning to their own kraals and maybe within a mile or two of it, and have had to put them right myself altho I was a stranger in the district; yet, I repeat, I have only once known a lad fail to find an animal I had shot. And that wretched youth didn't hear the end of it for months. When he finally quit the search that day and started back thru the forest, he came across one of the other beasts I had shot that morning and was greeted with yells of derision by the men cutting it up. One of them instantly grabbed his spear and shouted to the butchers to come on, that he would show them where the animal was. And so he did. I certainly did not blame the lad for failing to find the dead beast—I very much doubt if I would have been able to find more than one or at the most two of them myself.

Auctor: Tell me, old timer, how come so much solicitation over the game laws out your way, when the actual law may be several hundred miles away from the lawless proceedings? Your niggers must be great gabbers. In the States *every* nigger plays "shet mouth" and he don't know nothin', not never. One would have thought it would have been much easier to dent the game laws a mite out your way and get away with it. Or do you really have these police agents nosing around, even away out in the "Blue"?

Lector: The African has no newspapers, news-reels or radios. Each and every African is his own broadcasting station. They are constantly wandering around and, having all eternity in front of them, stop and pass the time of day, and any news they may have, with every other coon they meet, either on the path or in the various kraals and villages they pass. A white man is such a rare occurrence that he is automatically N$\underline{\underline{o}}$ 1 news-interest—his every doings are watched and related; his habits, actions, customs, mannerisms, temper and domestic arrangements are endlessly discussed.

Naturally, everything he shoots is known and his ability as a hunter and rifleman is compared with that of every other hunter that had ever been known to enter the district during at least the previous half century. Travelers carry all this news and information around with them and spread it far and wide wherever they go. It inevitably reaches the ears of the nearest government official sooner or later.

These government officials, Commissioners, as they are usually called, are little tin gods in their respective districts—lords of all they survey. Yet in spite of the airs they put on, some of them are not above running a considerable graft in their district. No local coon would even dream of complaining about them to still higher authority with the result that they can do pretty much as they please—their word is absolute law thruout maybe several hundreds or thousands of square miles and amongst maybe several hundreds of thousands of natives, men, women and children. In most parts a hunter is obliged to send his licence and permits along to the nearest official to be franked. If the official is of a snotty disposition, or is running some kind of graft amongst his "people," it is almost certain that a native police detective in "plain clothes"— possibly a strip of loin cloth—will be sent along to ask for a job or to just act as camp follower, doing odd jobs in return for an occasional bellyfull of meat, and nose around generally. Then the various chiefs and headmen of villages will probably be instructed to report on the hunter's activities. The official will not be above taking advantage of the most trivial misdemeanor to frame an excuse for ordering the hunter out of his district in case he happens to spot the racket.

The vast majority of white men do not take the trouble to keep in with the local chiefs and others—possibly they consider it beneath their dignity, and anyway few men spend much time in the Bush nowadays. Elephant-poaching on a large scale is almost a thing of the past—at any rate in British territory, owing to the fact that you must produce a permit authorizing you to be in possession of so much ivory before you can find a buyer for it, and the buyer must also produce papers before he can export it. Personally, I have always made a point of being on friendly terms with all coons from the paramount chief downwards, and have made it a hobby to learn all languages and dialects spoken by the different tribes amongst which I am hunting, as well as the customs of the peoples generally. The result is that when on a poaching expedition news of my whereabouts does not get around anything like so quickly—it eventually *will* get around, inevitably, owing to travelers and to the meat being distributed thruout the villages but I have the goodwill of the locals and they will let me know if the district official is making any move in my direction, and will willingly help me to get my ivory across the Border. I've been doing it all my life out here and have never yet been caught. But it's solely thanks to the good name I have made for myself amongst the various tribes. They do not look upon elephant-poaching as a crime, and take a genuine delight in helping a white man to outwit the government officials—it's so rarely they find one who plays their own game; the vast majority of white men with whom they have had any acquaintance have either been government officials or else have been one hundred per cent law-abiding and pro-government.

The African from "outside" is something of a sportsman and by no means a bad fellow—handle him the right way and he is your man. And there is one thing about these coons—once they have thrown in their lot with you they will not "squeal." I have had coons take a pretty severe beating-up—as I subsequently heard —from police and other government officials, such as District Officers, rather than squeal on me. They sure can play "shet mouth" as effectively as their cousins in the Southern States when they want to. It's a pity they don't always do it but the government officials have them pretty well under their thumb—all of them from the paramount chief downwards, since even he is only there at the pleasure of government—they can remove him any time they like if they reckon he's not playing ball the way they want it played. That's called indirect government.

Mind you, all that refers chiefly to British territory—the British are infernally "nosey" and spinsterishly "straight-laced" (outwardly!); everybody in their territory must conform to their ideas of how the "pukkha sahib" should comport himself—even to the clothes he wears. If any fella, disagreeing with their notions and stupid, petty conventions, decided to live and dress in the manner that best suits him, he soons earns not merely the cold eye of suspicion but that of very definite and real hostility. If he continues to be independent he will sooner or later find that the authorities have been brought into the silent, underground fight that is being waged against him, and he will be informed that he is considered undesirable in the territory and "a bad influence on the Natives." That last is their Ace of trumps and they never fail to use it.

However, there are still parts of Africa where a man can disappear entirely from the ken of civilization if he wishes but if he wants to remain in peace he will have to cultivate the goodwill of the local coons. I have done it myself for three-four year stretches at different times and on one occasion had to re-appear because rumours had gone around to the effect that I had been killed by elephant and the Powers-that-Be were kicking up a fuss about my guns and kit not having been brought in! On another occasion a fool of a British Consul wrote my folks, who were still alive, back home in Eire, to know if they would like him to send out a search party to see if they could find any relics of me to send them as souvenirs!

The trouble with Africa is that none of these folks has enough to do to keep their minds occupied—everything is done for them by numerous Africans, Indians, Goans, and half-breeds, with the result that they have nothing to do themselves but gossip about their neighbors and stick their noses into other men's business. Altho Africa is a mighty big continent, there are precious few white men in it, and everyone knows everyone else and all about them—and to try and find out a bit more, are not above spying on him thru the agency of the native servants of both parties. Nice, isn't it? I live in Portuguese territory myself, where conditions are very much pleasanter, the Portuguese motto apparently being, "Live and let live" or words to that effect—"Leave him alone so long as he leaves us alone." Which suits me.

Afterthoughts

Being
some sidelights on the situation
in the African big-game hunting world
as it exists today (May, 1948)

together with
a few useful tips
and personal experiences

This Big Game Racket

Here is an article I wrote for Britain's *GAME & GUN* immediately after getting out of uniform and hitting the trail to where I belong. It gives some idea of my feelings after what I had seen thruout Africa whilst serving in the Intelligence, which job kept me moving around quite considerably.

Back once more in the peace of the Bush after five years of the recent fantastic, senseless exhibition of Western lunacy, one has time in which to sort out one's impressions.

True, the whole idiotic business did certainly permit me to get on reasonably familiar terms with various parts of Africa and the world with which I had previously had only a nodding acquaintance, other than that gleaned from books and talks with others more familiar with those parts than I was.

One of the first and most outstanding impressions forced upon me concerned the Elephant and Game question. Nobody has a greater admiration than I have for the Elephant Control staffs of Tanganyika and Uganda, and the work they have done; so much so, in fact, that a few years ago I wrote various articles concerning them for *GAME & GUN* and other journals. Every word that I wrote then, I still stand by. But the point is, so well have these men done their work in teaching the elephant the boundaries of their reserves, and that they will not be molested in there, that the herds are breeding away to their hearts' content and thereby increasing their numbers to such an extent that it has been found necessary to slay some thousands of them each year in both of these territories for the past ten or twelve years. Otherwise, it has been stated, their reserves would not be able to support them and they would, therefore, be compelled to break out and go raiding in the cultivated areas. These cultivated areas are increasing

357

annually since the natives are also increasing in numbers. Accordingly, thousands of elephant will still have to be shot every year to preserve the balance between them and Man.

I have always understood that Government trading monopolies went out of existence somewhere in Queen Elizabeth's day or shortly after yet here are these East African Governments running a very nice ivory-trading monopoly which brings them in a revenue of close on £25,000 per annum each, year after year, after paying all expenses. This annual slaughter of elephant is all in the hands of the government hunters, and the ivory belongs to government. An outsider can still only get a permit for two elephant a year (three in Uganda).

Now, with the whole world reorganizing things, surely it's about time there was a little reorganizing in this direction. Nobody who realized the necessity for elephant control objected in the slightest to the Department collaring all the available money they could when the scheme was first started, because they had precious little in the way of funds in those days—twenty years or so ago. But the position is very different today—unless, of course, they have been using the money for other purposes than those directly concerned with the Game Department.

There are still a few individual hunters left with just as much, and possibly even considerably more, experience than any of the existing government men. Why should they not be given a chance, in the shape of a sufficiently generous permit, to enable them to make a living off the comparatively small ivory that has to be shot during Control operations? If it is claimed that there are not enough of these men able and willing to do the work and pay themselves out of the ivory—well, the government men are still there; nobody is suggesting that they be fired. The idea is merely to give the individual hunter a less raw deal. (I'm not grinding any personal axes—I live in Portuguese territory, and have my own arrangements with the powers-that-be.)

With regard to lesser game one views with grave concern the probable, if not indeed certain, introduction of full-powered self-loading or automatic rifles into the realms of sport (sic) in the near future. As various articles of mine in different sporting journals in the past have clearly shown, I have always condemned the ordinary magazine rifle for purely sporting purposes. It may be necessary from time to time for a professional hunter to use one when he is called upon to wipe out a bunch of marauding elephant, buffalo or lion that are making a nuisance of themselves but there cannot be the slightest necessity for such weapons in the hands of inexperienced sportsmen shooting solely for sport and pleasure. The psychological effect of the knowledge that he has several shots in immediate reserve tends to make him much more careless in the placing of those shots in the hope of making a big bag whereas with a single-loader, having nothing in reserve, he would take the utmost care to place his bullet where it was wanted. But just think what would happen with self-loading or automatic rifles! (I've seen Bren guns and Tommy guns turned on game during the war—I sincerely hope I shall never see anything of the sort again!)

Regularly, and without fail, up goes a moan that the various hunting tribes are a definite menace to the game. These tribes hunt principally with spears, and with bows and poisoned arrows. They also trap game.

The African hunts solely for food for himself and his family—skins are a secondary consideration and are only taken because they cover the meat. His methods, taken by and large, are relatively less cruel, in that they inflict less suffering, than the use of magazine rifles in the hands of inexperienced sportsmen firing expanding bullets at long ranges.

Take, for instance, his poisoned arrows. If the poison is fresh and strong, it kills in an altogether extraordinarily short space of time. There is no pain, so far as one can judge—the poison appears to have a paralyzing effect on either the nerve centres or muscles surrounding the respiratory system and/or heart. (I am no toxicologist.) At any rate, having run a little way after receiving the arrow, the animal stops, sways and collapses. Death is very rapid indeed; in fact, I have seen animals that appeared to be dead before they touched the ground after collapsing. The poison, in my experience—and I used it quite a lot—was invariably fatal. I did not lose a single beast hit. I did not have an opportunity of using it on anything larger than buffalo, but I see no earthly reason for disbelieving the natives when they tell me that it is equally effective on elephant or rhino. Compare that with concentrated magazine fire as three of four sportsmen (save the mark!) blaze off with their rifles into the brown of a herd.

These hunting tribes have no rifles or guns. They are very, and quite justifiably, discontented at the raw deal they are getting. They have hunted, and quite literally lived by hunting, since the world began, but are now thrown into gaol if caught doing so. In spite of their hunting, however, the country was alive with game when the first white men set foot there. Every one of them remarked on it. It was only after the advent of the white man with his magazine rifles that the extermination of the game became an accomplished fact in many parts of Africa, and its threatened extinction a serious possibility in other parts.

The Wandorobo, who are those most generally blamed in Kenya, and the Wakamba, who are probably the greatest exponents of the poisoned arrow (and the Shilluk in the Sudan, altho they only use spears), for being a danger to game preservation, have seen all this taking place. They see the car-loads of white men driving across the plains, cluttered up with rifles. They see the wounded game staggering and limping along—they know perfectly well that the white man is not shooting for meat because he is hungry, but only for the horns which he cannot eat. They know that the white man kills and wounds—particularly wounds —far more with his rifles than he (the Dorobo) does with his bows and arrows. Yet in spite of it all, it is he and his people who are blamed for decimating the herds!

For heaven's sake, let's have a little common sense on the matter. If the indubitable diminution in the game numbers that has taken place during the last fifty years or so can honestly be placed on the shoulders of the hunting tribes—who have been there for centuries—then imagination reels at the thought of the conditions that must have existed there in days gone by! It must have been literally impossible to move a step in any direction without stubbing one's toes on an animal! What did they all live on?

This is a perfectly logical assumption, if indeed the rapid thinning out of the game numbers in East Africa during the last half century is due to native hunters. But the very idea is absurd.

A parallel can be taken from South Africa or, better still, North America. Who wiped out the vast herds of American bison? The original redskin of the hunting tribes, with their bows and arrows, or the rifle-armed white man?

There is limitless game of every description thruout Africa for the genuine sportsman. Originally, before there was any attempt at settlement or anything but quite nominal game laws, the visiting sportsman with his insane desire to make a bigger bag than some other fella he knew back home who had been out here the previous year, was by far the worst offender. But that is a thing of the past. Today, things are quite different; ninety-nine times in a hundred the visiting sportsman is a genuine sportsman— particularly if he hails from America. The American hunter is here because he is a hunter at heart but all too often the visiting Britisher, especially if he happens to have a handle to his name, is not here because he wants to be but because it is "the thing to do," it is "expected of him." How often has one heard some such remark as: "Well, thank goodness we've got our rhino; now what's next?" One's sympathies go out to the unappreciated rhino who wasn't doing anybody a scrap of harm anyway.

No, today it's the resident who is responsible for any wanton slaughter that takes place, and above all, for the constant, needless wounding of game that can be directly laid to his stupid insistence on light, magazine rifles and featherweight, high-velocity, copper-pointed bullets. I have wandered over parts of the Athi plains in Kenya, rather less than a million miles from Nairobi, the capital, and have seen the ground literally littered with empty shells from small-bore, high-velocity rifles. I have seen the same thing around Naivasha, where in one particular place it was practically impossible to take a step without treading on an empty cartridge case.

The modern generations in Africa are not hunters. The few that ever go out with a rifle will only go as far as they can get by car, and they will only shoot what game they can see around their camp. The intending visitor need fear no lack of sport. Except for those, admittedly rare, occasions when ignorant South African and British Imperial troops machine-gunned large herds of game, little hunting took place thruout the years of the war, owing to lack of ammunition. That lack has not yet been filled (Dec. '47), so that one can safely say that there has been no hunting for the last seven or eight years. During the war in Africa, and later when I returned from farther East for discharge, I wandered extensively from the far north of the Sudan to south of the Zambezi, in Portuguese East, and nowhere did I find a scarcity of game where game might reasonably have been expected—and this applies to everything from elephant downwards. On the contrary, there was every evidence on all sides, both from my own observations and from talks with the local natives, that every species was more numerous. In particular, elephant and buffalo were doing extensive damage thruout the continent.

I cannot tell you what the cost of license is at the moment. Those Game Wardens whom I have asked say that nothing definite has yet been decided upon. However, it may be taken for granted that they will not be less than they were before the war. In British Africa the pre-war costs were as follows:—

	£ (Sterling)
Kenya.	
For the first elephant	50
For two elephant	150
Uganda.	
For one elephant	10
For second elephant	20
For two elephant	30
Tanganyika.	
For first elephant	20
For second elephant	30
Nyasaland.	
For first elephant	10
For second elephant	15
For third elephant	15
Northern Rhodesia.	
For first elephant	30
For second elephant	10
For third elephant	10
Sudan.	£ (Egyptian)
For first elephant	10
For second elephant	10

NOTE: Only two elephant may be shot on the big license in the Sudan after the additional fee has been paid, and not more than six elephant in all shall be killed by any one person, however long the period the license-holder may be in the Sudan, or however many licenses he may hold.

All the above elephant permits are only issued after the full game license has been taken out. It varies slightly in the different territories but generally runs (pre-war) from £50 to £75; the elephant permits are additional.

By paying a Customs deposit, which will be refunded when you leave the territory within a stipulated time, you can import your guns and rifles without any trouble. But note that the .450 caliber (rifle, revolver or pistol) is prohibited in the Sudan and the .303 prohibited thruout British East Africa, the Sudan and Nyasaland.

Here, in Portuguese East, where I live and have hunted for so many years, conditions are very much better. I chose it after wandering pretty well the length and breadth of Africa because it is about the only place left where a man can live on his rifles as a genuine hunter should. We do not get many visitors here because the conditions are pretty tough, as compared with British East Africa. There are no automobile "champagne safaris" here. Roads have only comparatively recently been built and, being bush and forest country, your car must keep to the road—you cannot go chasing across country in your truck or car here. In this neck o' the woods we tramp around with a string of porters or carriers humping our kit, just as they had to everywhere in days gone by. But licenses are very much cheaper here than they are in British territory, and the conditions and regulations very much easier. At the present time, for the equivalent of about $200.00 (American dollars), you can take out a special license that permits you to shoot pretty well anything you like, and as many bull elephant as you can. For some reason that no one can fathom, they have put hippo on the protected list but they and cow elephant are about the only things you can't shoot. Buffalo are classed as varmints, and you may shoot them for the mere price of a gun permit—$25.00 American. The Portuguese wish it to be clearly understood that they have no policy of game extermination, as Southern Rhodesia would seem to have but that the elephant and buffalo have increased to such an extent and do such an incalculable amount of damage every year, that it is imperative that they be thinned out somewhat. For a long time I have been impressing upon them the urgent necessity for this to forestall any fear of them passing panic legislation which might well lead to virtual extermination.

There are many keen hunters in the States who reckon they would willingly trade their souls, if they could only find someone who traded in that commodity, for a chance to get out to Africa for a big game hunt. If you ask them why they don't come anyway, the answer is invariably, "Hell! that's a rich man's game—where would I get the mazuma to pay for that?" But you know, it need not be only a rich man's sport. It's true that it can cost you just as much as you like to spend, and I have known parties who reckoned they were roughing it if they spent less than from $5,000 to $10,000 a month on their hunting—it's one of life's little mysteries to me what they found to spend it on!—but those sort of parties do most of the hunting in an easy chair in camp with a long, fat cigar and plenty of iced drinks.

But the keen hunter can get some of the finest sport in the world at no greater cost than it would cost him to live at home, if he just knows the right way to go about it. For instance, I knew a very keen sportsman who came out to Cape Town in South Africa. He bought himself a Ford delivery van, loaded his kit into it, and headed north. Fellows he met in Johannesburg invited him to visit at their farms, which were merely private game preserves for the owners and their friends. He had some good sport there amongst the larger varieties of non-dangerous game and was enabled to get his eye in. After a week or ten days there he packed up and again headed north. Once he got into the game country he took out the necessary gun permits and sought permission to hunt varmints such as lion, leopard, and, in many parts, buffalo. Nobody would object to him dropping an occasional buck for the pot, even if they knew and so he gradually worked his way up thru Africa. Settlers and farmers here and there were only too glad to see a new face, and insisted on him staying with them, and gladly gave him permission to do all the shooting he liked over their land, and the more lion and leopard he shot for them the more pleased they would be. If there were no farms about, well, his delivery van made a safe and cozy caravan for the night. He finally arrived in Nairobi, in Kenya, nearly a year after leaving Cape Town. He sold his van for two-thirds of what it cost him twelve months before. He told me that the entire expedition cost him $2,750.00 American but that there were many ways in which he could have saved on that—for instance he did not have to travel first class on the ship, both ways, and could have saved many a hotel bill by camping in his van. He figured that a man who was really keen could have the finest twelve months big game hunting he ever dreamt of for fifteen hundred dollars or thereabouts, and he wouldn't need to stint himself or rough it unduly. That was not very long before the outbreak of World War II. Under existing conditions it could be done even more cheaply right here in

Portuguese East, and there's no need to have to stay the full twelve months either, if you don't want to.

The best season for hunting is from August till the end of the year. In August they start burning the long grass which hides most of the lesser game.

The Facts Concerning Elephant Control

Looking thru back numbers of various sporting journals I am repeatedly seeing the fear expressed that the African elephant is in grave danger of extermination. So it would seem both opportune and desirable to place the actual facts of the matter before as large a public as possible, in order to dispel these fears once and, I hope, for all.

Let us consider the conditions prior to control.

For something like a hundred years Africa has been the happy hunting ground of the ivory-hunter, and the result of this has been the disappearance of elephant from many parts of the continent (notably South Africa and Southern Rhodesia), and the greatly decreased numbers in most other parts with the possible exception of Uganda and the Belgian Congo. Nobody can, or would attempt to, deny this. But it must be remembered that elephant in South Africa were very much easier to hunt and kill—in spite of the vastly inferior weapons of those days—because, not having become accustomed to firearms, they spent the greater part of their time in the open. The old-timers shot practically all their elephant from the saddle. In addition it must be remembered that in the past the natives slew literally tens of thousands of elephant every year; they had to protect their food-crops.

It has been estimated by those who have studied such matters that anything from 75,000 to 100,000 elephant were slain thruout Africa every year in the past. I have it on unimpeachable authority that the quantity of ivory passing thru Khartoum annually fifty years ago must have required some 20,000 elephant from Uganda and the Sudan to supply it. The present annual bag in Uganda of around 2,000 elephant compares very favorably with those figures. When control measures were first started in Uganda the annual bag was in the vicinity of from 500 to 600. Each year it was found necessary to increase this number since, as was stated in a recent report of the acting Game Warden, "that for every elephant shot two more seem mysteriously to spring into being." Critics beg leave to doubt this statement, or at least say that it fails to impress them, which amounts to the same thing. But if the habits of wild elephant are considered, it is not so extraordinary; on the contrary, it is precisely what one might expect.

In the past it was rarely, very rarely, that one saw a really young calf with the herd. The elephant had no real sanctuaries and were constantly and eternally being battered and chivvied about from pillar to post. The result was that in a very large measure the cows ceased breeding entirely or, when a cow was near her time, she cleared off by herself far from all habitation and likelihood of encountering her persecutors, and there remained until her calf was old enough to look after itself—possibly ten years or so. The result was that most of the cows encountered either had no calves or else well-grown youngsters standing at least 6–7 feet at the shoulder.

But nowadays, where the elephant have vast sanctuaries wherein the report of a rifle is never heard and man seldom if ever encountered, the cows have again begun breeding at normal intervals of from 2½ to 3 years. So that when meeting with a herd now it is noted that practically every cow has at least one calf and usually two or even three. These will all be from eighteen inches to two feet taller than the next in size (the period of gestation in elephant is now known to be from 18–20 months for a female calf and from 21–23 months for a male calf; the cow will take the bull again some 6 months or so after delivery). This means that the cows have from three to four calves nowadays for every one that they had in the past. Is it then any wonder that the herds are increasing and that increased killing has been found necessary to prevent the country becoming over-run with elephant? Particularly when it is born in mind that ivory-hunting by the individual is a thing of the past in British territory owing to the cost of licenses, the poor price of ivory, and the restriction to two per annum in the number of elephant that may be killed on a license, and above all, that all native methods of killing have been rigorously suppressed.

A good point of the Elephant Control Scheme is that only marauding elephant are killed, and they are killed in the most humane manner possible; when death is not literally instantaneous

—and it frequently is—it generally takes place within a matter of minutes—a very different thing to the long-drawn-out agonies of the past.

But the fact that I wish to emphasize is that *ten times as many elephant were killed every year prior to Elephant Control as are killed nowadays by the government hunters*. But in those days nobody gave a thought to such matters whereas now, government publishes details concerning the work carried out by the department and makes no secret of the number of elephant killed or the revenue which it derives from the sale of the ivory so obtained.

After all, it must be remembered that these government hunters have no pecuniary interest whatsoever in the ivory collected; they receive no additional bonus for making a big bag; they have been, in many cases, hunting elephant all their lives (but not so many of those are left now), so that it is no novelty to them to kill a good bull. They are not going to kill any more than is necessary to impress upon the remainder of the herd that it is dangerous and inadvisable to raid. Elephant-hunting is considerably more strenuous than bolting rabbits with a ferret, particularly nowadays.

When the scheme was first started I frankly admit that, as an ivory-hunter, I was bitterly opposed to government taking unto itself the monopoly of ivory-hunting and cutting myself and others like me out of the field entirely. But what else could it do? One of the first schemes tried was to give a limited number of hunters a free license to shoot twenty-five elephant on the understanding that they reported to the District Commissioner and shot where he told them that elephant were raiding and doing damage. But this permission was abused by some; they just went to the best elephant country and shot their twenty-five—and sometimes considerably more than twenty-five—irrespective of whether they were raiding or not. The result was disastrous, because the elephant were driven down to the cultivated areas instead of away from them. It was as a result of this that government decided to employ salaried hunters.

After all, since the native is not permitted to kill, government is under the obligation of protecting his food-crops and cotton-gardens. His food-crops *must* be protected.

With regard to the efficacy of elephant control, I should like to quote Blunt's excellent book *Elephant*, which incidentally is one of the very few books on big-game and big-game hunting I have ever read in which I cannot pick a hole or two, just to show that I am not entirely alone in my ideas.

". . . the result of the drastic punishment of a big herd by shooting a good many of them usually means that that herd will not have to be shot over again. This was proved by a *safari* I carried out in the height of the raiding season in a district where, about a year before, I had shot seven elephant in one morning. On the second occasion I walked for six weeks thru the district along the valley of a big river, and never fired my rifle. In every village I passed through or camped at, the natives said that no raiding had taken place, and yet every morning within a mile of the villages I came upon fresh spoor of elephant which had been down to water at the river in the night and had returned to the bush to feed and lie up. Those elephant had learned their lesson; they knew that if they worried human beings they would be punished, and that now that they were not raiding they were left alone."

The question of the number of elephant which it is deemed necessary to shoot each year might surely be left to the considered opinion of the experts on the spot who have been studying such matters year in and year out. What on earth can a man, living on the other side of the globe and considering game preservation in the light of the conditions apertaining in his territory, possibly know of the conditions in elephant country in Africa?

As I have stated before, the Elephant Control Scheme in force in Tanganyika and Uganda is the only means by which elephant and man can live and flourish side by side in one and the same territory. There is not the slightest fear of the elephant being exterminated.

Inspanning the African Elephant

There is a widespread belief that the African elephant has never been even tamed much less trained to work; that he is ferocious and unmanageable.

This is far from being the case. More than two thousand years ago African elephant were trained for war purposes. Hannibal used them in the wars in Macedonia and in the Punic wars across the Alps. After the fall of Rome, however, the secret of domesticating this species appears to have been lost until the end of the last century. Fifty years or so ago the London (England) Zoo had, I believe, the distinction of possessing the only African elephant in captivity at that time—"Jumbo," a magnificent specimen standing just over eleven feet at the shoulder.

In 1899 Leopold of Belgium commissioned Commandant Laplume to capture elephant in the Congo Free State and see if he could not succeed in taming them.

Laplume had no experience whatever in such matters, and his first attempt, utilizing the "kraal" or "keddah" method employed in Ceylon, proved impossibly disappointing. He then essayed another scheme. Accompanied by his hunting boys he approached a herd of elephant and, at a given signal, every man broke into cries, raising such a clamour as only natives can. The whole herd stampeded, leaving behind all those calves that were too young to follow. The natives then hurled themselves upon the youngsters and roped them up.

This method proved pretty successful from the point of view of captures, some thirty-five calves being taken during the nine or ten years that it was employed. Unfortunately, however, it was pretty costly in human lives, because as the calf was grabbed it immediately loosed a series of piercing cries which brought its mother back to the rescue. The unarmed natives fled for their lives but were not infrequently caught by the infuriated and vengeful parent. Many valued assistants were killed when Laplume used this method.

Then, in 1910, he devised another plan which proved equally successful and very much safer. It is in use at the present time, and is worked as follows:

The *safari*, which is out for several months, consists of two parties each of twenty native hunters armed with modern rifles, two squads of rope carriers of similar numbers, and from six to twelve trained elephants and their *mahouts*. As soon as a herd with calves is located the entire cortège sets off. On closing the herd they assume crescent formation, the armed hunters forming the body of the semi-circle and the rope-carriers the horns. The leader of the party then indicates the calves that he wants taken and the rope men, with their ropes twisted around their bodies, creep noiselessly towards their quarry. A shrill whistle is the signal for a fusilade of shots to be fired into the air over the herd which, needless to say, instantly clears off. At this signal the rope-carriers fling themselves on the nearest of the desired calves and slip the rope around one of its hind legs. The other end of the rope is tied to a tree if there is one, if not then it is held. The armed hunters now approach the captives, ready to fire on the mother if she attempts a rescue. They fire volleys over her head as she comes, and if this fails to stop her—and it seldom succeeds— then they fire to kill. (An elephant cow is probably the most devoted mother in the animal world, so that it is generally necessary to kill her. I never saw them succeed in driving her away.)

Two monitor elephants are now brought up and the captive is fastened between them and brought back to camp. Naturally, he puts up a fight, but a wallop from one of the monitor's trunks teaches him manners and, if this is not sufficient, then a little body pressure is brought to bear which very quickly has the desired effect!

Calves running from four to five feet at the shoulder are caught by this method. Larger than that they are too powerful to hold and manage before the monitors arrive on the scene; smaller they are too young to be taken from their mothers and invariably die.

The Belgians have now somewhere in the vicinity of 100 elephant working and in training. The system of training is very simple and can be summed up in the one word—kindness. At first, of course, they are invariably accompanied by a monitor who helps considerably in the training of the youngster. When fully trained, some eight of nine months after capture, they are docile and perfectly obedient to the word of command.

In the past several men were intentionally killed by elephant in training, but since on investigation it was proved that the men had ill-treated the elephant, nothing was done, nor did the elephant ever attempt to harm anybody else.

It is said that the elephant cannot stand noise of any description but I cannot see this. In the past they were trained for war purposes, and altho there were no firearms in those days, nevertheless, there must have been a pretty fair din all the same. Also, the monitor elephant that accompany the hunters when capturing the calves have obviously accustomed themselves to gun-fire. Accordingly, I see no reason whatever why it should not be possible to train them as *shikar* elephant for lion-hunting in long grass and scrub when it is practically impossible to get a shot on foot—just as the Asiatic elephant is trained in India.

I have caught young elephant myself, but naturally, not having a government behind me to pay all expenses, I used a very much less costly method than they do in the Congo. My method is just to drop the mother in her tracks with a brain shot and make friends with the youngster. He, not knowing yet that his mother is dead, makes no attempt to get away and likes you to rub him behind the ears. I camp down right there beside the dead mother for a couple of days or so, feeding the youngster out of a basin with thin porridge and plenty of condensed or evaporated milk. He will love his daily bath, particularly if you have a stiff brush with which to scrub his back! In a couple of days or so he will follow you anywhere with a halter around his neck. You can lead him back to your base camp and he will show intense interest in everything he sees there, and will come plodding across to tell you about something he has found. You can lead him up a plank into the back of your truck and he will bed down without any trouble on an armful of grass and thoroly enjoy his ride to wherever you want to take him.

The best day's hunting of my career, from the pecuniary point of view, was when I encountered two cows—incidentally, both tuskless; the only tuskless cows I had ever seen, and here they were together!—each with a grand little calf, just the right size to capture. I dropped the two mothers with a right and left, and there were my two calves. And as luck would have it, they turned out to be male and female. I knew somebody who wanted just such a pair and who had offered me a few thousand American if I could get them for him. So that those were the best two shots I ever fired in one morning in my life but I must admit that those two youngsters worked their way into a soft spot in my heart to such an extent that I grudged parting with them.

The African elephant is almost invariably described, even by those who ought to know better, as sloping down from the shoulders like a hyena, whilst the Indian elephant is described as having a flat back. As a matter of fact, the African elephant is as high over the hips as he is over the shoulders; his back is very definitely saddle-like and seem to have been deliberately made for a *howdah*. The Indian elephant, on the other hand, has a convex back.

Chinkhombero

Every now and then a question is asked concerning multiple-tusked elephant: Do they exist, or don't they? Well, I think it has been pretty conclusively proved that they do—or at least, that they occasionally appear and have been killed by natives in the Congo. There is a skull of a four-tusker, with the tusks still in place, in the Natural History Museum in New York, or there was. In addition, there is a large double tusk in the Museum of the Royal College of Surgeons in London. However, as far as I know, no white man has ever actually seen, much less shot or photographed, a multiple-tusked elephant. The natives in the Congo say that they are not so very rare but I cannot believe that they are common, or surely some hunter would have shot one by this time.

Thruout the districts in which I have hunted and roamed, pretty well wherever elephant are to be found in Central and Eastern Africa, from the Limpopo to the Sudan and from the Indian Ocean to the Central Congo, the natives assure me that there is a monster elephant with four gigantic tusks, whose name is "Chinkhombero"—the four-tusked Father of all Elephant. He is known by this name thruout all that vast stretch of territory, and by all the different tribes that inhabit the districts frequented by elephant. And the curious thing is, that in spite of all the different languages and dialects spoken, his name is the same and all the numerous legends attached to him are likewise the same.

I have hunted this mighty fellow off and on for somewhere around a quarter of a century now. Sometimes I might only be a few hours on his spoor then, encountering others worth shooting, would open fire. On other occasions, I might be two or three days or more on the spoor, but always something happened—either I ran out of food and had to shoot something else, or possibly again met good tuskers. The ivory-hunter must take what the gods offer and be thankful to get a shot at all. But on one occasion I struck his fresh spoor in the Lower Moravia district, to the north of the Zambezi and not very far from the Luia. I had been told that the big fellow was in the district and consequently was ready. Every day I would leave camp with three or four coons carrying food and a blanket or two, so that should I strike Chinkhombero's spoor, I should be able to follow no matter where it led. I might add that by this time Chinkhombero had become something of an obsession with me.

As I say then, I struck his spoor when it was maybe two or three hours old—the biggest pad-marks I had ever seen—and followed. He was heading south and slightly west and eventually, a day or so later, reached the Zambezi. It was close on sundown by the time we came to the river, and I felt certain that I would find him in the dense bush along the north bank the following day. But to my surprise I could not find the spoor leaving the water; it went in all right, but altho we hunted a considerable distance along the bank, there was no sign of it leaving. Accordingly, I got me some natives to take me across in a dugout and, sure enough, there were the hugh pad-marks leaving the water on the south side.

They led me southwest and over the border into the Lomagundi district in Southern Rhodesia; there they circled around and back again into Portuguese territory; along the Daki, around thru Chioco, and back again into the Chikoa district. He re-crossed the Zambezi to the west of Chikoa and headed north again, zig-zagging up thru the Asenga and Moravia districts into Angoniland. Thru that into the Lilongwe district in Nyasaland, and then north-west into Northern Rhodesia to the north of Fort Jameson. There he continued his wanderings into the southwest corner of Tangan-yika and then back again thru a corner of northeastern Rhodesia and so up towards the Congo.

For six solid weeks I followed him, sleeping on the spoor whenever I came to water around sundown, and then on again next day as soon as it was light enough to see. And yet, not once in all that time did I so much as get a glimpse of him. There were times when I was so close behind that I could see the bush or the grass just closing in as he passed thru, like a curtain falling into place behind him. Sometimes I could have sworn that I could make out his shape, just the dim, faint outline but in my heart of hearts I don't really think I did—it was just that the wish was father to the thought.

He never ran. Occasionally, of course, he got my wind and stepped out but not actually stampeding. Most of the time I am

sure he did not know that I was following unless he sensed it—
and that is neither impossible nor improbable because, having
gotten my wind once and then, perhaps days afterwards, gotten it
again, he would at once realize that he was being followed by the
same man. On these occasions he would keep up a fast walk,
hopelessly out-distance me, and gain maybe a day. Then he would
halt, as the indications showed, for sometimes over half a day or
more, and then wander on. He never gave me a chance in all the
miles I followed him—I must have tramped almost a thousand
miles in those six weeks.

Altho I never saw his teeth, he must have beauties—because
every now and then, where the going was clear as, for instance,
when crossing a dry river-bed or following a big elephant path for
a bit, there would be two long grooves, one on either side of his
spoor, which could only have been made by his tusks as he skidded
them along like a sledge to rest his neck from the weight.

Any natives I met assured me that it was in truth the mighty
four-tusker—but it may only have been because of the size of the
pad-marks and those deep furrows on the spoor; and the fact that
they knew that I wanted Chinkhombero, altho they assured me
that no man could kill him.

I was able to keep after him so long because I came to know his
habits and, after he had gotten my wind, I would branch off a bit,
shoot a buck, trade a bit of the meat for meal in the nearest native
village if there was any sign of one, jerk the remainder and then
step out in forced marches until I caught up again. Because each
time the big fellow gained a day on me, he would halt, himself,
for a while to rest. I was determined to have a smack at him but
unfortunately his determination not to become a trophy was
stronger than the circumstances which governed my determination
to make him one!

Eventually, since I had no business to be in British territory,
and no license to hunt there, I was so far from any border that I
was reluctantly compelled to abandon the chase and face the
weary trudge back again to the Zambezi to where I had left the
main body of my coons with a dead elephant to keep them going.

I would happily have poached old Chinkhombero had he given
me even one chance at him but when he led me so far from the
Portuguese frontier I might have had difficulty in getting those

mighty tusks back without being caught by the Powers-that-Be.

From my observations, spread out over the many years during which I have been hunting him off and on, and from many talks with keen and observant natives of elephant-hunting tribes, it would appear that this mighty bull made what can only be described as a circular tour of inspection, about once every three or four years. Had he come more frequently I would almost certainly have heard because I was and am well-known to all the coons in those parts and they, knowing how keen I was to bag the big fellow, invariably notified me, even from away so far as fifty or a hundred miles or so, if he appeared in those districts. He is not a resident of the Zambezi country, of that I am convinced; he invariably comes from the north and, after he has done his tour, returns again from whence he came.

He is due again now and I have little doubt but that when the rains are over, and it's possible to leave this district, I shall pack up, on some excuse or another, and drift up that way—one never knows! More than one skeptical eyebrow has been raised whenever I have mentioned the deep groves occasionally seen on Chinkhombero's spoor. African natives, anxious to entice some hunter to come along and shoot back the elephant that are devastating their food crops, not only for the sake of the crops but because they know that they will get the meat, not infrequently speak of elephant whose tusks reach the ground in the hope of thereby awakening the white man's cupidity. Since these tusks are merely figments of the natives' imagination, the unbelieving white man soon becomes skeptical of all such reports.

Nevertheless, altho such tusks must be very rare amongst the great grass and bush dwelling elephant, they are not so very rare amongst the forest elephant of the great Ituri forest system in the Belgian Congo. These elephant grow very long, very straight teeth that are carried very much closer to their knees than the tusks of the bush and grass elephant. Some years ago there were several full and half-page photos in the weekly edition of the London *Times* showing a group of five of these forest bulls having a drink in a shallow ford. The water was barely over their feet, yet the tips of the tusks of the big fellow facing the camera were under water. His head was not unduly lowered. His tusks were so straight, however, that he would have been unable to skid them along in front of him, as the points would have stuck in the ground.

That multiple-tuskers exist is proved by the fact that the teeth occasionally find their way in to Mongalla, in the Congo, and are sold there. The natives express surprise that the white man should be so interested in them. Now Chinkhombero indubitably hails from up there somewhere. He is in every way such an exceptional animal that I tentatively suggest he may be some kind of cross between the forest elephant and the big gray bush type. That might conceivably help him to possess tusks having the characteristics of both types, and also habits acceptable to both.

That heavy-tusked elephant will rest their teeth in the fork of a suitable tree, when dozing thru the heat of the day, is well-known but I have even more frequently seen some big fellow resting his on the back or hips of a somewhat smaller companion. And there was one fine tusker I saw several times before I managed to shoot him, who used to look around for a suitable antheap on which to rest his—they were very long and much straighter than is usually the case with the bush elephant; I opine he had difficulty in finding a suitable tree, and would have been quite unable to rest them on a companion's back.

Now since the legends concerning Chinkhombero go back, so far as my researches have been able to carry me, to the early part of the last century, and quite possibly considerably beyond, and that he was described as a monster even then, it will be apparent that he is very, very old. We know that the elephant's tusks continue growing after he himself has stopped growing and altho we do not know to what age an African elephant lives in his natural state, I should not be at all surprised to hear that it was well over 200 years—maybe 250-300 in exceptional cases. Consequently, this mighty animal we are discussing must have enormous tusks—far surpassing the existing World's Record of 236 lbs. and 225 lbs.; 10 ft. 4 in. on the curve. The longest known tusks run 11 ft. 5½ in. on the curve. Mammoth's tusks ran close on 15 ft. on the curve and nearly 250 lbs. in weight.

Accordingly, altho it is certainly unusual to see these grooves on the spoor, it is not inherently impossible. On more than one occasion in the Congo I clearly saw where a big bull had rested the points of his tusks on the ground.

Anyway, the grooves were there, and if they weren't caused by the tusks then I should be glad to hear just what did cause them—the human imagination is incredibly fertile (when it doesn't want to believe something!) and it would be intensely interesting to me to hear the explanations that are put forward to account for these grooves—if the obvious explanation is not accepted.

Why a Bevy of Natives with You When Hunting?

This is a question I have very often been asked by those who have done their own hunting in America, but have never yet hunted in Africa. And the reason is that when after elephant you may be days on the spoor. You must have somebody to carry food and water and possibly blankets. You cannot clutter yourself up with that sort of stuff on your own back when hunting dangerous game. Besides, when you have shot your elephant you cannot chop the tusks out yourself without assistance, and if they were worth shooting you certainly can't carry them back home all by yourself along with your rifle and the rest of the stuff. Consequently, to avoid the stupid and unnecessary waste of time that would ensue if you went out alone, shot your beast, returned to camp, collected what help was wanted, and then tried to find your way back to where you shot your game, you take these people with you when hunting. Normally they follow a short distance behind you. If you are in a good district with plenty of elephant all around, it may not be necessary to take either food or bedding but water is essential. Many a fine pair of tusks has been lost thru the hunter running out of water and having to quit. If you have been following all day in dry country and have finished the contents of your water-bottle by sundown, you cannot continue hunting next day because you have all that long way to go to get back to camp. And your elephant may be only half a mile in front!

And in the same way with trackers. It is far less tiring to leave the actual tracking to your men. It is your job to keep your eyes constantly searching the surrounding bush for the first glimpse of your quarry. If your men happen to lose the spoor, your eyes, not having been peering at the ground all the time, can frequently pick up the lost spoor before theirs can. You put them back on the trail and continue as before.

When following up a dangerous beast that you have been unlucky enough to only wound, it is imperative to use a tracker. An elephant is very cunning and highly intelligent. If he decides to ambush you he will choose his ground so as to give himself every possible advantage. If your eyes are glued to the ground you stand a very good chance of bumping your nose into him before you see him—his very bulk is his best camouflage. More than one man, too impatient to wait for his trackers, has been killed by the elephant he had wounded without having time to fire a shot at all—he must have run right into him.

There are men who boast about going out alone (but not after elephant) to hunt their game. Well, in Africa, I don't consider it's anything to boast about; on the contrary, I reckon it plain, damned foolishness, other than to pick up a bird or two for your own pot.

The Temperament of the Black Rhino

It is extremely interesting when wandering about Africa, to note the wide difference in the temperament of the common "black" rhino (*rhinocerous bicornis*) in different parts of the continent.

Some authorities of the last century on Central African game inclined to the belief that there were two distinct varieties of black rhino—the "Borili," in which the front horn was longer than the back horn, and the "Keitola," in which the back horn was the longer. This view, however, now finds little support, the occasional variation in the horns being no more than those seen in the horns and tusks of any species of game.

But there is a vast difference in their temperament in different districts, and it is interesting to speculate on the reasons for this.

It is a well-known fact that the rhino of the great open plains of Kenya and Tanganyika are of very uncertain temper and are just as likely to attack as not—if not even more so. Of course, these beasts have been hunted and worried to an infinitely greater extent than have the rhino living in the dense bush zones of Central and Southeast Central Africa, and it is possible that, realizing their limitations in the matter of eyesight and ease of being spotted on those great open plains, they have developed an aggressive manner in the hope of thereby causing their hated enemy to keep his distance and steer clear of them.

It has also been suggested, and not without reason, that the long, straggling safaris so characteristic of East Africa, are themselves responsible; that the rhino on encountering part of the safari dashes off and stupidly blunders into another portion of the long line of porters and, immediately jumping to the conclusion that he is being hemmed in by man, promptly converts his stampede into a charge.

In another place I mentioned how when elephant-hunting in a certain district to the south of the Zambezi I was constantly being charged by rhino but subsequent experience convinced me that the pugnacity of the rhino in that particular district was entirely exceptional and totally at variance with the usual characteristics of the bush-dwelling members of the species. During the five years immediately prior to the outbreak of the recent war I was hunting on the opposite side of the river—to the north and slightly to the east, of that same district. True, it is a very different type of bush, but the rhino are identical in everything except temperament. In that district there were more rhino than I had ever previously encountered in all the years of my wanderings. I shot about a couple of hundred of them, yet I did not once experience a charge. There were so many that it was possible to pick and choose—shooting only the best and leaving the others as breeding stock. In spite of the fairly heavy shooting, however, it would seem that my yearly bag was far more than covered by the normal annual increase, as there certainly did not appear to be any falling off in their numbers. This means that I encountered many more rhino than those I shot yet, I repeat, I did not have a single one do more than make faces at me. Further, the natives are constantly roaming in the forest looking either for wild honey or for trees to fell and subsequently hollow out into "dugout" canoes. These men, needless to say, frequently encounter rhino yet I cannot remember ever hearing one return in the evening and relate how he was attacked by one.

It's true that those beasts had never been hunted since the world began, prior to my advent. The natives told me that, altho an occasional white man had passed thru the district long before—before the tsetse fly arrived—I was the first hunter to work the place, and possibly that is the explanation. You say that I had been hunting them for five years and claim to have shot a considerable number, and that many others which I hunted I left alone as they weren't worth shooting? Sure, but then I belong, as I have already mentioned, to that school which never attempts to press trigger until it can clearly see its way to place the bullet exactly where it is wanted—either to kill instantly or, if that isn't possible, then definitely to cripple, when a second shot can be slammed in on the heels of the first to finish off the wretched beast and save the beastly business of following up and, maybe, losing the animal. The result was that I did not have a single wounded rhino get away from me in that district—all I shot I killed; the others I did not molest.

Accordingly, it may be said that all those rhino that are still roaming around there have never been hunted. Admittedly, an occasional one is shot by some native armed with an old gas-pipe muzzle-loader but such occurrences are mighty few and far between and, bearing in mind the numbers of rhino, can only be considered as a negligible factor in its effect on the animals' temperament. Because it is not the encountering by man that makes animals either vicious or else inclined to abandon a district so much as the constant wounding and battering about they receive at the hands of excitable and inexperienced sportsmen, probably using insufficiently powerful weapons, who are inclined to blaze off at an animal the instant they see any portion of his body and then fire wildly, ripping off the contents of their magazines, at his disappearing form. This, I'm convinced, is what does the damage and my observations incline me to the belief that it is this, and this only, that accounts for the wide difference in the temperament of the plains-dwelling rhino of East Africa, and the bush-dweller of Central and the Southeast Central portion of the continent.

And subsequent experience has tended to confirm this opinion. The Wakamba are amongst the best of the East African hunting tribes, and are probably the greatest exponents of the poisoned arrow. The rhino in their territory are notoriously vicious, and the same can be said for those that frequent the dry, thorn-bush-covered Tana running north of the Ukambani. Here I am quite certain that the Wakamba themselves are to blame. If an arrow hits squarely it will have no difficulty in penetrating even a rhino's tough hide, and if the poison is at all fresh it will kill him just as surely as it will kill a smaller beast but the African being what he is, it must frequently happen that the arrow only glances, inflicting a surface wound, and then if the poison is stale it may easily fail to kill, but will almost certainly cause the wound to fester. Hence the viciousness of the rhino around those parts.

Concerning Lions

Whenever hunters from Africa and India foregather, the inevitable argument crops up as to the comparative ferocity and killing powers of lion and tiger. It is all hypothetical, of course, of mere academic interest since nothing can be proved. Personally, I consider that whatever difference there may be is negligible.

Speaking generally, both beasts are of approximately the same size, altho a good maned lion may look bigger; that, I think, is principally due to the mane, tho we know that lions are usually somewhat heavier. And taking muscle for muscle their strength must be, more or less, the same.

The argument that, as tiger are known to kill full-grown elephant (captive) out East, whereas lion will only—on rare occasions—pull down a very young elephant calf in Africa, the tiger must be both stronger and a better killer than the lion, is easily answered.

Nobody can deny that there is considerably more game per lion in Africa than there is per tiger in India. Consequently, the lion has never had to devise methods of killing the larger beasts such as elephant and rhino.

His favorite method is to spring on a beast's shoulders, close his teeth on the back of the neck and bite, at the same time as one mighty-muscled forearm grabs the animal by the nose and wrenches the head around; this breaks the neck and death is instantaneous.

Should anything, such as a slight eddy of wind, warn the quarry of the lion's proximity and make him spring forward in alarm at the instant of the attack, causing the lion to miss his target and land abaft the shoulders, nine times out of ten the lion will just allow himself to slide to the ground. It does not seem to occur to him to bite thru the spine and paralyze the animal's hindquarters; nor does he think of grabbing a hind leg and pulling the animal down. He is satisfied to let the beast go and hunt on a bit farther. He will almost certainly be given another opportunity before the night is out.

As proof of this, I have frequently shot animals that have been scored diagonally right down the ribs by a lion's claws. I remember once I had shot a fine big roan-antelope bull, up on the Angoni plateau. On examining him I found that he had been scored right down one side only a day or two before and, on turning him over, that he was carrying similar wounds on the other side. But they had obviously been made some years previously. The freshly-made wounds clearly showed that the lion had landed well up on the roan's back, but some distance behind the shoulders. He had just allowed himself to slide off.

I admit I have been told by cattle-owners of lion grabbing oxen by one hind leg and pulling the beast down but I have never actually seen it myself. That, I might add, was in a district in which all game had been shot out.

I have often been asked the reason why so many lion have the long tushes at the corners of their mouths broken off. I do not think that there can be much doubt about the answer.

As I have already explained, the lion's favorite method of killing is to bite into the neck at the same time as he grabs the animal's nose and pulls the head around. As the beast crashes to the ground, the lion springs clear. But it must frequently happen that one or more of his long tushes have become jammed between the joints of the vertebrae. The jolt as the animal comes down, and the lion's own movements, would be sufficient to snap off the jammed tooth.

The greater my experience with lion, the more emphatically do I state that he is both a sportsman and a gentleman. (I am not, of course, referring now to man-eaters.) He does not kill for the sheer love of killing—as a leopard will; he does not kill from blood-lust. He kills solely for food or in self-defence. And, he only kills as much as he needs.

I have been told that a troop of lion will, occasionally, kill far more than they need when attacking a herd of cattle. But that is exceptional. Quite possibly, on the cattle breaking out of the *kraal*, the lions started in to kill without knowing that their pals were all similarly occupied. Time and again I have come across two or more lions hunting together. Almost invariably the actual killing is left to one. In the case of those cattle as they broke out and rushed amongst the lions, the temptation to kill and make sure of a feed, proved too much for some of the latter and accounts for the unnecessary blood being spilt. When hunting game, of course, things are different.

I have seen several lion resting in the shade and a large mixed herd of zebra and hartebeeste feeding in the immediate vicinity. On another occasion I saw a zebra pulled down out of a troop. His companions, naturally, stampeded at the attack, but very soon pulled up and looked around. On seeing that the lions had all they wanted, they began grazing again as tho nothing had happened. They knew that they were perfectly safe from further attack.

The ordinary hunting lion will never attack man unless provoked into doing so. He does not want to fight; he does not want trouble. He will leave you alone if you leave him alone. He does not like having to get out of your way, naturally, but he will do so rather than start a row. He simply does not want to have anything to do with man.

Apart from wild dogs, man is the lion's only enemy. All wild animals have a natural, instinctive, hereditary fear of man. The lion is no exception. He knows that man is the only creature that can kill from afar—without coming to actual grips—and he fears him as the ordinary man fears a deadly snake.

Altho the experience may not be a particularly pleasant one, you may quite safely meet a lion face to face when you are quite unarmed. Provided that you do not do anything foolish or lose your head, the chances are a hundred to one that he will not molest you—even if there are several of them. I have on several different occasions met lions in just such a manner when I had nothing more lethal on me than a walking stick; we just stood and gazed at one another until his curiosity was appeased—having seen plenty lions before, I was not curious but I most certainly was not going to move until he did. This business of jumping for the nearest tree, as some men say they would do, is just the very thing you must *not* do under such circumstances. Even if there was a suitable tree close by, unless the lion was a good distance away, nothing but a monkey or a squirrel could get up it in time if the lion was definitely after you.

If the lion is not hunting he won't interfere with you; if he *is* hunting you won't see him. Having realized that it is a man he is looking at, he will move off into the grass with a little grunt and give you the road. And later will probably tell his pals about the encounter in exactly the same slightly-breathless manner in which you would tell yours.

Coincidences

Curious coincidences take place in the Bush. I shot a big wart hog one day which had been attacked simultaneously by two leopards the night before. He was very sick and had only traveled about fifty yards from the spot on which he had been attacked. I back-spoored him—for it is very rarely, in this part of the world anyway, that leopards hunt in pairs—and found that he had been approached from both sides.

It seemed pretty clear that neither leopard knew of the existence of the other. They both sprang together and in their surprise and confusion on finding that they were each trying to take what must have seemed another's kill, the hog managed to make good his escape.

It is by no means unusual that an animal should be stalked simultaneously by two different enemies.

A number of years ago I was stalking a fine sable bull up Barotseland way. He was feeding on the far side of a small clearing and I was able to approach to with about thirty yards or so. I was on the point of firing, when I noticed a magnificent black-maned lion stalking the sable. He was almost within springing distance, so I very cautiously exchanged my rifle for a camera. With any sort of luck, I was going to obtain a unique photograph.

Inch by inch, the lion crept closer. And when at last I saw his hind feet wriggling for a sure foot-hold, I prepared to snap the picture. He sprang; I clicked the shutter of my camera; and picked up my rifle.

The lion had broken the bull's neck by his favorite method and was walking around his kill licking his chops and lashing his tail. I waited until he exposed his broadside and a single shot was sufficient.

It was a most successful morning—a fine sable, a magnificent lion, and a unique photograph. Unfortunately, a hippo upset my canoe not very long afterwards, and my precious photo, together with rifles, cameras, kit, and pretty well every darned thing I owned in all the world, went to the bottom of the Zambezi. Twice hippo have done that to me.

On another occasion, at Mangwendi—in the lower Zambezi valley—I was looking for some fresh meat for my men. I came on a bunch of kudu in the open, some fifty yards away or thereabouts. The grass was knee-high. On the heels of the shot, as the remainder of the troop stampeded, there came a series of angry, baffled grunts as a big tawny-maned lion bounded away. He had been stalking the kudu—between me and them—and must have been almost within springing distance. No wonder he was peeved!

Yet another, somewhat similar, coincidence gave me one of the finest sights that I have ever witnessed in the African bush. It also took place in the Zambezi valley, in the Moravia district.

I was returning to camp about midday, after a successful elephant-hunt, when, on crossing a clearing in which the grass was up to my chin, I heard a kudu bull coughing in a small, but very dense, thicket on the far side of the clearing. The little thicket was only about a quarter of an acre in extent, so I proceeded to advance straight across the clearing. When I was within about fifteen feet of the bush, I heard a shot on the far side. It was a shot gun so my cook boy was apparently trying to get me a guinea-fowl in the native lands which commenced there.

The shot was answered by a crash in the thicket, and the next second a fine kudu bull came full tilt thru the bush, straight for me. I swung up the double-rifle which I was carrying, and waited for the bull to win clear to the open. As he bounded out, not more than five yards from where I was standing, he saw me and slewed around. My heavy slug (I was loaded for elephant) smashed both his shoulders and he turned a complete somersault, and lay facing the way he had come.

As I fired, out of the corner of my eye I saw a tawny shape come streaking thru the bush after the bull. Naturally, I reckoned that it was one of his cows, as it was only a glimpse that I caught. I had all the meat that I wanted now, so did not intend to shoot. I brought the rifle down from my shoulder with the intention of reloading that barrel, when I suddenly found myself looking straight into a lioness's open mouth! It was on a level with my own.

The tawny shape that I had glimpsed was not a kudu cow. The

lioness must have been stalking and pretty close to the bull when the shot on the far side of the thicket had stampeded him—right onto the muzzles of my rifle. In baffled fury and a wild hope of being able to catch him, the lioness had come tearing after the bull. She must have been ravenously hungry to have been hunting so close to a large native village in the middle of the day. She did not see me, altho she seemed to be looking right at me and I am convinced that she never heard the roar of my elephant rifle, so great was her anxiety to find and catch the bull.

She leaped high in the air to see over the grass and then, seeing her quarry lying almost at her feet, but facing her, and not wishing to land on his horns—for she could not know that he was dead— she gave her body one mighty twist, turned completely over in mid air—her heels over her head—and came down on the bull's shoulders.

It was all so utterly unexpected—the finding of a lioness when I was expecting a kudu cow; the utter improbability of finding lion so close to a large native village at that hour of the day; the speed with which it all happened; prevented any possibility of my getting in a shot. For altho it takes some time to tell, the whole thing only lasted for a split second.

Now, altho she was eating my meat, she doubtless figured that it was hers and, in that grass, wherein I could not have seen her until I was within a matter of two or three feet (and she would undoubtedly hear me approaching), I had not the slightest intention of arguing with a ravenously hungry lioness as to the rightful ownership of the kill!

She had possession of it, wanted it badly, and would almost certainly refuse to part with it without a struggle. So I retreated a short distance, made a detour around her, and looked for a tree to climb which would enable me to see her in the grass.

Man-Eaters

Normally, with rare exceptions, lions only take to man-eating when very agéd. Then, with their teeth worn down, their claws blunted, and their great strength and agility failing them, they sometimes take to haunting the vicinity of native villages in the evenings, to catch the women that go to draw water.

There can be no doubt, however, that the great majority of

lions do not take to man-eating when old age comes on. They starve to death on rats and rabbits and even frogs, rather than force down their natural aversion to man. Were it not so, then Africa would be infested with man-eaters; since, as there are lions born every year, so must there be lions aging all the time. It is only in districts in which the balance of Nature has been upset— by the extermination of game by man—that the younger lions take to man-eating. They are forced to do so by hunger, and if they have cubs will bring up the youngsters with similar propensities.

Even then it is, more often than not, sheer accident that starts a lion off on his man-eating career. He is prowling around, ravenous with hunger, and comes across a native or two sleeping out without a fire or any other protection. The temptation is irresistible—probably, before he quite realizes what he is doing, he has sprung on one of the sleepers and carried him off. Then, finding how easy man is to kill and how easy to eat—no tough hide here to be torn off—he tries again. His efforts meeting with success, he gradually overcomes his instinctive fear of man, and becomes that most feared and dreaded of all beasts—the man-eater.

Not long ago, at my old camp at Mangwendi, I had an unfortunate coon carried away from within a few feet of where I was sleeping. It had once been a notorious district for man-eaters and, only a few miles away, over the Nyasaland border, it still is. But just here we had not been troubled for some eight or nine years or so. There would be lions roaring every night but as there was plenty of game about we took no notice, and never bothered to keep up the fires at night.

On this particular night the beast had come right along the path from over the border (as we found by his spoor next day) and on arrival here had first of all prospected the village by which I was camped, and then come sneaking over to where we were sleeping. Curiously enough, he stepped right over two lads to get a third who was actually sleeping closer to the glowing remains of the fire. It was thru the lion treading on one of those two lads and waking him up, that the hue and cry was raised. The boy woke up to find the lion standing on his legs and in the act of grabbing the third boy.

At the first yell, I was up and out of bed—for I had had previous experience of man-eaters—and had lit the hurricane lamp. It was a pitch-black night, and the grass was long around the little clearing in which the camp was pitched. A rifle would have been useless to me, as I'd run out of cells for my torch, but there was just a chance with the lamp of saving the wretched lad's life, if only I could be quick enough. Fortunately, there was not a breath of wind to blow out the match and I doubt if a hurricane lamp was ever lit quicker.

I then rushed after the lion—naked and all as I was—waving the lamp and yelling at the top of my voice. Luck was with us, both me and the boy, for I caught up with them at the very edge of the clearing. The lion having grabbed the boy by one knee only, had had to keep his head turned sideways as he ran so as to drag the lad along and not trip over him. I could see the boy, as he skidded along on his backside, punching the lion in the ribs in an effort to make him let-go. The result of it all was that the lion could not see any too well where he was going, and ran his own chest into the sharp stump of a small tree that had been felled two or three feet from the ground. The jar caused him to drop the boy, and before he could grab him again I had appeared on the scene. And I guess the spectacle I must have presented proved too much for his nerves!

He leaped around to face me but, with a vicious snarl, wheeled again and bounded into the grass. It is extremely improbable that he had ever previously faced a stark-naked white man, yelling and roaring at the top of his voice and waving a lighted lamp in one hand, wildly rushing straight towards him!

Now that was probably that lion's first attempt at man-eating. He had been prowling along, mad with the hunger, and had found us sleeping in the open right in his path. He was in the last stages of starvation—as we found a couple of days afterwards when he broke into a hut, killed a woman and three kids, and was shot for his pains before he could get out again.

That a lion's hereditary fear of man takes a whale of a lot of overcoming is, I think, pretty conclusively proved by the fact that when a wounded lion gets hold of a hunter he does not seem to know what to do with him. He appears completely to lose his head. Of course, the pain of his wound—to say nothing of the shock if, as is usual, a dum-dum bullet has been used—will tend to produce this condition but on top of that, it seems as tho his old fear of man is still battling, even against his berserk rage. He will grab a hand in his mouth and chew it, or an arm, or a leg, but it does not appear to enter his head to just take the man by the throat and shake him. One very rarely hears of a hunter being killed outright by a wounded lion. Those who lose their lives generally doing so thru blood-poisoning setting in as a result of the mauling.

Certain districts have always been notorious for their man-eaters. In this neck o' the woods they generally go around in threes—a male and two females. They create a positive reign of terror in a district, and when you finally succeed in making contact with them and wiping them out, the sigh of relief that goes around the district has hardly time to fade away amongst the trees, when another three arrive to take their place! The reign of terror created by Patterson's *"Man-Eaters of Tsavo"* pales into insignificance beside what takes place in various parts of this territory (Mozambique, Portuguese East Africa) every year, and has done as far back as we can trace—back beyond the days of David Livingstone.

The man-eaters of this territory have all the advantages on their side. The nature of the dry thorn scrub lends itself to their concealment, and spooring or tracking is impossible. It is infernally difficult to contact the lions in such stuff. Most men who go after them fail because they haven't studied the habits of the brutes sufficiently; they almost invariably make for the scene of the latest tragedy—which has the lions laughing at them. By the time the hunter gets there the lions are anything from twelve to twenty miles away. They circle around a large area with plenty of native villages in it, killing usually two or three times a week. Their cunning seems to increase in direct ratio with their success. They seldom attempt to kill on two consecutive occasions in the same village. On word coming in that the lions have killed a dozen miles away, the inexperienced sportsman dashes off there and the lions continue their laughing.

I knew one man who hunted them on and off for eight months without getting a shot at them. I suppose I could count on the fingers of one hand the number of times I have been lucky enough to meet up with the brutes in daylight. At that tho, it is generally more satisfactory to contact them by night, since they are usually sufficiently accommodating to stand and let you wipe them out when you get them in the beam of your torch.   But you've got to contact them first!

Buffalo-Killing Lions

If you hunt in good buffalo country you will almost invariably see from the spoor where one or two lions have been following the herds.   These lions will seldom lower themselves to kill lesser game.   When the herds leave a district they follow.   I have never seen more than two of them at this game—magnificent big, tawny-maned fellows, they seem to be almost a different breed from the ordinary lion.   I once shot one, a lone one, and have ever since regretted it.   He crossed my path without seeing me, about fifteen or twenty paces away, and I swung up my rifle without thinking what I was doing—a kind of reflex action—and killed him.   He never knew what hit him.

These lions do an immense amount of good by following the herds and killing off those that have been wounded and not finished off by careless or nervous hunters.   Where the buffalo are shot up to the extent that they are here by inexperienced, thoughtless, and hopelessly inadequately armed men, many native women and children are killed and mauled every year by wounded buffalo when they go out to collect wild fruit.   Accordingly, I do not hunt or shoot or otherwise interfere with these great buffalo-killers.   They do not interfere with man.   On several occasions I have had them pass within ten feet of my bed at night, stop—as their spoor clearly showed—and have a look at me sleeping there, and go on their way.

In that very fine buffalo district to which I have previously referred, I used to meet up with two of these splendid animals on countless occasions when following the spoor of the buffalo herds. I met them so often that I almost knew them by their first names. They knew perfectly well that I would not molest them, and when I came along and overtook them, they would just draw aside off the trail of the herd, sit down under a tree not more than twenty or thirty yards away, and watch me go past.   There was no trace of fear in their attitude; there were no threatening growls.   They would just gaze placidly at me with those beautiful, golden eyes of theirs as I waved and greeted them with a "Good hunting, brothers!" I am quite certain that those lions got so they could recognize me and my men. I won't go so far as to say that they would lift a paw and wave back to my greeting, but it often looked as tho they would like to!

It is perfectly incredible the apparent ease and rapidity with which a buffalo-killer can slay so mighty a beast as a full-grown African buffalo bull. He can break his neck, a mass of bone and sinew and muscle as thick as a big man's body, as easily as I could break a match-stick. Quite recently, here in this same camp wherein I am typing this, I heard a buffalo give a small grunt quite close by one night. As it is a magnificent district for buffalo, and they are around the camp every night, I thought nothing of it, as buffalo usually grunt contentedly when wandering along feeding at night. But I was amazed the following morning to find that a lion had killed a mighty bull just where I had heard this fellow grunt—perhaps fifty yards from the camp. It was obviously the same bull because there was no other fresh spoor just there, and I have no doubt whatever that that small and somewhat strangled grunt was all that the bull had time to give or do before his neck was broken. Because the spoor clearly showed that the lion had been lying in wait behind a small bush, had just reared up, grabbed the big fellow and killed him then and there—there was no sign of there having been a struggle.

As with lesser game, the lion breaks the neck but the accomplished buffalo-killer does not actually spring on the buffalo, but rather rears up against his shoulders and grabs with his forearms only, keeping his hind feet on the ground for greater leverage. At least, judging by the tracks on several occasions this is what appears to be his method.

But lions are not born with the technique for buffalo-killing. They have to learn it just as man has to. I have had ample proof of this. On more than one occasion I have come on the remains of lions that have been killed by buffalo and was reading only the other day where no less than four lions were killed by a herd of buffalo within either twelve or twenty-four hours, all fairly close together.

If an inexperienced lion springs on a buffalo in his usual manner where lesser game are concerned, the buffalo gallops full-tilt into a tree, swerving slightly as he reaches it so as to crush the lion. The wretched lion falls to the ground with his back either broken or severely injured and probably several ribs crushed as well. The bull then turns and tramples and savages him to death.

One night we heard a terrific battle being waged about 150 yards from camp—the pounding of hooves, crashing of bush and furious bellowing of a buffalo. I naturally imagined that two bulls were fighting about something, because we had a troop of five monsters that used to regularly visit with us at night, and they would often be fighting amongst themselves. Just the same sounds, but there would, of course, also be the crash and rattle of horns. On the occasion I mention, however, I could hear no clash of horns, but hardly realized that fact until next morning. The battle raged for upwards of an hour, by which time it was just light enough to see. So I took a rifle and went out to see what on earth was happening, as it was most unusual for a fight to last so long and continue into daylight.

I did not have to go far before reaching the scene of the action. It was not a fight between two buffalo bulls—it was a maneless lion trying to kill a big buffalo. The wretched bull was covered with blood and it was obvious that it was his own, because his sides, both of them, from neck to flanks, were deeply scored by the lion's claws. When I arrived on the scene the lion was crouching with his eyes on the buffalo and obviously just waiting for an opening; the buffalo, badly winded, was blowing steam from his gaping nostrils, pawing the ground and shaking his head, but always facing his enemy. Presently the lion pretended to draw off and as he partially disappeared behind a bush, the buffalo reckoned that this was his opportunity to make a get-away. He swung around to go, but that was just what the lion was hoping for. No sooner did the bull expose his broadside than the lion made his rush and sprang on the bull's shoulders. The bull must have seen him coming out of the corner of his eye and realized that he could not avoid him, because he attempted to swing back again so as to meet the lion head on. In this he was too late so, bellowing hoarsely, charged towards a tree. But the lion wasn't waiting to be crushed—he let himself slide off, giving the unfortunate buffalo another set of long and deep claw marks.

Once again they faced each other and, feeling sorry for the poor old buff (which would one day fall to my rifle, when I wanted him), I felt that he had had about enough, so dropped the lion with a bullet thru the shoulder.

For a moment the bull stood stock-still obviously unable to believe either his eyes or his ears. Then, with a look in my direction, he moved off, halted a short distance farther on, and looked back. And I should dearly have loved to know just what was passing thru his head then!

I back-spoored him and the lion to see what had happened. It appears that he and a companion had been ambling along thru the tall reeds on the bank of a dry river, and just as they reached the small native foot-path that crossed the river there, two lions had literally walked right into them—the lions having just crossed the river-bed and come up the path thru the reeds. One buffalo had immediately swung around and dashed back the way he had come, one lion going after him (I reckon he probably got away, as I could find no trace either of him or of the lion altho I followed them for a long way). My buff had come galloping along towards my camp with the second lion after him.

It is obvious that neither of those lions was an experienced buffalo-killer.

Lion and Leopard

Looking back thru my journals I have just come across a most curious thing that took place near here just before the rains began around the end of '38—one for which it is difficult to find an adequate explanation.

The natives told me that they had heard a leopard coughing and belching close by, but took no notice as that was quite a common occurrence. Suddenly the leopard's song changed and rose to a shrill, high-pitched scream, choked—and then silence. Nothing further happened that night and in the morning they went out to look for spoor and found a dead leopard.

From the tracks, which I examined myself, it appears that a lion had been strolling along and for some reason best known to himself took exception to the leopard making such a noise in his presence. He just gave one bound, grabbed the leopard by the back of the neck, killing him practically instantaneously, took two or three bounds with the leopard in his mouth and halted suddenly. Probably he swung his head at the same time because the leopard must have sailed some distance thru the air to fall where we found him. There were no pug marks nearer than the deep impressions made by the lion where he halted.

Having thrown the dead leopard away, the lion just turned around and wandered away himself in the direction in which he had originally been heading. He never made a sound of any sort.

What strikes me as being so extraordinary is that the leopard never saw the lion, or surely he would not have permitted such a close approach (the grass was all burnt off and there was no cover). Further, it's most unusual for a lion to kill without provocation and when not hungry—had the lion been hungry surely he would have shown more interest in his kill because a lion will think nothing of eating a dead companion.

The reader is doubtless waiting expectantly for some explanation of this extraordinary occurrence. So am I. The whole thing seems to be inexplicable; but the leopard's skin is actually under my feet as I type this!

A Tip on " Following Up"

I suppose the principal ambition of every visiting sportsman and hunter setting foot in Africa is to shoot a good lion. It is customary for wealthy sportsmen to retain at least one professional hunter, part of whose job it is to see that his patron does not get hurt. So that in the case of a lion being wounded and taking refuge in a difficult place, he will generally do his best to dissuade the visitor from following up, and will suggest he return to camp. Personally, I should feel it pretty galling if I was in the place of that visitor and had a decent rifle in my hands.

There is no question about the risk you are running when following a wounded lion into thick scrub, reeds or long grass but where would the attraction be in big game hunting if there was no risk attached to it? (I use the African interpretation of the expression "big game" which implies dangerous game. I can appreciate the hunting of any game animal which tests my bushcraft but if there was no risk attached to the shooting of lions there would be no more thrill in it than there is in the shooting of zebra.)

At some time or another, and there is no telling when, any man with a rifle may be called upon to follow up a wounded lion—and I doubt if there is a more dangerous pastime on earth.

The following little trick, which can be played on a wounded lion (or, for that matter, on a tiger, panther or leopard, given reasonably suitable conditions), was told me by an old-timer who, I gathered, devised it himself. At least, altho I have been hunting for years and have discussed such matters with innumerable sportsmen and hunters, I have never heard anyone else mention using it. Accordingly, tho others may quite possibly have evolved a somewhat similar method, I shall endeavor to describe this procedure which, I might add, I have used with the greatest possible success on several occasions in the past, in the hope that it may be of service to others. Since I had occasion to play it again but a short while ago, I think it may be best if I just describe that small adventure because the conditions were literally ideal for the success of the deception.

A breathless and perspiring runner arrived in my camp one morning to tell me that his master, a Portuguese, camped in a native village some two or three miles away, had wounded a lion and wanted me to come along and help him follow it up and finish it off. Well, I knew what that meant—I should have to do all the dirty work, whilst he remained well back from the danger zone, in all probability with the safety catch of his rifle in the firing position, his finger on the trigger and the muzzle pointing straight at the small of my back!

It appeared that on the goats being released from the *kraal*, a lion had pounced on one of them, carried it off a small way and then commenced feeding. The herd boys had called the Portuguese and he had gone out and fired a hasty and somewhat wild shot which had hit the lion, but nobody knew where or how badly. The lion had decamped and, galloping across the open, had disappeared in a dense clump of bush. The village was situated on the edge of a large plain on which the grass was burnt off. Some 250 yards or so from the village, however, there was this small but very dense, circular thicket—only perhaps forty or fifty yards in diameter—consisting of large trees and almost impenetrable undergrowth. Here and there were small passages, or tunnels rather, running into the centre of the thicket. Around the edge there was a fairly thick fringe of four-foot grass that had somehow managed to escape the fires. The tunnels could be seen running thru this grass.

The natives told me that the lion had been seen entering one of these passages in the grass, but that he had not gone on into the bush. They swore that having entered about the length of his own body, he had turned around and was now lying down at right angles to the passage with his nose almost on the track. They vowed that they could discern his shape thru the grass, which was not very thick at that particular spot.

So, since it would be sheer lunacy for anybody to attempt to follow a wounded lion into that bush, wherein one would have to progress on hands and knees, and the rapid use of a rifle would be a physical impossibility, I decided to play my small trick on the lion and see if I could not entice him out so as to get a fair chance at him.

There was a grizzled old warrior standing beside me arrayed in a couple of yards of what had once upon a time, in the dim and distant past, been white calico. It is extremely doubtful if it had ever seen either soap or water during all the years he had had it, and it was just the thing I wanted. On my promising to give him a new piece, the old hero, altho surrounded by the entire population of the district, including women and children, with a charming lack of self-consciousness, disrobed himself and handed me his entire wardrobe.

There were no stones to be had, but with knives and assegais my lads prised me up a lump of sun-baked clay rather larger than a polo-ball. This I tied in the old fellow's rags, leaving a generous "tail" to flutter behind. Then, telling everyone, including the Portuguese, to remain where they were, I and my gun-bearer advanced across the open. As we got closer it certainly looked as tho there was something in the grass just where the natives had said that they could discern the lion, and so I began to feel more optimistic of our chances of success.

When we were within about twenty-five yards of the grass, I dropped to one knee and my tracker, who knows the game as well as I do, for he has been with me many years, moved a pace or so to one side so as not to interfere with my line of fire. He then looked towards me and I nodded my head. That was the signal, so he lobbed the decoy into the mouth of the little passage-way

in the grass. It landed with a thud and then trundled forward
with its tail flapping behind it.

And sure enough, it did not get far before, with a grating snarl,
the lion hurled himself upon it. Hearing the thud and the flutter-
ing movement, to say nothing of the strong whiff of man which
he almost certainly received, he was undoubtedly convinced that
he had his enemy nicely. His head and shoulders were now clearly
exposed, and a single round from my .375 Magnum was all that
was required.

On re-reading what I have written, I am afraid that I have not
been quite as coherent as perhaps I might have been. But so long
as the principle of the trick is made clear, that is the main thing.

But there is one warning that I would give, and it is one that
cannot be too strongly emphasized:

If you are following up a wounded lion in ordinary continuous
scrub and practise this trick wherever you think it possible that
it may come off successfully, only to find that on lobbing your
decoy nothing happens at all, *let nothing induce either you or your
tracker to speak, laugh, or otherwise advertise your presence* and above
all, do not get off your guard or ease your alertness because you
think the lion must be much farther ahead. It is quite possible
that he has circled around and is lying up on one or the other side
of you. Follow up the spoor in complete silence and, if you find,
as you may, that he is circling around, then double your alertness,
slow up your speed to half, and again throw your decoy into
likely spots.

The great danger is in choosing the wrong spot and then ad-
vancing carelessly to pick up the decoy with the lion maybe watching you all the time, but sufficiently far off to spot the deception.

Inquisitiveness in Wild Animals

It's strange the ideas that some men develop. I am thinking
at the moment of those men who will tell you that wild animals
are entirely devoid of curiosity. One is compelled to the assumption that they have had no real experience with wild animals, or
else are grossly unobservant.

That deer and antelope, especially the smaller species, are
intensely inquisitive is, I always thought, a well-known fact. I
remember when I was out in New Zealand being told by a man

that when he wanted a shot at a deer he reclined in a tub or half-barrel with his feet waving about in the air, and that if there were any deer within sight they would come up to investigate. I saw no reason to disbelieve him, as he was a well-known and successful poacher, and his only weapon was a smooth 12-bore.

That, I think, was the first I ever heard of the inquisitiveness of wild animals but it remained in my mind and proved exceedingly useful on one of the two occasions when a hippo upset my canoe and sent my entire battery of rifles and, for that matter, everything else I possessed, to the bottom of the Zambezi.

I had recently sold a man living not far away an old shot gun and some N $\stackrel{\circ}{=}$ 4 shells, so despatched a runner to tell him of my predicament and ask for the loan of the gun to enable me to feed myself and my coons. He very decently sent it along and altho there was plenty of game about, the grass had been burnt and it was impossible to get close enough to kill—N $\stackrel{\circ}{=}$ 4 shot, even in a magnum 3-in. 12-bore, was never intended to kill anything on four legs much bigger than a rabbit except at almost point-blank range.

Accordingly, I commandeered all my heroes' loin-cloths and these, of practically every hue in the rainbow, with the addition of my shirt, I knotted together so as to make something which would more or less conceal me when I stooped down. I then wandered around until I spotted a herd of impala, got down-wind of them and stalked up as close as possible. I could not get closer than about 100 yards, but that was close enough.

I now draped my covering over myself, so as to hide my head and body, and crouching half on hands and feet advanced into the open in small hops something between the gait of a lame frog and a rabbit. The impala threw up their heads and snorted and whistled their astonishment. I did not continue the advance, but put my hands on the ground (more or less concealed under my covering) and pretended to be busily feeding, hopping about and moving my backside up and down. It must have been a screamingly funny performance to watch, but it served its purpose for it had the little impala guessing; they would come a few paces towards me, and then stand snorting and blowing, the rams tossing their heads and stamping their little fore-feet, and the ewes jostling each other forward.

I found that if I attempted to approach them, they stayed still but that if I just continued my evolutions without apparently taking any notice of them, they would gradually move towards me. And so it went on until they were snorting and stamping within fifteen yards or so. Whether they would have come right up to me or not I do not know, but I dared not experiment any further because some of the ewes were nearly down-wind of me now. They were nervous of coming quite so close as the rams, and had circled around a bit.

I hate shooting these prettiest and most graceful of all African game, and in normal circumstances never do so but "the troops must be fed," so I had no alternative. I dropped two of the rams and away the rest went. My naked coons, who had been watching the performance from points of vantage in the background, now came hurrying up delighted at the success of my stratagem.

That "curiosity killed the cat" in this instance, is undeniable.

Further, I had heard that a bright red cloth, suspended where he can see it, proves an irresistible attraction for a hippo. So on one occasion I hung a couple of yards of vivid scarlet *limbo* on the bank of a pool wherein some half-dozen hippo were disporting themselves. Whether it was just coincidence, or whether it was really the red rag, I cannot say, because for some reason or another I have never tried it since, but one of those hippo, a big bull, came over our way and paid the price.

Then take the case of a large herd of buffalo which have not heard a rifle speak for some considerable time. If you come across them right out in the open, in the centre of a large plain where the grass has been burnt off so that there is no cover at all, and want a shot, the only thing to do is to walk slowly straight towards them. When you are within 150 yards or thereabouts they will begin to jostle towards you, the master bull or bulls in front and the remainder of the herd forming a great black semi-circle behind. And they will continue to jostle each other until they break into a trot. It is apt to be a trifle alarming until you become accustomed to it, because every now and then they will stop and the bulls will snort and blow and toss their horns and paw the ground until the dust flies. You need a stout lad as gun-bearer to stand it unless he knows you and knows the game.

Now is that not curiosity? True, the antics of the bulls are, of course, bluff—to try and scare you away, and if your heart was to fail and you were to turn tail and run, I have no doubt but that the herd would change their trot to a gallop and, maybe, run you down. If, however, you stand your ground, they will approach to within about forty or fifty yards, maybe less, and again jostle each other to try and see what it's all about. This curiosity is not so apparent with the smaller herds but you will see it more and more markedly as the herds increase in size from fifty or so to perhaps several hundreds.

Then what about rhino? I have had rhino come snorting and blowing towards me at a slow walk—I standing perfectly still and, of course, down- or across-wind. The rhino had probably seen some movement but could not make out what it was. Surely that can only be described as curiosity? The rhino has no enemies other than man—if he suspects man then surely he would be more inclined to clear off rather than approach for a closer inspection because in normal circumstances a rhino will put as great a distance as he can with the least possible delay between himself and his hated enemy. He may charge, of course, but that is only when he thinks that you are so close that he cannot get away. I have never known a rhino charge other than from close quarters.

In the same way I have had elephant, perhaps one individual out of the herd, come slowly towards me because he had seen some movement and wanted to know what it was. There was no sign of fear—his ears were out and his head up—but his trunk was down. He obviously wasn't alarmed—just curious.

Imaginative Hunting

It always seems a very great pity to me that those who write books on big game hunting, with but mighty few exceptions, render their observations, which would otherwise be of intense interest, utterly valueless by claiming to have seen things which have been proved, over and over again, to be impossible.

I am thinking in particular of that statement which practically all writers seem to imagine is expected of them: "they saw the lion's eyes glowing in the dark."

Now I have indulged in every conceivable kind of experiment in an attempt to prove or disprove this statement: I have let the fire burn down so that the lions which I could hear prowling and

purring around the camp might close in then flung a cup of gaso-
line, kerosene, or a handful of gunpowder on the glowing embers.
I have sat up in a tree or on a *machan* on pitch-black nights and on
moon-lit nights, and deliberately made a noise when the lions approached close so as to make them look up at me. But in spite of
all this I have yet to see a lion's eyes glowing in the dark.

No animal has phosphorescent eyes, consequently they cannot
glow unless a spot-light is turned directly towards them and even
then, unless the light is an extremely powerful one, you will not
see the eyes glowing unless they are very close to you.

Another remark that is also very common is that someone has
seen a native with an arm or a leg—in one account it was *both* legs—
which had been bitten clean off by a croc as neatly as tho by an axe.

Now a croc invariably grabs his prey and pulls it under water.
He drowns his victim always. I have been instrumental in rescuing
two persons from crocs—one an Englishman and the other a native
woman—and have seen several other natives that had been grabbed
and saved by their companions. Of the two that I was fortunate
enough to rescue, one had been grabbed by the arm, and the other
by the leg. In neither case did the croc bite off the limb as a shark
would have done—he just pulled. The result was that the limb
was badly lacerated by his teeth, and, in the case of the white man,
the arm rendered practically useless owing to the tendons and
muscles being so badly torn. When you come across some native
fisherman with the half of one arm gone and are told that a croc
took it, do not jump to conclusions; this is how such things happen: The fisherman is in the water with his part of the net; the
water may be anywhere up to his neck; a small croc grabs him by
the arm—it must be a small one; he wouldn't have a hope if it
was a big one—he yells for help and hangs onto the top rope of
the net; his pals come along and grab his other arm and pull. In
the struggle the arm the croc has in his mouth is broken and the
lower part torn off. The croc has not actually bitten it off.

I read a book some time ago wherein the author tells us how
he saw the lions' eyes glowing, took a hasty shot at them, and then
jumped into the tent on his wagon and fumbled in the dark for
his shooting lamp. Obviously, therefore, he did not have it lit
when he claims to have seen the glowing eyes. In a later chapter[1]
he goes on to talk about hippo and describes amongst other things

how a hippo bit a native in two halves. Now is it possible for a hippo to do this? From an examination of his mouth I, personally, fail to see how he could. He can bite a small iron-wood canoe in two pieces as easily as I could bite thru a cracker—as I know from bitter experience, when my canoe was splintered to matchwood by one bite from a hippo and I lost a perfectly good battery of expensive rifles. But biting thru a hard substance which offers resistance to the bite, is a very different thing from biting thru a soft, pliable substance like a human body—when the formation of a hippo's mouth and teeth are borne in mind.

Be that as it may, however, the man in question claims to have seen some extraordinary things in the Bush. We all know that wild animals will occasionally show remarkable traits utterly opposed to the usual habits and customs of their respective species and, of course, it is not impossible, tho perhaps improbable, for one fortunate man personally to witness several of these "freaks" but the point is that he makes it impossible for us to credit these sights, which otherwise would be of such intense interest, by also claiming to have seen a lion's eyes glowing in the dark when he did not have his spot-light trained towards them.

A most interesting letter from the pen of that well-known observer, D. D. Lyell, brings to mind a somewhat similar experience of mine. In his letter Lyell mentions how a friend of his was sitting up for a panther in India one night. On the panther approaching, the sportsman fired. The two other men who were present maintained that the animal loosed a shrill scream on feeling the lead, bounded forward and then dropped dead. But the sportsman who had fired never heard a sound (he was using a .577 B. P. Express).

The first time I ever tackled a large herd of elephant (at a rough estimate there were, I should say, anything from 100-120 of them, spread out in horse-shoe formation in fairly open forest), I closed in to within about twelve to fifteen paces of the two best, up at the top end of the "horse-shoe." This meant that I had elephant on both sides of me as well as in front. Eyes were obviously going to be of greater assistance to me than ears.

I fired and saw the muzzles of the rifle jump slightly under the shock of discharge; I distinctly heard the "clup" of the bullet (I was listening for that, and in view of what follows this is interesting) but I am convinced that I never heard the roar of the rifle. And I know that I did not hear another sound, not even when I fired for the other big tusker tho I again saw the muzzles jump.

As the herd stampeded there was, of course, the usual pandemonium—but I heard nothing. Yet I am certain that there wasn't a thing that I did not see—the corrugations on the elephants' hides; one big fellow with very small tusks and an abnormally long trunk; another with queerly-shaped tusks, one pointing upwards and the other very straight; another with a broken tusk; two monsters with no tusks at all; the dirt and clay and small stones thrown up as trees were pushed over quite close to me; the splinters flying as another tree was snapped off several feet above the ground; yet, I repeat, I never heard a sound. The din must have been terrific —my boys told me that it was and, of course, I have frequently heard it since. But on that occasion my eyes must have completely robbed my ears to aid my sight, since I had realized the necessity for it before opening fire. As I have mentioned, it was the first time I had tackled a large herd and I was, I suppose, a trifle nervous.

Of course, it is not a thing, I should imagine, you could consciously do altho I have several times since then had somewhat similar experiences. But never quite so pronounced as on that first occasion.

Radiating Danger

We have all seen how ordinary domestic animals, dogs, cattle, horses, etc., know perfectly well if a man is nervous of them or not. How many wretched mailmen and messenger boys get bitten by dogs which never attempt to bite an ordinary social visitor to the house simply because the social visitor has probably had considerably more experience in handling dogs and does not show the slightest signs of fear.

Altho I have no fear of dogs or horses, I have always been terrified of cattle (other than milch cows) and there is not the slightest doubt that they know it. I have vivid recollections of a farm in Canada where I had to attend to a mob of bullocks in a barn, and how I had to run the gauntlet every time I passed along one of the alleys, as these brutes "cow-kicked" back at me but they never attempted to do so if the owner came around. I have had similar experiences in Australia and New Zealand.

Now, even if so comparatively dull an animal as a stall-fed bullock can sense that fear in man, how much more so could wild animals with their highly sensitive receiving apparatus—particularly elephant. Sutherland in his book *The Adventures of an Elephant-Hunter* refers repeatedly to the number of times that he was charged. He used a pair of double .577 Nitro-Expresses. Blunt, who later shot in the same districts, states in his book *Elephant* that he was charged so seldom that he does not feel qualified to discuss or give an opinion on charging elephant. Blunt obviously was not the least bit frightened, and says that he never had the slightest difficulty in either stopping or at least turning a charge. Selous had said the same thing years previously. Sutherland, on the other hand, says that he was never certain of stopping a charge. Accordingly, with all due respect to the late Jimmy Sutherland, I contend that he must have been nervous and that the elephant sensed it and consequently feared him less than they did Blunt.

This may seem a fantastic thing to say of a man, one of the only five in history, and probably the first of them to do it, who have killed more than a thousand elephant. But on reflection it may not seem quite so absurd. If a man, possessing any more imagination than a hen, and armed with a pair of such tremendously powerful rifles, admits that he was never certain of being able to stop a charge, then he *must* have felt nervous when approaching a herd. It's a positive insult to his intelligence to suggest otherwise. From my own experience I have not the slightest doubt that this is the explanation. Many years ago, before I learned the lesson that a man cannot drink heavily and shoot dangerous game at one and the same time, I found myself amongst elephant after being on a vulgar and somewhat prolonged jag. I was very nearly killed by an elephant I had wounded and the shock put the finishing touches to the ragged ends of my nerves. I became so terrified that I could not hold the rifle steady and had to carry an assegai shaft and with its aid try and prevent the muzzles from dancing about. It was positive agony to approach a herd, and time after time I was charged. However, by sticking to it, I gradually overcame my fear and realized that with a good rifle in my hands there was no earthly need to be nervous. Nowadays, hunting in those same districts, I seldom have to face a charging elephant.

But there is another side to this question—just as a man radiates fear if he is nervous, so, I contend, does he radiate danger when hunting. As any elephant-hunter can tell you, it is astonishing how often and at how close ranges you can encounter lesser game when following elephant spoor. These animals do not show fear, and even if they do move off, it will not be a frantic stampede, and they will not go far before pulling up again. They do not sense real danger because, since the hunter has no intention of molesting them, the danger signals are in this instance not being broadcast, but are concentrated and focused on the elephant. On the other hand, if he just wants meat and is out to shoot anything, then he will have to be far more careful, because the game will sense the danger very much sooner and will not permit anything like such a close approach unless carefully stalked. The same thing can frequently be seen if one is just walking along without a rifle—game are often encountered at close quarters and just stand and stare as one passes.

We all know the contempt that rooks show for a man armed with nothing more lethal than a walking-stick, even tho he may deliberately carry it as tho it was a gun but let him try an approach with a genuine gun, even as tho he tries to carry it as tho it was a walking-stick, and the birds will not let him come within range. They cannot possibly distinguish between steel and wood, so the only possible explanation is these danger radiations.

Then, we must all have experienced at some time or other an irresistible impulse to turn around and look behind when sitting in an hotel lounge or verandah, and invariably one's eyes go directly to those of some stranger who is staring straight at us. So if a man is capable of feeling that he is being watched, how much more so will the highly sensitive receiving apparatus of wild animals register the presence of danger—principally, of course, those animals which have the greatest number of enemies. And there cannot be the slightest doubt that the well-known, steady, wide-eyed, unwinking stare, so characteristic of the felines, saves many an animal from an untimely death.

I have been aware for a long time now that it is very unwise to keep your eyes fixed on your quarry when stalking, and have long made a practice of cautioning my trackers and gun bearers against doing so.

Averages

I have several times had non-professional hunters tell me that I ought to have a very much better average of kills-to-cartridges than they have, because I am at the game all the year around whereas they are lucky to get a couple of months a year in the Bush and generally only a bare six weeks or even less.

Out here in the big game shooting districts of Africa you sometimes hear impossible claims being made—tho almost always they are made by the inexperienced man. The hunter who knows his job also knows that extravagant claims of what he has shot with his last hundred rounds are just so many insults to the intelligence of any other experienced hunters within earshot. But when considering a man's average, there is one point which is frequently overlooked—is the man a professional hunter or only an amateur? It sums up in those words, "professional" and "non-professional."

The amateur wants good trophies, good tusks, good heads and good skins. He need not fire unless he likes and there are rarely two really good heads standing together, altho, of course, there are exceptions. In other words, he is out essentially for quality whereas the professional hunter, far more often than not, must shoot for quantity if he is to do his job thoroly—particularly in the case of an Elephant Control Officer or Cultivation Protector.

Let us take the two cases separately—an average day in the life of an amateur sportsman in good game country and a similar day in the life of a government hunter.

The non-professional man leaves camp and sooner or later encounters game of a certain species. If there is a good head amongst them he stalks. If the animals wind him and stampede, he need not tire himself out following them unless he likes. He can branch off and wander around until he encounters something else. Even if there is more than one good head, he is under no obligation to kill more than the one. As far as that one is concerned, he should be able to kill it cleanly with a single shot, since he can take his own time and not worry about the others maybe wandering into the bush. He only wants the one. He drops it and moves on. In good game country he will almost certainly meet up with another species before long. He again kills with a single shot, and may quite possibly spot yet another type of game, before reaching camp, and again secure his trophy without trouble—three heads for three rounds fired.

Now take the case of the Elephant Control man. A troop of elephant have raided the natives' food-crops over-night. He gets on the spoor at daybreak and follows the troop. As all elephant-hunters know, it is astonishing how often, when following elephant, you can encounter other game at absurdly close quarters—and they always seem to be particularly fine specimens but you cannot fire for fear the elephant will hear the shot, and it's the government man's job to catch up with those elephant and teach them their lesson.

If the wind is favorable, he may do so and get back to camp by 9 or 10 o'clock or thereabouts, but if the wind is contrary, he may close them in thick bush and approach to within a matter of a few paces, only to have a wee whiff of air come from the wrong direction and stampede the herd. And this may happen time and again during the day. At length, perhaps towards the middle of the afternoon, he gets his chance. The breeze has died down and he can move around and count the beasts and determine how many he should kill to impress upon the remainder that it is dangerous and inadvisable to raid, and also which to select as examples.

If the herd consists of ten or a dozen persistent raiders, then he will probably attempt to kill three of them. Now this would be comparatively simple if the elephant were standing in the open but during the midday heat they will almost certainly be in thick bush or heavy forest. Since they know that they have been followed all day from the scene of their depredations, they will be more or less on the alert—at least, they will certainly stampede on the heels of the first shot, which elephant that are not on the alert very often will not do, owing to the difficulty of placing the danger zone in thick cover. But the point is that the first step will take most of them out of sight. So, altho the hunter might be able to drop the leader with a clean brain-shot from a certain position, it might not be possible for him to fire from there since, if he did, he might not get another shot. Accordingly, he must maneuver into such a position that he has a fair chance of bagging his three, even if it can only be done by crippling the first two or the first and third.

Judging the most likely line to be taken by the herd when it stampedes and the most probable actions of his chosen three, he takes up his position and opens fire.

His first shot may be for the point of the shoulder—to break the bone. His second a side brain-shot as the second "example" exposes his broadside and the third either a side heart- or lung-shot or, possibly, an anchoring shot by the root of the tail if the animal is travelling directly away from him.

Now, assuming that these three shots have come off as he wanted them to, he has, surely, bagged three elephant with three shots for an elephant with a broken shoulder must fall sooner or later and, once down with a broken shoulder, he cannot rise again. But he must be given another shot to put him out of his misery and finish him off, as also must the "anchored" one. So the professional man has also collected his three tails that day, but—it has taken him five rounds to do it.

The hunter retained by government for Elephant Control purposes that can show his 55–60 tails per 100 rounds of ammunition fired has no need to be ashamed of himself. From 60–70 is darned good shooting whilst anything over 70 spells phenomenally good luck more than anything else, in finding the elephant in easy country. (I am, of course, assuming a keen hunter who does his work conscientiously for its own sake and not just for the few pounds a month that his salary brings him in.)

The ivory-hunter should show a better average than the government man and the non-professional sportsman a still better record (assuming that he is not a mere beginner). But when you hear men speak of an *average* of from 96–97 animals killed per 100 rounds of ammunition fired, a large, a very large, pinch of salt is more than indicated.

Man-Eating Leopards

The man-eating leopard is a rare thing in Africa. It is only once in a very, very blue moon that you hear of him, and then, curiously enough, it is rather "man-killing" than "man-eating." True, leopards every now and then kill man, but that is when they are being hunted and have been wounded—a very different thing. As I mentioned in another place, I once had an unwounded and unprovoked leopard maul me, and heard of a native being killed in South Africa in a similar manner. But I am convinced that that was only because the leopard was unable to get away and so considered attack its best defence. I wasn't hunting it, knew nothing of its existence, in fact, but it could not have been aware of that.

The first I ever heard of a definite man-eating leopard was at a native village on the bank of the Revugwe—a tributary of the Zambezi. The natives told me that the previous night a big leopard had sprung onto the roof of a hut, worked his way thru and killed an old crone who was sleeping inside. A young lion, maybe, I thought, but not a leopard. However, on examining the roof, the leopard's hairs were indisputable. I never heard of that leopard again. What happened to him I don't know but so far as I know he never returned to the village, nor did I hear of him killing anyone else. Needless to say, the natives swore that it was some enemy of the old crone who had transmogrified himself (or herself) into a leopard for the purpose of killing the old daisy. Which, of course, was conclusively and unassailably proved by the fact that nobody else was killed and that the leopard had no existence after killing the crone.

I heard no more of man-killing leopards then for a number of years. Not, in fact, until some three years before the war, when I was in that great buffalo district to which I have several times referred. When I arrived that year the rains were just over and the natives told me that they had been greatly troubled by a big leopard which had mauled several of them and killed one or two. Again I rather doubted the leopard and guessed that it might have been one of the small man-eating lions that are such an infernal nuisance around these parts. But the natives were most emphatic; they vowed that they had seen the brute. Nothing happened during the dry season, and when the rains came on again I moved my camp some miles to the southwest to where there was slightly higher ground near the foot-hills and where I knew that I would have no difficulty in keeping the old wolf from the door during the wet season.

Whilst I was there, rumours reached me to the effect that the leopard had returned and was causing something of a reign of terror in that same district. If the brute could not kill during the night, it waited until the natives were working in their lands and then attacked in broad daylight. It was out of the question for me to go there, as I had but a skeleton staff in camp, and the entire country in between was under mud and water, practically impassable for anything but frogs and wild-fowl. In any case, I guessed the reports were grossly exaggerated.

However, as soon as the rains eased and made it possible to do so, I packed up and returned to my previous camp. On arrival I was met by a deputation from all the surrounding villages and gathered from them that the leopard had indeed been busy. Some eight or ten people had been killed, men, women and children, and twice as many more had been mauled. This was certainly serious, as several of the injured natives died of blood-poisoning in spite of all I could do for them—I had, of course, arrived much too late. But with my arrival, the leopard vanished. I hunted for him by day, altho there wasn't one chance in a thousand of finding him; and sat up for him by night. But since it's tsetse-fly country there are, of course, no goats or sheep or even dogs, so that I had to shoot something for bait and no telling where to put it, as the brute roamed from village to village over a fairly large area.

Nothing more was heard of him whilst I was there and again I left when the rains came on as my quarry, the buffalo, then evacuated the district and I had to go after them. That season the leopard was worse than ever—he would sit up in a tree from which he could see along the main path and, on any unfortunate travellers appearing, drop down and ambush them from behind a small bush that grew at the foot of the tree. I examined this tree later when I returned, and from the number of claw marks and the amount of spoor and leopard hair on the ground and on the bark of the tree, there was no earthly doubt that it was regularly used by the brute.

That season, when the rains came on, I did not shift my camp as usual but remained where I was, because the reign of terror had been so bad that five entire villages evacuated their homes and cleared out of the district, abandoning their villages. That may seem incredible but it is a plain statement of fact. I now had great hopes of getting a smack at the brute, because there was only the one small village, consisting of two or three families, left in the area and so if the leopard wanted man he would have to come here.

However, he failed to put in an appearance. It's just possible that there may be something in the natives' theory that, since I had to occasionally kill something to feed myself and my coons, the leopard had heard the shots, realized there was danger hanging around, and consequently lay low. I do not know but it is quite possible. And I'm afraid I cannot finish the yarn as you would doubtless like me to, and as in fiction I should inevitably have to, and tell you how I successfully beat him at last because this is not fiction and candour compels me to admit that—surely during a moment of mental aberration?—I left everything and went off to the war!

Avoidable Accidents

What, precisley, constitutes an "accident"? In the African Bush any unpleasantness or fatality is almost invariably referred to as an "accident," but is it? If a man makes a habit of tackling dangerous game with a rifle which he knows frequently misfires, and gets himself mauled or killed thru the rifle refusing to go off, that to my way of thinking is no "accident"; "unfortunate occurrence" perhaps, but not "accident." As I look at it, a genuine accident is something unavoidable and I contend that not more than, at the very most, one out of ten of the so-called shooting or hunting "accidents" are other than due to carelessness, thoughtlessness, inexperience, or something of the sort.

If a man, facing a charging buffalo, has the ground give way under his foot, due to the machinations of some burrowing animal, at the very moment of pressing the trigger, so that he loses his balance and the shot is thrown high, that would be a genuine accident if he was injured or killed. I have known this happen to a man. But to take the case of a well-known sportsman in Kenya, Colonel M, who was motoring himself, his wife and family somewhere. Before they were halfway the car either broke down or became bogged or something—at any rate they could neither get it forward nor back—so abandoned it and set out to walk back.

M had a double-barreled rifle and, on crossing a clearing, found himself being charged by a rhino. He shouted to his wife and family to get behind him and endeavored to push forward the safety slide on his rifle—but could not budge it. There was no cover, no available tree to climb, nothing—an extremely unpleasant position, bearing in mind the wife and family. M did the only thing he could do—waited until the rhino was practically on him, side-stepped and, holding his rifle as tho there was a bayonet on the end of it, drove the muzzles into the brute's eye. This caused the rhino to swerve slightly, and so saved his wife and children from being run down.

Now, had anybody been hurt, it would almost certainly have been described as an "accident" but I contend there was nothing accidental about it at all—the gallant colonel himself was, or rather would have been, solely and entirely to blame, and nobody else. It is palpably obvious that he had permitted the safety slide on his rifle to rust fast—a safety slide will not jam of its own accord; there is nothing to jam. In view of the sportsman's position, standing and experience, it is extremely improbable that he was carrying anything but a really fine quality weapon—such rifles are 100% reliable. But the finest piece of mechanism on earth will rust if it is not cleaned and oiled.

I have described in an earlier chapter how I might very easily have been killed by a wounded buffalo which charged me in long grass, if I had not made it a habit to test the safety slide of my rifle before leaving camp. Had I omitted to do so and had that buff smashed me up, I certainly would not have considered it an "accident." Yet when I showed two other men the account of that sportsman in Kenya, they both made the same remark, and blamed the rifle.

Some time ago in Tanganyika a sportsman was badly mauled by a wounded buffalo. It appears that he had wounded the bull and then followed it into long grass, carrying a magazine rifle. The buffalo charged, he fired, failed to stop the beast, and then endeavored to reload and only succeeded in giving himself a hopeless jam. His own words were, "for the first time the rifle let me down." Later, when he was in the hospital, the affair was referred to as a "grievous accident." But with all due respect to him, I contend that it was his own fault. If his rifle was a cheap, mass-production abomination hailing from the Continent, such as one sees being used on all sides in Africa, then quite possibly it did really jam—in which case it was the man's own fault for tackling dangerous game with a weapon of that description; on the other hand, if it was a decent quality weapon then the jam was probably due to his failing to draw the bolt back sufficiently when reloading, owing to his excitement and hurry. In which case I consider it mighty unfair to blame the rifle. It is the man who is at fault.

If your son and heir was in the habit of hurtling around the country in his Dusenberg with his foot hard down on the accelerator and a new copy of this book propped up on the steering wheel before him to help while away his boredom, when the inevitable crash took place it is extremely unlikely that, fond and indulgent parent tho you may be, you would have the gall to refer to the regrettable affair at the subsequent inquest as an "accident"!

A Plea for the Porter

At first glance it might appear as tho the subject contained in the above heading is rather outside the scope of such a book as this. But since some of the best big game hunting districts cannot be reached by anything on wheels and, therefore, the humble and long-suffering native porter must be substituted, I contend that that lowly individual must be considered as being a most necessary and indispensable accessory to big game hunting. For there can be no doubt that were it not for the assistance rendered by this two-legged beast of burden, the vast majority of the magnificent trophies which adorn the walls of many a fine house and hunting lodge in America and Europe would still be roaming the mountains, forests, plains and swamps on their original owners' shoulders. And so the carrier is deserving of occasional consideration.

At one time or another, thruout the years I have been hunting and wandering around Africa, I have had a considerable and fairly representative selection of African coon in my trail, and I do know what an altogether astounding amount of hardship, suffering and overwork the African porter can and will stand, for a pitifully meagre wage, provided his belly is filled at not too infrequent intervals. Give him his fill of meat, and something must be radically wrong if he is not happy—and so long as he is happy, all is well.

A man will boast that he can average his twenty, twenty-five or even thirty miles a day, day after day, on foot, in tropical Africa. His carriers must also tramp the same distance but the small point that he so often forgets is that he is well and comfortably shod and, in all probability, has carried nothing heavier than a walking-stick, which has definitely helped him when walking up-hill, whereas his coons have had to carry heavy, awkward, ungainly and sharp-cornered boxes and packing cases weighing half-a-hundredweight or so under exactly similar conditions. And further, having arrived at his destination, the white man can throw himself down in a comfortable chair, stick his feet up on one of those same boxes and completely relax, with someone to bring him a cup of tea or coffee and, later, something reviving out of a bottle which, incidentally, was also carried in one of those boxes.

Others again, to save walking, use a "bush-car," a well-sprung seat mounted on a motorcycle wheel, complete with tire and tube, with shafts running fore and aft, and trundled along by two coons, whilst many use a bicycle—and there are few better ways of getting around Africa in the dry season than a bicycle. These men can complete a twenty-five mile trek and arrive fresh enough to go out for an evening shoot. If they kill, their wretched porters will have to help bring in the meat, cut it up, collect firewood and water, clear a spot for the camp, and so on. But they will willingly and cheerfully do all this on top of their day's work for the sake of a good feed of fresh meat—there will be the deep hum of voices, spontaneous laughter and song around the fires and the camp a picture of savage content.

It is so easy and costs so little to keep the African happy, and makes such an enormous difference to the pleasure and even success of your expedition, that it passes my comprehension why every-body does not try to do it. For instance, it is by no means unusual to see a man marking his boys' tickets in the evening, and if there was only half-a-day's work, then only half a day is marked on the ticket—in other words, the man is saving maybe a penny or a little more out of the boy's wages—yet thinks nothing of drinking at sundown a couple of dollars' worth of the whiskey which the boy carried for him!

But even this will not upset the coon provided he gets his bellyful of meat. And this is where so many men make the mistake —especially visiting sportsmen. I have more than once come across them and listened to them bellyaching, they had heard so much about the willingness and cheerfulness of the African native, they couldn't see it—there was nothing but discontent and grum-bling and possibly even desertions in his camp; "What's the matter with the bastards, anyway?"

And it usually transpired that the sportsman was frightfully anxious to secure a few record heads, and was determined to shoot nothing small. The result of this was that time after time his trackers had brought him up close to game, but after examining them thru his glasses, he had refused to shoot because there didn't appear to be an exceptional head amongst them. And in one case that I remember this man had left his unfortunate hunters, trackers, porters and servants for a solid three weeks without giving them any meat at all, and for the two previous weeks had only shot one fairly small beast. So that actually you might say those coons had been working for five weeks with only one small feed to cheer them. Is it any wonder they grumbled, with plenty game about? What if you have vowed to shoot nothing small—what is there to prevent you occasionally dropping a beast with a *bad* head for the sake of your staff? If it wasn't for them you wouldn't have a chance at all of bagging that record.

But this question of record heads is greatly overdone. The exception must obviously be mighty few and far between. When the vastness of the territory is borne in mind, there is a much better chance for your $2.00 ticket to win a first prize in one of these huge sweepstakes that are being run nowadays, than there is for you to run up against a record head of any particular species of game—a million-to-one chance.

The shooting of record heads is entirely a matter of luck—just luck and nothing more. It is of no use trying to tell an experienced hunter that it is anything else. You can boast to yourself and to your friends that it is merely a question of perseverance but it is nothing of the sort. The redoubtable Selous, in all the years he hunted, and amongst all the thousands of animals he must have shot, never had a single, solitary record head to his name. After all, even if you do manage to get one record, or a head running close to the record for that particular species, the chances of you getting equally good ones of all the other species to complete your collection must be infinitesimal.

Surely it is much better to concentrate on bagging a fair, average, representative head of each and every species. I have never been in a position to hunt solely and entirely for sport and pleasure, but I should imagine that the great attraction, excluding the excitements and thrills associated with the hunting of dangerous game, is the wild, free, unfettered and unconventional life at the back of Nowhere, the seeing of Nature in the raw, the close approach after a careful stalk to some great wild creature, the pause before the shot to watch and admire, and then—the crack of the rifle and the accurately placed bullet, ensuring a clean kill to complete the story.

The head? What if it does not equal the record? It's a fine trophy and will bring back memories just as effectively as would some "freak." And your poor devils of porters—to say nothing of your trackers who found the game for you—will be happy; they don't eat the horns anyway, and won't care a hoot whether they're "records" or not!

How NOT to Shoot Elephant

Here now is an adventure that occurred almost exactly twenty-five years ago, after I had had maybe twelve months experience. I relate it as an Awful Warning and a Horrible Object-Lesson, since it has taken me a full quarter of a century to get so I can even think of it without getting hot around the ears! Let me hasten to assure you that there is no word of exaggeration in what follows—I am much too keen on my chosen profession to ever write anything about it that was not strictly accurate.

Here it is, then; take note of the points:

Now, here in the Zambezi valley, some hundreds of miles from the coast, the elephant-hunting is good. But, like that hoary old curate's egg, it is only good in parts; in other parts it is not so good. Some of it consists of the toughest going I have ever experienced. It consists of dry, thorn-bush country. The thorn, of the "hawk's-bill" variety, rises in a dense, matted, utterly impenetrable mass to an average height of about twelve feet or so. You can only get along by following one of the paths beaten out by the feet of the big gray ghosts themselves. These paths are more or less clear for a height of maybe three and a half or four feet from the ground, but from there up they are draped by the overhang of the thorn. The big fellows can merely brush thru this, but the hunter in his grey or khaki drill and his naked trackers and gun-bearers have to struggle along, hour after hour, all doubled up in the sweltering heat, because not a breath of cooling breeze can reach him in there, but the sun can. It's desperately tiring work but the prizes are good when the god of hunters reckons that you have earned one.

My first attack on this district took place twenty-five years ago. Naturally, I knew very much less about elephant-hunting then than I know now; nevertheless, in the year's experience I had had there were some things I had learned that could no more be broken with impunity than the laws of the Medes and Persians. And one of these was that you must never, no matter what the temptation, fire both barrels of a double-rifle in thick cover without first reloading the right. In other words, you must always have your left barrel in immediate reserve. That was one thing I had learned; unfortunately there was another which I hadn't! It was that you cannot drink heavily and hunt dangerous game at close quarters in thick cover at one and the same time.

I had been hitting it up some in a small township just a few days before, and my nerves were still somewhat ragged at the edges. It was this, I am certain, which caused me to make the mistake that so nearly cost me my life—to say nothing of the life of my gun-bearer. This is how it happened:

We had had a damnable day's hunting without getting a shot, and had returned to camp somewhere around 4:30 in the afternoon, very hot and very tired, cursing all elephant and all fools who were foolish enough to spend their lives elephant-hunting. However, after a pot of coffee and a stiff drink, I began to feel better. I was camped by a small native village, and presently a woman came along to say that she and her sisters had encountered elephant on their way down to fetch water from the waterhole. She said that three big bulls had crossed the path right in front of her. It was less than a couple of hundred yards away.

Instantly, all fatigue vanished like magic—the news of elephant invariably does that to the weary hunter—and I grabbed the nearest rifle, a double .470, yelled for my tracker, and started down the path. All this was taking place in a deep bowl-shaped valley surrounded by fairly high hills. The light was failing rapidly. It was still fairly good on the path which the natives had hacked out to the waterhole by enlarging an old elephant-path but as soon as we turned off that onto the small track which we could see the elephant had just used, it was very bad.

I made my way cautiously along, stopping every now and then

to listen, because hunting under such conditions is conducted entirely by ear, visibility being limited to a matter of three or four feet. Suddenly, without the slightest warning, something swished against my left shoulder. It was an elephant's tail—nothing else was visible of him. He had turned into the bush off the track and halted. A shot was out of the question—he was much too close. I would have risked his having small tusks, because I knew that practically all bulls in here were well worth shooting but it would have meant that I would have had to stand immediately behind him to enable my bullet to have a straight run thru his long body to reach the heart. I would have had to shoot with the muzzles of my rifle less than six inches from his backside, there was no room to do anything else. It was more than probable that his hind quarters would have given way and he would have sat on me before I could have gotten clear. It was most aggravating in view of the failing light. Then suddenly I heard a great swish of leaves and the crack of a breaking branch a little way farther along the track—one of his companions must be having a feed there.

I edged past this big fellow and continued along the track. Sure enough, in a small depression on my left, there was another big bull. But only bits of him were visible, and they were not vital bits. Maneuvering for position was a physical impossibility. I crept quietly up only to find that his head and shoulders were completely concealed behind a large baobab tree. The light was failing so rapidly here in this saucer that I knew I must take my shot within the next few minutes or go without. I got down on hands and knees and crawled along a beastly little tunnel under the intervening thorn. It looked as tho it might be a possibility. I snaked up to within eight feet or thereabouts of the elephant's starboard quarter. It was infuriating! I could see the tip of a magnificent tusk protruding beyond the tree, the heel of one forefoot and one huge hip, and that's all. I couldn't move from under the bush where I was crouching on my knees, except slightly forward and to the right which would put me on another elephant-path but with the baobab tree then entirely covering the bull.

Now had I been fully *compos mentis* I would have withdrawn and left the elephant alone for the night—if they weren't disturbed I would probably get a shot at them sometime on the morrow—but my brain was by no means its usual reasonably bright self. And so occurred the first of the series of mistakes that so nearly ended disastrously both for me and my wretched gun-bearer who, faithful lad, was squatting at my heels. I decided to take the kidney-shot. It's an extremely difficult shot at the best of times, but from a kneeling position not more than eight or ten feet away it was sheer madness to attempt it. It's mortal, of course, if you succeed in getting it, but not immediately so; your elephant can be a hideously dangerous proposition for some little time after receiving the bullet, because I guess it is about the most painful of all shots.

And then came mistake number three. Bearing in mind how close I was, the density of the thorn, and the fact that there were at least two other elephant in the immediate vicinity, of all occasions this surely was one on which I should have kept my left barrel in reserve, and reloaded the right after firing. I knew that perfectly well, yet I went and emptied both barrels into that beast's flank just as fast as I could slip finger from one trigger to the other! He loosed a screaming yell that put my hair on end and whipped around that tree like a young pig. It does not take long to think under such circumstances. Had I had my left barrel, all would have been well but I had emptied it. The elephant was only a few feet away and coming; nor was he loitering. Whether he was actually charging the sound of the shots or merely trying to get away just at first, is immaterial. As tho moved by the same string, I and my gun-bearer legged it down the elephant-path immediately in front of us, there was nowhere else to go; our mistake was in trying to go anywhere. As we ran I broke the breech with the intention of trying to reload. This brought the rifle across my body. These modern high-velocity rifles have a very high foresight block, and mine got itself hung up on a trailing vine or creeper or something which whipped the rifle out of my hands. It would have been suicide to stop and try to pick it up, because the elephant was immediately behind and screaming like a stuck hog. My boy, who was just in front of me, tripped and fell right in the path. I wheeled around and flung my helmet into the elephant's face, and then turned to jump over whatever it was had tripped the boy, only to catch my own foot in it and come down full length; as I fell I struck the boy behind the knees and brought him down again. As I fell I distinctly heard a voice say: "Well, this is the end." I suppose it was mine.

All fear departed as I realized that there was absolutely nothing, nothing under the sun, that I could do. Very cautiously I looked up and instantly froze. The bull's feet were only about a foot from mine, his tusks and trunk were right over me. His trunk was up and waving about over his head trying to get our wind and his little, pig-like eyes, red as signal-lamps with rage and pain, were blazing down the path. I slid one hand up to my boy's shoulder to press him down and prevent any possible movement. Poor devil, he told me afterwards that he thought it was the elephant that had gotten him down! And so we lay for what appeared to be several ages, but I doubt if it was quite as long as that. Had the bull lowered his trunk he must inevitably have winded us, and then "good night" but by the mercy of Allah he didn't.

It was the most extraordinary sensation. One step forward and he would tread on my feet—and I wondered if it would hurt much as they were squashed like tomatoes; yet, I repeat, I felt no fear. It was a curious impersonal feeling—how can I put it?—as tho I was sitting up in a tree and watching the predicament in which some other fella found himself. Since we were so very close to him, the elephant could not see us. An elephant cannot see things down at his feet unless his trunk tells him they are there and he turns his head sideways and looks down with one eye. Otherwise he must squint appallingly on account of the distance his eyes are apart and the fact that his tusks and trunk all protrude from between his eyes. And that was what saved us.

Possibly my helmet, hitting him as it did slap between the eyes, caused him to flinch momentarily and so lose sight of us as we fell then, not being able to see us he may have had dim recollections of elephant-pits and feared to take another pace forward in case he also fell into one. I don't know; all I do know is that he finally swung around and moved slowly away. And then, for the first time in a couple of centuries, I drew a breath and sat up. And there we sat, I and my boy, just looking at one another and breathing. It took a little while to recover, and it was only when I realized that it was nearly dark that I suggested a move. We crept back along the path to see if there was anything left of the rifle; but the gods had been kind. It had fallen parallel with the path so the elephant had not trampled it. There was nothing the matter with it, so after glancing thru the barrels, I reloaded and we crept along to where we could hear the bull. And hear him we certainly could! He was no longer giving voice, but was tearing branches off trees and hurling them around. He must have been in a thundering rage.

We crept up close, and then hared away like hell as a large branch came crashing thru the thorn overhead. However, we pulled up after going some ten or fifteen yards and realizing what darned fools we were making of ourselves. Again we approached, and this time there was no mistake. I was offered a clean brain-shot from about fifteen paces, a long shot in that neck o' the woods, and altho I was trembling from head to foot I succeeded in dropping him.

Well, there it is. A superlative example of how *NOT* to shoot elephant.

Ending with a Perfect Day

Well now, after that bit of self-exposure, both in justice to myself and also to encourage the inexperienced sportsman who may think that having lost his nerve he might as well quit, let me describe another, much more recent, hunt to show that a man can recover his nerve if he sticks to it and can develop utter, absolute and complete confidence in himself and that once-fickle nerve of his.

This hunt took place in a district that might almost be described as "virgin," since it had not been shot up for at least fifteen years. It consisted of what I would describe as delightfully easy, open bush. I was hunting with my friend and partner, the man who called himself Lincoln Cadillac, and it was our custom to hunt separately, pool the ivory, sell it and split the proceeds 50–50. We had an arrangement with government whereby we got an unrestricted permit on the understanding that we shot raiders and marauders and similar varmints, including man-eaters, and paid ourselves out of the ivory.

We had just arrived in this district, the home of my boy Ali, the previous evening. At first crack of dawn we were drinking a pot of coffee and wiping the oil out of our rifles. Ali had sent around the word that we were there to hunt marauding elephant, and as soon as it was light enough to see two local natives arrived to say that two different lots of elephant had been raiding the crops overnight. Good enough. We were just starting off, each following one of the guides, when a third man arrived with news of yet another lot of raiders. I told him to wait until one of us got back, and if all was well it might be possible to get a smack at them also. These raiders, not having been shot up for so long, would probably not bother to go far.

As it transpired, I found mine still on the outskirts of the native gardens, as tho reluctant to go. The wind being favorable, the approach was easy. It was a family party of about fifteen elephant and I could see two good bulls, just good average herd bulls carrying between 80 and 90 lbs. of ivory apiece. It was necessary to be careful, however, because there were a number of cows with calves between me and the bulls. On this account I made my approach across wind. I walked quietly up to within about fifteen paces of the two bulls who were standing under a tree with the remainder of the troop scattered about waiting for these, the leaders, to give the word to go.

There was no need to get any closer. I had a perfectly clear view of both beasts from here, and the range and angle were both suitable for clean brain shots; besides, if I attempted to get any closer, I would almost certainly give my wind to some of those cows as I was very nearly up-wind of them now. There was one with a young calf that looked as tho it might be advisable to keep an eye on her. The big leader had the tree between me and him, but that didn't matter because his head was exposed and I wanted a brain shot. With a bullet thru his heart he would run fifty yards before falling, and the rest of the herd would go too but if I dropped him in his tracks the others would almost certainly stand around, ears out and trunks up, undecided what to do without his leadership, and so give me a second shot.

I was using a pair of double .465s, Nasib-bin-Risik, my head gun-bearer, standing beside me with the second in case I needed it and ready to reload the first when I had fired it. I am very fond of this method where the conditions permit and I have three staunch and well-tried men whom I have trained myself to act as gun-bearers—two always remaining with me, whilst the third takes a spell in his village. In thick cover I rely on myself and the rifle in my hands. I took deliberate aim for the side brain shot and squeezed the trigger. The big bull dropped instantly, as dead as a kippered herring before he hit the ground and the second bull swung up his trunk and took a pace back from the tree. He was also exposing his broadside, so I gave him the contents of the left barrel and dropped him beside his erstwhile companion.

There was a great commotion amongst the cows and I swung around to exchange rifles with Nasib. One, that same cow that I had decided needed watching, gave every evidence that she was about to make a vicious charge—and a cow's charge can be just as dangerous as that of a bull—so I turned to face her. I did not want to kill her if I could possibly avoid it, because her ivory was small and so was her calf. Two or three times she demonstrated, trumpeting shrilly and making short runs towards me. With her ears back she looked very vicious and bad-tempered, but could not work herself sufficiently to press home the charge. She hadn't yet gotten my wind and probably couldn't see me distinctly, and was just trying to scare me away; nevertheless, she was in a very dangerous mood and it would not do to forget about her.

I looked around amongst the others, and finally was tempted to drop a third, a nice young bull. At the shot, the peevish cow at last made up her mind to drive me out of it or kill me. She made a most determined rush, but I had moved from the spot where I had originally been standing and she had not seen me do so. The shot now coming from a different direction from that towards which her suspicions were directed, upset her calculations. She charged up to the spot from which I had shot the two leaders, stopped, swung around with her trunk up and twisted from side to side trying to wind or see me. Had she done so, she would undoubtedly have charged again, but Nasib and I remained motionless and wished the herd would clear off. Finally they did so, and we were enabled to examine our kills.

Not having heard the song of Cadillac's rifles, it would seem that his quarry had left the scene of their depredations and he would be following them up now. I hoped that the sound of my three shots would not scare them unduly and give him an excessively long tramp after them. We cut off the tails of my three bulls in the usual manner, both as proof that they were ours and to convince those in camp that we had really shot the number claimed. We then returned to camp as I figured that if we were to have a try for the third party of raiders it might be advisable to have a feed first, since by the time we picked up their spoor the sun would be warming up and they might have gone some considerable distance to seek shade for the midday siesta.

Accordingly, after cleaning my rifles, I had breakfast and my men also had something to eat. The man who had reported the troop of raiders had accompanied us on the first hunt, and was now ready to guide us to his garden, full of pleasant anticipations after seeing how effectively I had dealt with the first lot. As I had guessed, the second party led us a long way. They didn't seem able to make up their minds where to settle down. Possibly they had heard my shooting earlier, which had disturbed them, and then somewhere around eleven o'clock, quite possibly when they had at last decided that it was safe, they would have heard Cadillac's rifles speak in the distance, and started off again. We also heard the shots, two followed by two more in rapid succession after a short pause. I could visualize what had happened—two shots at the leaders, such as I had taken, grab the second rifle and get in another two shots at the hearts or lungs of two more as the herd began to move. I wished him success but the shooting must have again unsettled my troop, because they wandered around all over the countryside and would not halt. It is possible too that on account of the apparent aimlessness of their wanderings they from time to time got a wee whiff of our wind, not enough to stampede them but just enough to keep them on the move.

We kept plodding along with just one short halt around midday for a smoke and a mouthful of water, and then on again. It was well into the afternoon before we at long last heard unmistakable elephant noises a short distance ahead of us and slightly to one side. Maybe it was a good thing we hadn't caught up with them any earlier, because the wind is usually fitful during the middle of the day, blowing from all points of the compass in turn, to settle down fairly steadily later on. The spoor had clearly shown that this was a much larger herd than the other we had hunted that morning. I figured there must be at least fifty of them here, with big pad marks indicating big bulls amongst them.

Once again the approach was easy. The herd was scattered about in an isolated patch of by no means dense bush in fairly open country. A little caution was needed when entering the bush to ensure that we did not stampede any of the cows in our search for the big tuskers. Eventually, after about twenty somewhat anxious minutes moving carefully around looking for them, we found them under a large tree some small distance from the main body of the herd.

The leader, a fine beast, had two big companions under the tree with him and I could see a number of other good tuskers scattered about here and there. They would be the leaders of the various families that made up the herd, whilst the old man under the tree would be the master bull that all would follow. If I could drop him in his tracks I stood a very good chance of making a big bag here, since the other bulls would not know that he was dead and would await his signal to give them the line of retreat.

I again closed in to within fifteen or twenty paces before firing. The big chap was facing me, the two others were more or less broadside on. I took the frontal brain shot and the big fellow sank down without a murmur, all four "knees" giving way simultaneously so that he remained in an upright position, his tusks supporting his head. As the other that was facing me threw up his trunk, I shot him at the base of the throat and grabbed my second rifle. The third bull was twisting around in an undecided manner; I waited my chance and blew out his brains when he offered me a fair shot.

Out of the corner of my eye I had noticed a good deal of movement amongst the remainder of the herd whilst I had been dealing with the big chap and his companions. That, of course, was to be expected. But there was no indication of a stampede. Ears out and trunks up, they were clustered in family parties each awaiting the signal from their respective leaders, and the leaders awaiting the word from the master bull. Not getting it, they were undecided what to do. This was what I had banked on. I moved quietly around from one party to another picking out the best and dropping them. At first the different groups would rush off a little distance and then stop again, but as the shooting continued they became completely demoralized and just stood around in dismay—they had been let down by the master bull, they had apparently been abandoned by their own leaders, they just didn't know what to do about it.

I dare say I could have wiped out the greater number of them had I wished but such, of course, was not my intention. I killed eleven of them and then was satisfied. If there were fifty or sixty of the herd to start with that was not too many in view of the long years of immunity they had enjoyed during which they had been raiding the wretched natives' food-crops to their hearts' content. Such a herd could cause positive devastation in the course of a single night's raiding. It is not the amount they eat—tho that is bad enough in all conscience—but the amount they trample down and utterly destroy.

Having cut off the tails we started the return to camp amidst great jubilation. Our first day's hunting having proved so successful was a splendid omen and augured well for the remainder of the expedition. But we were not yet finished with the elephant. It was getting along towards sundown and we were all a trifle leg weary when, within a long mile of camp, we suddenly heard an elephant's tummy rumbling and his ears flop against his shoulders. The sounds were coming from a fairly dense patch of shady bush. I snicked forward the safety catch and headed straight for the place whence the rumbling had come. There were two quite nice bulls standing with their heads together taking things easy in the shade of a tall tree.

One bull was practically facing me; I was satisfied with his position, but wanted the other to come around a bit. So, with my lips almost touching Nasib's ear, I just breathed a word. He, knowing, stooped and picked up a couple of dry twigs. Gently he cracked one. In the absolute stillness that followed, huge ears swung out till they stood at right angles to the head—the bulls were listening. Again a twig cracked. Slowly, ponderously, and in absolute silence except for the faintest rustling of his hide against something, the monster moved around. And then, as he exposed his broadside, I slammed a heavy slug into his brain, bringing him down instantly. The crashing roar of the rifle was drowned in the trumpeting yell of the second bull as he threw up his trunk in alarm. But I gave him no chance to do anything. I fired the left barrel into his chest, which caused his hindquarters to give way so that he squatted there like a huge hog whilst I exchanged rifles with Nasib. But there was no need to waste another shell. He made but one effort to get to his feet, found it hopeless, and resigned himself to the end.

Index

John Howard "Pondoro" Taylor was born in 1904 in Dublin into a very respectable family. His father was a famous Irish surgeon and his mother, Lady Taylor, was reported to be a beauty who orignally hailed from Louisiana. Although Pondoro came from a socially well-thought of family, he was a bit of a scamp who longed for adventure.

He was sent by his parents to Canada, but almost immediately found himself in disgrace when it was discovered that he had joined a smuggling ring. On returning to Ireland, he again got himself into trouble—and this time it was deadly. He somehow got on the wrong side of the Sinn Fein, and Lord and Lady Taylor realized that it was only a matter of time before someone would take revenge on their son and kill him.

Since Pondoro had developed an urge to go to Africa from an early age, his parents decided to pay for his passage to Cape Town. John-Pondoro had decided to become a profesional hunter. He quickly discovered he wanted to hunt elephants for a living and hunted in what was then Rhodesia and Portuguese East Africa until WWII. During that period he experimented extensively with calibers and rifles and gained a vast knowledge on the subject. He enlisted for service during the war, thinking that he would resume his elephant hunting career later.

During his life Taylor claimed to have shot between 1,200 and 1,500 elephants. Many of the episodes of his life are described in *PONDORO: LAST OF THE IVORY HUNTERS*. Pondoro became an authority on big game rifles, writing *BIG GAME AND BIG GAME RIFLES* and *AFRICAN RIFLES AND CARTRIDGES*. His last hunting title is *MANEATERS AND MARAUDERS*.

In 1957 Taylor arrived in London, coming from Rhodesia, with the idea of leaving shortly for French Equatorial Africa, but a series of negative circumstances, bad information, and shortage of capital proved fatal. London became a deadly trap, from which he was never able to escape. Given his rather specialized qualifications, he could only find menial-type jobs in London; consequently, for years he could barely make a living. He died, destitute, in 1969.

*In 1994, Safari Press will publish the long-awaited biography of John H. Taylor's life, titled *A MAN CALLED LION*, by Peter H. Capstick.